Principles of Visual Attention:

Attention:

Linking Mind and Brain

_TURN

Oxford Psychology Series

Editors: Mark D'Esposito, Daniel Schacter, Jon Driver, Anne Treisman, Trevor Robbins, Lawrence Weiskrantz

Principles of Visual Attention:
Linking Mind and Brain

Claus Bundesen and Thomas Habekost
University of Copenhagen

OXFORD
UNIVERSITY PRESS

OXFORD

UNIVERSITY PRESS

Great Clarendon Street, Oxford OX2 6DP

Oxford University Press is a department of the University of Oxford.
It furthers the University's objective of excellence in research, scholarship,
and education by publishing worldwide in

Oxford New York

Auckland Cape Town Dar es Salaam Hong Kong Karachi
Kuala Lumpur Madrid Melbourne Mexico City Nairobi
New Delhi Shanghai Taipei Toronto

With offices in

Argentina Austria Brazil Chile Czech Republic France Greece
Guatemala Hungary Italy Japan Poland Portugal Singapore
South Korea Switzerland Thailand Turkey Ukraine Vietnam

Oxford is a registered trade mark of Oxford University Press
in the UK and in certain other countries

Published in the United States
by Oxford University Press Inc., New York

© Oxford University Press 2008

The moral rights of the author have been asserted
Database right Oxford University Press (maker)

First published 2008

A catalogue record for this title is available from the British Library

Data available

Library of Congress Cataloguing in Publication Data

Data available

Typeset by Cepha Imaging Private Ltd., Bangalore, India
Printed in Great Britain
on acid-free paper by
Biddles Ltd., King's Lynn, UK

ISBN 978–0–19–857070–7

10 9 8 7 6 5 4 3 2 1

Preface

Visual attention has long been a major subject in cognitive psychology. With the advent of cognitive neuroscience, the brain mechanisms underlying visual attention have also been studied extensively. Today, research on visual attention is arguably one of the most advanced areas in the current bridge building between mind and brain sciences. This book contains an overview of this multidisciplinary field. As a central organizing principle, the book presents a theoretical framework that unites the psychological and neural lines of research: the theory of visual attention (TVA). This integrating feature distinguishes the book from traditional textbooks that give more fragmented presentations of the field. Also, presenting one of the most wide-ranging theories of visual attention to date, the book represents a research contribution in itself.

The TVA framework has been supported by five *Psychological Review* articles (Bundesen 1990; Logan 1996, 2002a; Logan and Gordon 2001; Bundesen *et al.* 2005). With a few simple equations, the TVA model provides close fits to a large set of attentional effects. Over the previous two decades TVA has stimulated a range of influential research, both theoretical and empirical (Bundesen 1993; Logan 1996, 2002a; Logan and Gordon 2001; Bundesen *et al.* 2003), also extending into clinical areas of research (Duncan *et al.* 1999; Habekost and Bundesen 2003; Peers *et al.* 2005; Finke *et al.* 2006). Recently, the TVA equations have been found to be highly compatible with attentional effects on a very different scale than the psychological: the firing patterns of individual neurons in the visual system (Bundesen *et al.* 2005). Building on this new 'neural TVA' interpretation, this book aims to bind together the diverse research on visual attention and give an integrated overview for the reader.

The intended primary audience for the book is advanced students of psychology or cognitive neuroscience and professional researchers interested in attention. Offering both a comprehensive overview and a novel theoretical synthesis of the field, the book should be of interest to both groups. In addition, with its demonstration of how simple mathematical principles underlie both psychological and neural functions, the book should appeal to readers more generally interested in cognitive neuroscience.

We would like to express our gratitude to a number of people who provided valuable comments on earlier versions of the manuscript: Daniel Barratt, John Duncan, Axel Larsen, Gordon D. Logan, Werner X. Schneider, and Signe Vangkilde. Special thanks go to Thomas Alrik Sørensen for his huge effort in producing the figures for the book.

Copenhagen, Denmark   C.B and T.H

Contents

Conclusion

Appendices

List of boxes

Parameters in the theory of visual attention (TVA)

$\eta\,(x, i)$ Strength of the sensory evidence that 'object x belongs to category i'

β_i Perceptual bias for making categorizations of type i

π_j Pertinence (current importance) of attending to objects that belong to category j

$v\,(x, i)$ Processing rate of the categorization 'object x belongs to category i'

w_x Attentional weight of object x

α Attentional weight of a distractor relative to a target (efficiency of selection)

K Storage capacity of visual short-term memory (VSTM)

C Total visual processing capacity

t_0 Threshold for visual perception

μ Persistence of the visual afterimage following an unmasked display

Introduction

1

Introduction

'Attention' is a common English word and in an intuitive sense everybody knows what it means. We are attentive when our minds are directed at something specific, such as when searching for a face in a crowd, keeping track of a particular conversation at a loud party, or trying to focus on the print on this page rather than one of the many other things in the room. In spite of this familiarity a scientific explanation of attention has remained elusive. Many have claimed that attention is simply an ill-defined term referring to a broad class of so-called 'attentional phenomena' (cf. Allport 1993). As suggested by John Duncan (2006), among others, any two attentional phenomena may show resemblances to each other, but—except for the name—no single property may be shared by all members of the class. Thus, the class of attentional phenomena may be kept together by nothing but *family resemblance* (Wittgenstein 1953). In a provocative article, *Die Nichtexistenz der Aufmerksamkeit*, the Danish psychologist Edgar Rubin (1925/1965) argued essentially the same point and concluded that attention does not exist; *attentional* is a generic term for a set of loosely related phenomena without any defining property. In this book we shall argue for a quite different position: Attention, at least in the visual domain, is the working of a few specific mechanisms that follow a unified set of mathematical equations. The purpose of these mechanisms is *selectivity*: to choose only the most important information for consciousness and behavioural response. The importance of selectivity becomes clear when one considers the severe capacity limitations that characterize humans: we can only be conscious of a small part of the information that is picked up by the eyes every moment, and our ability to make visually guided actions is similarly limited to one or a few objects at a time. Without attention we would not be able to function.

This book presents and elaborates the theory of visual attention (TVA) introduced by Bundesen (1990) and the neural theory of visual attention (NTVA) of Bundesen *et al.* (2005). TVA is a formal computational theory that accounts for attentional effects in mind and behaviour reported in the psychological literature. The theory is based on the principle that Desimone and Duncan (1995), in a later, highly influential article, called 'biased competition': all possible visual categorizations ascribing features to objects *compete* (race) to become encoded into visual short-term memory before it is filled up. Each possible categorization is supported by the sensory evidence that the categorization is true. However, the competition is *biased* by attentional weights and perceptual biases, so that certain objects and categorizations have higher probabilities of being consciously perceived. The way sensory evidence and attentional biases interact is specified in two equations: the rate and weight equations of TVA. Thus, TVA represents a mathematical formalization of the biased competition principle.

NTVA is a neural interpretation of the rate and weight equations of TVA. The equations jointly describe two mechanisms of attention: *filtering* (which is selection of objects) and *pigeonholing* (which is selection of features). In NTVA, filtering changes the number of cortical neurons in which an object is represented. Complementary to this, pigeonholing scales the level of activation in individual neurons coding for particular features. The probability that a particular visual categorization is selected, and thus may influence consciousness and response, depends on the total neural activation supporting the categorization. This activation is directly proportional to both the number of neurons representing the categorization (which is controlled by filtering) and the level of activation in the individual neurons representing the categorization (which is controlled by pigeonholing). This way, the two mechanisms jointly determine the attentional selection process. The details of this idea will be made clear during the course of the book.

The appeal of TVA lies not only in its simplicity, but also in its power to account for the empirical literature on attention, spanning cognitive psychology, neuropsychology, and neurophysiology. For this reason the book includes comprehensive reviews of the main areas of attention research, to provide the full background for TVA theory.

Part 1 of the book concerns the psychology of visual attention. In Chapter 2 we present an overview of cognitive research on visual attention from the pioneering studies in the 1950s to the mature psychological field of today. Classical empirical phenomena and findings are described alongside theories that have shaped the field. The long-standing debate between serial and parallel models of visual attention is given special emphasis. We also describe the signal detection and biased choice theories, which represent early attempts at describing attention and categorization in mathematical terms. In Chapter 3 the TVA theory is presented. We describe how TVA was developed by integrating simpler models of attentional selection into a unified mathematical frame and explain the basic concepts of the theory. In Chapters 4 and 5 it is shown how the TVA model accounts for a wide range of empirical findings on divided and focused attention, respectively, including many of the classic effects presented in Chapter 2.

Part 2 of the book covers the neurophysiology of visual attention. In the past two decades, manipulations of visual attention have been shown to correlate systematically with the firing patterns of single neurons in the visual system. Chapter 6 presents an overview of this area, organized according to four major effects in the literature: the strong attentional effects found when a neuron can potentially respond to more than one stimulus, the more modest activity modulation seen with a single stimulus in the receptive field, shifts in the neuron's baseline firing rate when a target is expected to appear, and increased firing synchronization between neurons responding to an attended stimulus. Prominent models of these findings are discussed. Whereas the models reviewed can typically explain one or other of the main effects in the literature, none of them can account for the whole range of findings. In Chapter 7 we present the neural interpretation of TVA (NTVA), a recent attempt to integrate behavioural and neural descriptions of visual attention. In NTVA, the mathematical principles of TVA are implemented in a set of neural networks that produce exactly the same attentional selection as described on an abstract psychological level in the original theory. In Chapter 8 it is shown how the NTVA model can account for a large part of the existing single cell research while remaining completely consistent with the TVA principles of psychological function. The NTVA model is unique in being highly constrained by data from both behavioural and neurophysiological research on attention.

Part 3 of the book targets research on the anatomy of visual attention. Following the recent advances in brain imaging technology [e.g. event-related potentials (ERP), positron emission tomography (PET), functional magnetic resonance imaging (fMRI)], the anatomical basis of visual attention has been subject to much interest. Chapter 9 presents an overview of this area of research and describes how visual selection depends on the integrated function of large networks of brain areas, including both subcortical and cortical structures. We also present a possible anatomical localization of the selection processes described in the NTVA model, where specific nuclei of the thalamus are given a central role. Another important approach to the relation between visual attention and the brain is the study of patients with neurological disorders. In Chapter 10 various disorders of visual attention, both generalized and limited to one visual field, are presented and related to current theories of brain function. A new line of research where lesions are simulated in healthy participants by magnetically stimulating their brains (transcranial magnetic stimulation; TMS) is also described. TVA has recently contributed to research on attention disturbances by forming the basis of a powerful neuropsychological test method, TVA-based assessment. In Chapter 11 we present this method and describe the broad range of neuropsychological studies it has already been used for. Together, the studies illustrate four major strengths of TVA-based assessment: sensitivity, specificity, reliability, and validity.

We conclude the book in Chapter 12 by summarizing how visual attention is expressed across the different levels in the human processing system: from the single neuron over the anatomical network to the selective behaviour manifest on the psychological scale. We argue that the equations of TVA provide a unifying framework for the whole field of visual attention research and point to further extensions of the theory into the psychological domains of memory, executive functions, emotion, and consciousness.

TVA allows for mathematical modelling of attentional phenomena in a highly detailed way. This means that some mathematical background is needed to fully appreciate the theory. However, to make the main points of TVA available to a wider audience, more technical mathematical issues are segregated from the main text and located in boxes (Chapters 3, 4, 5, 7, and 8). Thus, without loss of continuity one can choose to read only the qualitative explanations in the main text, but for the deepest level of theoretical understanding we recommend that material from the boxes is included. Also, TVA can be applied to a large number of individual studies in the attention literature, which we have done in Chapters 4, 5, and 8. One may choose to read these empirical reviews selectively; for example, based on the overviews given at the start of each chapter. However, in this case also, reading the full text should be rewarded by a thorough understanding of the relevance of TVA for the complex field of visual attention research.

Part 1

The psychology of visual attention

2

Psychological research on visual attention

Visual attention is at play in almost every situation of our waking lives. Whether driving a car, shopping, or doing any other daily activity, the eyes constantly pick up a massive, rapidly changing set of inputs, far too much to be analysed in full or responded to by the organism. To function, we continuously need to locate the most significant objects and direct our mental resources at these. Fortunately we are equipped with a highly efficient system for this operation—visual attention—so that under most circumstances we do, in fact, focus on what is relevant and respond appropriately. The attentional system is so efficient that typically its activity goes unnoticed; selection appears effortless. Yet, it is no small feat to swiftly pick out the essential components of any visual environment, and for a long time psychologists have tried to uncover the mechanisms of this process.

Visual attention evolved to handle the information that is present in our natural environment, but the complexity of real-world situations is typically too large to be studied scientifically. Therefore, using an approach from the natural sciences, experimental psychologists try to isolate a few essential properties of a real-life situation to study under controlled conditions in the laboratory. For example, the common task of searching a room for a particular object may be idealized in the form of a two-dimensional computer display with a fixed number of simple distractor objects and a target. In this chapter we describe the main results obtained from half a century of such experimental studies of visual attention.

Section 2.1 presents pioneer attempts in the 1950s and 1960s at modelling attentional selection: the filter theories of Broadbent and Treisman and the late-selection model of Deutsch and Deutsch. In the same decades two classic frameworks for mathematical analysis of perceptual decision making were developed, signal detection and choice theory (Section 2.2). Both were later integrated in general theories of attention. Another important development in the 1960s was George Sperling's demonstrations of strong capacity limitations in visual processing (Section 2.3). In the decades following this early work, visual search became the dominant paradigm in attention research. The results were often analysed by simple serial models of selection, the most prominent example being Anne Treisman's feature integration theory (Section 2.4). An important alternative framework was simple parallel models of selection (Section 2.5). Both types of models did well to explain the findings from certain experimental paradigms, but as more aspects of visual attention were studied using new paradigms, the simple models proved inadequate. These empirical developments included distractor interference tasks (Section 2.6), studies of attentional capture versus voluntary control (Section 2.7), and many types of experiments on the dynamics of attention shifting (Section 2.8). A new generation of theoretical models evolved to account for these findings: selective serial models (Section 2.9) and selective parallel models (Section 2.10). Connectionist models also became popular in the 1980s, in an attempt to theorize at a level closer to neurobiology (Section 2.11). In spite of clear theoretical progress in the field, many problems still remain, especially with the selective serial models. One of the fundamental issues in the field—the dichotomy between parallel and serial models—may, however, be resolved by the FIRM model, a direct predecessor of the TVA theory (see Section 2.12).

2.1 Setting the stage

Modern research on attention dates back to the early 1950s, when Cherry and other pioneers investigated selective listening. Cherry (1953) studied the ability to attend to one speaker without being distracted by other speakers (the *cocktail party problem*). For example, subjects were asked to repeat (*shadow*) a prose message while they heard it, rather than waiting until it finished. When the message to be repeated was presented to one ear while a message to be ignored was presented to the other ear (*dichotic* presentation), subjects were unable to recall the content of the unattended message. If the message to be ignored consisted of human speech, the listening subjects could identify it as such, but they could not report any word or phrase heard in the rejected ear. They also were unable to make definite identification of the language as being English. Thus, except for simple physical characteristics, the message to be ignored appeared to be 'filtered out'.

The studies on selective listening inspired the first modern theory of attention, the *filter* theory of Broadbent (1958). This theory pioneered the use of flow-chart models (block diagrams) in cognitive psychology (Fig. 2.1). In Broadbent's conception, information flows from the senses through many parallel input channels into a short-term memory store. The short-term store can hold the information for only a few seconds. Further transmission to response systems requires access to a *limited-capacity channel*, the ability of which to transmit information is much smaller than the total capacity of the parallel input channels. Therefore, a selective filter operates between the short-term memory and the

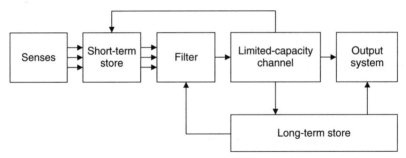

Fig. 2.1 Architecture of the filter model of Broadbent (1958). Arrows depict the flow of information from the senses through short- and long-term memory stores towards the output system. Multiple arrows represent parallel channels with a high capacity for information transmission.

limited-capacity channel. The filter acts as an all-or-none switch, selecting information from just one of the parallel input channels at a time.

Broadbent (1958) defined an input channel as a class of sensory events with a common simple physical feature (e.g. a common location, a common pitch, or a common colour). Except for analysis of such features, stimuli on unattended channels should not be perceived. This conjecture accounted for the main results of the early studies on selective listening, but it was soon challenged.

Moray (1959) and others showed that subjectively important words (e.g. the subjects's own name) tended to be recognized even when they were presented on the non-shadowed channel. To accommodate such findings, Treisman (1964a,b) proposed a variation of filter theory in which the filter operates in a graded rather than an all-or-none fashion. In Treisman's theory, unattended messages are weakened (*attenuated*) rather than blocked from further analyses. Both selected and attenuated messages are transmitted to a recognition system containing word recognition units. Since thresholds of recognition units for important words are lowered, these words tend to be recognized even when they appear in attenuated messages.

In the filter theories of Broadbent and Treisman, attentional selection occurs before stimulus recognition. Such theories are called *early-selection* theories. In *late-selection* theories, attentional selection occurs only after stimulus recognition. The first late-selection theory was proposed by Deutsch and Deutsch (1963), who assumed that attended and unattended messages receive the same amount of analysis by the recognition system. Only after a stimulus has been recognized is the importance of the stimulus retrieved, and the stimulus with the greatest importance is selected for further processing, including conscious awareness.

The qualitative theories of Broadbent, Treisman, and Deutsch and Deutsch set the stage for the development of more precise, quantitative models of attention. Most of these models were based on studies of performance in simple visual tasks, which afforded more rigorous experimental control of time relations between stimuli. Auditory studies remained an active field of research, but with less impact on mainstream discussions of attention.

2.2 Classic formal frameworks

At the same time as Cherry (1953) and Broadbent (1958) were investigating auditory selection of one among a number of messages (filtering), two formal theories were being developed for quantitative analysis of perceptual decision making: signal detection theory and choice theory. To begin with, both theories were restricted in scope to single-stimulus detection and recognition (pigeonholing). Later on, signal detection theory and choice theory provided formal frameworks for more general theories of attention comprising both filtering and pigeonholing (for a comprehensive review, see Logan 2004).

2.2.1 Signal detection theory

The theory of signal detection was developed by W. P. Tanner Jr and his colleagues in the 1950s and 1960s (see Tanner and Swets 1954; Swets *et al.* 1961; Green and Swets 1966). The theory aims at separating sensitivity (the observer as a sensor) from decision bias due to the observer's values and expectations (the observer as a decision maker). The basic conceptualization goes back to L. L. Thurstone's (1927) model of comparative judgment: the presentation of a stimulus produces a sensory representation that can be summarized by a number. Due to internal noise, the number varies from presentation to presentation. For example, the distribution generated by repeated presentations of the same stimulus may be Gaussian in shape. When the observer discriminates a signal from noise (i.e. a time interval filled by a signal from an empty time interval without any signal), he or she compares the sensory representation produced in the trial in question with a decision criterion, categorizing the stimulus as a signal if the numerical value of the sensory representation is greater than the criterion, but as noise if the value is smaller than the criterion.

The observer's sensitivity depends on the degree of overlap between the signal distribution (the distribution generated by repeated presentations of the signal) and the noise distribution (the distribution generated by repeated presentations of empty time intervals). The smaller the overlap, the greater is the sensitivity. In case the two distributions are Gaussian, the sensitivity is measured by parameter d', defined as the distance between the means divided by the standard deviation of the noise distribution (Fig. 2.2).

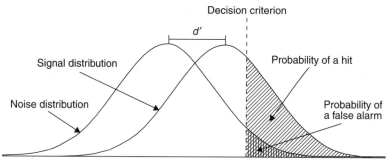

Fig. 2.2 Signal detection theory. Typical normal probability density distributions of sensory representations of signal and noise. A stimulus is categorized as a signal if, and only if, the numerical value of the sensory representation exceeds the decision criterion.

The observer's decision bias corresponds to the position of the decision criterion on the decision axis. The lower the criterion, the stronger is the bias in favour of categorizing stimuli as signals rather than noise. Thus, as the criterion is shifted to the left along the decision axis, the probability that a signal is correctly detected (a *hit*) increases but so does the probability that noise is categorized as a signal (a *false alarm*). In case the signal and noise distributions are Gaussian with equal variances, the decision bias is measured by parameter β, defined as the (likelihood) ratio between the heights of the signal and noise distributions, respectively, at the position of the criterion on the decision axis—the height of the signal distribution being the probability density that a signal produces a sensory representation with the given numerical value, and the height of the noise distribution being the probability density that noise produces a sensory representation with the given numerical value.

The actual position of the criterion on the decision axis depends on the observer's values and expectations. For example, the criterion may be positioned so that the expected value of the observer's response is maximized. It can be shown that in order to maximize the expected value, the decision criterion must be positioned at a point (numerical value) on the decision axis at which a particular ratio is found between the height of the signal distribution and the height of the noise distribution. For this reason, a large part of the theory of signal detection is based on the assumption that the numbers on the decision axis are either identical to the likelihood ratios or given by a monotonic function of the likelihood ratios (e.g. a logarithmic function). Possible neural mechanisms for computing log likelihood ratios have been considered by Gold and Shadlen (2001).

2.2.2 Choice theory

Choice theory was developed in the 1950s and 1960s by R. N. Shepard, R. D. Luce, and others (see Bradley and Terry 1952; Shepard 1957; Luce 1959, 1963). It describes choices among alternative categorization responses to a given stimulus x. According to the so-called Luce (1959) choice rule, there is a ratio scale v such that the probability $P(i)$ of selecting alternative i from a given choice set, R, equals the v value of i, $v(i)$, divided by the sum of the v values of all the elements in R:

$$P(i) = \frac{v(i)}{\sum_{j \in R} v(j)}. \tag{2.1}$$

The biased choice model of Luce (1963) is a specialization of equation 2.1 in which each v value is a product of two factors:

$$v_x(i) = \eta(x,i)\beta_i. \tag{2.2}$$

The first factor, $\eta(x, i)$, can be interpreted as a measure of the similarity between the presented stimulus, x, and stimuli belonging to category i. The second factor, β_i, is a bias in favour of choosing response category i. By equations 2.1 and 2.2,

$$P(i) = \frac{\eta(x,i)\beta_i}{\sum_{j \in R} \eta(x,j)\beta_j}. \tag{2.3}$$

By equation 2.3, the probability of selecting response category i for stimulus x increases with the product of

(1) the similarity between stimulus x and stimuli belonging to category i; and

(2) the bias in favour of using response category i.

Conversely, the probability of selecting category i for stimulus x decreases with increasing degree of match between stimulus x and any alternative response category j, and with increasing bias in favour of using any alternative response category. Further discussion of equation 2.3 is found in Chapter 3.

2.3 Early demonstrations of capacity limitations in vision

Despite the massively parallel architecture of the brain's visual system (emphasized by Allport 1989, among others), we can identify only a small number of objects within the same instant. This limited capacity creates a need for selective attention—an ability to distribute processing capacity so that behaviourally important objects are allocated more capacity than are unimportant ones. Classical demonstrations of capacity limitations in visual attention were provided by Sperling (1960, 1963) using the *whole report* paradigm. The whole report task dates back to nineteenth-century investigations on the 'span of apprehension' (Cattell 1885) but Sperling's experiments were conducted more rigorously than those of his historic predecessors.

Sperling (1963, 1967) instructed subjects to report as many letters as possible from a briefly exposed array of unrelated letters followed by a pattern mask. The number of correctly reported letters (the score) depended on the *stimulus–onset asynchrony* (SOA) between the letter array and the mask. For each subject, there seemed to be a minimal effective exposure duration, t_0, below which the score was zero (corrected for guessing). As the SOA exceeded t_0, the mean score initially increased at a high rate (about one letter per 10–15 ms) and then levelled off as it approached a value of about four letters or the number of letters in the stimulus, whichever was smaller. This last finding was termed the *whole report limitation* and indicated a visual immediate memory span of about four letters, a result that has been generally replicated since (e.g. Shibuya and Bundesen 1988; also see Luck and Vogel 1997).

Sperling (1963) proposed a simple model to account for the initial strong, and approximately linear, increase in mean score as SOA exceeded t_0. By this model the subject encodes one letter at a time, requiring 10–15 ms for each. This *serial* encoding is interrupted when the stimulus is terminated by the mask, or when the number of encoded letters reaches the immediate memory span of the subject. The model was later rejected by Sperling (1967), based on the observation that, as exposure duration increases, all items in a display are reported with above-chance accuracy before any one item can be reported with perfect accuracy. The observation that all locations begin to be reported at better than chance levels, even at very brief exposures, could be accommodated by Sperling's original model, if the order of scanning were allowed to vary from trial to trial (Sperling 1967, Footnote 1). However, Sperling preferred to interpret the results in terms of *parallel* processing, implying that multiple items were attended simultaneously.

The interpretation of Sperling's data was an early example of the controversy about models assuming serial (one-at-a-time) processing of displays with multiple objects versus models assuming parallel (simultaneous) processing. Although the issue has been discussed widely, it still constitutes a major division line in attention research, as will be obvious from the general review in this chapter (also see Logan 2002b).

2.4 **Simple serial models**

In the 1960s and the following decades, *visual search* became the dominant experimental paradigm for attention research and gave rise to a new generation of models. In a typical experiment on visual search, the subject must indicate 'as quickly as possible' whether a target is present in a display. The target either belongs to a predesignated category such as *red* or letter type *T* or must be determined by the subject from display to display as the 'odd one out'. The display contains either one or no occurrences of the target as well as a varying number of distractors. Positive (present) and negative (absent) reaction times are analysed as functions of display size. Following Nickerson (1966) and Sternberg (1967), *simple serial models* have been used extensively in analysing reaction times from visual search experiments. The method of analysis was spelled out by Sternberg (1966, 1969*a,b*, 1998). It can be summarized as follows.

By a simple serial model, items are scanned one by one. As each item is scanned, it is classified as a target or as a distractor. The selection of items is random in the sense that the order in which items are scanned is independent of their status as targets versus distractors. A negative response is initiated if and when all items have been scanned and classified as distractors. Hence, the number of items processed before a negative response is initiated is equal to the display size, N, and the rate of increase in mean negative reaction time as a function of N equals the mean time taken to process one item, Δt. In an *exhaustive* search process, a positive response is made if a target is found, but the response is not initiated until all N display items have been processed. Therefore, the rate of increase in mean positive reaction time as a function of N also equals Δt. However, in a *self-terminating* search process, the search is terminated and a positive response is initiated as soon as a target is found. As the order in which items are scanned is independent of their status as targets versus distractors, the mean number of items processed before a positive response is initiated equals the average of 1, 2, … , and N, which is $(1 + N)/2$, so the rate of increase in mean positive reaction time as a function of N equals $\Delta t/2$. Thus, for self-terminating search in accordance with a simple serial model, the effect of display size for target-present displays should be half that for target-absent displays. This notion soon received extensive support in empirical studies.

2.4.1 **Feature and conjunction search**

Treisman *et al.* (1977) made an influential distinction between feature and conjunction search. In *feature search*, the target differs from the distractors by having a simple physical feature not shared by any of the distractors.

For instance, the target can be a white X among distractors that are black Xs (Fig. 2.3a). In such conditions, the target may appear to pop out from the background of distractors without any need to scan the display by saccadic eye movements or shifts of attention. Behaviourally, search can be fast and little affected by display size.

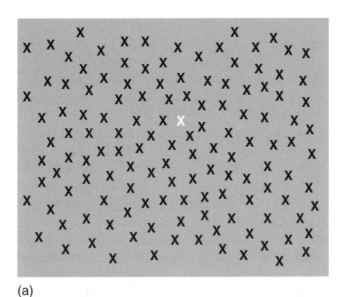

(a)

(b)

Fig. 2.3 Typical stimulus displays for visual search. (a) Feature search; (b) conjunction search. In both displays the target is a white X.

In *conjunction search*, the target is not unique in any simple physical feature, but the target differs from the distractors by showing a particular conjunction of physical features (e.g. a particular colour combined with a particular shape). For instance, the target can be a white X among black Xs and white Os (Fig. 2.3b). In such conditions, the search process may be effortful and appear to consist in scrutinizing the display part by part or even item by item. Behaviourally, search times tend to be longer, and positive and negative mean reaction times tend to be approximately linear functions of display size with substantial slopes and positive-to-negative slope ratios of about 1:2. This pattern conforms to predictions by simple serial models of visual search.

2.4.2 Feature integration theory (FIT)

The most important simple serial model is the feature integration theory (FIT) by Treisman and her associates (Treisman and Gelade 1980), which was the most influential model of attention in the 1980s. According to FIT, simple stimulus features such as colour, size, and orientation are registered automatically, without attention, and in parallel across the visual field. The features are stored in separate *feature maps*, each of which is organized retinotopically (i.e. in such a way that features depicted side by side on the retina are represented in adjacent areas on the map; see, for example, Zeki 1993). Localizing a feature requires spatial attention, but merely determining whether a feature is present can be done preattentively. Thus, a feature search can be done in parallel across the visual field.

The central hypothesis of FIT is that spatial attention is necessary for correct integration (*binding*) of individual features into whole-object representations (*object files*). The feature integration is done by moving an attention window (or *spotlight*) within a *master map of locations* and selecting from the feature maps whatever features are currently represented at the attended location. The selected features are conjoined to form an object, which in turn is compared with stored representations for recognition. After binding the features, the attention window moves to another location and initiates a new recognition process. In this way attention proceeds serially from object to object, at a rate typically estimated at 40–60 ms per item. Thus, whereas feature search should be a fast, parallel process, conjunction search should be a relatively slow, serial process, integrating the features of only one object at a time.

Besides early studies of visual search (see Treisman 1988), empirical support for FIT has come from demonstrations of *illusory conjunctions*, in which features of one object are erroneously attributed to another (Treisman and Schmidt 1982; Treisman and Paterson 1984; Robertson *et al.* 1997). In FIT, illusory conjunctions are explained by failures of focusing attention (see Treisman 1999; but see also Tsal *et al.* 1994; Ashby *et al.* 1996; Logan 1996; Donk 1999; Kyllingsbæk and Bundesen 2007).

2.4.3 Problems with FIT

From studies showing nearly linear search reaction time functions of display size with positive-to-negative slope ratios of about 1:2, Treisman and her associates conjectured that conjunction search is done by scanning items one at a time. However, rather similar predictions can be made if attention is shifted among small, non-overlapping groups of items, such that processing is parallel within groups, but serial between groups, and shifting is random with respect to the distinction between target and distractors. In this case, the total processing time should be an approximately linearly increasing function of the number of processed groups, which itself should be approximately linearly related to display size for both positive and negative displays, with a positive-to-negative slope ratio of 1:2. Pashler (1987*a*) suggested this sort of explanation for conjunction search, and Treisman and Gormican (1988) proposed the same sort of explanation for feature search with low target–distractor discriminability.

Other findings have argued against the original formulation of FIT. Both Nakayama and Silverman (1986) and Wolfe *et al.* (1989) reported that, contrary to the predictions of FIT, some forms of conjunction search can be conducted very rapidly. Duncan and Humphreys (1989) varied the similarity between stimuli and found that the slopes of the functions relating reaction time to display size showed no clear division between (fast, parallel) search for features and (slow, serial) search for conjunctions. Instead, they found a continuum of search efficiency such that the efficiency increased with decreased similarity of targets to distractors and with increased similarity between the distractors. Likewise, in summarizing a great number of search experiments, Wolfe (1998) found no indication of a bimodal distribution reflecting parallel versus serial search patterns. In the light of such findings, FIT has been revised (Treisman and Sato 1990) and is now more aptly characterized as a selective serial model (see Section 2.9 for related theories).

2.5 Simple parallel models

Alongside the development of serial models of selection, models assuming parallel processing were always an important alternative. In parallel models, several objects can be attended simultaneously. If processing times for individual stimuli in a display are statistically independent (in the sense that they are mutually independent random variables), the model is called an *independent* parallel model. If the processing time distributions for the stimuli are independent of the size and constituency of the displays in which they are presented, the model is said to have *unlimited processing capacity* (cf. Townsend and Ashby 1983; Bundesen 1987; for more discussion on this issue, see Chapter 4). An independent parallel model with unlimited processing capacity is called a *simple* parallel model (Bundesen 1996). The first simple parallel models of visual processing of multi-element displays were the *independent channels models* developed by C. W. Eriksen and his colleagues (Eriksen and Lappin 1965, 1967; Eriksen 1966; Eriksen and Spencer 1969). In these models display elements are processed in parallel at levels up to and including the level of stimulus recognition.

Eriksen and Lappin (1967) investigated an independent channels model for whole report. Their stimulus displays contained one, two, three, or four letters, each of which could be an A, an O, or a U, and the participants were instructed to report as many letters as possible from the displays (whole report). The possible stimulus positions formed the corners of an imaginary square centred on the fixation point. The probability that a particular letter occurred at a particular corner was independent of whatever other letters appeared in the display. Figure 2.4 shows a fit of the independent channels model to the proportions of trials without errors, with one error, and with two or more errors, respectively, as functions of display size with level of exposure duration as the parameter. The three exposure duration conditions were determined so that they yielded about 75%, 85%, and 98% correct reports, respectively, at a display size of 1. As can be seen, the fit is good for all display sizes and all three exposure–duration conditions.

Simple parallel models have been used extensively to account for cases in which visual search is highly efficient (i.e. effects of display size are small). As pointed out by Treisman and Gelade (1980), among others, this includes cases of feature search with high target–distractor discriminability. In an influential theory proposed by Schneider and Shiffrin (1977) and Shiffrin and Schneider (1977), it also includes cases of search for more complex targets after prolonged, consistent training in detecting those particular targets (also see Czerwinski *et al.* 1992; Kyllingsbæk *et al.* 2001).

Although successful in some respects, the simple parallel models have failed in other respects. Notably, the linear relations often found between mean reaction time and display size in visual search are hard to explain by simple parallel models (for a proof, see Townsend and Ashby 1983, p. 92; for a contrasting view, see Palmer 1995; Palmer *et al.* 2000). This problem led to the development of more refined parallel models (see Section 2.10), analogous to the evolution from simple to selective serial models. A more general problem was that the early serial and parallel models related to a rather limited number of experimental paradigms, such as whole report and visual search. As more

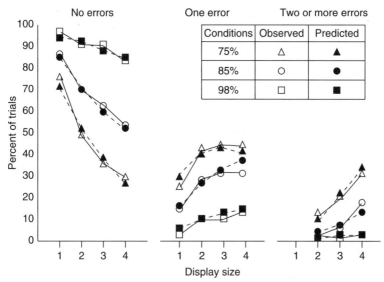

Fig. 2.4 Mean proportion of trials having no, one, and two or more errors as a function of display size and level of exposure duration in the whole report experiment by Eriksen and Lappin (1967). Group data were for four subjects. Exposure duration conditions were determined for each subject so as to yield about 75%, 85%, and 98% correct reports, respectively, at a display size of 1. Adapted with permission from Eriksen and Lappin (1967). Independence in the perception of simultaneously presented forms at brief durations. *Journal of Experimental Psychology*, **73**, 468–472. Copyright 1967 by the American Psychological Association. The use of APA information does not imply endorsement by APA.

aspects of attention were studied using new paradigms, the field gradually grew more complex, and a much larger pool of empirical data had to be accounted for. These new findings often served to elaborate the classical discussions on serial versus parallel processing or early versus late selection, and provided stronger empirical constraints for new generations of models. In the following three sections, we summarize the empirical developments in the most central areas of investigation.

2.6 **Distractor interference**

The extent to which irrelevant stimulus information is processed is a long-standing issue in attention research. It relates to fundamental theoretical questions such as serial versus parallel processing and early versus late selection. As an example, Treisman's feature integration theory predicts that ignored items are analysed only at the level of simple features. Conversely, high-level semantic processing of distractors is prima-facie evidence for parallel processing of objects. Many experimental paradigms have been used to investigate the extent of processing of irrelevant stimulus information. Most of the paradigms provide measures of more or less automatic interference from the irrelevant information.

2.6.1 Stroop and flanker interference

In a classical task introduced by Stroop (1935), the participants are requested to name the colour of the ink used to print a word. Stroop showed that the task is more difficult when the printed word is the name of a different colour than that of the ink (e.g. 'red' printed in blue) than when the word does not refer to a colour or refers to the colour of the ink ('blue' printed in blue). The Stroop effect has been studied widely (for a review, see MacLeod 1991) and it is generally considered to result from conflict in late, response-related stages of processing. In the Stroop task, the participant attends to a particular feature of an object (*featural attention*) while ignoring another feature of the same object, and the Stroop effect indicates semantic processing of the feature to be ignored. Other tasks have been devised to study the extent to which distracting objects are processed.

In the *flankers task* of B. A. Eriksen and C. W. Eriksen (1974), participants are instructed to focus attention on a target presented at fixation (*spatial attention*). Usually the target is a letter, and the participant is asked to make a speeded binary classification (e.g. move a lever in one direction if the letter is a T or a K, but in the opposite direction if the letter is an S or a C). The target is flanked by letters that are irrelevant to the task (flankers). However, compared with the condition with neutral flankers (letters other than T, K, S, and C), the task is more difficult when the flankers are *response-incompatible* with the target (Ss or Cs flanking a T) but more easy when the flankers are *response-compatible* with the target (Ts or Ks flanking a T). Eriksen and Eriksen concluded that the flankers are processed in parallel with the target up to and including the stage of letter recognition.

Flanker interference decreases in strength as the spatial separation of the flankers from the target is increased (B. A. Eriksen and C. W. Eriksen 1974). The effect also decreases if the flankers appear in another colour than the target, even when colour is completely irrelevant to the task (Harms and Bundesen 1983; see also Kramer and Jacobson 1991; Baylis and Driver 1992). Harms and Bundesen (1983) conjectured that the strength of flanker interference depends on the extent to which a flanker is perceptually grouped with the target (for related discussion, see Cave and Bichot 1999).

Paquet and Lortie (1990) questioned if flanker interference is clear evidence of late selection. When the conditions for focusing attention on the target were improved by displaying a cue exactly at the target position at the start of each trial, the effects of the flankers were markedly reduced. This finding supports the possibility of early filtering. However, absence of flanker interference does not exclude the possibility of semantic processing of distractor items. Evidence for such processing has been found by the method of negative priming (Driver and Tipper 1989; Fox 1995*b*).

2.6.2 Negative priming

Responses to a stimulus presented as a target (on a *probe* trial) tend to be slower and less accurate if the same stimulus has been presented as a distractor on a preceding (*prime*) trial. This phenomenon is called *negative priming*. In the 1990s negative priming attracted strong interest, partly because the effect appeared to provide direct evidence of inhibitory mechanisms in attention.

The first demonstrations of negative priming were made by Dalrymple-Alford and Budayr (1966) and Neill (1977) by use of the Stroop colour–word task. The effect was replicated in other experimental conditions by Tipper and Cranston (1985) and Tipper (1985). When discovering the generality of the phenomenon, Tipper (1985) labelled the effect 'negative priming'. In the experiments of Tipper (1985) and Tipper and Cranston (1985), the participants were presented with outline drawings of pairs of overlapping objects, each pair formed by a target and a distractor. The target always appeared in a predesignated colour. In the *attended repetition* condition, the target in a probe display was the same as the target in the preceding prime display. In the *ignored repetition* condition, the target in the probe display was the same as the distractor in the prime display. In the control condition, stimulus repetitions did not occur. Response times were shortest in attended repetition, intermediate in the control condition, and longest in ignored repetition.

In subsequent years, negative priming has been investigated by many different experimental methods (for reviews, see Fox 1995*a*; May *et al.* 1995). The priming effect was shown not only for identical objects, but also for objects that were merely similar to each other in physical properties or even in only semantic properties. For semantic negative priming to occur, the ignored object must have received high-level processing in the prime trial.

The empirical literature on negative priming is extensive and quite complex. The generality of the effect has been firmly established, but no theory explains all the findings. On the whole, the negative priming effect seems consistent with an inhibitory account (Tipper 2001) without providing clear evidence of inhibitory mechanisms. Thus, the role of inhibitory mechanisms in attention remains controversial (Milliken and Tipper 1998).

2.6.3 The locus of selection revisited

From the time the stage was set by Broadbent (1958), Deutsch and Deutsch (1963), and Treisman (1964*a,b*), the *locus of selection*, early versus late, has been widely debated in attention research. In line with Johnston and Heinz (1978), Lavie (1995) suggested that the extent to which distractors are processed depends on the perceptual load of the task. If perceptual load is low, distractors are processed automatically, which gives rise to interference effects. This corresponds to late selection. If perceptual load is high, distractors receive little processing, which corresponds to early selection. Other researchers have argued that the question of early versus late selection is ill-posed (e.g. Allport 1989, 1993). On the one hand, selectivity may be found at multiple levels of processing. For example, electrophysiological studies have provided strong evidence of attention effects at early stages of visual processing (see, for example, Hillyard *et al.* 1999), while a large body of behavioural evidence points to selectivity at later stages. On the other hand, attentional selection and stimulus recognition may be two aspects of the same process rather than two different stages of processing. This idea of *simultaneous selection* is central in the TVA model (see Chapter 3).

2.7 Attentional capture and voluntary control

Another main issue in attention research is the competing influence of stimulus properties versus subjective control on selection: *bottom-up* and *top-down* factors in attention, respectively. Leibniz described this fundamental dichotomy in 1765 (Leibniz 1996) and, more recently, much work has been done to clarify the interaction between external and internal factors in attentional selection.

2.7.1 Attentional capture

Studies of bottom-up mechanisms focus on the phenomenon *attentional capture*, where the object of attention is more or less automatically determined by certain properties of the stimulus. Most studies have concerned the propensity of salient feature discontinuities or abrupt onsets to attract attention. Theeuwes (1992, 1994, 1995) provided evidence that when the target of search is a featural *singleton* (e.g. a single red item among black ones), attention will be captured by the most salient singleton in the display, regardless of whether this singleton is relevant to the subject's task. Bacon and Egeth (1994) argued that when subjects are looking for a featural singleton in a given dimension, they adopt a strategy (*singleton-detection mode*) of directing attention to the locations with the highest feature contrast, regardless of the dimension in which the contrast is found. Thus attention should be guided by the output of a general feature-contrast detector.

Yantis has argued that, in the absence of a deliberate attentional set for a featural singleton, a visual stimulus of abrupt onset will capture attention (Jonides 1981; Yantis and Jonides 1984; Jonides and Yantis 1988; Remington *et al.* 1992; Yantis and Hillstrom 1994), but other types of stimuli will not (Jonides and Yantis 1988; Hillstrom and Yantis 1994). However, even capture by abrupt onsets seems not entirely automatic. Yantis and Jonides (1990) found that when subjects had focused attention on a particular spatial location, no stimuli appearing elsewhere captured attention. Folk *et al.* (1992, 1994) argued that all cases of attentional capture are contingent on *attentional control settings*: Abrupt-onset stimuli tend to capture attention when subjects look for abrupt-onset targets, but not when they look for colour targets, and vice versa (for further discussion, see Folk *et al.* 1993; Yantis 1993; but also see Theeuwes 1994).

2.7.2 Partial report

Partial report is an experimental technique for studying the efficiency of top-down control of selection. In a partial-report experiment, the subject is instructed to report as many targets as possible from a briefly exposed display containing a mixture of targets (items to be reported) and distractors (items to be ignored). The targets are defined as those items that satisfy a particular selection criterion. For selection by simple criteria such as location, colour, or size, early studies (Sperling 1960; von Wright 1968, 1970) demonstrated a phenomenon termed *partial-report superiority*: the probability that a given target is correctly reported is higher in partial report than in whole report from displays with the same total number of items.

In later studies (Bundesen *et al.* 1984, 1985; Shibuya and Bundesen 1988; Shibuya 1993; see also Duncan 1980, 1983, 1985), the number of targets and the number of distractors in the stimulus displays were varied independently for different selection criteria, such as brightness, colour, shape (curved versus straight), alphanumeric class (letters versus digits), and conjunctions of colour and alphanumeric class. With each of these criteria, the probability that a target was correctly reported decreased as the number of other items (targets or distractors) was increased. The decrement caused by a distractor was less than the decrement caused by another target, so processing was selective. Measured by the difference in effect between a distractor and another target, the efficiency of selection varied widely with the selection criterion; but even with a fairly difficult selection criterion such as alphanumeric class, the difference in effect between a distractor and another target was also demonstrated when effects of storage limitations should be negligible (e.g. with postmasked displays and exposure durations so brief that mean scores were a small fraction of one item and at most two items were ever reported; see Duncan 1983; Shibuya and Bundesen 1988). The results suggest that allocation of processing capacity is selective so that the available processing capacity allocated to a distractor is less than the capacity allocated to a target.

2.8 Attentional orienting, shifting, and dwelling

Attentional orienting, shifting, and dwelling concern the way attention is allocated over the visual field and reallocated from time to time. The dynamics of deploying and reallocating attention bear directly on the issue of serial versus parallel processing. Thus, a typical serial model assumes that attention is focused on one object in the visual field at a time but moved about at a high speed. A typical parallel model assumes a broad distribution of processing resources over the visual field, shifting slowly, but comprising many objects simultaneously.

2.8.1 Set for spatial position

C. W. Eriksen, Posner, and others developed a simple cuing paradigm for studying spatial orienting of attention. In this paradigm, the participant is presented with an attentional cue followed by a target that requires a speeded response (Fig. 2.5). Usually, the target appears in a peripheral location, and the cue tells the participant where the target is likely to appear, but the participant must maintain fixation at a central fixation point. Thus attentional orienting is *covert* (i.e. without eye movements; cf. Eriksen and Hoffman 1973; Posner 1980; for evidence on close coupling between attention and saccadic eye movements, see Deubel and Schneider 1996).

Two types of attentional cues are commonly distinguished: central versus peripheral. *Central* cues are presented at fixation and give symbolic information about the occurrence of the target. A typical example is an arrow pointing at the likely location of the target, telling the subject to 'push' attention (*endogenously*, i.e. voluntarily) to the indicated location. *Peripheral* cues appear in the periphery of the visual field, 'pulling' attention (*exogenously*, i.e. automatically) to the location of the cue. The pull can be generated by the abrupt onset of the cue (see Section 2.7.1).

The version of the cuing paradigm developed by Posner and his associates (e.g. Posner *et al.* 1978, 1980) provides measures of both attentional cost and attentional benefit. With central cuing, the *attentional benefit* is measured

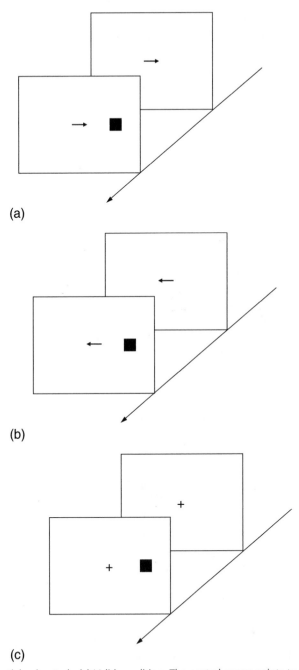

Fig. 2.5 Spatial cuing task. (a) Valid condition. The central arrow points to the location where the target appears subsequently. (b) Invalid condition. The central arrow points to a different location than where the target will appear. (c) Neutral condition. The subject is not given prior information about the location of the target.

by the decrease in reaction time to a target that follows a *valid* cue (i.e. an informative cue that turns out to be true) as compared with the reaction time to a target that follows a *neutral* (i.e. non-informative) cue. The *attentional cost* is measured by the increase in reaction time to a target that follows an *invalid* cue (an informative cue that turns out to be false) instead of a neutral cue.

Posner and Cohen (1984) observed that a non-informative peripheral cue that was followed by a target at the same location facilitated responses to the target when the cue–target interval (SOA) was short (e.g. 100 ms). They suggested that the cue produced an automatic orienting of attention that facilitated detection of targets at the cued location. However, when the cue–target interval was longer than a few hundred milliseconds (e.g. 300 or 500 ms), responses to the target were slower when the target appeared at the cued location as compared with uncued locations. Posner and Cohen proposed that in this case, attention was initially captured by the cue, but then shifted away from the cued location so that the initial facilitation was replaced by inhibition. The phenomenon is called *inhibition of return.* Posner and Cohen found the inhibition to persist for more than 1 s after cuing. Inhibition of return has been demonstrated in many different paradigms (see, for example, Gibson and Egeth 1994; Pratt and Abrams 1999). The phenomenon may reflect a 'novelty bias' that makes visual exploration proceed efficiently without revisiting previously searched locations (Milliken and Tipper 1998).

2.8.2 Spotlight and zoom-lens models

Posner (1980) described his findings on spatial orienting in terms of a spotlight model of attention. In this model, attention is unitary (like a single spot of light), delimited in space at a particular time, and moved about in visual space from time to time. The similarity between shifts of attention and eye movements is not coincidental, as there are strong connections between the oculomotor system and visual attention. Eriksen and Yeh (1985) and Eriksen and St. James (1986) proposed a closely related model, a zoom-lens model of the visual attentional field. According to this model, the attentional field can be varied in extension from covering a spot subtending less than 1 of visual angle to covering the entire visual field. As the total visual processing capacity is limited, the amount of processing capacity allocated to a given attended location decreases as the extension of the attentional field is increased. However, the attentional field cannot be split among non-contiguous locations (for a contrasting view, see Shaw 1978). Direct tests of this assumption have been attempted, but the issue is still controversial (cf. Eriksen and Webb 1989; for a review, see Cave and Bichot 1999).

The spotlight and zoom-lens models describe visual attention as a spatial phenomenon. This *space-based* conception has been highly influential (cf. feature integration theory), but *object-based* theories of attention have also been proposed (see Kahneman 1973; Duncan 1984). According to these theories, processing capacity is allocated to objects rather than the locations at which the objects appear. Traditionally, space- and object-based accounts of attention have been rival theories, but integrated accounts have been proposed by Logan (1996) and Humphreys (1999).

2.8.3 Set for size and orientation

Attentional sets for size and orientation have also been demonstrated. Larsen and Bundesen (1978) (see also Cave and Kosslyn 1989) presented subjects with a sequence of letters in various sizes. The sequence was constructed such that following the presentation of a letter in a given size, the probability that the next letter appeared in the same size was high (80%). The time taken to respond to the letter increased with divergence between the cued size (given by the size of the preceding letter) and the actual stimulus size. Specifically, when letters were not repeated, the increment in latency was approximately proportional to the logarithm of the ratio between the cued size and the actual size.

In a closely related experiment showing attentional set for orientation, Jolicoeur (1990) presented subjects with two letters in rapid succession. Each letter appeared at the centre of the visual field in one of two possible orientations. The participants were instructed to name the two letters at the end of the trial. The responses to the second letter were more accurate when its orientation was the same as the orientation of the first letter than when it was different.

2.8.4 Attentional blink and dwell time

The *attentional blink* refers to the following phenomenon. When two masked targets are presented sequentially with a separation of more than 500 ms, the presentation of the first target (T1) has little effect on the report of the second target (T2). However, when T1 and T2 are presented within approximately 500 ms of each other, and both targets are to be reported, report of T2 is impeded.

The attentional blink has been investigated extensively by presenting subjects with a rapid sequence of stimuli (e.g. 6–20 items/s) at a fixed location (*rapid serial visual presentation*, RSVP). In a pioneering study, Broadbent and Broadbent (1987) instructed subjects to report two target words from an RSVP stream of words (see also Weichselgartner and Sperling 1987). The target words were indicated by capital letters. Broadbent and Broadbent found a clear deficit in reporting both words when the temporal interval between the words was less than about 400 ms. Subsequent research has addressed the precise time course of the effect (Shapiro *et al.* 1994; Chun and Potter 1995). The probability that T2 is reported correctly is typically a U-shaped function of the SOA between T1 and T2 (Fig. 2.6). Performance is lowest when T2 is presented about 300 ms after the onset of T1, but relatively good when T2 is presented within 100 ms of T1 onset.

Raymond *et al.* (1992) showed that identification of T1 disturbed not just identification but also simple detection of T2 items, even when these were fully prespecified. Furthermore, Raymond *et al.* reported that T1 processing must be interrupted by another visual stimulus in order for the attentional blink to occur. When a blank interval was substituted for the item immediately following T1, the attentional blink was substantially reduced. Finally, Raymond *et al.* established that detection of T2 was impaired only when a response to T1 was required. When the subject was instructed to ignore T1, T2

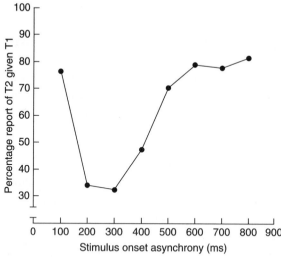

Fig. 2.6 Percentage report of the second target (T2) given report of the first target (T1) as a function of stimulus onset asynchrony in Experiment 1 of Chun and Potter (1995). Adapted with permission from Chun and Potter (1995). A two-stage model for multiple target detection in rapid serial visual presentation. *Journal of Experimental Psychology: Human Perception and Performance*, **21**, 109–127. Copyright 1995 by the American Psychological Association. The use of APA information does not imply endorsement by APA.

was readily detected, so the effect seemed not to be due to sensory masking. Raymond *et al.* therefore coined the term *attentional* blink. Later studies have confirmed the non-sensory nature of the basic phenomenon (Shapiro *et al.* 1997; Vogel *et al.* 1998), although some masking effects have been reported (Brehaut *et al.* 1999).

Chun and Potter (1995) proposed a *two-stage* model of the attentional blink. At the first stage of processing, features of each item in the RSVP stream are detected in parallel. At the second stage, processing is serial: items detected at the first stage receive full semantic processing and are consolidated for report, but only one at a time. The attentional blink results from the limited capacity of the second stage of processing. During the consolidation of a selected item, other items are still being detected at the parallel stage. However, representations generated at the parallel stage of processing are short-lived and vulnerable to interference from other items. Therefore, as long as T1 occupies the serial stage of processing, subsequent targets tend to be lost (see McLaughlin *et al.* 2001, for possible modifications of the two-stage model; for a recent, formal version of the two-stage model, see Bowman and Wyble 2007).

Shapiro *et al.* (1994) suggested an *interference* model. Like the two-stage model of Chun and Potter, the interference model assumes unlimited-capacity parallel preprocessing of all items followed by full processing in a limited-capacity system. However, in the interference model, the limited-capacity system works in parallel, so that several items undergo semantic processing at the same time. More specifically, the attentional blink results from competition among several items for processing resources in visual short-term memory. Initially items are compared with an attentional template (cf. Duncan and Humphreys 1989) and good matches (i.e. targets) receive greater weight in the competition for conscious retrieval. T1 is a strong competitor, and until it can be transferred to a more durable memory store, it reduces available capacity for subsequent items, including T2. This results in frequent intrusion errors, T2 being mixed up with distracting items (see Isaak *et al.* 1999, for empirical support for the interference model; for a recent, formal version of the interference model, incorporating aspects of the two-stage model, see Shih in press).

The dynamics of attention can be described as a time series of distributions of processing resources across objects in space, linked by reallocations of processing resources from one distribution to the next one (see Sperling and Weichselgartner 1995; Shih and Sperling 2002). The *attentional dwell time* is the time during which a particular distribution of processing resources is maintained. The attentional blink has been regarded as evidence for a dwell time of several hundred milliseconds (Ward *et al.* 1996). Duncan *et al.* (1994) provided further support for an estimate of this order of magnitude by use of a simplified version of the RSVP task. Moore *et al.* (1996) argued that the dwell time estimated by Duncan *et al.* (1994) was inflated by masking effects, but the estimate seems consistent with electrophysiological results obtained in monkeys (Chelazzi *et al.* 1993, 1998). A dwell time of several hundred milliseconds is inconsistent with simple serial models of visual search, in which attention moves from object to object at a speed of a few dozen milliseconds per item. In the next section more recent types of serial models are considered. Although still hard to accommodate, the findings on attentional dwell time are more compatible with these models.

2.9 Selective serial models

In serial models of attention, only one stimulus is attended at a time. Within this framework there has been a theoretical evolution from simple serial models (described in Section 2.4) to selective serial models. In selective serial models, items in the stimulus display are attended one at a time but, unlike simple models, the sequential order in which items are attended depends on their status as targets versus distractors: When a target and a distractor compete for attention, the target is more likely to win.

2.9.1 Hoffman's model of visual search

The first selective serial model of visual search was published in 1978 by James Hoffman. The model was based on findings from C. W. Eriksen's laboratory on the time taken to shift attention in response to a visual cue (e.g. Colegate *et al.* 1973; see also Section 5.3.3). The findings went against the assumption that attention can be shifted from item to item at the high rates required by simple (non-selective) serial models of processing.

In Hoffman's (1978, 1979) model, visual search is a two-stage process. At the first stage, the entire stimulus display is evaluated in parallel. The evaluation is preattentive and quick, but rough. For each item in the display, it yields a measure of the likelihood that the item is a target. The parallel evaluation guides a slow serial mechanism that transfers items one by one (about one item per 100 ms) to the second stage of processing. Although the serial transfer mechanism is slow, it makes search efficient by transferring items in order of decreasing likelihood that the items are targets. Hence, if there is a target in the display, the target is likely to be among the first items that are transferred to the second stage of processing.

2.9.2 The guided search model

Jeremy Wolfe and his collaborators have proposed a highly influential selective serial model called *guided search* (cf. Wolfe *et al.* 1989; Cave and Wolfe 1990;

Wolfe 1994). The guided search model combines elements of the two-stage model of Hoffman with elements of the feature integration theory of Treisman and her associates (Treisman and Gelade 1980; Treisman 1988). Like feature integration theory, the guided search model assumes that simple stimulus features such as colour, size, and orientation are registered automatically, without attention, and in parallel across the visual field. Registration of objects (i.e. items defined by conjunctions of features) requires a further stage of processing at which attention is directed serially to each object. Like Hoffman's model, the guided search model assumes the outcome of the first, parallel stage of processing guides the serial processing at the second stage. The guidance works as follows.

For each feature dimension (e.g. colour, size, or orientation), the parallel stage generates an array of activation values (attention values) forming a map of the visual field. Each value is a sum of a bottom-up and a top-down component. In a map for a given feature dimension, the bottom-up component for a particular location is a measure of differences between the value of the feature at that location and values of the same feature at neighbouring locations. The top-down component for the location is a measure of the difference between the value of the feature at the given location and the target value for the feature dimension. When activations have been calculated in separate maps for each feature dimension, they are summed across feature dimensions to produce a single overall activation map. In computer simulations, a certain level of Gaussian noise is also added at each location. The final overall activation values represent the evaluation given by the parallel stage of how likely the stimulus at each location is to be the target (Fig. 2.7).

The serial stage processes the items in order of decreasing activation in the overall activation map. When an item is processed, it is classified as a target or as a distractor. The processing continues until a target is found or until all items with activations above a certain value have been processed.

The guided search model accounts for many findings from experiments on visual search. The model was motivated, in part, by demonstrations of fast conjunction search. The model explains some demonstrations of fast conjunction search (e.g. Nakayama and Silverman 1986) by assuming that for some feature dimensions, top-down control is very effective. Other demonstrations (e.g. Wolfe *et al.* 1989) are explained by assuming that in some subjects, the level of Gaussian noise is very low.

2.9.3 Problems with the guided search model

In selective serial models, the conflict between data suggesting that attention shifting is slow and data showing only slight effects of display size in visual

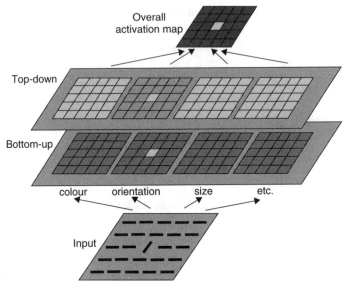

Fig. 2.7 Parallel stage of processing (during a feature search task) in the guided search model. The bottom figure represents the visual input. The vertical line in the centre of the input pattern is the target and the distractors are all horizontal lines. Above the input pattern are separate feature maps for each feature dimension. Each feature map is split into two maps to show the effects of bottom-up and top-down activation separately. Each location of the maps is shaded according to its activation: Lighter shading represents a higher activation level. All objects in the visual input have the same colour and size, so the bottom-up maps that represent these features have low activation. However, there is one element that differs from the rest in orientation, which leads to high bottom-up activation at the location corresponding to this object in the orientation map. The top-down activation at each location of a feature map is given by the similarity between the feature at that location and the target value ('vertical line'). This produces high top-down activation at the centre location in the orientation map, but does not lead to activation differences in the other feature maps. The combined bottom-up and top-down activations of each feature map are summed up to produce an overall activation map (top figure) that represents the parallel stage's 'opinion' of how likely the stimulus at each location is to be the target. Adapted with permission from Cave and Wolfe (1990). Modeling the role of parallel processing in visual search. *Cognitive Psychology*, **22**, 225–271. Copyright 1990 by Elsevier.

search (e.g. 10ms per item; Sperling *et al.* 1971) is resolved by assuming that the serial processing is limited to targets and target-like items. However, a closely related problem for serial models remains: the conflict between data suggesting that attention shifting is slow and data suggesting processing rates of up to one item per 10–15ms in whole report (e.g. Sperling 1963), that is, in a task in which all items are targets.

The guided search model also has problems in accounting for search slopes. Wolfe (1994) considered 708 pairs of corresponding positive (target present) and negative (target absent) search slopes from subjects tested on many different search tasks. Out of the 708 pairs, 167 pairs had positive slopes greater than 20 ms per item. These pairs showed a mean positive-to-negative slope ratio of 0.50. Another 187 had positive slopes less than 5 ms per item. For these pairs, the mean positive-to-negative slope ratio was nearly the same (0.53). The guided search model has difficulty explaining these findings. The model predicts a 1:2 slope ratio in the limiting case in which activations caused by targets and distractors are identically distributed so that search is non-selective ('blind' with respect to the distinction between target and distractors). However, when target activations are stronger than distractor activations, targets should be more likely to be among the first items scanned. Thus, when search becomes guided, both the positive search slope and the positive-to-negative slope ratio would be expected to decrease. The results of Wolfe's (1994) study of 708 pairs of search slopes went counter to this expectation.

Horowitz and Wolfe (1998) reported evidence against another basic assumption in the guided search model: that items are sampled in series without replacement. Subjects searched for a rotated T among rotated Ls, which yielded a search slope of 20–30 ms per item with normal, 'static' displays. In the critical condition, all letters in a display were relocated at random every 111 ms. In this condition, subjects should be unable to keep track of the progress of search in such a way that the letters could be sampled without replacement. Nevertheless, search slopes were unaffected. This finding goes against serial models that assume display items are sampled one by one without replacement. The finding also contradicts parallel models that assume that information about the identity of display items is gradually accumulated over time. As argued by Horowitz and Wolfe, the result is consistent with a 'memory-less' serial model in which items are sampled with replacement so that the same item may be sampled again and again. The result also agrees with a parallel model in which processing times of display items are distributed exponentially. The exponential distribution is the only distribution endowed with complete lack of memory (i.e. a constant 'hazard function'; for a proof, see Feller 1968, p. 459). However, the generality of the results is uncertain. A study by von Mühlenen *et al.* (2003) suggests that subjects may have adopted a different strategy in the 'dynamic' condition than in the static condition; in the dynamic condition observers may have attended to a subregion of the display and waited for the target to appear there. Also, studies of eye movements during overt search suggest that oculomotor visual search does have memory, at least for the past few items (see Peterson *et al.* 2001; McCarley *et al.* 2003).

2.10 **Selective parallel models**

In parallel models of attention several stimuli can be attended at the same time. Like serial models, parallel models have progressed towards more complex and powerful accounts, from simple parallel (independent-channels) models to limited-capacity and race-based parallel models of selection. These latter types of models can be characterized as *selective* in that processing capacity is distributed intelligently (i.e. with respect to what is important for the perceiver) among the objects in the visual field.

2.10.1 **Limited-capacity parallel models**

Compared with simple parallel models, models of parallel processing with limited capacity account for a wider range of experimental findings. For example, as noted in Section 2.5, the linear relations between mean reaction time and display size in visual search cannot be explained by simple parallel models. However, the linear relations can be explained by independent parallel models with limited processing capacity (Atkinson *et al.* 1969; Townsend 1969).

Shaw and co-workers (Shaw and Shaw 1977; Shaw 1978) proposed an *optimal capacity–allocation model*, which extended the limited-capacity model of Atkinson *et al.* (1969) and Townsend (1969) to situations in which a target is more likely to occur in some display locations than in others. An *allocation policy* (cf. Kahneman 1973) is a way of allocating and reallocating the total processing capacity C across display locations. For any distribution of the probability of target occurrence across the display locations, there is an optimal allocation policy, that is, an allocation policy that maximizes the probability that the target has been recognized by time t, for any time t (cf. Shaw 1978; see also Townsend and Ashby 1983, pp. 139–45). After extensive experience with a given probability distribution, the subject is assumed to adopt the optimal allocation policy.

Shaw (1978) fitted the optimal capacity–allocation model to differences in mean reaction time between high- and low-probability locations in a detection task. The model provided reasonable but not really good fits. However, the principle of optimization seems important (Sperling 1984), and goodness of fit might be improved by including time costs of reallocations of processing capacity (shifts of attention; see Section 5.3).

2.10.2 **Race models of selection**

In *race models of selection* from multi-element displays (Bundesen *et al.* 1985; Bundesen 1987, 1993), display items are processed in parallel, and attentional selection is made of those items that finish processing first (the winners of the race). Thus selection of targets rather than distractors is based on processing of targets being faster than processing of distractors.

Shibuya and Bundesen (1988) proposed a fixed-capacity independent race model (FIRM). The model describes the processing of a stimulus display as follows. First an attentional weight is computed for each item in the display. The weight is a measure of the strength of the sensory evidence that the item is a target. Then the available processing capacity is distributed across the items in proportion to their weights. The amount of processing capacity that is allocated to an item determines how fast the item can be encoded into visual short-term memory (VSTM). Finally, the encoding race between the items takes place. The time taken to encode an item is assumed to be exponentially distributed with a rate parameter equal to the amount of processing capacity that is allocated to the item. The items that are selected (i.e. stored in VSTM) are those items whose encoding processes are complete before the stimulus presentation terminates and before VSTM has been filled up. FIRM was the direct predecessor of TVA theory, which inherited many of the basic notions and mathematical principles of FIRM. We describe these principles in much more detail in Chapter 3.

2.11 Connectionist models

In traditional cognitive theories, functional mechanisms are described at a highly abstract level. Connectionist models represent an attempt to theorize at a level that is closer to neurophysiology (McClelland and Rumelhart 1986; Rumelhart and McClelland 1986). In connectionist models, information processing is implemented as a flow of activation through a network of neuron-like units, which are linked together by facilitatory and inhibitory connections. Connectionist models of visual attention include, among others, the selective attention model (SLAM) of Phaf *et al.* (1990; see also van der Heijden 1992, 2004), the multiple object recognition and attentional selection (MORSEL) model of Mozer (1991), the search via recursive rejection (SERR) model of Humphreys and Müller (1993), the neurodynamical model of visual search proposed by Deco and Zihl (2001), and the selective attention for identification model (SAIM) of Heinke and Humphreys (2003).

As an instructive example, consider the neurodynamical model of Deco and Zihl (2001). In this model, the elementary units are *populations* of neurons. The mean firing activity of each population is governed by a set of differential equations (cf. Usher and Niebur 1996). The architecture of the model is shown in Fig. 2.8. Visual input to the system is represented in a *retina map* that

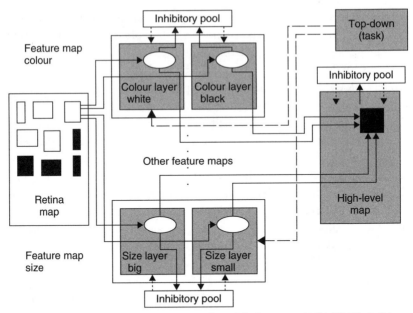

Fig. 2.8 Architecture of the neurodynamical model of Deco and Zihl (2001). Solid and long-dashed arrows represent excitatory connections between modules, short-dashed arrows represent inhibitory connections. Adapted with permission from Deco and Zihl (2001). Top-down selective visual attention: a neurodynamical approach. *Visual Cognition*, **8**, 119–141. Copyright 2001 by Psychology Press.

has excitatory connections to a set of *feature maps* (representing colour, size, etc.), with separate layers for each value of the feature (e.g. white, big). The feature maps are organized retinotopically; in each layer, the neuron population at a particular position receives excitatory input from the corresponding position in the retina map. In this distributed way, activity in the feature maps encodes values of features at specific locations on the retina. For each feature map, there is a pool of inhibitory neurons. Each layer of the feature map sends excitatory connections to this pool, which indirectly inhibits activity in other layers of the feature map. In this way feature values compete for activation in a winner-take-all fashion. Conjunctions of features are represented in a retinotopic *high-level map*. In this map, a unit representing a conjunction at a certain location receives excitatory inputs from representations of the components of the conjunction at corresponding locations in feature maps. Like the feature maps, the high-level map is connected to a pool of inhibitory neurons, which produces competition among conjunctions at different locations. A *top-down module* provides memory information about the feature values of the target item (cf. Duncan and Humphreys 1989), which is transmitted by excitatory inputs to the relevant feature layers. For example, if the target is 'small' and 'white', all activations in these layers of the feature maps are enhanced.

The model works as follows. In a visual search task, the system is given both a sensory input and a memory specification of target attributes. In response to these inputs, the parallel competition mechanisms in the feature and conjunction maps eventually produce a stable pattern of activity throughout the system. In this stable state, only the neuron populations receiving both bottom-up and top-down excitatory inputs (i.e. units with sensory inputs matching the target features) are highly activated. The convergence of activity towards the stable state corresponds to focusing of attention at the target object. An important dependent variable is the *latency* of the system, that is, how long it takes for convergence to develop in a given search task. In simulations of human performance this corresponds to reaction time. Deco and Zihl (2001) found that the performance of the system was qualitatively similar to human performance in various feature and conjunction search tasks. Specifically, the 'serial' search pattern observed in many cases of conjunction search (i.e. linearly increasing reaction time functions of display size) emerged from the parallel dynamics of the system without assuming an explicit priority map or a serial scanning mechanism (cf. Wolfe 1994).

2.12 Summary

Modern research on attention sprung from the theoretical framework developed by Broadbent, Treisman, and other pioneers. Since the early work, most research has concerned visual attention, and by now a wide range of empirical findings has accumulated in this field. Studies have described capacity limitations, interference by distractor objects, automatic and voluntary influences on selection, the temporal dynamics of processing, and numerous other aspects of attention. Significant theoretical development has occurred, from purely qualitative models in the early years towards quantitative accounts with much higher empirical specificity. The emergence of connectionist models represents an important theoretical development, directed towards modelling the underlying neural processes.

Despite the wealth of empirical findings, the fundamental theoretical question of serial versus parallel processing of multi-element displays continues to arouse debate. Many studies have provided support for parallel processing, many others for serial processing. Of course, a serial processor of a certain type of items need not be capable of parallel processing of the same type of items, and a parallel processor need not be capable of serial processing. However, as noted by Bundesen (1990), a selective parallel processor such as the one described in the FIRM model of Shibuya and Bundesen (1988)—a parallel processor with spatially selective allocation of processing resources to a certain type of items—is also capable of serial processing of the same type of items. The serial processing can be done by first using a spatial selection criterion for sampling one or more items from one part of the stimulus display, then shifting the selection criterion to sample items from another part of the display, and so on, with or without eye movements. Each individual sampling of items can occur in parallel, but the search process as a whole has a strong serial component. Thus, as elaborated in Section 5.3, the choice of serial or parallel processing may be partly strategic (i.e. under cognitive control), and the optimal strategy may be one of shifting attention between subsets of items with a set size that depends upon the task.

3

A psychological theory of visual attention (TVA)

The theory of visual attention (TVA) proposed by Bundesen (1990) was an attempt to devise a *general mechanism* for attentional selection. When surveying the psychological literature, Bundesen (1990) noticed a vague appeal to an intelligent force or agent in many explanations of attentional phenomena. For example, in the influential theory developed by Shiffrin and Schneider (1977) the subject was equipped with an *attention director*—an agent that directs attention to internal representations of stimulus items. As noted by Johnston and Dark (1986, p. 68), the same questions that were asked about how individuals pay attention now had to be asked about how the attention director pays attention. The theory of Shiffrin and Schneider (1977) addressed such questions only in very general terms. In particular, no mechanism for selecting among representations that compete for attention was specified. Such vagueness concerning the mechanics of attention was not unique to the theory of Shiffrin and Schneider; on the contrary, it was characteristic of nearly all attentional models at the time. Although this state of affairs has improved in recent years, few models rival the explicit modelling of the selection process given by TVA.

TVA does not discard the notion that attentional selection is influenced by an intelligent agent, but relieves the burden on the agent by providing it with a powerful mechanism. In essence, TVA describes a computational system that does the tasks of *filtering* and *pigeonholing* given sensory input from a (front-end) visual system and control parameters from a (high-level) executive system. The filtering mechanism *selects inputs* by criteria specified by one control parameter, while pigeonholing *classifies the selected inputs* with respect to categories specified by another parameter. As we shall describe in Chapters 4 and 5, the choice mechanisms not only work in principle, but also seem to correspond closely to the way humans select visual information: TVA explains a wide range of empirical findings on human performance in visual recognition and attention tasks. In the present chapter we describe the conceptual and historical background for the development of TVA and present the general theory. In addition to our main line of presentation, which describes the elements of TVA in largely qualitative terms, the chapter includes more formal expositions marked out as boxes. These sections should be considered optional, but they offer a deeper understanding of TVA for the mathematically interested reader.

3.1 A new approach to visual selection

As explained in Chapter 2, theories of attention are commonly classified by their assumptions on the relationship between attentional selection and pattern recognition ('the locus of selection'). In *early-selection* theories (e.g. Broadbent 1958; Rumelhart 1970; Treisman and Gelade 1980; LaBerge and Brown 1989), attentional selection occurs before pattern recognition. Early selection is based on simple 'physical' features (e.g. location or colour) extracted by prerecognition processes, and affects the following perceptual processing. Traditionally, the recognition system is supposed to have limited capacity and selective attention is viewed as a way of distributing this capacity among several input channels (e.g. elements in the visual field).

In *late-selection* theories (e.g. Deutsch and Deutsch 1963; Posner 1978; Duncan 1980; van der Heijden 1981), attentional selection takes place only after pattern recognition. The selection can be based on complex properties such as meaning or categorical information (e.g. alphanumeric class) as well as simpler stimulus characteristics, and it does not affect perceptual processing. Thus, except for sensory interactions such as masking, the quality of perceptual processing of information on a given input channel should be the same regardless of information presented on other input channels. TVA draws on both early- and late-selection theories (in particular, Rumelhart 1970; Duncan 1980), but belongs to neither of the pure types described. Instead, the theory represents a possible solution to the controversy about the locus of selection.

Taking a new look at the relationship between visual recognition and attentional selection, consider an experiment in which a target category and a number of report categories are specified, a display is presented, and the task is to assign every element in the display that belongs to the target category to one of the report categories. For example, the task may be to report the identity of every red digit in a mixed display of red and black digits. Analytically, two decision problems can be distinguished: a search problem and a recognition problem. The search problem is to select only the red targets from the total set of elements in the visual field. The recognition problem is to select the appropriate report category, the identity of the digit, for each of the target objects.

The search and the recognition problems are closely related. First, both are decision problems and the information that is required for successful search is similar to the information that is required for successful recognition. Presumably, information required for search consists in sensory evidence for categorizations of the form 'x has property i', where x is an element in the visual field and i is the target category (e.g. 'x is red'). Information required for recognition consists in sensory evidence for categorizations of the form 'x has property i', where x is an element in the visual field and i is a report category (e.g. 'x is the digit 4'). Thus, if both target and report categories are perceptual categories, the type of information required for search is essentially the same as the type of information required for recognition. Second, as elaborated in later sections, both decision problems have been treated very well by formalisms based on the Luce (1959) choice model, and the way in which sensory information is used in choice models of search is similar to the way in which sensory information is used in choice models of recognition.

Despite the similarity between decision problems in search (does x belong to target category i?) and decision problems in recognition (does x belong to report category i?), those early- and late-selection theories that have attempted to account for filtering assume two separate stages of processing, one for selection (search) and one for recognition. In late-selection theories, the recognition stage precedes the selection stage: first the recognition problem is solved for every element in the visual field, then elements are selected on the basis of whether they belong to the target category or not. The scheme implies that selection can be based on any categorization done at the recognition stage, so selection can be intelligent. From a biological point of view, this implication is attractive. On the other hand, by assuming that the recognition problem is solved for every element in the visual field, the scheme implies a very large amount of perceptual decision making. This implication is less attractive. In early-selection theories, the selection stage precedes the recognition stage: first simple physical features are extracted, then selection is done on the basis of these features, and finally (full) recognition takes place for the selected elements. By restricting most perceptual decisions to those elements that are selected, the scheme reduces the demand for perceptual decision making. On the other hand, selection is implied to be rather primitive.

In this chapter we present a unified theory of visual recognition and attentional selection, TVA. The theory was constructed by integrating previous theories of visual recognition and attentional selection derived from the Luce (1959) choice model. The account has features in common with both early- and late-selection theories, but selection and recognition are viewed as *two aspects of the same process* rather than two different stages of processing. In other words, selection and recognition are neither early nor late in relation to one another but occur *simultaneously*. The key to resolving the search and the recognition problem at the same stage of processing is the mechanism proposed for selection. The mechanism selects among possible perceptual categorizations of the form 'x belongs to i', and the probability that a particular categorization is selected depends jointly on the strength of (1) the sensory evidence that x belongs to i and (2) the strength of the sensory evidence that x belongs to the current target category. Note that there is a crucial difference between holding a representation of (more or less strong) sensory evidence and achievement of full recognition (*explicit recognition*): only in the latter case is a categorical decision about the nature of the object made by the perceptual system. In agreement with late-selection theories, TVA assumes that strengths of sensory evidence (η values) for perceptual categorizations of the form 'x belongs to i' are computed before selection takes place; since i need not be defined by a simple physical feature, intelligent selection is possible. However, in agreement with early-selection theories, the categorical recognition problem is resolved only for those elements that are selected (encoded into visual short-term memory, VSTM; see Section 3.4.1).

In the next section we first review choice models for visual recognition (categorization) and for visual search (partial report). Roughly speaking, these models are *non-process models* (cf. Townsend and Ashby 1982); they provide descriptive equations with strong empirical constraints, but make little or no attempt to specify the temporal course of the information processing underlying performance. Following the presentation of the choice models, we review a *race model* for selection from multi-element displays. The race model is a *process model*; it specifies temporal characteristics of processing. Further, the race model is perfectly consistent with the descriptive choice model for visual search, which can simply be derived from it mathematically. Finally, the unified theory of visual recognition and attentional selection (TVA) is developed by integrating choice models for recognition into the race model framework. In a mathematical sense, TVA includes the previous models as special cases, and hence inherits their success in accounting for empirical findings. Further, TVA is not only a process model, but is also *computational*; it specifies the computations by which selection is supposed to be done.

3.2 Choice models of recognition and selection

Attention research has mainly been occupied with selection of objects in multi-element displays (filtering) and cared less about how the selected objects are categorized. Conversely, investigations of categorization have looked primarily at how individually presented objects are classified (pigeonholing) while largely ignoring the problem of selecting between objects. However, as argued above, both types of task—whether one or multiple objects are displayed—involve similar decision problems. In the following we describe historically successful models for each of these two choice situations: the biased choice model and the choice model for partial report.

3.2.1 The biased choice model

In a categorization experiment, there are n distinct stimuli and n appropriate responses, one for each stimulus. A typical stimulus set is the alphabet or the ten digits. In each trial, a single stimulus is presented briefly and the subject attempts to make the appropriate response. Because of the brief exposure condition, incorrect categorizations (confusions) occur with certain probabilities. The results of a categorization experiment are tabulated in an $n \times n$ confusion matrix where cell (k, i) gives the frequency with which stimulus k evoked response i (i.e. the response appropriate to stimulus i) (for an example, see Fig. 3.1).

	0	1	2	3	4	5	6	7	8	9
0	99.3	0.0	0.1	0.2	0.0	0.1	0.1	0.0	0.2	0.0
1	0.0	99.4	0.2	0.1	0.0	0.1	0.1	0.1	0.1	0.0
2	0.7	0.1	97.9	0.1	0.1	0.0	0.4	0.6	0.4	0.0
3	0.0	0.0	0.3	97.7	0.0	0.5	0.0	0.5	0.7	0.3
4	0.1	0.0	0.4	0.0	98.4	0.0	0.2	0.0	0.0	0.9
5	0.2	0.0	0.0	1.0	0.1	97.8	0.3	0.1	0.2	0.2
6	0.5	0.2	0.2	0.0	0.2	0.5	98.1	0.0	0.2	0.0
7	0.0	0.6	0.9	0.1	0.1	0.0	0.0	97.5	0.1	0.8
8	0.4	0.0	0.2	0.4	0.3	0.2	0.1	0.4	97.6	0.3
9	0.2	0.4	0.0	0.4	0.9	0.4	0.0	0.4	0.3	97.0

Fig. 3.1 Example confusion matrix for digits. Each row of the matrix represents a particular type of stimulus, whereas each column represents a particular type of response. In this example, digits of type 0 were categorized as digits of type 0 with a frequency of 99.3%, never categorized as digits of type 1, categorized as digits of type 2 with a frequency of 0.1%, and so on.

The biased choice model (Luce 1963; see also Shepard 1957) was designed to account for the data observed in such confusion matrices. It explains the choice probabilities by a simple combination of two factors: *perceptual similarity* and *decision bias*. A particular categorization is likely to occur if (1) the displayed stimulus is perceived to be similar to the representation linked to the categorization response, and (2) the observer has a significant bias for making this response in general (i.e. independent of the displayed stimulus). The probability also depends on the rest of the stimulus set, specifically the sum of the tendencies to make any of the other possible categorizations. To express this notion more exactly, the probability $P(k, i)$ of obtaining response i to a presentation of stimulus k is given by

$$P(k,i) = \frac{\eta(k,i)\beta_i}{\sum\limits_{j=1}^{n}\eta(k,j)\beta_j} \qquad (3.1)$$

where $\eta(k, i)$ is the similarity of stimulus k to stimulus i. Parameter β_i, which is independent of the actual stimulus, represents a measure of the perceiver's general bias toward identifying any presented stimulus as stimulus i. The numerator of equation 3.1 implies that the probability of responding i for object k increases with both the similarity between i and k as well as the observer's bias for responding i. On the other hand, the denominator implies that the probability decreases with the similarity between k and the total set of other stimuli in the set, as well as with the biases for making each of these alternative identifications.

The biased choice model has been remarkably successful in predicting confusion matrices from identification experiments (Luce 1963; Lupker 1979; Smith 1980; Townsend 1971a,b; Townsend and Ashby 1982; Townsend and Landon 1982). For example, in an extensive test of ten mathematical models of visual letter recognition against data from a letter confusion experiment with brief presentations, Townsend and Ashby (1982) found that the biased choice model consistently provided the best fits. To quote Ashby and Perrin (1988), such results have made the biased choice model 'the long-standing "champion" identification model' (p. 124).

A simple interpretation of the parameters in the biased choice model is as follows: performance in the identification task is based on comparison of the presented stimulus (stimulus k) against a number of alternative memory representations, one for each member of the stimulus set. The memory representation or *template* for a particular member of the stimulus set, say, the template for stimulus i (template i), is a specification of the sensory characteristics of stimulus i. The template for stimulus i is associated with a conceptual code, namely, a *perceptual category* (category i) subsuming stimulus i but no other members of the stimulus set. The outcome of comparing stimulus k against template i is a certain degree of match, which is measured by parameter $\eta\,(k, i)$. Regardless of the outcome of the comparison process, the subject is more or less strongly predisposed to assign stimuli to category i, and the strength of this perceptual decision bias is measured by parameter β_i. As specified in equation 3.1, the category-related decision bias β_i acts as a weight on the outcome of the sensory comparison process, $\eta\,(k, i)$, in determining response probabilities.

3.2.2 The choice model for partial report

In a partial report experiment, the subject is shown a brief display containing a mixture of targets and distractors and must report as many targets as possible while ignoring the distractors (see also Section 2.7.2). Scores for displays without distractors provide a whole-report baseline. Bundesen *et al.* (1984, 1985) developed a choice model to account for performance in this multi-element paradigm. The model assumes that, whether partial or whole report is required, performance reflects the number of targets that enter a limited-capacity short-term memory store (cf. Sperling 1967), say, VSTM. Elements entering the store may be targets, distractors, or extraneous noise, but the total number of elements in the store is limited by its maximum storage capacity, K elements. The value of parameter K is typically about 3–4 elements (see Sperling 1960; Bundesen *et al.* 1984, 1985; Shibuya and Bundesen 1988; Luck and Vogel 1997; Lee and Chun 2001; although recently disputed by Alvarez and Cavanagh 2004; Wilken and Ma 2004). The choice model for partial report further assumes that any target entering the store is correctly reported with probability θ (typically close to 100%), regardless of the fate of other elements.

Read-in to VSTM is conceived as selective sampling, without replacement, of the elements in the display. The selective sampling continues until K elements have been sampled and VSTM has been filled up. Thus, the choice model assumes that the display is shown long enough for the subject to fill up VSTM; typically this may be achieved using unmasked exposures lasting several hundred milliseconds. The selection occurs in accordance with the Luce (1959) choice rule (see Section 2.2.2). The rule implies that elements are assigned weights or *impacts* (v values), such that the probability that any not-yet-selected element will be the next one to be selected equals the impact of that element divided by the sum of the impacts of all those elements that have not yet been selected. Put formally, for a given selection criterion there is a scale v with the following property: if S is the set of all elements remaining after selection of $k - 1$ elements ($1 \leq k \leq K$), and i is a member of S, then the probability that element i is the kth to be selected equals

$$\frac{v(i)}{\sum_{j \in S} v(j)}. \tag{3.2}$$

3.2.2.1 Four-parameter model

A four-parameter version of the choice model for partial report is obtained by adding two simple assumptions. First, all targets have identical impacts and all distractors have identical impacts, so the impact of a target can be set to 1 and the impact of a distractor to α, where α is a constant between 0 and 1. Parameter α is a measure for *efficiency of selection* (i.e. the efficiency of selecting targets rather than distractors). If α is zero, selection is perfect. If α equals one, sampling is non-selective. As a second assumption, the number of extraneous noise elements (in the experimental situation or in long-term memory) is large in relation to K, and each one has a small probability of being sampled on a given trial. This implies that the total impact of all the not-yet-selected extraneous noise elements, ε, is essentially constant as more and more items are sampled into VSTM.

The two assumptions mentioned above leave the following four parameters in the choice model: the storage capacity of VSTM, K; the impact of a distractor, α; the total impact of extraneous noise elements, ε; and the probability that a target that has entered the short-term store will be reported, θ. These parameters of the model can be used for computing the probability that a particular set of elements will be selected, as described in Box 3.1.

3.2.2.2 Three-parameter model

A further simplification can be made when the numbers of targets and distractors are large in relation to K and the analysis is based on observed mean scores (rather than the underlying frequency distributions of scores). When the numbers of targets and distractors are large, the predicted mean score (the mean number of targets reported) is closely proportional to the product of parameters K and θ (given that parameters α and ε are kept constant, as described above). Accordingly, when the analysis is based on observed mean scores, the four-parameter model effectively reduces to a three-parameter model with a single parameter K' representing the product of K and θ. Computationally, the three-parameter model is identical to the four-parameter model with parameter θ kept constant at a value of 1 and $K = K'$.

Box 3.1 Selection probabilities in the four-parameter model

To see how the four-parameter model works, consider a subject trying to select as many targets as possible from a display containing T targets and D distractors. Let K equal four. Regardless of T and D, a total of four elements is transferred to the short-term store. If both T and D are greater than one, the probability that the first element selected is a target, the second a distractor, the third an extraneous noise element, and the fourth a target is given by the product of $T/[T + \alpha D + \varepsilon]$, $\alpha D/[(T-1) + \alpha D + \varepsilon]$, $\varepsilon/[(T-1) + \alpha(D-1) + \varepsilon]$, and $(T-1)/[(T-1) + \alpha(D-1) + \varepsilon]$. In the case where two targets enter the short-term store, the expected probability distribution for the number of targets correctly reported is the binomial distribution for two Bernoulli trials with probability θ for success.

3.2.2.3 Goodness of fit

The choice model has accounted very well for partial report performance as a function of number of targets, number of distractors, and selection criterion (Bundesen et al. 1984, 1985; Bundesen 1987). Bundesen et al. (1984) fitted the three-parameter version of the model to mean scores observed in a variety of conditions with partial reports based on brightness, colour, shape, and alphanumeric class. In all conditions, exposure time was kept constant, pre- and postexposure fields were dark, and the subject was informed about the selection criterion before the stimulus display was presented. Estimates for parameter K' (the product of K and θ) showed little variation across conditions, indicating a general limitation in storage capacity. Estimates for parameter ε were small, so noise extraneous to the experimentally defined situation had little effect. In contrast, estimates for parameter α varied widely across conditions, and the variation in this one parameter accounted for changes in performance with different selection criteria. In data obtained by averaging across conditions, the model accounted for 99% of the variance with the numbers of targets and distractors.

Bundesen et al. (1985) fitted the four-parameter version of the model to data representing the number of correctly reported targets as functions of varying numbers of targets and distractors. Selection was either done by colour or by alphanumeric class. Again, excellent fits were obtained with parameter ε kept constant near zero, while estimates for K, θ, and α were plausible and consistent with previous findings. To illustrate, estimates for K averaged 3.57 for the colour conditions and 3.52 for the alphanumeric conditions.[1] Estimates for θ averaged 0.92 for colour conditions and exactly the same for alphanumeric conditions. Estimates for α varied widely with the selection criterion, averaging 0.05 for colour and 0.36 for alphanumeric conditions.

3.3 Race models of selection

Although typically very rapid, visual information processing is extended in time. This follows from the fact that cognitive processes are implemented in a physical system, the human brain, where signal transmission cannot exceed certain maximum rates. *Process models* aim to incorporate the temporal aspect of attentional selection and thus are wider in scope than *non-process models* of choice (such as the models presented in the previous section), which predict only the end result of selection. Race models of visual selection (Bundesen 1987) form a prominent type of process models, in which the selection process is viewed as a race between individual elements in the visual field toward a state of 'having been processed', as the first elements reaching this state are the ones selected for consciousness and response. Unless otherwise specified, it is assumed that all elements in the visual field begin to be processed (start the race) at the same moment in time ($t = 0$). In real-life perception, this situation should occur every time the gaze lands on a new position following a saccade.

3.3.1 Central concepts of the race model framework

Certain functional properties are crucial in characterizing race models: statistical independence, processing capacity, attentional weighting, and exponential processing. These concepts can all be given an exact mathematical interpretation which, among other things, can be used to show that particular types of race models make exactly the same predictions as the choice model for partial report described above. In other words, the two modelling frameworks (choice versus race models) can be made entirely consistent (see Box 3.5).

3.3.1.1 Independence

An *independent* race model is a race model in which processing times for individual elements in the visual field (the times at which individual elements

---

1 All parameters were treated as continuous; for non-integral values of K, predicted values were calculated as weighted averages such that, for instance, a value of 3.57 for K was treated as a mixture of values of 3 and 4 with a probability of 0.57 for sampling four elements on a trial.

reach the state of having been processed) are mutually independent random variables. Intuitively, the independence assumption means that the individual elements are processed in parallel without interfering with each other during the race. The independence assumption greatly simplifies the derivation of selection predictions, as described in Box 3.2. (However, Boxes 3.2–3.5 are mathematically more demanding than any others in this book. Remember that the boxes can be omitted without loss of continuity.)

3.3.1.2 Processing capacity

The notion of *processing capacity* is also central to race models. Intuitively, when selection is determined by a race, variations in the amount of processing capacity allocated to an element concern the rate at which the element is processed, but not the type of processing that is done. It is often assumed that the total amount of processing capacity is *limited* and perhaps even *fixed*, so that it sums up to a constant (see Box 3.4). However, it is also theoretically possible for processing capacity to be *unlimited* in the sense that processing of each individual element is unaffected by adding other elements to the display. (A more extreme notion of unlimited capacity: instantaneous processing of all elements in the visual field, is hardly applicable to physical systems.) See Box 3.3 for a formal quantification of processing capacity.

3.3.1.3 Attentional weights

Rumelhart (1970) introduced the notion of *attentional weights* to describe the way processing capacity is distributed among the elements in the

Box 3.2 Selection probabilities in independent race models

Selection probabilities for independent race models can be computed as follows. Consider selection from a choice set S consisting of elements $1, 2, \ldots,$ and n. Let $f_i(t)$ and $F_i(t)$ be the probability density and distribution functions, respectively, for the processing time of element i ($i = 1, 2, \ldots, n$) when selection is from S. By the independence assumption, the probability P that element 1 is the first element that completes processing, element 2 is the second element that completes processing, ... , and element k ($k < n$) is the kth element that completes processing is given by

$$P = \int_0^\infty f_1(t_1) \int_{t_1}^\infty f_2(t_2) \int_{t_{k-1}}^\infty f_k(t_k) \prod_{j=k+1}^n [1 - F_j(t_k)]dt_k \quad dt_2 dt_1. \qquad (3.3)$$

Box 3.3 Quantification of processing capacity

To analyze independent race models with *limited processing capacity*, a quantitative notion of processing capacity is needed. More specifically Bundesen (1987) proposed that the effect of processing an element from time 0 to time t with a capacity of k units should equal the effect of processing the element from time 0 to time kt with a capacity of 1 unit. Thus, if $F_i(t)$ is the conditional distribution function for the processing time of element i given that the capacity allocated to element i is k units and $G_i(t)$ is the conditional distribution function for the processing time of element i given that the capacity allocated to element i is 1 unit, then for any time t,

$$F_i(t) = G_i(kt). \tag{3.4}$$

The quantitative notion of capacity expressed in Equation 3.4 is closely similar to the notion of capacity in the multicomponent model of Rumelhart (1970). Formally, an independent race model is *unlimited* in *processing capacity* if, for every element i, the distribution function for the processing time of element i is independent of the size and constituency of the choice set in which element i is presented. In this case, Equation 3.3 gives selection probabilities P for any choice set S in terms of density and distribution functions that are fixed for elements across choice sets.

choice set: for any display elements i and j in the visual field, there are attentional weights w_i and w_j such that the ratio between the amount of capacity allocated to element i and the amount of capacity allocated to element j equals the ratio between w_i and w_j. The amount of capacity allocated to a particular element is supposed to depend upon the choice set in which it is presented, but the attentional weight of the element is supposed to be constant across choice sets (see Box 3.4 for an explanation of what this assumption means for selection probabilities).

3.3.1.4 Exponential processing

The race for attentional selection is assumed to be a stochastic process, governed by statistical probabilities. It is therefore interesting to consider which probability distribution the race might follow. From a mathematical point of view, the most simple distribution of latencies is the *exponential distribution*, which is characterized by the so-called 'memory-less' property: an object's probability of being selected at any given instant (provided that the object has

Box 3.4 Selection probabilities with constant attentional weights

Consider an independent race model with limited processing capacity and constant attentional weights (i.e., attentional weights w_i, w_j that are constant across choice sets). As before, let $f_i(t)$ and $F_i(t)$ be the probability density and distribution functions for element i ($i = 1, 2, ... , n$) when selection is from a choice set S consisting of elements $1, 2, ... ,$ and n, and let the total processing capacity distributed among the elements in S equal C. Then the processing capacity allocated to element i in the choice set S equals

$$C \frac{w_i}{\sum\limits_{j=1}^{n} w_j},$$

which may be rewritten as cw_i, where

$$c = \frac{C}{\sum\limits_{j=1}^{n} w_j}.$$

By Equation 3.4, therefore,

$$F_i(t) = G_i(cw_i t), \qquad (3.5)$$

and accordingly,

$$f_i(t) = cw_i g_i(cw_i t), \qquad (3.6)$$

where c is independent of i, and $g_i(t)$ and $G_i(t)$ are the conditional probability density and distribution functions for element i given that the capacity allocated to element i equals 1 unit. Substitution of Equations 3.5 and 3.6 into Equation 3.3 yields

$$P = \int\limits_{0}^{\infty} cw_1 g_1(cw_1 t_1) \int\limits_{t_1}^{\infty} cw_2 g_2(cw_2 t_2) \quad \int\limits_{t_{k-1}}^{\infty} cw_k g_k(cw_k t_k) \prod_{j=k+1}^{n} [1 - G_j(cw_j t_k)] dt_k \quad dt_2 dt_1.$$

By using the substitution $u_i = ct_i$, $du_i = cdt_i$, for $i = 1, 2,..., k$, and finally writing t_i for u_i, we get

$$P = \int\limits_{0}^{\infty} w_1 g_1(w_1 t_1) \int\limits_{t_1}^{\infty} w_2 g_2(w_2 t_2) \quad \int\limits_{t_{k-1}}^{\infty} w_k g_k(w_k t_k) \prod_{j=k+1}^{n} [1 - G_j(w_j t_k)] dt_k \quad dt_2 dt_1,$$

Box 3.4 Selection probabilities with constant attentional weights *(continued)*

regardless of the total processing capacity C. Thus, for an independent race model with limited processing capacity and constant attentional weights, selection probabilities P for any choice set S are given by Equation 3.3 if, for every element i, $f_i(t)$ and $F_i(t)$ are replaced by $w_i g_i(w_i t)$ and $G_i(w_i t)$, respectively.

---

not yet been selected) is completely independent of how long the object has undergone processing (i.e. time t since onset of the display). Thus, what has happened previously in the selection process is not 'remembered': there is no accumulation of information during the race, just the same probability of selection in each instant. The exponential distribution is well known from other natural phenomena, such as, for example, the decay of radioactive substances, where the probability of particle emission at any given moment is also constant. As explained in Box 3.5, a race model with this property can make exactly the same predictions as the choice model for partial report. (As previously mentioned, Box 3.5 can be omitted without loss of continuity. However, the three general properties of exponential distributions listed in the first paragraph of the note are extremely useful in arguments and calculations.)

3.3.2 FIRM: an exponential fixed-capacity model

Considering the close relationship that exists between the Luce choice rule (expressed in equation 3.2) and exponential independent race models (see Box 3.5), the good fits of the choice model for partial report to the data of Bundesen *et al.* (1984, 1985) may be interpreted as fits by exponential independent race models with either (1) unlimited processing capacity or (2) limited processing capacity and constant attentional weights. To discriminate between these two possibilities, one has to consider temporal characteristics of processing: limited-capacity models predict that a given element will be processed *slower* if more elements are added to the display ('stealing capacity'), whereas unlimited-capacity models predict no effect of this added processing load. These two general hypotheses were tested by Shibuya and Bundesen (1988), who studied partial report performance as a function of exposure duration by using stimulus displays terminated by pattern masks. Each display was a circular array of letters and digits, centred on fixation, and the task was to report the digits. Exposure duration ranged from 10 to 200 ms. Testing was very extensive: each participant served in 60 trials for each of the 108 conditions in the experiment. The results strongly suggested that performance was constrained by limitations in both processing capacity and storage capacity

Box 3.5 Exponential race models and the choice model for partial report

An independent race model is *exponential* if processing times for individual elements are exponentially distributed. Three general properties of exponential distributions are used very widely in arguments and calculations. Consider n mutually independent parallel processes: Process 1, Process 2, ... , and Process n, with exponentially distributed processing times. Let the rate parameters for the processes be $v_1, v_2, ... ,$ and v_n, respectively, such that, for instance, the probability that Process 1 completes at or before time t equals $1 - \exp(-v_1 t)$ for $t > 0$. First, the mean time taken by Process 1 equals $1/v_1$. This property is used extensively in calculations of mean reaction times. Second, the probability that Process 1 is the first to complete equals $v_1/(v_1 + v_2 + ... + v_n)$. This property is used extensively in calculations of selection probabilities predicted by race models. Third, the minimum of the n processing times is itself exponentially distributed with rate parameter $v_1 + v_2 + ... + v_n$. This property is used extensively in calculations of the time taken to win a race.

The choice rule expressed in Equation 3.2 of the choice model for partial report is implied by exponential independent race models with unlimited processing capacity or with limited processing capacity and constant attentional weights (Bundesen 1987; Bundesen *et al.* 1985). The implication can be seen as follows. First, consider an exponential independent race model with unlimited processing capacity. The processing time for element i has probability density function

$$f_i(t) = v_i\exp(-v_i t)$$

and distribution function

$$F_i(t) = 1 - \exp(-v_i t),$$

where v_i is constant across choice sets. Selection probabilities P are given by Equation 3.3; P equals

$$\int_0^\infty v_1 \exp(-v_1 t_1)\int_{t_1}^\infty v_2 \exp(-v_2 t_2) \quad \int_{t_{k-1}}^\infty v_k \exp(-v_k t_k) \prod_{j=k+1}^n \exp(-v_j t_k)dt_k \quad dt_2 dt_1$$

$$= \int_0^\infty v_1 \exp(-v_1 t_1)\int_{t_1}^\infty v_2 \exp(-v_2 t_2) \quad \int_{t_{k-1}}^\infty v_k \exp(-\sum_{j=k}^n v_j t_k)dt_k \quad dt_2 dt_1.$$

Box 3.5 Exponential race models and the choice model for partial report *(continued)*

By solving the innermost integral,

$$\int_{t_{k-1}}^{\infty} v_k \exp\left(-\sum_{j=k}^{n} v_j t_k\right) dt_k = \frac{v_k}{\sum_{j=k}^{n} v_j} \exp\left(-\sum_{j=k}^{n} v_j t_{k-1}\right),$$

P reduces to

$$\int_{0}^{\infty} v_1 \exp(-v_1 t_1) \int_{t_1}^{\infty} v_2 \exp(-v_2 t_2) \quad \int_{t_{k-2}}^{\infty} v_{k-1} \exp\left(-\sum_{j=k-1}^{n} v_j t_{k-1}\right) dt_{k-1} \quad dt_2 dt_1 \frac{v_k}{\sum_{j=k}^{n} v_j}.$$

By repeating the procedure a total of k times, P reduces to

$$\frac{v_1}{\sum_{j=1}^{n} v_j} \frac{v_2}{\sum_{j=2}^{n} v_j} \cdots \frac{v_k}{\sum_{j=k}^{n} v_j},$$

which is equivalent to Equation 3.2.

Next, consider an exponential independent race model with limited processing capacity and constant attentional weights. Let $g_i(t)$ and $G_i(t)$ be the conditional probability density and distribution functions for the processing time of element i given that the capacity allocated to element i equals 1 unit, and let w_i be the attentional weight of element i. As previously shown, selection probabilities P are given by Equation 3.3 if, for every element i, $f_i(t)$ and $F_i(t)$ are replaced by $w_i g_i(w_i t)$ and $G_i(w_i t)$, respectively. Let

$$g_i(t) = \mu_i \exp(-\mu_i t)$$

and

$$G_i(t) = 1 - \exp(-\mu_i t).$$

Then

$$w_i g_i(w_i t) = w_i \mu_i \exp(-w_i \mu_i t)$$

and

$$G_i(w_i t) = 1 - \exp(-w_i \mu_i t).$$

By substitution of these expressions for $w_i g_i(w_i t)$ and $G_i(w_i t)$ into Equation 3.3 and repetition of the argument used above for race models with unlimited processing capacity, P reduces to

$$\frac{w_1 \mu_1}{\sum_{j=1}^{n} w_j \mu_j} \frac{w_2 \mu_2}{\sum_{j=2}^{n} w_j \mu_j} \cdots \frac{w_k \mu_k}{\sum_{j=k}^{n} w_j \mu_j},$$

which is equivalent to Equation 3.2 with $v_i = w_i \mu_i$ and $v_j = w_j \mu_j$.

(see Section 4.2.2 for details). A simple four-parameter exponential independent race model (FIRM) that assumes fixed processing capacity, fixed storage capacity, and time-invariant selectivity fitted the intricate pattern of data extremely well (see details later in this section).

The assumptions of the model may be spelled out as follows. At a first stage of processing, sensory evidence is collected for each element (letter or digit) in the stimulus display that the element is a target (digit). The strength of this evidence is (1) approximately the same, w_1, for any target in the display as for any other target in the display; and (2) approximately the same, w_0, for any distractor in the display as for any other distractor in the display. At the next stage of processing, elements are sampled into VSTM by a process with limited capacity. The total capacity of the sampling process is fixed at C elements/s and distributed over the elements in the stimulus display so that the capacity allocated to an individual element is directly proportional to the strength of the evidence (w_1 or w_0) that the element is a target. Thus, w_1 and w_0 serve as attentional weights, and targets tend to receive more processing capacity than distractors. Once distributed over a given display, processing capacity is not redistributed in that trial. A schematic illustration of the FIRM model is shown in Fig. 3.2.

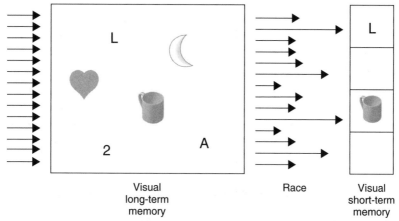

Visual long-term memory   Race   Visual short-term memory

Fig. 3.2 Schematic illustration of the fixed-capacity independent race model (FIRM) of Shibuya and Bundesen (1988). For each stimulus, evidence is collected that the item is a target (i.e. an object to be attended) by comparing the item against representations in visual long-term memory. The stronger the evidence, the more processing capacity is devoted to the item, so the faster the item can be processed in the ensuing race to become encoded in visual short-term memory (VSTM) before it has been filled up with other items and before the effective exposure duration has expired.

The sampling process is activated t_1 ms after the onset of the stimulus display. During the period in which the sampling process is active, the probability density that an individual element will be sampled at a given moment of time, provided that the element has not already been sampled, is a constant. The constant simply equals the amount of processing capacity allocated to the element. Formally, this implies that as long as the sampling process is active, the time it takes to sample an element is exponentially distributed. The sampling process continues until either (1) the number of elements sampled equals K, where K is the storage capacity of VSTM, or (2) t_2 ms have elapsed after onset of the mask. The difference between delays t_1 and t_2 (i.e. $t_1 - t_2$) is denoted t_0. Parameter t_0 is the minimum effective exposure duration (or, to be completely precise, the maximum ineffective exposure duration). t_0 can be considered a measure of the *threshold of conscious perception*. Finally, overt responses are based on the contents of VSTM: the number of targets correctly reported from a given display (the score) equals the number of targets sampled from the display.

With the above assumptions, FIRM predicts the entire probability distribution of the score as a function of (1) number of targets, (2) number of distractors, and (3) exposure duration for any observer's values of four parameters: C (processing capacity), α (efficiency of selection; $\alpha = w_0/w_1$), K (storage capacity of VSTM), and t_0 (minimum effective exposure duration). As illustrated in Fig. 3.3, maximum likelihood fits to the data obtained by Shibuya and Bundesen (1988) were remarkably good. The figure is a *cumulative frequency diagram* for an individual subject showing the relative frequency of scores of j or more (correctly reported targets) as a function of exposure duration, with j, number of targets (T), and number of distractors (D) as the parameters. The theoretical fit is represented by smooth curves. According to FIRM, this complex set of data can be explained by just four simple characteristics of the subject's attentional capabilities: the data fit was obtained with parameter C at about 49 elements/s, α at 0.40, K at 3.74 elements, and t_0 at 19 ms.[2]

3.4 **TVA: a unified theory of recognition and selection**

As noted previously, decision problems in search (does x belong to target category i?) and decision problems in recognition (does x belong to report

---

2 Parameters ε (ratio between the amount of processing capacity devoted to extraneous noise elements and the amount devoted to a target) and θ (probability that a target that has entered the short-term store will be reported) were not included in the model. Omitting these parameters from the model corresponds to setting $\varepsilon = 0$ and $\theta = 1$ under the conditions of the experiment.

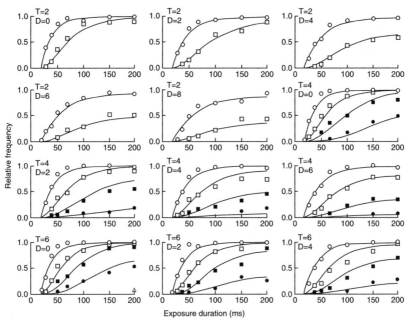

Fig. 3.3 Relative frequency of scores of *j* or more (correctly reported targets) as a function of exposure duration with *j*, number of targets (*T*), and number of distractors (*D*) as parameters in the partial report experiment of Shibuya and Bundesen (1988). Data are shown for Subject M.P. Parameter *j* varies within panels; *j* is 1 (open circles), 2 (open squares), 3 (solid squares), 4 (solid circles), or 5 (triangle). *T* and *D* vary among panels. Smooth curves represent a theoretical fit to the data by the FIRM model. For clarity, observed frequencies less than 0.02 were omitted from the figure. Adapted with permission from Shibuya and Bundesen (1988). Visual selection from multielement displays: measuring and modelling effects of exposure duration. *Journal of Experimental Psychology: Human Perception and Performance*, **14**, 591-600. Copyright 1988 by the American Psychological Association. The use of APA information does not imply endorsement by APA.

category *i?*) are highly similar. In view of the success of the biased choice model in accounting for recognition, and the success of the choice model for partial report in accounting for selection from multi-element displays, an attempt to develop a unified theory of visual recognition and attentional selection by integrating the two choice models seemed well motivated. TVA is this unified theory.

Since the race model framework provided a plausible process interpretation of the choice model for partial report, TVA was developed in this framework. The theory was developed by integrating the biased choice model into the race model framework and linking the parameters of the exponential FIRM model of Shibuya and Bundesen (1988) to the η and β parameters of the biased choice model. The resulting theory is general in scope, but simple in structure. Mathematically the theory is tractable, and it specifies the computations by which selection is performed.

3.4.1 Central assumptions and equations

In TVA, visual recognition and attentional selection consist in making *perceptual categorizations*. A perceptual categorization has the form 'object *x* has feature *i*' or, equivalently, 'element *x* belongs to category *i*', where object *x* is a perceptual object (an element in the visual field), feature *i* is a perceptual feature (e.g. a certain colour, shape, movement, or spatial position) and category *i* is a perceptual category (the class of all objects that have feature *i*). The perceptual categorization is made (or, equivalently, *selected*) if and when it enters a limited-capacity visual short-term memory store (VSTM; as in the FIRM model). When the perceptual categorization '*x* belongs to *i*' is made, element *x* is said both to be selected and to be recognized as a member of category *i*. Similarly, an element is said to be represented in VSTM when some categorization of the element is represented in VSTM. Selection and recognition are two sides of the same coin; they occur simultaneously.

Selection is determined by temporal characteristics of processing. At the moment a perceptual categorization of an element *finishes processing* (or, equivalently, *is sampled*), the categorization enters VSTM, provided that memory space is available in the store. VSTM can hold at most *K* elements, and space is available for a categorization of element *x* if (1) element *x* is already represented in VSTM or (2) fewer than *K* elements are represented in VSTM. Otherwise (i.e. if VSTM is filled up with elements, and *x* is not among the elements in VSTM), the sampled categorization of element *x* is lost. Thus the VSTM system is limited in terms of the number of objects it can retain rather than the number of categorizations made of the objects.

Before the race for selection takes place, an attentional weight must be computed for each element in the visual field. This is necessary to distribute processing resources intelligently during the race. Attentional weights are derived from *pertinence* values. Every perceptual category *j* is assigned a pertinence value π_j, which is a measure of the current importance of attending to elements that belong to category *j* (cf. Norman 1968). For instance, if one is looking for a red object, the pertinence value of the category red should he high. According to one of the two central equations of TVA, the *weight equation*, the attentional weight of every element *x* in the visual field is determined by summing up products of two factors across all perceptual categories:

$$w_x = \sum_{j \in R} \eta(x,j)\pi_j,$$ (3.7)

where R is the set of all perceptual categories, $\eta(x, j)$ is the strength of the sensory evidence that element x belongs to category j, and π_j is the pertinence value of category j. By the weight equation, the current selection criterion is represented by the distribution of pertinence values over perceptual categories: the pertinence of category j is the weight assigned to sensory evidence that x belongs to j in determining the attentional weight of element x.

When attentional weights have been computed, the race for selection into VSTM occurs. Observe the course of processing from the moment the race is initiated (time $t = 0$) and consider the event that a certain perceptual categorization, 'x belongs to i', finishes processing at time t (where $t > 0$). $v(x, i)$ denotes the *hazard function* of this event (i.e. the conditional probability density that the perceptual categorization finishes processing at time t, provided that the categorization has not finished processing before time t). Put less formally, the v value represents the moment-to-moment probability that the categorization will be selected, and can also be considered a measure of the 'speed' with which a particular categorization races towards VSTM. The other main equation of TVA, the *rate equation*, assumes that the v value is determined by a combination of three factors:

$$v(x,i) = \eta(x,i)\beta_i \frac{w_x}{\sum_{z \in S} w_z},$$ (3.8)

where $\eta(x, i)$ is the strength of the sensory evidence that element x belongs to category i, β_i is a perceptual decision bias associated with category i ($0 \leq \beta_i \leq 1$), and w_x and w_z are attentional weights of elements x and z, respectively. S is the set of all elements in the visual field; since the denominator sums up attentional weights for all elements, the third factor of the rate equation expresses the *relative* attentional weight of element x and, by implication, how large a part of the total available capacity is allocated to this element.

Looking at the rate and weight equations combined, $v(x, i)$ is a function of η (strength of sensory evidence), β (perceptual bias) and π (pertinence) values. When these values are determined, processing times for individual perceptual categorizations are independent random variables. In most applications to experimental paradigms, η, β, and π values are supposed to be constant during the period in which the stimulus is exposed. When η, β, and π values are constant, v values also are constant. In this case, processing times for perceptual categorizations are exponentially distributed, and $v(x, i)$ is the exponential rate parameter associated with the categorization that x belongs to i.

The TVA theory evolved as a combination of the biased choice model for visual recognition and the FIRM model for attentional selection. Each of these models can be derived as a special case of TVA (see Boxes 3.6 and 3.7, respectively) and the unified theory thus inherits their success in accounting for single stimulus identification and selection from multi-element displays.

3.4.2 Mechanisms of attention

TVA is a generalization of the FIRM model of Shibuya and Bundesen (1988). It extends the race model in scope by accounting for many more empirical findings. It also extends the race model in depth by providing an account of the mechanisms by which selection is supposed to be done. TVA contains two mechanisms of attention: a mechanism for selection of objects and a mechanism for selection of features or, equivalently, categories. Following Broadbent (1971), selection of elements is referred to as *filtering* and selection of categories as *pigeonholing*.

3.4.2.1 Filtering

The filtering mechanism is represented by attentional weights. To see how the mechanism works, suppose perceptual category i is a target category. Selection of elements in the visual field that belong to category i is favoured by letting the pertinence value of category i, π_i, be high in relation to pertinence values of other categories. For, if π_i is increased, then the attentional weight of any element x is increased by an amount proportional to $\eta(x, i)$, the strength of the sensory evidence that the element belongs to category i (cf. the weight equation). The effect is to increase attentional weights of elements that belong to category i rather than attentional weights of other elements and, accordingly, to favour selection of elements belonging to category i by speeding up processing of such elements at the expense of any other elements.

Importantly, as shown in Box 3.8, the filtering mechanism does not bias perception in favour of perceiving the selected elements as belonging to any particular category. In other words, filtering determines *which* objects are selected, but not *how* the selected objects are classified. Having a mechanism with this property—to increase the probability that a target element is selected without changing the probability that the element is classified into a particular category, given that the element is selected—seems highly desirable for a system developed for veridical perception.

Box 3.6 TVA and the biased choice model

The biased choice model of Luce can be derived directly from TVA. To see this, consider an identification experiment with n distinct stimuli. For $i = 1, 2,..., n$, let category i be a perceptual category subsuming stimulus i but no other members of the stimulus set. On each trial, one of the n stimuli is exposed from time zero until the subject responds. With a single element k in the visual field, the rate equation implies that, for any i,

$$v(k, i) = \eta(k, i) \, \beta_i.$$

Let η and β values be constant during the period of stimulus exposure, and let β_i be zero unless $i = 1, 2, ... ,$ or n. Then, for $i = 1, 2, ... , n$, the processing time of the categorization that k belongs to i is exponentially distributed with rate parameter $v(k, i)$. Accordingly, the probability P that the categorization "k belongs to i" is the first categorization that completes processing is given by

$$P = \int_0^\infty v(k,i)\exp[-v(k,i)t]\prod_{\substack{j=1 \\ j\neq i}}^n \exp[-v(k,j)t]dt$$

$$= \int_0^\infty v(k,i)\exp[-\sum_{j=1}^n v(k,j)t]dt$$

$$= \frac{v(k,i)}{\sum_{j=1}^n v(k,j)}$$

$$= \frac{\eta(k,i)\beta_i}{\sum_{j=1}^n \eta(k,j)\beta_j}.$$

Thus, assuming that the subject's response is based on the first categorization that completes processing, Equation 3.1 of the biased choice model for identification is obtained.

Box 3.7 TVA and the FIRM model

The exponential fixed-capacity independent race model for selection from multielement displays (Shibuya and Bundesen 1988) can also be obtained from the equations of TVA. Consider the experimental task of Shibuya and Bundesen: report of digits from a mixed array of letters and digits terminated by a pattern mask. Suppose visual short-term memory (with a capacity of K elements) is empty at the moment a stimulus display is presented and add the following assumptions.

Within the experiment, β (bias) and π (pertinence) values are constant over time. For any character type (i.e., for any type of letter or any type of digit) i, the bias parameter β_i equals a positive constant β_0, but for all other perceptual categories, the bias parameters are zero.

η (strength of sensory evidence) values for elements in the stimulus are constant for a period equal to the effective exposure duration of the stimulus, but before and after this period, the η values are zero. The effective exposure duration, τ, equals the physical exposure duration (= the stimulus-onset asynchrony between the stimulus display and the pattern mask) minus a nonnegative constant t_0, provided that the physical exposure duration is longer than t_0; otherwise, t equals zero.

During the period of effective exposure, any token x of character type i has an η value, $\eta(x, i)$, which equals a positive constant η_0. The attentional weight of x, w_x, depends upon the alphanumeric class of x. For any digit (target) in the stimulus, the attentional weight is a positive constant w_1. For any letter (distractor), the attentional weight is a constant w_0. The ratio w_0/w_1 defines parameter α.

Let $i(x)$ be the character type (the identity) of stimulus character x in display S. During the period of effective exposure, the conditional probability density that the perceptual categorization "x belongs to $i(x)$" finishes processing at a given moment of time, provided that the categorization has failed to finish processing before this moment, is a constant. By the rate equation, this constant is

$$v[x, i(x)] = \eta[x, i(x)]\beta_{i(x)} \frac{w_x}{\sum_{z \in S} w_z}$$

$$= \eta_0 \beta_0 \frac{w_x}{\sum_{z \in S} w_z}.$$

Box 3.7 TVA and the FIRM model *(continued)*

Suppose that, for any character type j other than $i(x)$, $\eta\,(x, j)$ is small and $v(x, j)$ is negligible. (In the study of Shibuya and Bundesen, intrusion errors were few, and they were not subjected to formal analysis.) If so, then the sum of v values across all perceptual categorizations of element x, $v(x)$, is given by

$$v(x) = \sum_{i \in R} v(x,i) \cong v[x,i(x)] = \eta_0 \beta_0 \frac{w_x}{\sum_{z \in S} w_z}.$$

Define the *processing capacity* C as the sum of v values across all perceptual categorizations of all elements in the display, that is,

$$C = \sum_{x \in S} v(x) = \sum_{x \in S} \sum_{i \in R} v(x,i). \tag{3.9}$$

Then

$$C \cong \sum_{x \in S} \eta_0 \beta_0 \frac{w_x}{\sum_{z \in S} w_z} = \eta_0 \beta_0, \tag{3.10}$$

regardless of the number of targets and distractors in the stimulus. Thus the exponential fixed-capacity independent race model is obtained with parameter C given by Equations 3.9 and 3.10.

3.4.2.2 Pigeonholing

The pigeonholing mechanism is represented by perceptual bias parameters. To see how the mechanism works, suppose perceptual category i is a relevant report category. Categorization of any element x as belonging to category i is favoured by letting the bias associated with category i be high in relation to biases associated with other categories. For, if β_i is increased, then for every element x in the visual field, the v value of the categorization that x belongs to i is increased (in direct proportion to β_i, as expressed in the rate equation), but other v values are not affected (see also Box 3.9).

3.4.2.3 Combined filtering and pigeonholing

Consider how filtering and pigeonholing may work together in a situation in which a target category and a number of report categories are specified, a display is presented, and the task is to assign every element in the display that belongs to the target category to one of the report categories. To use the same

Box 3.8 Filtering does not bias recognition

A change in the pertinence value of a perceptual category causes a change in the distribution of attentional weights over elements in the visual field (cf. the weight equation), and a change in the relative attentional weight of an element x,

$$\frac{w_x}{\sum_{z \in S} w_z},$$

changes the v value for any categorization of element x (cf. the rate equation). However, for every perceptual category i, the ratio between the v value for the categorization that x belongs to i and the sum of all v values for categorizations of element x is invariant under this transformation. The ratio

$$\frac{v(x,i)}{\sum_{j \in R} v(x,j)}$$

is the conditional probability that the first categorization that finishes processing is the categorization that x belongs to i, given that the first categorization that finishes processing is a categorization of element x, so conditional probabilities of this form are not affected by filtering.

Box 3.9 Pigeonholing does not bias selection of objects

Pigeonholing is a pure categorical-bias mechanism. To be specific, consider the first selection of a categorization. That element x is selected means that, for some category i, the categorization that x belongs to i is selected. By analogy, let us say that category i is selected if, for some element x, the categorization that x belongs to i is selected. In these terms, filtering changes the probability that element x is selected, without affecting the conditional probability that category i is selected given that element x is selected (as explained above). Conversely, pigeonholing changes the probability that a particular category i is selected, without affecting the conditional probability that element x is selected given that category i is selected.

example as in Section 3.1, suppose the task is to report the identity of every red digit in a mixed array of red and black digits. A plausible strategy for doing this task is as follows.

To select red rather than black elements, let the pertinence value of the perceptual category red be high, and let other pertinence values be low; the effect is to increase the rate of processing of every categorization of a red element relative to rates of processing of categorizations of black elements. To recognize the identity of the red digits rather than other attributes of the elements, let each of ten perceptual bias parameters, one for each type of digit, be high, and let other perceptual bias parameters be low; the effect is to increase the rate of processing of every categorization with respect to type of digit relative to rates of processing of categorizations with respect to other attributes. The combined effect of the adjustments of pertinence and bias parameters is to increase the rate of processing of every categorization of a red element with respect to type of digit relative to rates of processing of any other categorizations. A numerical analysis of the digit report example is given in Box 3.10.

The numerical analysis in Box 3.10 was simplified in at least two respects. First, any consequences of extraneous noise stimuli were neglected by implicitly assuming that the choice set consisted exclusively of experimenter-defined targets and distractors. Second, it was implicitly assumed that pertinence and perceptual bias parameters could be manipulated freely to optimize performance in the experimental task (thus, most parameters were set to zero). This assumption is useful in demonstrations of principles of selection, but, as argued later on, it appears to be a gross simplification. In reality, we cannot exert such perfect control over attentional selection.

Although the analysis presented in this section is idealized, it demonstrates the power of the mechanisms of attention contained in TVA. Coupled to a front-end system that supplies measures of strength of sensory evidence concerning the nature of elements in its visual field, and given adequate settings of pertinence and perceptual bias parameters, the specified system will do the tasks of filtering (i.e. selecting targets rather than distractors) and pigeonholing (i.e. classifying the selected elements with respect to those categories that are relevant for action) by elementary algebraic operations (summarized in the rate and weight equations) that determine the rate parameters in a race. In this sense, TVA gives a computational account of selective attention.

3.5 Elaboration of the basic concepts

In the preceding statement of TVA, the notions of elements in the visual field, strength of sensory evidence, and perceptual categories were treated almost as primitives. In this section we indicate how the theory fits in with some broader

Box 3.10 Combined filtering and pigeonholing

Suppose the pertinence of red is given a value of one, but all other perti-nence values are zero. By the weight equation, the attentional weight of any element x in the visual field, w_x, becomes equal to η (x, red) (i.e., the strength of the sensory evidence that the element is red). Suppose, further, that for each of the 10 types of digits, the perceptual bias parameter is given a value of one, while all other bias parameters are zero. By the rate equa-tion, then,

$$v(x,i) = \eta(x,i)\frac{\eta(x,\text{red})}{\sum_{z \in S} \eta(z,\text{red})} \tag{3.11}$$

if i is one of the 10 digit categories, but otherwise $v(x, i)$ is zero.

By Equation 3.11, performance is limited by visual discriminability between red and black and between types of digits. In particular, if there are constants η_r and η_b such that η $(x, \text{red}) = \eta_r$ if x is a red element, and η $(x, \text{red}) = \eta_b$ if x is a black element, then the efficiency of selecting targets rather than distractors is determined by the ratio η_b/η_r (which in this case corresponds to parameter α of the choice and race models for partial report). To make filtering perfect, η_b should be zero; in this case, no catego-rizations of black elements would be selected. For optimal performance, discriminability between types of digits also should be perfect in the sense that, for every digit type i, η (x, i) should be zero unless element x was a token of type i. In this case, only correct identifications of red digits would be selected.

conceptualizations of visual processing. Following the original sketch by Bundesen (1990), the conceptualizations make the notions of elements, sensory evidence, and perceptual categories more concrete. In Section 7.6 we present another, less conventional conceptualization of basic functional elements in TVA.

3.5.1 Sensory processing

Visual processing of stimulus objects begins with registration of retinal images at the level of photoreceptors and proceeds through a number of stages. Broadly speaking, the first major stage of processing (the *sensory* stage) con-sists of extraction of information about the visible surfaces (cf. Gibson 1950, on 'literal perception'; Marr 1982, on 'early vision'). Presumably it produces a representation (a *visual impression*) in which local surface colour and depth are made explicit for each position in the visual field (cf. Marr 1982, on 'the 2.5-D sketch').

Sensory processing is parallel across the visual field and, to a first approximation, it is automatic and 'bottom-up' or 'data driven' (for a review, see Wagemans *et al.* 2005). The approximation is not perfect: there is evidence that, under certain conditions, the formation of visual impressions is guided by higher-level, conceptual processes (see, for example, Ittelson 1951, on familiar size as a cue to distance). There is also evidence that, in some respects, formation of visual impressions may be controlled voluntarily. For example, when subjects are instructed to will seeing a particular orientation of a reversible figure such as the Necker cube, they can affect the reversal rate somewhat (Bruner *et al.* 1950), even when the retinal image is stabilized by viewing it as an afterimage (Washburn and Gillette 1933).

3.5.2 Unit formation

Following Neisser (1967), Kahneman (1973), Julesz (1981), and others, Bundesen (1990) supposed that the next stage of processing generates a part–whole organization of the visual input by Gestalt grouping operations. At this stage, parts of the scene represented in the total visual impression are defined as separate *perceptual units* by criteria based on proximity, similarity, and continuity. By defining groups of perceptual units as higher-level perceptual units, a hierarchical part–whole organization of perceptual units is created (cf. Palmer 1977; Feldman 2003). The set of perceptual units is the set of *elements in the visual field*. These are the objects of selection in TVA. The process of defining elements in the visual field (i.e. unit formation) is mainly data driven (cf. Pomerantz 1981); however, 'top-down' effects of familiarity and perceptual set have long been recognized (see, for example, Wertheimer 1923).

3.5.3 Perceptual testing

For some psychological categories i, a measure of the strength of the sensory evidence that an element x in the visual field belongs to category i is computed by comparing element x (actually, a structured visual impression of element x, formed at the previous stage of processing) against a memory representation of visual characteristics (such as colour or shape) of members of category i. A category i with this property is said to be a *perceptual category*, and the memory representation of visual characteristics of members of category i is referred to as a *template* for category i. TVA is neutral as regards the exact representational format of such 'templates' (e.g. 'pictorial' versus 'propositional';

'multiple views' versus 'structural descriptions'; for reviews, see Ullman 1996; Hayward and Tarr 2005; Graf 2006).

Templates may be held in either short- or long-term visual memory. Short-term visual templates are supposed to be the same as mental images. Presumably they can be generated in three ways:

(1) by encoding perceptual units from the visual impression into visual short-term memory (for a classic demonstration, see Posner and Keele 1967);

(2) by transferring visual representations (through activation or coding) from long-term memory into visual short-term memory (cf. Posner *et al.* 1969); or

(3) by transforming images already present in visual short-term memory (see Shepard and Cooper 1982; see also Bundesen and Larsen 1975; Bundesen *et al.* 1981).

Once a mental image has been generated, it can be compared with an element in the visual field. The comparison yields a degree of match that can be used as a measure of the strength of the sensory evidence that the element belongs to a perceptual category associated with the short-term template (the mental image). To a considerable extent, formation and transformation of mental images is under voluntarily control, and perceptual tests based on mental imagery may be programmed flexibly by the subject for the task at hand.

The nature of long-term visual templates is not well understood. Theoretical simplicity favours the view that a long-term template for a perceptual category is similar in format to a short-term template (i.e. a mental image) or a set of short-term templates for exemplars of the category, but the issue is not resolved (Biederman and Gerhardstein 1995; Tarr and Bülthoff 1995; see also Larsen and Bundesen 1978, 1998).

3.5.4 Attentional selection

$\eta(x, i)$, the computed strength of the sensory evidence that element x belongs to category i, may be regarded as a measure of a level of activation representing the degree of match between a visual impression of element x and a template associated with category i. As the retinal stimulation varies over time, the visual impression varies, and η values are supposed to be updated continuously to reflect the momentary state of the visual impression. However, the temporal resolution of the visual system is limited, and the update of η values occurs with a latency due to the limited speed of neural conduction and computation. Thus, in the TVA-based analyses presented in Chapters 4 and 5, we assume that when a bright stimulus display is abruptly replaced by a dark postexposure field, decrease in η values is gradual rather than abrupt.

In the theory of attentional selection expressed in the rate and weight equations, increase in the computed strength of the sensory evidence that element x belongs to category i has two interacting effects. The first effect directly concerns *search* for members of category i: as $\eta\,(x,\,i)$ increases, the attentional weight of element x is automatically increased by an amount proportional to the pertinence of category i. By increasing the attentional weight of element x, the v value (processing speed) of the categorization that x belongs to j is increased by the same factor for every perceptual category j. The second effect directly concerns *recognition* of element x: as $\eta\,(x,\,i)$ increases, the v value of the particular categorization that x belongs to i is increased in relation to v values for other categorizations of element x. As previously shown in detail (see Section 3.4.2) the two effects interact to yield faultless selection (i.e. selection of only correct identifications of targets) when visual discriminability (with respect to target and report categories) is perfect and settings of pertinence and perceptual bias parameters are optimized for the task at hand. Under such conditions, only v values for correct identifications of targets are different from zero.

Under less ideal conditions—that is, in typical real-life situations—the set of positive v values is likely to be large, perhaps very large, and it is worth considering how the system works in such circumstances. Presumably, v values are continually being updated to reflect the momentary state of the set of η values. The task of the attention system, then, is to select a few categorizations capturing the most important aspects of the visual scene, given a choice set consisting of a large number of possible categorizations, each of which is supplied with a time-varying, continuous v value indicating its relevance. The task might be solved by having a special processor read every v value at a given moment of time, compare the v values, and select categorizations in order of decreasing v value; accounts of this general sort have been offered by Deutsch and Deutsch (1963), Norman (1968), Hoffman (1978), Shaw (1980, 1984), Wolfe (1994), and many others (cf. Chapter 2). In TVA, however, no processor is required to read or to compare v values. Rather, selection is simply determined by a race between the possible categorizations. When memory space is available in the short-term store, the instantaneous v value of a categorization defines the momentary probability that the categorization enters the short-term store, provided that the event has not occurred before that instant.

3.5.5 **Mediate perception**

When stimulus discriminability is high, the first perceptual categorization made of a stimulus (the *immediate* perception of the stimulus) tends to be accurate. However, when stimulus discriminability is low, false perceptual categorizations become more frequent. Thus, when discriminability is low, the fact that a certain perceptual categorization has been made (encoded into VSTM) provides only weak evidence concerning the true identity of the stimulus. In this case, accurate performance cannot be based on the first categorization that 'comes to mind' (i.e. is encoded into VSTM).

Suppose that, once a perceptual categorization has become represented in the short-term store, the same categorization may be confirmed by being sampled anew. This supposition provides a natural way of accounting for gains in both confidence and correctness by prolonged viewing of a stationary display. For example, performance may be based on the categorization that first reaches a criterion of having been sampled a particular number of times, r, where $r > 1$. In this case, the observer behaves in accordance with a so-called *Poisson counter* or *accumulator* model (for general reviews, see Townsend and Ashby 1983, Chapter 9; Luce 1986; for a TVA-based counter model, see Logan 1996). As the criterion r is raised, speed is traded for accuracy: The system waits for additional confirmation of the categorical decision, which makes it more reliable. A related possibility is to base performance on the categorization that first reaches a criterion of having been made r times *more* than any alternative categorization. This possibility leads to so-called *random-walk* models with exponential interstep times (for general reviews, see Townsend and Ashby 1983, Chapter 10; Luce 1986; see also Bundesen 1982; Nosofsky and Palmeri 1997; Ratcliff and McKoon 1997; for TVA-based random-walk models, see Logan and Gordon 2001; Logan 2002a). Again, as the criterion r is raised, speed is traded for accuracy. Given the well-defined mathematical structure of both the Poisson counter and random-walk models, the selection mechanisms described in TVA can easily be extended to include such mediate perception processes (see Bundesen *et al.* 2005).

3.6 Summary

In this chapter a general theory of visual attention, TVA, has been presented. The development of TVA was motivated by the success of the biased choice model (Luce 1963) in accounting for single-stimulus recognition, and the success of the choice model for partial report (Bundesen *et al.* 1984) in accounting for selection from multi-element displays. Both choice models were originally non-process models and so did not describe the temporal course of attentional selection, but a plausible process interpretation of the choice model for partial report has been proposed (Bundesen *et al.* 1985; Bundesen 1987) and substantiated (Shibuya and Bundesen 1988). The process interpretation was provided by a race model, where attentional selection is assumed to occur in parallel and follow an exponential probability distribution. TVA—a unified theory of visual recognition and attentional selection—was formed by integrating the biased choice model into the race model framework. The historically preceding models can thus be considered special cases under the TVA framework and can be derived mathematically from it.

In TVA, visual recognition and attentional selection consist in making perceptual categorizations of elements in the visual field. A perceptual categorization is made (selected) if and when it enters a limited-capacity short-term memory store. When the categorization is made, the element is said both to be selected and to be recognized as a member of a particular category. Thus, attentional selection and recognition are neither early nor late in relation to one another, but occur simultaneously. Selection is determined by a processing race between possible perceptual categorizations toward the short-term store. By the two central equations in TVA, the weight equation and the rate equation, processing rates of categorizations depend upon three types of parameters: η (strength of sensory evidence), β (perceptual decision bias), and π (pertinence; i.e. the current importance of particular types of objects). When η, β, and π values are kept constant over time, processing times follows the memory-less (non-accumulative) exponential distribution.

The specified system in TVA contains a mechanism for filtering (selection of target objects rather than distractors) and a mechanism for pigeonholing (classification of objects with respect to particular categories that are relevant for action). Coupled to a sensory system that supplies measures of the strength of sensory evidence concerning the nature of elements in its visual field, and given adequate top-down settings of pertinence and perceptual bias parameters, the system will do the tasks of filtering and pigeonholing by elementary algebraic operations (summarized in the weight and rate equations) that determine the rate parameters in a race. In this sense, TVA gives a computational account of selective attention. As we have also shown, this account can be coupled with elaborate notions of sensory processing, perceptual testing, and other issues related to attentional selection. In the following chapters, we shall see how the TVA framework can account for many of the central findings on human attentional performance.

4

Explaining divided attention by TVA

Chapter 3 described how the theory of visual attention (TVA) integrated several models that each had strong explanatory power for either single stimulus identification or partial report. However, TVA is actually much broader in scope. In this chapter and Chapter 5 the theory is applied to empirical data from across the attention literature, covering some of the classic and well-established findings in the field. Besides demonstrating the empirical span of TVA, these chapters give an impression of how to apply the concepts of the model to specific experimental designs, which may inspire readers to try this out for themselves. As in Chapter 3, detailed mathematical expositions are provided in (optional) boxes, whereas the main text presents a more qualitative explanation of the cognitive modelling.

A useful organizing principle for the empirical literature on attention is the distinction between tasks that require *focused* and *divided* attention. Studies of focused attention concern the ability to direct attentional resources at target rather than distractor objects; this research area is covered in Chapter 5. The present chapter deals with divided attention: the limits on our ability to split attention between multiple, simultaneous targets or between multiple information channels to be monitored simultaneously. Central issues in this research area are *processing independence*, the extent to which inputs interfere with one another, and *capacity*, the amount of resources available for information processing. Major experimental paradigms for investigating these questions are whole report and target detection; both are readily analysed by TVA.

Attentional processing of objects seems to be limited in a different way than processing of features (see Section 4.1). A central result was reported by Duncan (1984), who found that several features of the same object can be simultaneously encoded without reductions in performance, whereas attention to multiple objects at the same time degrades the perception of each individual object. Bundesen *et al.* (2003) went on to show that even when attending to several objects at the same time, processing of different features can occur in a completely independent manner. Both results are in close accordance with the rate equation of TVA.

Duncan's observation of impaired performance with attention to multiple objects suggests that attentional capacity is a limited resource, and the nature of this limitation has been characterized by the whole report studies described in Section 4.2. Sperling (1960) showed that participants can typically report only about four targets from a brief visual display, a result that also holds if the stimulus display is terminated by a pattern mask (Shibuya and Bundesen 1988). Strong effects of the position of individual elements are also possible (Sperling 1967). Each of these classic whole report findings can be accounted for by the two main capacity parameters of TVA, C and K, used in slightly different models depending on the specific experiment.

As described in Section 4.3, when several locations are monitored for the appearance of a target, detection can be improved both by pre-cuing of the spatial location of the target (Posner *et al.* 1978) and by target redundancy (e.g. presentation of the target at several locations simultaneously; van der Heijden *et al.* 1983). In TVA, spatial pre-cuing corresponds to manipulating the pertinence of particular locations, whereas target redundancy effects can be explained by having several targets racing in parallel towards visual short-term memory (VSTM). Some studies of target redundancy suggest a sampling process with unlimited capacity (in the sense that the rate of processing for a given target is unaffected by the presence of other targets), apparently in contradiction with other findings on divided attention. However, as explained in Section 4.4, the paradox can be resolved within TVA.

4.1 Processing independence for objects versus features

4.1.1 Object integrality

Duncan (1984) presented subjects with small, foveal displays, each consisting of two overlapping objects (a box with a line struck through; see Fig. 4.1). The task was (a) to report one (prespecified) aspect of (a prespecified) one of the objects (e.g. the tilt of the line); (b) to report two aspects of one of the objects (e.g. the tilt and texture of the line); or (c) to report one aspect of one of the objects and one aspect of the other object (e.g. the tilt of the line and the size of the box). Accuracy was the dependent variable and stimulus presentations were brief to avoid ceiling performance.

It was found that, for each aspect, performance in Condition b was equal to performance in Condition a, but performance in Condition c was inferior to performance in Condition a. Thus the results supported the hypothesis that 'two judgments that concern the same object can be made simultaneously without loss of accuracy, whereas two judgments that concern different objects cannot' (Duncan 1984, p. 501; for related results, see Treisman *et al.* 1983;

(a)

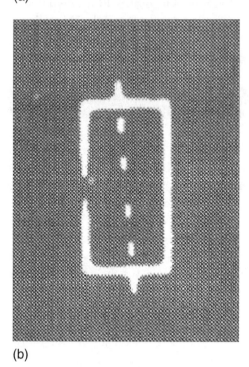

(b)

Fig. 4.1 Displays used by Duncan (1984). (a) Small box with gap on the right, dotted line with tilt clockwise; (b) large box with gap on the left, dashed line with tilt counterclockwise. Adapted with permission from Duncan (1984). Selective attention and the organization of visual information. *Journal of Experimental Psychology: General*, **113**, 501–517. Copyright 1984 by the American Psychological Association. The use of APA information does not imply endorsement by APA.

also see Treisman 1969; Kahneman 1973; Kahneman and Henik 1981). Duncan's (1984) results are often taken to imply that all features of an attended object are selected together ('all or none' encoding), but in fact the study simply shows *lack of interference* between encoding of different features that belong to the same object.

The results can be explained in a straightforward way by TVA. According to the rate equation of TVA, the processing speed (v value) of a particular categorization is not affected by varying the perceptual biases (β values) for other types of categorizations; these factors are simply not included in the computation of the v value in question. Thus perceptual biases can be set high for several different features without affecting the processing speed of each type of categorization. On the other hand, the rate equation also implies that it makes a negative difference to attend to two (or more) objects rather than one. Compared to the situation when only one object is attended, this object's relative attentional weight—all other things being equal—is lowered by increases in the attentional weight of other objects. By the third factor in the rate equation (the ratio between attentional weights) this means that all v values of categorizations of the object are decreased accordingly. A formal proof of this general point is given in Box 4.1.

Box 4.1 Duncan (1984)

Suppose the tilt of the line is an aspect to be reported, suppose the line is tilted to the left (i.e. counterclockwise from the vertical), and consider the determinants of $v(x_1$, tilted left) [i.e. the processing rate of the categorization that element x_1 (the line) is tilted to the left]. Let β (tilted left) (i.e. the perceptual decision bias associated with the category 'tilted left') be a constant across all conditions in which the tilt of the line is to be reported; let $\eta(x_1$, tilted left) (i.e. the strength of the sensory evidence that element x_1 is tilted to the left) be a constant across all conditions in which the line is tilted to the left; and let $\eta(x_1$, line) (i.e. the strength of the sensory evidence that element x_1 is a line) and $\eta(x_2$, box) [i.e. the strength of the sensory evidence that element x_2 (the box) is a box] be constant across all conditions. Further, suppose there are constants π_{hi} and π_{lo}, where $\pi_{hi} > \pi_{lo} \geq 0$, such that π (line) (i.e. the pertinence value of the perceptual category 'line') equals π_{hi} when aspects of the line are to be reported, and π (box) (i.e. the pertinence value of the perceptual category 'box') equals π_{hi} when aspects of the box are to be reported, but π (line) equals π_{lo} when no aspect of the line is to be reported, and π (box) equals π_{lo} when no aspect of the box is to

---

Box 4.1 Duncan (1984) *(continued)*

be reported. Finally, for simplicity, let all other pertinence values be zero, and let all η values for false perceptual categorizations be zero. By the rate and weight equations of TVA, $v(x_1, \text{tilted left})$ is given by

$$\frac{C\,\eta(x_1, \text{line})\,\pi(\text{line})}{\eta(x_1, \text{line})\,\pi(\text{line}) + \eta(x_2, \text{box})\,\pi(\text{box})},$$

where $C = \eta(x_1, \text{tilted left})\,\beta(\text{tilted left})$. Hence, when the task is to report the tilt of the line (Condition a) or both the tilt and another aspect of the line (Condition b), $v(x_1, \text{tilted left})$ equals

$$\frac{C\,\eta(x_1, \text{line})\,\pi_{\text{hi}}}{\eta(x_1, \text{line})\,\pi_{\text{hi}} + \eta(x_2, \text{box})\,\pi_{\text{lo}}}.$$

When the task is to report the tilt of the line and some aspect of the box (Condition c), $v(x_1, \text{tilted left})$ takes on a lower value, namely,

$$\frac{C\,\eta(x_1, \text{line})\,\pi_{\text{hi}}}{\eta(x_1, \text{line})\,\pi_{\text{hi}} + \eta(x_2, \text{box})\,\pi_{\text{hi}}}.$$

Thus, as found by Duncan (1984), performance in Condition b should equal performance in Condition a, but performance in Condition c should be inferior to performance in Condition a.

According to Duncan's (1984) results, different features of the same object can be recognized without interference, but features of different objects cannot. The above explanation of Duncan's (1984) results rests on the assumption that attentional weights are assigned to elements (objects rather than features) so that (1) the rate of processing of a perceptual categorization of an element is directly related to the attentional weight of that element, but inversely related to the attentional weight of any other element (cf. TVA's rate equation) and, by implication, (2) an increase in the attentional weight of an element facilitates recognition of any feature of that element, but interferes with recognition of any other element. Note that, according to this account, probabilities of recognizing (selecting) different features of the same element should be positively correlated if the attentional weight of the element is varied. Thus, if the attentional weight is increased, the probability of encoding any categorization of the element becomes higher. By the same account, probabilities of recognizing features from different elements should show negative correlations when the attentional weights of the elements are varied: if one element receives a higher attentional weight, the relative weights of other elements go down, which makes any categorization of these elements less likely. However, if attentional weights (as well as η and β values) are kept constant across trials, processing times for different perceptual categorizations should be stochastically independent (i.e. uncorrelated), even when attending to several objects at the same time.

4.1.2 Stochastic independence

There is substantial evidence of such stochastic (statistical) independence (see Kyllingsbæk and Bundesen 2007). In one experiment (Bundesen *et al.* 2003), each stimulus display showed a pair of coloured letters, one to the left and one to the right of fixation (Fig. 4.2). The exposure was brief (29 ms), and the letter pair was followed by a mask. The observer was asked to pay equal attention to the two letters and try to report the colour and the shape of each letter, but to refrain from pure guessing. Order of report was free, but the observer should indicate whether a report of a feature referred to the letter on the left or the letter on the right.

The 16 possible combinations of correctly and not correctly reported features are listed in Table 4.1. On the strong assumption that reports of the four individual features (the left shape, the left colour, the right shape, and the right colour) were mutually independent, the probabilities of each of the 16 possible combinations of correctly and not correctly reported features should be predictable from the probabilities of report of the four individual features. By the definition of stochastic independence, the probability of a particular combination of reports should then simply be given by multiplying the probabilities for each individual report. For example, for a given participant, the probability of correct report of both the shape and the colour of the left-hand letter and the shape but not the colour of the right-hand letter (report type 12 in Table 4.1) should equal the product of (1) the (overall) probability (for the given participant) of correct report of the shape of the left-hand letter, (2) the probability of correct report of the colour of the left-hand letter, (3) the probability of correct report of the shape of the right-hand letter, and (4) the complement of the probability of correct report of the colour of the right-hand letter.

Fig. 4.2 Typical stimulus display used by Bundesen *et al.* (2003).

Table 4.1 Possible types of report in experiment of Bundesen *et al.* (2003)

Type	Left		Right	
	Shape	**Colour**	**Shape**	**Colour**
1	0	0	0	0
2	1	0	0	0
3	0	1	0	0
4	0	0	1	0
5	0	0	0	1
6	1	1	0	0
7	0	0	1	1
8	1	0	1	0
9	0	1	0	1
10	1	0	0	1
11	0	1	1	0
12	1	1	1	0
13	1	1	0	1
14	1	0	1	1
15	0	1	1	1
16	1	1	1	1

1, correctly reported; 0, not correctly reported.

Some of the eight observers showed systematic deviations between the observed and predicted probabilities of this model, but the majority of the observers showed close fits (Fig. 4.3). Three among the eight observers (including those whose data are depicted in Fig. 4.3a and b) seemed able to keep the attentional weights of the two letters perfectly constant across trials. For each of these observers, the agreement between observed and predicted probabilities was virtually perfect, with correlations exceeding 0.99. Thus, for these observers, the likelihood that one of the features (colour or shape) of a given letter was correctly reported seemed completely independent of whether the other feature of the letter was correctly reported, and also completely independent of whether features of the other letter were correctly reported.

Kyllingsbæk and Bundesen (2007, Experiment 1) extended the findings of Bundesen *et al.* (2003) to reports of orientation and colour of pairwise-presented bar-shaped stimuli. In a further experiment, Kyllingsbæk and Bundesen (2007, Experiment 2) showed virtually perfect stochastic independence between reports of colours and directions of motion of pairwise-presented

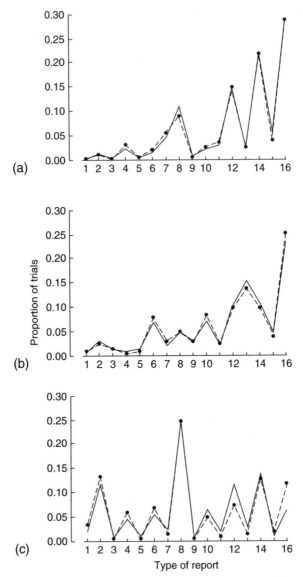

Fig. 4.3 Observed and predicted probability distributions of reports of pairs of coloured shapes across 16 types of report. (a) Data for Observer S1. Observed probabilities are shown by solid circles connected with dashed lines. Predicted probabilities are indicated by unmarked points connected with unbroken lines. The predictions were derived from observed probabilities of correct identification of the left shape, the left colour, the right shape, and the right colour, respectively, by assuming mutual independence between reports of the four features. The 16 types of report are defined in Table 4.1. (b) and (c) Similar data for Observers S3 and S5, respectively. Adapted with permission from Bundesen, Kyllingsbæk and Larsen (2003). Independent encoding of colors and shapes from two stimuli. *Psychonomic Bulletin & Review*, **10**, 474–479. Copyright 2003 by the Psychonomic Society.

circular discs at each of three levels of exposure duration that varied unpredictably from trial to trial. As argued in detail by Kyllingsbæk and Bundesen, the findings from this experimental design provide strong evidence that the reported features of the two stimuli were identified and localized in parallel across the display.

4.2 Whole report: number and spatial position of targets

4.2.1 Number of targets

Sperling (1960, Experiment 1) measured the number of elements (letters) correct in whole report as a function of display size. Results obtained with an exposure duration of 50 ms and dark pre- and postexposure fields are shown in Fig. 4.4. As can be seen, the mean score (the mean number of letters correctly reported, averaged across five subjects) was close to the number of elements in the stimulus when the display contained four or fewer elements, and averaged between four and five elements for displays containing five or more elements. The data can be closely fitted by a parallel processing model with limited capacity, such as TVA. The general idea is that all the elements in the display race for encoding into a VSTM store that can hold at most K items. The speed at which each element is processed varies over time: it is zero until onset of the display, then rises immediately to a specific value and stays at this level for the duration of the display, only to decay exponentially after the element has been replaced by a blank screen (and only a positive afterimage remains in the visual system). Parameters τ and μ denote the duration of the physical display and the effective duration of the visual afterimage, respectively. Given these simple constraints the probability of encoding (and reporting)

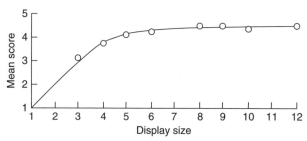

Fig. 4.4 Mean score (number of targets correct in whole report) as a function of display size in Experiment 1 of Sperling (1960). Open circles, group data for five subjects. A theoretical fit by TVA is indicated by unmarked points connected with straight lines. The observed data are from Fig. 3 of Sperling (1960). The information available in brief visual presentations. *Psychological Monographs*, **74** (11, Whole No. 498). Copyright 1960 by the American Psychological Association. Adapted with permission. The use of APA information does not imply endorsement by APA.

each individual element in the display can be computed exactly by TVA, as described in Box 4.2.

Box 4.2 Sperling (1960)

Let the short-term memory store be empty at the moment a stimulus display is presented. Assume that, for any letter types i and j, the perceptual decision bias parameters β_i and β_j equal a positive constant β_0, but for any other perceptual categories, the bias parameters are zero. Assume that, for any token x of letter type i in a stimulus exposed for τ ms, $\eta(x, i)$ (i.e. the strength of the sensory evidence that x belongs to i) varies over time such that (1) $\eta(x, i)$ is zero until, say, time zero; (2) from time zero until time τ, $\eta(x, i)$ equals a positive constant η_0; and (3) after time τ, $\eta(x, i)$ decays exponentially with a fixed time constant, μ. Assume that, for any letter token x which is not of type i, effects of $\eta(x, i)$ are negligible (intrusion errors will not be analysed). Finally assume that, for any elements (letter tokens) x and z in the stimulus, the attentional weights w_x and w_z are positive and equally great, but for any other elements in the visual field, the attentional weights are zero.

Applying the assumptions to a display with T targets, the rate equation implies that T identical v values must be considered, one for each target. Each of the v values is a function of time given by

$$v(t) = \begin{cases} 0 & \text{for } t \leq 0 \\ C/T & \text{for } 0 < t \leq \tau \\ (C/T)\exp[-(t-\tau)/\mu] & \text{for } \tau < t, \end{cases}$$

where C stands for $\eta_0\beta_0$.

Because $v(t)$ is the conditional probability density that (the correct categorization of) an individual target finishes processing at time t provided that the target has not finished processing before time t, the unconditional probability that the target finishes processing at or before time t is given by

$$F(t) = 1 - \exp\left[-\int_0^t v(s)ds\right]$$

(for an applicable proof, see Parzen 1962, p. 168). Taking the limit of $F(t)$ as t tends to infinity and solving the integral yields

$$s = F(\infty) = 1 - \exp[-C(\tau + \mu)/T], \tag{4.1}$$

where s is the probability that, sooner or later, the target finishes processing.

Box 4.2 Sperling (1960) *(continued)*

If T (i.e. the number of targets in the stimulus) is less than or equal to K (i.e. the capacity of the short-term store), then the number of targets entering the short-term store obeys the binomial probability law for T Bernoulli trials, with probability s for success. In this case, the theoretical mean score (= the expected number of targets entering the short-term store) is given by

$$E(\text{score}) = Ts. \tag{4.2}$$

If T is greater than K, the theoretical mean score is given by

$$E(\text{score}) = \sum_{j=0}^{K} jp(j) \quad, \tag{4.3}$$

where

$$p(j) = \begin{cases} \binom{T}{j} s^j (1-s)^{T-j} & \text{for } j = 0, 1, \quad , K-1 \\ \sum_{i=K}^{T} \binom{T}{i} s^i (1-s)^{T-i} & \text{for } j = K. \end{cases} \tag{4.4}$$

In general, the theoretical mean score is a function of display size T, short-term storage capacity K, and the product $C(\tau + \mu)$. The meaning of parameter $C(\tau + \mu)$ is clarified by noting that, if storage capacity were unlimited, the expected score would approach an asymptotic value of $C(\tau + \mu)$ elements as display size increased (to see this, substitute from equation 4.1 into equation 4.2 and let T tend to infinity). The theoretical mean scores shown in Fig. 4.4 represent a least squares fit to the data; the fit was obtained with $K = 4.34$ elements and $C(\tau + \mu) = 9.85$ elements.

The theoretical fit to Sperling's (1960, Experiment 1) data on the number of elements correct in whole report as a function of display size implies that, for displays with five or more elements, the score was limited mainly by storage capacity (parameter K) rather than processing capacity and effective exposure duration [parameter $C(\tau + \mu)$] (the latter, composite term represents the total amount of processing accumulated over the duration of the display: the processing rate multiplied by the effective exposure time). Specifically, for displays with six or more elements, both observed and theoretical mean scores exceeded four; since the estimate for K was less than five elements, little improvement should be expected from increase in exposure duration (parameter τ). A further experiment by Sperling (1960, Experiment 2) confirmed this expectation: as exposure duration was increased from 50 ms up to 500 ms, the mean score (for displays with six or eight elements) increased by only half an element. Related studies (e.g. Mackworth 1963; Sperling and Speelman 1970) have supported a conjecture that, once about four elements have been selected (so that the short-term store has been filled up with elements), further increase in the score as exposure duration is prolonged occurs at only the slow rate of implicit speech. Implicit speech should provide articulatory read-out from the visual short-term store to auditory short-term memory, thus making space available in VSTM for additional information.

4.2.2 Stimulus followed by mask

Experiments 1 and 2 of Sperling (1960) were done with dark pre- and postexposure fields. The results change dramatically if the target display is followed by a pattern mask rather than a dark field. The number of elements correct in whole report (the score) then becomes critically dependent on the stimulus-onset asynchrony (SOA) between the target display and the pattern mask. When the SOA is less than or equal to some critical value, t_0, the score via non-guessing appears to be zero. As the SOA exceeds t_0, the mean score initially increases at a high rate of about one element for every 5–30 ms of SOA (in case of young, healthy participants), and then levels off as it approaches the span of around four elements, or the number of targets in the stimulus, whichever is smaller (cf. Sperling 1963, 1967; Allport 1968; Merikle *et al.* 1971; Townsend and Ashby 1983, Chapter 11; Shibuya and Bundesen 1988). Representative mean score functions for displays with two, four, and six targets terminated by pattern masks (group data for two subjects, replotted from Shibuya and Bundesen 1988) are shown in Fig. 4.5.

A theoretical least squares fit to the data in Fig. 4.5 is indicated by smooth curves. It was determined by the same assumptions as those used in fitting the data of Sperling (1960, Experiment 1) except for the following two modifications. First, parameter t_0 (minimum effective exposure duration) was introduced and parameter τ was interpreted as *effective* exposure duration: when the physical exposure duration of the target display (= the SOA between the target display and the pattern mask) was shorter than t_0 (i.e. below threshold), τ was assumed to be zero. When the physical exposure duration was longer than t_0, τ was equated with the physical exposure duration minus t_0 (i.e. the time passed since the visual threshold was crossed).

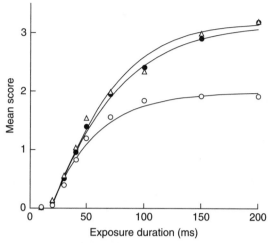

Fig. 4.5 Mean score (number of targets correct in whole report) as a function of exposure duration, with display size T as the parameter, in the experiment of Shibuya and Bundesen (1988). Group data for two subjects. T was 2 (open circles), 4 (solid circles), or 6 (triangles). A theoretical fit by TVA is indicated by smooth curves. The observed data are replotted from Fig. 1 of Shibuya and Bundesen (1988). Visual selection from multielement displays: measuring and modelling effects of exposure duration. *Journal of Experimental Psychology: Human Perception and Performance*, **14**, 591–600. Copyright 1988 by the American Psychological Association. Adapted with permission. The use of APA information does not imply endorsement by APA.

Second, the pattern mask was assumed to interrupt processing. Thus, for any stimulus x of type i with an effective exposure duration of τms, $\eta(x, i)$ was assumed (1) to be zero until time zero; (2) to equal a positive constant η_0 from time zero until time τ; and (3) to be zero after time τ. Thus, the processing speed (v value) is zero except during the interval of τms just before the onset of the mask.

With the two modifications to take account of the effect of the pattern mask, the theoretical predictions for whole report performance become identical to predictions by the fixed-capacity independent race model (FIRM) of Shibuya and Bundesen (1988; see Section 3.3.2). The account has three free parameters: minimum effective exposure duration t_0, storage capacity K, and processing capacity C (which equals the product of η_0 and the corresponding perceptual bias, β_0). For any values of the three parameters, theoretical mean scores can be calculated by equations 4.2–4.4 and a modified version of equation 4.1

$$s = 1 - \exp(-C\tau/T) \tag{4.1'}$$

(see Box 4.2; the modification of the equation relates to the fact that, due to the interrupting effect of the mask, no gradual decay of processing occurs following stimulus offset. The μ parameter therefore disappears from the equation). The least squares fit to the data in Fig. 4.5 was attained with processing capacity C at 51.8 elements/s, storage capacity K at 3.20 elements, and minimum effective exposure duration t_0 at 19 ms. The fit accounted for 99.4% of the variance in the observed mean scores, which is nearly perfect. In contrast, other exponential models assuming unlimited capacity make predictions that deviate systematically from the experimental results (see Box 4.3).

Box 4.3 Comparison with unlimited-capacity models

It is instructive to compare predictions by TVA (i.e. an exponential race model with fixed processing capacity C and fixed storage capacity K) with predictions by otherwise similar exponential models that assume (a) unlimited processing capacity, but fixed storage capacity; (b) fixed processing capacity, but unlimited storage capacity; or (c) unlimited processing capacity and unlimited storage capacity (recall from Chapter 3 that the term 'unlimited processing capacity' signifies that the amount of capacity allocated to each object is unaffected by additional objects in the display, not that an infinite amount is allocated to each object). In Case a (unlimited processing capacity, but fixed storage capacity), theoretical mean scores can be calculated by equations 4.2–4.4 and a new version of equation 4.1,

$$s = 1 - \exp(-C\tau). \qquad (4.1'')$$

A least squares fit to the data of Shibuya and Bundesen is shown in the upper panel of Fig. 4.6. [The fit was obtained with C (exponential processing rate per element) at 16.7 elements/s, storage capacity K at 2.84 elements, and minimum effective exposure duration t_0 at 25 ms.] Accounting for 93.3% of the variance in the data, the model captures the basic shape of the mean score functions (the functions mapping exposure durations on to mean scores), but the model overpredicts the effect of the parameter (the number of targets T) on the initial rate of increase as a mean score function rises from zero.

In Case b (fixed processing capacity, but unlimited storage capacity), theoretical mean scores can be calculated by equations 4.1′ and 4.2 (for any value of T). A least squares fit to the data of Shibuya and Bundesen is shown in the lower left panel of Fig. 4.6. (The fit was obtained with processing

Box 4.3 Comparison with unlimited-capacity models *(continued)*

capacity C at 33.7 elements/s and minimum effective exposure duration t_0 at 10 ms.) In this case, the theoretical mean score functions for four and six targets are size scaled versions of the function for two targets; the four- and six-target functions are obtained from the two-target function by geometric multiplications with factors 2 and 3, respectively, about the point $(t_0, 0)$ on the time axis. The model accounts for 94.6% of the variance in the data. As can be seen, the model overpredicts the effect of the parameter (the number of targets T) at long exposure durations.

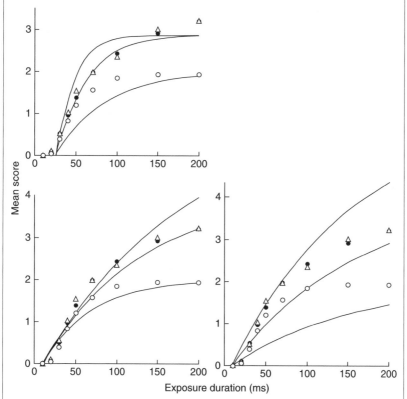

Fig. 4.6 Mean score (number of targets correct in whole report) as a function of exposure duration with display size T as the parameter in the experiment of Shibuya and Bundesen (1988). Group data for two subjects. T was 2 (open circles), 4 (solid circles), or 6 (triangles). Theoretical fits are indicated by smooth curves. Upper panel: fit by model with unlimited processing capacity, but fixed storage capacity. Lower left panel: fit by model with fixed processing capacity, but unlimited storage capacity. Lower right panel: fit by model with unlimited processing and storage capacity. The observed data are the same as in Fig. 4.5.

Box 4.3 Comparison with unlimited-capacity models *(continued)*

In Case c (unlimited processing capacity and unlimited storage capacity), theoretical mean scores can be calculated by equations 4.1″ and 4.2 (for any value of T). A least squares fit to the data of Shibuya and Bundesen is shown in the lower right panel of Fig. 4.6. [The fit was obtained with C (exponential processing rate per element) at 6.7 elements/s and minimum effective exposure duration t_0 at 8 ms.] In this case, the theoretical mean score functions are constrained so that, for any given exposure duration, the mean scores for four and six targets are 2 and 3 times as high, respectively, as the mean score for two targets. The model accounts for 77% of the variance in the data. As would be expected from the previous fits, the model overpredicts the effects of the parameter (the number of targets T) at both short and long exposure durations.

4.2.3 Position of targets

The Shibuya and Bundesen (1988) data were obtained with circular arrays that yielded little effect of serial position (i.e. spatial position in the array). In whole report of linear arrays, however, strong serial position effects have been found (e.g. Sperling 1967; Merikle *et al.* 1971; Townsend and Ashby 1983, Chapter 11). The results provided by Sperling (1967) are reproduced by the solid curves in Fig. 4.7, which shows the accuracy of report as a function of exposure duration for each location in a horizontal array of five letters terminated by a pattern mask (data for one typical subject). As noted by Sperling, all locations begin to be reported at better than chance levels, even at brief exposures. and the accuracy of report increases continuously as a function of exposure duration, but the rate of increase varies widely between locations. In TVA, this corresponds to different processing rates (v values) for each element. Looking at how v-values are computed in the rate equation, the most plausible reason for this is that both sensory effectiveness (parameter η) and attentional weights (parameter w) vary with the stimulus location. Supposedly, variation in η reflects sensory factors such as differences in retinal acuity (see Eriksen and Schultz 1978) or differences in strength of lateral masking (see Bouma 1978; Pelli *et al.* 2004; Kyllingsbæk *et al.* 2007; also see Intriligator and Cavanagh 2001; Tripathy and Cavanagh 2002; Strasburger 2005). Variation in w may reflect an attentional factor, namely, differences in the pertinence ascribed to different spatial locations (cf. Merikle *et al.* 1971; Townsend and Ashby 1983, Chapter 11). However, parameters η_m and w_m are not separately identifiable from the serial position curves in Fig. 4.7 (see equation 4.5 in Box 4.4 for details).

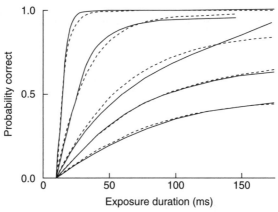

Fig. 4.7 Probability correct in whole report as a function of exposure duration for each display location in a horizontal array of five letters (Sperling 1967). Observed data for one typical subject are represented by five solid curves. A theoretical fit by TVA is indicated by dashed curves. If display locations are numbered from left to right and observed curves or theoretical curves are numbered from top to bottom, Curve 1 = Location 1, Curve 2 = Location 2, Curve 3 = Location 3, Curve 4 = Location 5, and Curve 5 = Location 4. Adapted with permission from Bundesen (1990). A theory of visual attention. *Psychological Review*, **97**, 523–547. Copyright 1990 by the American Psychological Association. The use of APA information does not imply endorsement by APA. Solid curves are adapted with permission from Sperling (1967). Successive approximations to a model for short-term memory. *Acta Psychologica*, **27**, 285–292. Copyright 1967 by Elsevier.

Box 4.4 Sperling (1967)

A close theoretical fit to the data in Fig. 4.7 is indicated by dashed curves. The fit was based on the following assumptions. First, for any letter types i and j, the perceptual decision bias parameters β_i and β_j equal a positive constant β_0, but for any other perceptual categories, the bias parameters are zero. Second, for any letter x of type i in stimulus location m ($m = 1, 2, \ldots, 5$), the strength of the sensory evidence that x is a token of type i, $\eta(x, i)$, (1) is zero until time zero; (2) equals a positive constant η_m from time zero until time τ; and (3) is zero after time τ. (As before, τ is the effective exposure duration of the target display: when the physical exposure duration is smaller than parameter t_0, then τ is zero; otherwise, τ equals the physical exposure duration minus t_0.) Third, for any letter token x which is not of type i, effects of $\eta(x, i)$ are negligible. Finally, for any letter in stimulus location m ($m = 1, 2, \ldots, 5$), the attentional weight equals a positive constant w_m, but for any element which is not a stimulus letter, the attentional weight is zero.

Box 4.4 Sperling (1967) *(continued)*

Applying the assumptions to a display with five stimulus letters, the rate equation implies that five different v values must be considered, one for each letter. For the letter in stimulus location m ($m = 1, 2, \ldots, 5$), the v value is a positive constant,

$$v_m = \eta_m \beta_0 \frac{w_m}{\sum_{n=1}^{5} w_n}, \tag{4.5}$$

in the interval from time zero to time τ, and the v value is zero outside this interval.

Effectively the assumptions leave seven free parameters: the storage capacity K, the minimum effective exposure duration t_0, and the v values $v_1, v_2, \ldots,$ and v_5. The theoretical fit to the data in Fig. 4.7 was attained with K at 4.00 elements, t_0 at 10 ms, and v values v_1 through v_5 at 169, 43, 17, 6, and 10 elements/s, respectively. A procedure for constructing the five theoretical serial position curves from the seven parameters is described in Appendix A.

4.3 Detection: number and spatial position of targets

4.3.1 Cued detection

Studies on covert spatial attention (selective attention to elements in particular spatial positions without the aid of eye movements) have investigated the effects of position uncertainty in detection and recognition with single-target displays. Facilitating effects of foreknowledge of the spatial position of the target have been found in analyses of latency of luminance detection (e.g. Posner *et al.* 1978, 1980), accuracy of luminance detection (e.g. Bashinsky and Bacharach 1980), latency of letter recognition (e.g. Eriksen and Hoffman 1974), and accuracy of letter recognition (see van der Heijden *et al.* 1985, for positive findings and for a discussion of negative findings by Grindley and Townsend 1968; see also Downing 1988, for related results).

According to TVA, foreknowledge of the spatial position of a target should facilitate selection of the target whether the background contains experimenter-defined distractors or only extraneous noise elements (including areas of 'empty' field in possible target locations; see Duncan 1981, 1985). Thus, if the location of the target is pre-cued, the subject may increase the attentional weight of any element in the cued location by increasing the pertinence value of the cued location. Increasing the attentional weight of an element (in relation to the weights of other elements in the visual field) speeds processing of that element at the expense of other elements. Accordingly, if the target does appear in the cued location, performance should improve in both latency (the time taken to sample the required information) and accuracy (the probability that the information is sampled from the display). Otherwise, if the cue is misleading, performance should degrade in both latency and accuracy.

Consider an experiment on luminance detection by Posner *et al.* (1978, Experiment 3). In this study, the subject was provided with a single response key, and the task was to press the key as quickly as possible when a signal (an above-threshold luminance increment) was detected in an otherwise blank field. The signal appeared either 7° to the left or 7° to the right of a central fixation point (see Fig. 4.8). The subject was pre-cued as to whether the signal would appear to the left or right, but eye movements were not permitted. If the pre-cue was an arrow pointing to the left or right, it was valid on 80% of the trials and invalid on 20%. If the cue was a neutral plus sign, the signal was equally likely to appear in either of the two locations.

As shown in Fig. 4.9, valid cues yielded faster detection responses (mean reaction times) than neutral cues (attentional *benefit*), and invalid cues yielded slower responses than neutral cues (attentional *cost*; cf. Posner 1978).

In this experiment, we suppose, subjects prepare for the detection task by adjusting the pertinence values of Locations L (7° to the left) and R (7° to the right) on the basis of the information provided by the pre-cue. With relatively high pertinence values of both Locations L and R and little pertinence of other locations, subjects sample (attend to) nothing but areas of blank screen in Locations L and R until the luminance increment is presented. At that point, sensory evidence is generated that one of the two areas shows a luminance increment, and once a categorization of the form 'x shows a luminance increment' has been made (sampled), the response is evoked. The response time is assumed to be a sum of two independent components: the time taken to encode a visual categorization of the signal (given by the rate equation) plus a residual response latency. The rate of visual encoding depends on the relative attentional weights of the two display locations, which are presumed set by the subject (using the information from the cue) so that average response time is minimized. Reaction time under different cuing conditions can thus be predicted from just two parameter estimates: the total processing capacity available, C, and the average residual response latency, b. A formal version of this simple model is developed in Box 4.5, together with equations for predicted reaction times.

Two general features of the TVA account of cued detection may be noted. First, as Broadbent (1982) would have it, the effect of foreknowledge of spatial

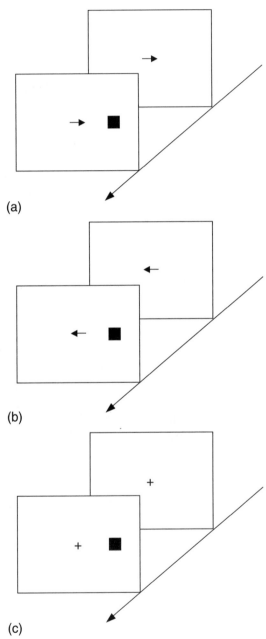

Fig. 4.8 Experimental procedure of Posner *et al.* (1978). (a) Valid condition. The central arrow points to the location where the target appears subsequently. (b) Invalid condition. The central arrow points to a different location than where the target will appear. (c) Neutral condition. The subject is not given prior information about the location of the target.

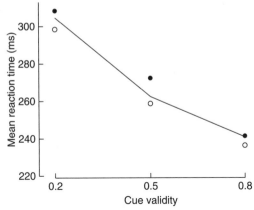

Fig. 4.9 Mean simple reaction time as a function of position uncertainty as varied by cue validity in Experiment 3 of Posner et al. (1978). Group data for eight subjects. The stimulus occurred to the left (solid circles) or to the right (open circles) of fixation. Cue validity was 0.2 (invalid cues), 0.5 (neutral cues), or 0.8 (valid cues). A theoretical fit by TVA is indicated by unmarked points connected with straight lines. The observed data are read from Fig. 5 of Posner, Nissen and Ogden (1978). Attended and unattended processing modes: the role of set for spatial location. In: H. L. Pick and I. J. Saltzman (eds), *Modes of perceiving and processing information*, pp. 137–157. Hillsdale, NJ: Lawrence Erlbaum Associates. Copyright 1978 by Taylor & Francis. Adapted with permission.

Box 4.5 Posner *et al.* (1978)

A theoretical least squares fit to the data in Fig. 4.9 is indicated by unmarked points connected with straight lines. The fit was based on the following, strong assumptions. First, under the conditions of the experiment, attention is purely spatial, in the sense that the attentional weight of an element (signal or noise) is determined by the spatial location of the element. Specifically, for elements (signal or noise) in Locations L and R, attentional weights w_L and w_R, respectively, are positive, but for any other elements in the visual field, attentional weights are zero. Second, the sensory evidence η_0 that a noise element (physically, a blank area) is a signal (i.e. an area with an above-threshold luminance increment) is vanishingly small in relation to the sensory evidence η_1 that a signal is a signal, and η_0 and η_1 are constant across the three experimental conditions (valid, neutral, invalid). Third, the perceptual decision bias β_1 associated with the signal category also is constant across conditions. Fourth, reaction time is a sum of two independent components; one component is the time taken to make (sample)

> **Box 4.5 Posner *et al.* (1978)** *(continued)*
>
> at least one categorization that an element x in the visual field is a signal, and the other component is a residual response latency X_b with mean b. Fifth, the information provided by the pre-cue is used for adjusting w_L and w_R (by adjusting the pertinence values of Locations L and R) so that expected reaction time is minimized.
>
> As shown in Appendix B, the rate equation and the five assumptions listed above imply that expected reaction times with valid (80% probability), neutral (50% probability), and invalid (20% probability) cues are given by
>
> $$E(\mathrm{RT} \mid \mathrm{valid}) = 1/(0.67\ C) + b,$$
>
> $$E(\mathrm{RT} \mid \mathrm{neutral}) = 1/(0.5\ C) + b,$$
>
> $$E(\mathrm{RT} \mid \mathrm{invalid}) = 1/(0.33\ C) + b,$$
>
> where the processing rate is given by $C = \eta_1\beta_1$. The least squares fit to the data in Fig. 4.9 was obtained with processing rate C at 24.7 elements/s and base reaction time b at 181 ms. Both estimates seem plausible.

position is supposed to be 'a genuine improvement in intake of information, not a criterion shift; filtering rather than pigeon-holing' (p. 270). Second, the account is consistent with evidence that subjects may set themselves for selecting stimuli from regions of space that are complex in shape (Egly and Homa 1984)—perhaps as complex as they can imagine (cf. Podgorny and Shepard 1978, 1983). In this respect, the notion of ascribing pertinence to spatial locations seems more adequate than the metaphor of spatial attention as a spotlight (cf. Section 2.8.2).

4.3.2 **Target redundancy**

Suppose the experiment by Posner *et al.* (1978, Experiment 3) had included trials in which two targets (luminance increments) were presented simultaneously, one in Location L (7° to the left) and one in Location R (7° to the right). In this case two identical signals, instead of just one, would be racing in parallel towards VSTM. The mean time taken for at least one of the two signals to reach its destination is readily predicted from the theoretical analysis described above. Regardless of the values of the attentional weights w_L and w_R (i.e. regardless of whether the pre-cue is neutral or not), the predicted simple reaction time to the redundant signals is the same (specifically, $1/C + b$), which is less than the predicted reaction time in trials with a single signal in the neutral condition $(1/(0.5C) + b)$. Thus the analysis predicts a substantial *redundancy gain* (viz., a gain of $1/C$, which is about 40 ms in case of the data from Posner *et al.* 1978).

We are not aware of studies extending the cost–benefit paradigm of Posner and his associates by presentation of redundant signals, but clear redundancy gains have been found in closely related reaction time experiments with incomplete foreknowledge of the spatial positions of targets (e.g. Miller 1982, Experiment 5; van der Heijden *et al.* 1983, 1984; a related experiment with accuracy as the dependent variable was reported by Eriksen and Lappin 1965). Consider the go/no-go experiment of van der Heijden *et al.* (1983). Subjects were presented with displays showing one, two, or three identical letters. For one group of subjects (high stimulus discriminability group), the letters were either Es or Os; for another group (low stimulus discriminability group), the letters were Es or Fs (see Fig. 4.10). The task was to press a button if, and only if, one or more Es were shown. Positions of individual letters in a display were determined by drawing at random (without replacement) from a set of only three possible positions (found at 4, 8, and 12 o'clock on an imaginary circle centred on fixation).

As shown for each group of subjects in Fig. 4.11, mean reaction time decreased as the number of targets (Es) increased. Analyses of reaction times to single-target displays showed no effect of spatial position. As detailed in Box 4.6, the data can be fitted by the rate and weight equations of TVA combined

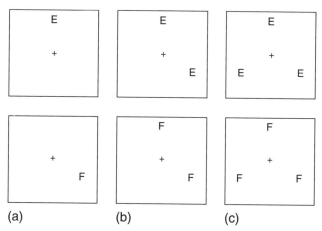

Fig. 4.10 Examples of stimulus displays used by van der Heijden *et al.* (1983) in the condition with low stimulus discriminability: (a) one-letter displays; (b) two-letter displays; (c) three-letter displays.

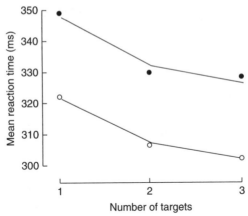

Fig. 4.11 Mean reaction times as functions of number of targets (target redundancy) for two groups of subjects in the go/no-go experiment of van der Heijden et al. (1983). There were six subjects per group. Stimulus discriminability was high for one group (open circles) and low for the other group (solid circles). Theoretical fits by TVA are indicated by unmarked points connected with straight lines. The observed data are taken from the appendix of van der Heijden, La Heij, and Boer (1983). Parallel processing of redundant targets in simple visual search tasks. *Psychological Research*, **45**, 235–254.

Box 4.6 van der Heijden *et al.* (1983)

Theoretical least squares fits to the data in Fig. 4.11 are indicated by unmarked points connected with straight lines. For either group of subjects, this TVA fit was based on essentially the same assumptions as those used in fitting the data of Posner *et al.* (1978, Experiment 3). First, under the experimental conditions, attention is assumed to be purely spatial, in the sense that the attentional weight of an element (a stimulus letter or a blank area) is determined by the spatial location of the element; specifically, for elements in Locations 1, 2, and 3 (the three possible stimulus positions), attentional weights w_1, w_2, and w_3, respectively, are positive, but for any other elements in the visual field, attentional weights are zero. Second, a response is presumed to be evoked if and when a perceptual categorization of the form 'x is an E' has been made, and the sensory evidence η_0 that a blank area is an E is supposed to be vanishingly small in relation to the sensory evidence η_1 that a letter token of type E belongs to this type. Third, like η_0 and η_1, the perceptual decision bias β_1 associated with letter type E is independent of the number of letters in the stimulus. Fourth, reaction time is a sum of two independent components: the time taken to make

---

Box 4.6 van der Heijden *et al.* (1983) *(continued)*

(sample) at least one categorization that an element x in the visual field is an E and a residual latency with mean b. Fifth, attentional weights w_1, w_2, and w_3 are adjusted (by adjusting the pertinence values of Locations 1–3) so that expected reaction time is minimized.

By the rate equation and these five assumptions, expected reaction times to displays with one, two, and three targets are given by (cf. Appendix B)

$$E(\text{RT} \mid T = 1) = 1/(0.33\ C) + b,$$

$$E(\text{RT} \mid T = 2) = 1/(0.67\ C) + b,$$

$$E(\text{RT} \mid T = 3) = 1/C + b,$$

where $C = \eta_1\beta_1$. For the high discriminability group, the least squares fit to the data in Fig. 4.11 was obtained with parameter C at 102.6 elements/s and base reaction time b at 292.8 ms. For the low discriminability group, the fit was obtained with C at 94.6 elements/s and b at 317.0 ms.

---

with the same basic assumptions about visual processing and reaction time as were used in accounting for the experiment of Posner *et al.* (1978).

4.4 Interference versus independence in the perception of simultaneous targets

The experiments on whole report reviewed in Sections 4.1 and 4.2 (e.g. Duncan 1984; Shibuya and Bundesen 1988) showed *interference* in the perception of simultaneous targets. The observed probability that a given target was correctly reported decreased with the number of targets in the stimulus display, and the nature of the decrement suggested that targets were sampled from the display by a process with *limited capacity*.

By way of contrast, the gains from target redundancy observed in detection and recognition experiments like that of van der Heijden *et al.* (1983) provided evidence of *independence* in the perception of simultaneous targets. Individual targets appeared to be processed in parallel and independently, in the sense that the rate of processing of a given target was independent of the number of simultaneous targets. This sort of independence is an earmark of *unlimited-capacity* parallel processing (cf. van der Heijden *et al.* 1983).

As emphasized in the foregoing paragraphs, results from the two types of experiments (whole report versus detection and recognition) may seem to be in conflict. Yet both types of results were fitted by TVA, and it is worth elaborating the resolution of the paradox. By the rate equation of TVA, interference prevails in the perception of simultaneous elements in the visual field. For any element with an above-zero attentional weight, the rate of processing decreases when the number of simultaneous elements (with above-zero attentional weights) are increased. However, the composition of the set of elements that compete for attention (the set of elements with above-zero attentional weights) depends upon the experimental conditions. Specifically, in the whole report conditions of Shibuya and Bundesen (1988), the set of competing elements is supposed to be the same as the set of experimenter-defined *targets*. Phenomenologically, attention is captured by the targets once the stimulus display is presented. Granted that processing parameters (η and β values) are the same for any target as for any other target, the results conform to predictions from a parallel model with fixed processing capacity.

In detection and recognition experiments like those of Posner *et al.* (1978, Experiment 3) and van der Heijden *et al.* (1983), the set of competing elements is supposed to consist of the fixed set of (two or three, respectively) *information sources* ('channels') to be monitored for the presence of experimenter-defined targets (luminance increments or Es, respectively). Phenomenologically, attention is directed to these information sources (particular parts of the surface of the display screen) *before* the targets are presented. Granted that attention is not reallocated once a target appears (i.e. once a channel that is monitored shows a luminance increment or an E, respectively), the rate of processing a given target depends upon the number and the attentional weights of the channels that are monitored, but not upon the number of simultaneous targets in these channels. Accordingly, so long as the distribution of attentional weights across channels is kept constant, redundancy gains conform to predictions from an unlimited-capacity parallel model.

In the suggested interpretation, the appearance of unlimited-capacity parallel processing in, for instance, the experiment of van der Heijden *et al.* (1983) reflects that (a) attention was directed to individual channels (defined by spatial locations) rather than targets (defined by shape); and (b) the distribution of attentional weights across channels was the same regardless of the number of targets in the stimulus. Supposedly, Condition (a) was favoured by the fact that the number of channels (possible stimulus locations) was small. Due to the small number of channels, distributing attention over channels before targets were presented yielded a high rate of target processing (i.e. a high value of the sum of the processing rates for the individual targets) even for single-target displays. Condition (b) prevailed on account of the nature of the position uncertainty in the task. Throughout the experiment, presentation probabilities for the three possible stimulus locations were equal, so optimal performance was attained by keeping constant the distribution of attentional weights across channels.

In related detection and recognition experiments, position uncertainty has been eliminated (C. W. Eriksen and B. A. Eriksen 1979; Krueger and Shapiro 1980) or manipulated between conditions (Posner *et al.* 1978, Experiment 3). In these experiments, performance was optimized by changing the distribution of attentional weights across channels between conditions. The impression of unlimited-capacity parallel processing then disappeared. When position uncertainty was eliminated, redundancy gains vanished (C. W. Eriksen and B. A. Eriksen 1979; Krueger and Shapiro 1980). When position uncertainty was manipulated between conditions, limitations on processing capacity showed up as attentional cost and benefit (Posner *et al.* 1978).

The proposed analysis suggests that, even in whole report experiments, results might conform to predictions from an unlimited-capacity parallel model if the set of possible stimulus locations is small and fixed and presentation probabilities for the possible stimulus locations are equal. Judging from the results on detection and recognition (e.g. van der Heijden *et al.* 1983), such conditions should favour a strategy of monitoring the possible stimulus locations by distributing attention equally among the channels in advance of the presentation of the target display. Support for this conjecture was found in the whole report experiment by Eriksen and Lappin (1967) (for related results, see Eriksen 1966). As described in Section 2.5, displays contained one, two, three, or four targets. Positions of the targets were chosen at random from a set of only four possible locations. In these conditions, individual targets appeared to be processed in parallel and independently, in the strong sense that the rate of processing a given target was independent of the number of simultaneous targets.

4.5 **Summary**

In this chapter TVA has been applied to classic experimental findings on divided attention. The theory proved useful in explaining effects of object integrality (e.g. Duncan 1984) and stochastic independence in simultaneous processing of multiple features (Bundesen *et al.* 2003). Both findings suggest important differences between attentional processing of objects and features, closely in line with the rate equation of TVA. TVA also provided a coherent account of diverse findings on limitations of attentional capacity, specifically the effects of number and spatial position of targets in whole report. In particular, the theory provided accurate fits to effects of number of targets in whole report with (Shibuya and Bundesen 1988) or without (Sperling 1960) masking. Also, TVA was used to fit the spatial position effects in whole report found by Sperling (1967). In relation to detection experiments, the theory proved useful in analysing the spatial cuing paradigm of Posner *et al.* (1978), and it correctly predicted effects of target redundancy (e.g. van der Heijden *et al.* 1983). The proposed TVA analyses reconciled apparently conflicting findings on interference versus independence in the perception of simultaneous targets.

5

Explaining focused attention by TVA

The experiments reviewed in Chapter 4 were studies of divided attention, the ability to process multiple targets or information channels simultaneously. The detection and search experiments to be treated in the present chapter are studies of *focused attention*. They deal with the ability to focus attention on targets rather than distractors (selectivity). Combined studies of divided and focused attention, in which capacity and selectivity are investigated in the same design, can provide strong empirical constraints for theoretical models (see Sections 5.1 and 5.4). Interesting examples of such studies were carried out by Estes and Taylor (1964, 1965). Historically, however, the main experimental paradigm for focused attention has been visual search, and many variations of this task have been investigated. If target–distractor discriminability is high, search can proceed very efficiently and in a single view, as described in Section 5.2. A famous example of this was presented by Treisman and Gelade (1980). The search process can be influenced by grouping effects (Bundesen and Pedersen 1983) as well as various mechanisms of attentional capture (Folk *et al.* 1992). If target–distractor discriminability is poor, search is relatively slow and often requires multiple different views of the display (cf. Section 5.3). In this case reaction time typically increases linearly with the number of items in the display (Treisman and Gelade 1980), an effect that may result from a number of different search mechanisms. Studies of the relatively long time required to shift attention between different locations (e.g. Colegate *et al.* 1973) suggest that attention is allocated to small groups of items at a time. Another question of timing concerns processing of (delayed) selection cues, which was investigated in a partial report design by Sperling (1960; see Section 5.5). Furthermore, selectivity can change with extended practice, effects that have been characterized by Shiffrin and Schneider (1977) and Schneider and Fisk (1982). These findings are described in Section 5.6. As in the previous chapter, we show how each of these effects can be accounted for by TVA. Finally, in Section 5.7, we describe three important extensions of TVA proposed by Logan and co-workers (Logan 1996, 2002a; Logan and Gordon 2001) that account for many findings from research areas neighbouring visual attention: effects of spatial distance, categorization, memory, and executive control of dual task performance.

5.1 **Selective detection compared with whole report**

A study by Estes and Taylor (1964) forms an interesting link between the work on divided and focused attention by incorporating both kinds of task in the same experimental design. They presented subjects with brief displays of randomly selected consonants. Two letters (e.g. B and F) were predesignated as targets ('critical elements') and the rest as distractors (see Fig. 5.1). Each display contained exactly one of the two targets, and the subject's task was to report the target that appeared in the display, guessing whenever unsure. Exposure duration was 50 ms, and pre- and postexposure fields were dark. The data obtained with this detection method were compared with whole report scores obtained with the same subjects in similar conditions. To facilitate the comparison, the observed detection probabilities were corrected for guessing, and the corrected probabilities were multiplied by the number of elements in the display, to get an estimate of 'the number of elements processed' for each display size.

The results are shown in Fig. 5.2, together with a fit to the data by TVA (unmarked points connected with straight lines). The theoretical whole report scores were determined by assumptions identical to those used in fitting the data of Sperling (1960, Experiment 1; see Section 4.2.1). The detection scores were modelled by the same assumptions, with the following exceptions. First, detection (via non-guessing) was assumed to occur if, and only if, the target was among the elements selected from the display. Second, the attentional weight of a distractor was supposed to be less than the attentional weight of a target, and the ratio between the attentional weight of a distractor and the attentional weight of a target was assumed to be a constant (parameter α). In addition to the selective detection parameter α, the assumptions leave only

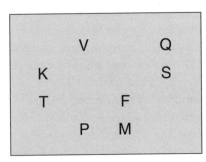

Fig. 5.1 Typical search display used by Estes and Taylor (1964).

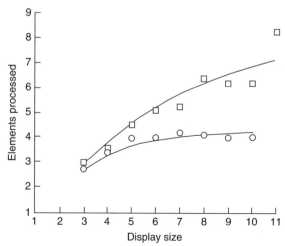

Fig. 5.2 Mean number of 'elements processed' as a function of display size for both whole report and detection procedures of Estes and Taylor (1964). Whole report data (circles) and detection data (squares) are for the same group of four subjects. A theoretical fit by TVA is indicated by unmarked points connected with straight lines. The observed data are read from Fig. 4 of Estes and Taylor (1964). Visual detection in relation to display size and redundancy of critical elements. *Perception & Psychophysics*, **1**, 9–16. Copyright 1964 by Estes and Taylor. Adapted with permission.

two free parameters, both of which are familiar from the fit to the whole report data of Sperling. One is the short-term storage capacity K. The other is the processing parameter given by the composite term $C(\tau + \mu)$. As noted previously, the latter term represents the total amount of processing accumulated over the duration of the display (i.e. the processing rate multiplied by the effective exposure time). The fit to the data in Fig. 5.2 was found with $K = 4.70$ elements, $C(\tau + \mu) = 6.90$ elements, and $\alpha = 0.43$. (Formulas for calculating the theoretical detection score as a function of display size for any values of the three parameters are given in Appendix C.) Thus, TVA yields a unified account of the data from whole report and selective detection.

5.2 **One-view search**

Visual search for a target among distractors varies greatly in efficiency. At one extreme, the target immediately calls attention to itself. Phenomenally, a single view suffices to make the target pop out from the background of distractors without any need to scan the display by saccadic eye movements or shifts of attention. At the other extreme, the display must be scrutinized in order to find the target. Phenomenally, the search process is effortful and appears to consist in serially scanning the display part by part or even element by element.

5.2.1 **Efficient feature search**

In feature search, the target differs from the distractors by possessing a simple 'physical' feature (e.g. a particular colour, size, or curvature) not shared by any of the distractors. If the target feature is highly discriminable, search can be very efficient (i.e. effects of distractors can be very small). A famous example was provided by Treisman and Gelade (1980, Experiment 1, feature condition). Subjects were presented with displays showing either one or zero targets (with equal probability) among a number of distractors. The distractors were brown Ts and green Xs, and the target was equally likely to be a blue element (a blue T or a blue X) or an S (a brown S or a green S). The task was to make a key press with the dominant hand if a target was present, and with the non-dominant hand if not, and to respond as quickly as possible 'without making any errors'. Display size (i.e. number of targets plus number of distractors) varied between trials, and each display was exposed until a response was made. Positive and negative mean reaction times as functions of display size are shown in Fig. 5.3. There were no systematic effects of display size on errors, and miss and false alarm rates were nearly equal (2.1% and 2.2%, respectively).

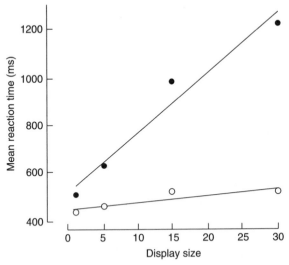

Fig. 5.3 Positive and negative mean reaction times as functions of display size in the feature search condition of Treisman and Gelade (1980, Experiment 1). Group data for six subjects. Positive reaction times are shown by open circles, negative reaction times by solid circles. A theoretical fit by TVA is indicated by unmarked points connected with straight lines. The observed data are read from Fig. 1 of Treisman and Gelade (1980). A feature-integration theory of attention. *Cognitive Psychology*, **12**, 97–136. Copyright 1980 by Elsevier. Adapted with permission.

A theoretical least squares fit to the data in Fig. 5.3 is indicated by two straight lines, one for positive and one for negative reactions. The fit was based on a *deadline model of one-view search* which was arrived at as follows. In the deadline model of one-view search, positive ('present') reactions are based on positive categorizations of target identity, whereas negative ('absent') reactions are made by default when a preset temporal deadline is reached, but no positive categorization has been made. For any deadline, there is a certain probability r of missing a target, because the deadline may be reached before a positive categorization has been sampled even if a target is present in the display. Of course, the longer the set deadline, the smaller the probability of a miss.

Reaction time is assumed to be given as a sum of two independent components. The first component is the time taken to encode a positive categorization of the target (or alternatively, to reach the deadline), which depends on both the general processing rate, C, and the ability to discriminate targets from distractors, α. The second component is a residual response latency that may vary between positive and negative responses (parameters a_1 and b_1, respectively). As detailed in Box 5.1, this yields a model with only four free parameters: r, the ratio α/C, a_1, and b_1. The least squares fit shown in Fig. 5.3 was obtained with r at 0.0002, α/C at 2.93 ms, a_1 at 448 ms, and b_1 at 536 ms.

The fit was made on the assumption that r (i.e. the probability that a target fails to be sampled before the deadline) was constant as display size N varied. As demonstrated in Box 5.1 (equations 5.2 and 5.6), this assumption implies that positive and negative mean reaction times are linear functions of N. It also implies that the residual response latencies a_1 and b_1 are independent of N (equations 5.4 and 5.8). The assumption that r was constant as display size varied is consistent with the fact that Treisman and Gelade (1980) observed no systematic effects of display size on errors. The small value of the estimate for r is consistent with the finding that miss rates (reflecting r) were small and no higher that false alarm rates. The estimate for α/C also seems plausible; it is consistent with a hypothesis that, say, $C = 45$ samples/s (as in the partial report experiment of Shibuya and Bundesen 1988) and $\alpha = 0.13$.[1]

The deadline model of one-view search makes several interesting predictions. Some predictions are generated by the way parameter r figures in

....

[1] Accounting for 97.8% of the variance in the observed mean reaction times, the least squares fit shown in Fig. 5.3 is quite good, but not perfect. The fit could be improved by relaxing the assumption that parameter r (the probability that a target fails to be sampled before the deadline) was constant as display size varied. For example, if parameter r was allowed to be slightly higher for display size 30 than for display sizes 1, 5, and 15, the percentage of variance accounted for by the model would increase from 97.8% to 99.8%.

Box 5.1 Treisman and Gelade (1980; feature search)

Let a positive categorization be a categorization of the form 'x is blue' or 'x is an S'. Let the strength of the sensory evidence that x is blue be η_1 if x is blue, but η_0 if x is brown or green, and let the strength of the sensory evidence that x is an S be η_1 if x is an S, but η_0 if x is an X or a T. Let the perceptual decision bias parameters associated with *blue* and S be β_1, and let all other perceptual bias parameters be β_0 or less. Finally, let the pertinence values of *blue* and S be equally high, and let the ratio of the attentional weight of a distractor to the attentional weight of a target be a constant α.

Suppose target–distractor discriminability is high so that η_1 is high, but η_0 is low. With little risk of false-positive categorizations, strong pigeonholing is warranted: let β_1 be high, but let β_0 be close to zero. By the rate equation, if η_0 and β_0 are sufficiently low, v values for categorizations other than correct positive ones are negligibly small. For a display with one target (a blue element or an S) and D distractors, the processing rate for the correct positive categorization can also be computed from the rate equation: because the attentional weight of the target is one and the weight of each distractor is α, the v value is given by

$$v = \eta_1\beta_1 * 1/(1 + \alpha D) = C/(1 + \alpha D),\qquad(5.1)$$

where $C = \eta_1\beta_1$.

In the deadline model of one-view search, positive reactions are based on positive categorizations, whereas negative reactions are made by default when a preset temporal deadline, d, is reached, but no positive categorization has been made. For any deadline d, there is a certain probability, r, of missing a target, because the deadline may be reached before a positive categorization has been sampled even if a target is present in the display. With a display of one target and $D = N - 1$ distractors, the probability is given by one minus the probability of making a positive categorization within the time interval from 0 to d, that is:

$$r = 1 - \int_0^d v\exp(-vt)dt = \exp(-vd),$$

where v is given by equation 5.1. By combining the two expressions and rearranging the terms, we arrive at

$$d = \frac{-\ln(r)}{v} = -\ln(r)\frac{1 + \alpha(N - 1)}{C}$$

Box 5.1 Treisman and Gelade (1980; feature search) (continued)

(because $D = N - 1$). The expectation of the negative reaction time, $E(RT_-)$, is assumed to be a sum of d and a residual component b_0 which is a constant. Thus,

$$E(RT_-) = -\ln(r)\frac{1 + \alpha(N - 1)}{C} + b_0, \tag{5.2}$$

which can be rewritten as

$$E(RT_-) = -\ln(r)\frac{\alpha}{C}(N - 1) + b_1, \tag{5.3}$$

where

$$b_1 = b_0 - \frac{\ln(r)}{C}. \tag{5.4}$$

Positive reaction times also depend upon the deadline d. With a display of one target and $N - 1$ distractors, the conditional expectation of the time taken to sample the correct positive categorization, given that the sampling occurs before time d, equals

$$s = \frac{\int_0^d tv\exp(-vt)dt}{\int_0^d v\exp(-vt)dt}, \tag{5.5}$$

where v is given by equation 5.1. Equation 5.5 reduces to

$$s = \frac{1 - \exp(-vd) - vd\exp(-vd)}{v[1 - \exp(-vd)]}$$

$$= \left[1 + \frac{r\ln(r)}{1 - r}\right]\frac{1 + \alpha(N - 1)}{C}.$$

The expectation of the positive reaction time, $E(RT_+)$, is assumed to be a sum of s and a residual component a_0 which is a constant. Thus,

$$E(RT_+) = \left[1 + \frac{r\ln(r)}{1 - r}\right]\frac{1 + \alpha(N - 1)}{C} + a_0, \tag{5.6}$$

Box 5.1 Treisman and Gelade (1980; feature search) *(continued)*

which can be rewritten as

$$E(RT_+) = \left[1 + \frac{r\ln(r)}{1 - r}\right]\frac{\alpha}{C}(N - 1) + a_1,$$ (5.7)

where

$$a_1 = a_0 + \left[1 + \frac{r\ln(r)}{1 - r}\right]C^{-1}.$$ (5.8)

---

equations 5.2 and 5.6 of Box 5.1. As noted previously, provided that r is kept constant as display size N varies, both positive and negative mean reaction times should be linear functions of N. If α is zero (i.e. target–distractor discriminability is perfect) the predicted functions are flat, regardless of r: in this case, the number of distractors does not make any difference for the mean reaction time. Otherwise, the slopes of the functions increase as r is decreased (i.e. as the subject becomes more cautious in not missing any target). Specifically, as r approaches zero, the slope of the positive reaction time function tends to a value of α/C, whereas the slope of the negative reaction time function tends to infinity. At the other extreme, as r approaches a value of one, the slopes of the positive and negative reaction time functions both tend to zero: in the limiting case the subject simply responds negatively to every display regardless of its characteristics. These predictions seem plausible, but direct evidence is lacking. In particular, the suggested strong dependence between the slope of the negative reaction time function and the rate of misses should be worth testing.

Other predictions by the deadline model of one-view search are more general in nature. Presumably they would follow from any reasonable model of efficient search based on the rate and weight equations of TVA. One concerns the importance of *target–distractor discriminability*: as the visual discriminability between targets and distractors with respect to features defining the targets is increased, search efficiency should also increase. The prediction is highly plausible and supported by empirical evidence. For example, the time taken to determine whether a predefined achromatic target is present among a number of chromatic distractors of constant brightness and saturation decreases monotonically as the difference in brightness between target and distractors is increased (Farmer and Taylor 1980). Similarly, positive and negative reaction times in the search for a line of a certain length among a number of shorter ones decrease as the difference in length between target and distractors is increased (Treisman and Gormican 1988, Experiment 1). Again, positive and negative reaction times in search for a predefined curved line among a number of straight lines decrease as the curvature of the target is increased (Treisman and Gormican 1988, Experiment 4; for early related findings, see Neisser 1963; see also Pashler 1987b; Duncan and Humphreys 1989).

Another general prediction of the deadline model of one-view search concerns the importance of sensory factors determining the *visibility* of targets and distractors. If target–distractor discriminability is kept constant, increasing the visibility of a target (e.g. by increasing the luminance contrast of the target to the background) should make search more efficient by increasing the strength of the sensory evidence for a positive categorization of the target. For this reason, search for a dark grey target among light grey distractors on a white background should be more efficient than search for a light grey target among dark grey distractors on the white background (a *search asymmetry* reported by Treisman and Gormican 1988, Experiment 2). For the same reason, search for an 8-mm line among 5-mm lines would be expected to be more efficient than search for a 5-mm line among 8-mm lines (another search asymmetry found by Treisman and Gormican 1988, Experiment 1).[2]

5.2.2 One-view search with perceptual grouping

Perceptual grouping of display elements (i.e. formation of higher-level units) is an important determinant of search efficiency (see, for example, Banks and Prinzmetal 1976; Prinzmetal and Banks 1977; Farmer and Taylor 1980; see also Harms and Bundesen 1983; McIntyre *et al.* 1970). Normally, adding more distractors to a search display causes reductions in performance (except when search is very easy, in which case the number of distractors makes no difference). However, perceptual grouping may reverse this effect. A particularly striking demonstration was provided by Banks and Prinzmetal (1976): displays were carefully constructed so that, as the number of distractors increased, the added distractors increased the degree to which the set of distractors formed a single perceptual group isolated from the target. With these displays, the time taken to find the target actually decreased as the number of distractors

---

[2] In a supplementary study with 'matched distractors', Treisman and Gormican (1988, Experiment 1a) found approximately the same efficiency of (a) search for a 10-mm line among 7.5-mm lines (size ratio 1.33) as of (b) search for a 5-mm line among 7.5-mm lines (size ratio 1.50). In our interpretation, this finding shows that the effects of an increase in target visibility (higher in Condition a) can be annulled by a decrease in target–distractor discriminability (lower in Condition a).

increased. Perhaps the simplest way of explaining this result is by assuming that, as the set of distractors formed a stronger perceptual group, individual distractors lost in attentional weight. This idea is explored below in relation to a study by Bundesen and Pedersen (1983).

Bundesen and Pedersen (1983, Block A) presented subjects with displays of alphanumeric characters in different colours. The task was to indicate the alphanumeric class (i.e. letter or digit) of a target character, singled out by appearing in a designated colour (the target colour) which varied across trials. The number of distractor characters (individual character tokens other than the target) and the number of distractor colours (colours other than the target colour) varied separately and unpredictably between trials. The displays were constructed to favour perceptual grouping by colour: the stimulus characters were bold-faced, their colours were highly discriminable, and in the main condition (Block A: organized displays), same-coloured characters appeared in spatial proximity so that, for each distractor colour, the set of characters in that colour could be seen as a single unit (see Fig. 5.4). However, as in the

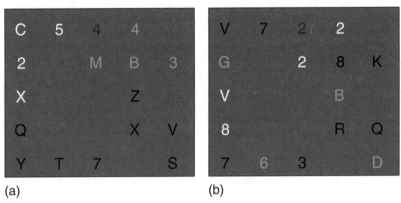

(a)   (b)

Fig. 5.4 Two search displays used by Bundesen and Pedersen (1983). Difference in colour between characters is represented by difference in brightness. (a) An organized display with 17 characters (one target plus 16 distractors) in four different colours. Same-coloured distractors appear in spatial proximity so that the set of characters in any given colour can be seen as a single perceptual group. With organized displays, the number of distractor characters and the number of distractor colours showed approximately additive effects in mean reaction times (depicted in Fig. 5.5). (b) A scrambled display partnering the organized one. Colours and spatial locations of distractors are unrelated, and no simple relationship is apparent between the number of distractor colours and the number of perceptual groups. With scrambled displays, search was comparatively slow, and the mean reaction times did not show additivity between effects of the number of distractor characters and the number of distractor colours, respectively.

study of Banks and Prinzmetal (1976), the perceptual grouping appeared to increase in strength as the number of distractor characters increased and the spatial distance between neighbouring characters concomitantly decreased. Each display was presented until a response was made.

The mean reaction time observed in the main condition is shown in Fig. 5.5 as a function of the number of distractor characters D with the number of distractor colours G as the parameter. As can be seen, the effect of D was non-linear, but the effect of G was linear, and the effects of the two factors were nearly additive. A theoretical least squares fit to the data is indicated by open circles connected with straight lines (see Box 5.2 for details). The fit was based on the following considerations. First, for an organized display of one target, D distractor characters, and G distractor colours, the set of elements in the visual field presumably included the target, the D distractor characters, and G perceptual groups of same-coloured characters, one for each of the distractor colours. In other words, the groups competed for attention on par with individual characters (the target and the individual distractors). Second, as the number of distractors increased

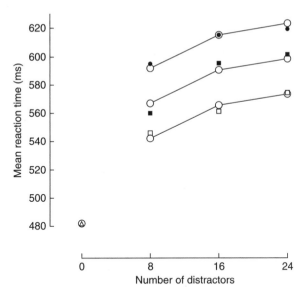

Fig. 5.5 Mean reaction time as a function of number of distractor characters, with number of distractor colours as the parameter, in the search experiment of Bundesen and Pedersen (1983, Block A). Group data for five subjects. Number of distractor colours was 0 (triangle), 1 (open squares), 3 (solid squares), or 5 (solid circles). A theoretical fit by TVA is indicated by open circles connected with straight lines. The observed data are taken from Table 1 of Bundesen and Pedersen (1983). Color segregation and visual search. *Perception & Psychophysics*, **33**, 487–493. Copyright 1983 by the Psychonomic Society. Adapted with permission.

Box 5.2 Bundesen and Pedersen (1983)

For an organized display of one target and D distractor characters in G colours, let constant w_1 be the attentional weight of the target, let constant w_0 be the attentional weight of a group of same-coloured distractor characters, and let $w(D)$ be the attentional weight of an individual distractor character. The relative attentional weight of the target equals

$$\frac{w_1}{w_1 + Gw_0 + Dw(D)},$$

which can be written as

$$\frac{1}{1 + \alpha_0 G + \alpha(D)D},$$

where $\alpha_0 = w_0/w_1$ (i.e. the weight of a perceptual group of distractors versus the target) and $\alpha(D) = w(D)/w_1$ (i.e. the weight of an individual distractor versus the target). In analogy with equation 5.1, the processing rate for the target can be written as

$$v = \frac{C}{1 + \alpha_0 G + \alpha(D)D},$$

where C is the processing rate when the target is presented alone. Because it is exponentially distributed, the expectation of the time taken to sample the target equals the reciprocal of the processing rate: $1/v$. Accordingly, the expected reaction time is a sum of $1/v$ and the residual response latency b:

$$E(\text{RT}) = \frac{1}{v} + b,$$

which can be rewritten as

$$E(\text{RT}) = \frac{\alpha_0}{C}G + \frac{\alpha(D)}{C}D + b_1, \qquad (5.9)$$

where

$$b_1 = b + \frac{1}{C}.$$

The least squares fit by equation 5.9 to the data in Fig. 5.5 was obtained with α_0/C at 12.4 ms, $\alpha(8)/C$ at 5.9 ms, $\alpha(16)/C$ at 4.4 ms, $\alpha(24)/C$ at 3.3 ms, and b_1 at 482 ms.

and the spatial distance between neighbouring characters concomitantly decreased, the perceptual grouping increased in strength. As a consequence, the individual characters making up the groups became less 'conspicuous' as individuals. Presumably, the individual distractor characters lost in attentional weight by suffering a general loss in η values (cf. the weight equation). Third, reaction time was a sum of two independent components: the time taken to sample the target and a residual response latency.

The fit to the data of Bundesen and Pedersen (1983, Block A) represents a first step in accounting for the effects of perceptual organization in visual search. It was based on two general hypotheses concerning effects of grouping. First, groups compete for attention on a par with those individuals that make up the groups. Second, by being embedded in a group, an individual suffers a general loss in η values, and the stronger the group, the greater is the loss. The simplicity of the first hypothesis is highly attractive. The second hypothesis affords a possible explanation for observations such as the following.

When viewing a display consisting of, for example, a number of green letters forming a strong perceptual group and a single blue letter that is isolated from the group, the likelihood of noticing the identity of a particular one of the green letters is less than the likelihood of noticing the identity of the blue letter. Neither perceptual bias nor difference in pertinence is supposed to favour the blue letter rather than the green letters. However, by the hypothesis proposed above, one reason that the blue letter (the deviant element) captures attention is that, by being embedded in a strong perceptual group, the green letters suffer a substantial loss in η values and, therefore, in v values. Attentional capture is analysed further in the next section.

5.2.3 Attentional capture

As described in Section 2.7, much work has been devoted to the relationship between automatic capture and voluntary control of attention. Some investigators (e.g. Theeuwes 1996) have drawn a sharp distinction between two types of attention—one type of attention variably being characterized as 'involuntary', 'automatic', 'stimulus-driven', 'exogenous', or 'bottom-up'; the other type being characterized as 'voluntary', 'controlled', 'goal-driven', 'endogenous', or 'top-down'. Other investigators (e.g. Folk *et al.* 1994) have distinguished between two types of attentional factors (stimulus-related versus goal-related) that can interact, instead of two distinct types of attention, and argued, for example, that all cases of attentional capture are contingent on attentional control settings.

As noted by Folk *et al.* (1992, p. 1042), the attentional mechanisms of TVA may be used for setting attentional controls for salient features and abrupt onsets. For example, if a general feature-contrast detector is available (see Section 2.7.1), attention can be guided by the output (η values) of the general feature-contrast detector by letting the perceptual priority (π value) of feature contrast be high and letting perceptual priorities of other properties be low. When TVA is configured in this mode (singleton-detection mode; Bacon and Egeth 1994), the attentional weight of an item depends primarily on the feature contrast of the item. Similarly, if separate detectors are available for static versus dynamic discontinuities (cf. Folk *et al.* 1992, 1994), then attention can be guided by the output (η values) of the detector for static discontinuities (e.g. colour and shape singletons) by letting the perceptual priority (π value) of static discontinuity be high, and attention can be guided by the output (η values) of the detector for dynamic discontinuities (e.g. onset and motion singletons) by letting the perceptual priority (π value) of dynamic discontinuity be high.

In TVA, attentional selection always depends on both stimulus properties (represented by η values) and control parameters (β and π parameters). The rate and weight equations of TVA are precise descriptions of the way in which bottom-up and top-down factors interact in attentional selection, and the equations should be true whether or not attention is effectively controlled by the observer (i.e. whether attention is primarily goal- or stimulus-driven). The way in which attentional capture by salient features and abrupt onsets (static and dynamic discontinuities) depends on pertinence (π) parameters was described above. Concerning the dependence on stimulus properties, it should be noted that η values can be increased by both simultaneous and successive stimulus contrast. Local feature contrast seems critical (cf. the guided search model, Section 2.9.2). Presumably, the computed strength of the sensory evidence that stimulus x has feature i, $\eta(x, i)$, increases with the local spatial and temporal feature contrast between x and its surroundings with respect to feature i. Colour contrast is an obvious example: The η value of the colour of an object is increased by presenting the object in the spatial or temporal vicinity of objects of the complementary colour.

Capture of attention by an abrupt onset is a different kind of example of how η values can be increased by successive stimulus contrast. When a stimulus appears abruptly (a kind of successive contrast), firing rates of typical neurons responding to the stimulus first increase rapidly, then reach a maximum, and finally decline and approach a somewhat lower, 'steady state' level. The corresponding η values presumably follow the same temporal course, and the 'overshoot' phenomenon (in the η values and, accordingly, in the corresponding v values) implies a tendency to see the abrupt-onset stimulus (i.e. encode the stimulus into visual short-term memory, VSTM) soon after the onset.

5.3 **Many-view search**

TVA may be described as a limited-capacity independent parallel-processing model, and parallel identification of several objects from a given fixation seems to be the rule rather than the exception (cf. Bundesen 1987, 1990; see also Bichot *et al.* 1999; Awh and Pashler 2000; McMains and Somers 2004, 2005; Thornton and Gilden 2007). In general, however, an attention system capable of parallel processing with spatially selective allocation of processing resources is also capable of serial processing (Bundesen 1990). As elaborated in this section, the serial processing can be done by first using a spatial selection criterion for sampling one or more objects from one part of the stimulus display, then shifting the selection criterion to sample objects from another part of the display, and so forth, with or without eye movements.

In developing the deadline model of one-view search, we presumed that target–distractor discriminability was high. When target–distractor discriminability is high, and pertinence values are appropriate, then α (the ratio of the attentional weight of a distractor to the attentional weight of a target) is small, and when α is small, searching in accordance with the model is highly efficient. In the limiting case where α is zero, both positive and negative search times are independent of the number of distractors.

However, if target–distractor discriminability is low, the deadline model of one-view search is not appropriate. Target–distractor discriminability may be low in either feature or conjunction search (cf. Section 2.4.1). In feature search, the target is distinguished from the distractors by a simple feature (e.g. a particular colour, size, or curvature). Plainly, if the target is defined by, for example, colour, and target and distractors are highly similar in colour, target–distractor discriminability is low.

In conjunction search, the target differs from the distractors by showing a predefined conjunction of simple features, but the target is not unique in any of the component features of the conjunction. For example, in a study by Treisman and Gelade (1980, Experiment 1, conjunction condition), the task was to search for a green T among distractors that were brown Ts and green Xs in (nearly) equal numbers. Since each distractor matched the target in one of the two defining features, target–distractor discriminability might be expected to be poor. Indeed, search was slow and inefficient in this task. The inefficiency can be explained by assuming that pertinence was not ascribed specifically to the conjunction, but only to its component features (i.e. the colour–shape conjunction was not treated as a single perceptual feature). As shown in Box 5.3, this assumption implies that the attentional weight of individual distractors was at least half as high as the weight of the target ($\alpha \geq 0.5$); their total impact

Box 5.3 Treisman and Gelade (1980; conjunction search)

A formal analysis of the task used by Treisman and Gelade (1980, Experiment 1, conjunction condition) can be made if we assume that (a) green and T are perceptual categories, but (b) green T is not a perceptual category. If so, then presumably the attentional weight of an element x (a target or a distractor) may be written as

$$w(x) = \eta\,(x, \text{green})\,\pi\,(\text{green}) + \eta\,(x, \text{T})\,\pi\,(\text{T}) + w^*, \tag{5.10}$$

where w^* is a residual weight component which is approximately the same whether x is a target or a distractor. Let $\eta\,(x, \text{green})\pi\,(\text{green})$ equal $w_1(\text{green})$ if x is green, but $w_0(\text{green})$ if x is brown, and let $\eta\,(x, \text{T})\pi(\text{T})$ equal $w_1(\text{T})$ if x is a T, but $w_0(\text{T})$ if x is an X. By equation 5.10, the attentional weight of a target (a green T) equals

$$w_1(\text{green}) + w_1(\text{T}) + w^*;$$

the attentional weight of a distractor that is a brown T equals

$$w_0(\text{green}) + w_1(\text{T}) + w^*;$$

and the attentional weight of a distractor that is a green X equals

$$w_1(\text{green}) + w_0(\text{T}) + w^*.$$

Thus the attentional weight of a green T (a target) cannot exceed the sum of the attentional weights of a brown T and a green X (two distractors). By this analysis, if green and T are perceptual categories, but green T is not, then the mean value of α (the ratio of the attentional weight of a distractor to the attentional weight of a target) is bound to be at least 0.5 in the search for a green T among distractors that are brown Ts and green Xs in equal numbers.

on the search process should thus be very substantial, especially in displays with many distractors.

5.3.1 Strategies for many-view search

When target–distractor discriminability is low, a plausible strategy for visual search consists of selecting and testing elements in the display until either (a) a target has been found or (b) every element in the display has been selected and tested, but no target has been found. In Case a, a positive response is made, and the response is said to be based on a *self-terminating* search through the display (cf. Section 2.4). In Case b, a negative response is made, and the response is said to be based on an *exhaustive* search of the display.

The search may be done with or without *reallocation* of attention. At one extreme, a multi-element display is processed in one view; that is, without scanning the display by overt eye movements or covert reallocations of attention. This is characteristic of the search tasks described in Section 5.2. At the other extreme, an N-element display is processed in N views, one for each element in the display (following a simple serial model of attention, see Section 2.4). Between the extremes, an N-element display (with $N > 2$) may be processed in k views, where $1 < k < N$. The processing may be done by first using a spatial selection criterion for sampling elements from one part of the display, then (with or without eye movements) shifting the selection criterion to sample elements from another part of the display, and so on, until a target has been found or the entire display has been searched exhaustively.

Several considerations are likely to determine the number of views taken to scan a multi-element display. First, the benefits of foveation by saccadic eye movements are an obvious consideration. Other things equal, the number of views taken to scan a display should increase with the size of the area over which the stimulus elements are spread. Second, the suggested way of processing presupposes that the subject knows when a set of elements has been searched exhaustively. Phenomenally, if the set of elements is large, it seems impossible to tell when the set has been searched exhaustively, unless one employs a strategy of scanning the set part by part. Intuitively, therefore, the need to know when an exhaustive search has been done favours taking many views and few elements per view rather than few views and many elements per view. Third, the subject may consider a trade-off between (a) time taken to shift (reallocate) attention between groups (subsets) of elements and (b) gains in sampling rate once attention has been reallocated. Given that each reallocation of attention takes a fixed amount of time, the most efficient search strategy (i.e. the optimal number of elements in each attended group) can be computed from TVA, as described in Box 5.4.

5.3.2 **Search reaction times**

Many experiments on conjunction search or feature search with low target–distractor discriminability have yielded positive and negative mean reaction times that are approximately linear functions of display size, with fairly steep slopes and positive-to-negative slope ratios of about 1: 2. For example, in the conjunction condition of Experiment 1 of Treisman and Gelade (1980), the positive reaction time function was approximately linear

Box 5.4 Optimal stimulus sampling in many-view search

For simplicity, suppose the time taken to shift attention to a group of n elements in a display is a constant s, regardless of n. Further suppose that, once attention has been shifted to the group, the total processing capacity C distributed over the elements in the group is independent of n. C is the sum of the v-values (processing rates) of the n elements. The mean time taken to sample the first element from the group equals C^{-1}. Provided that the n v-values are equal, the mean time taken to sample a second element from the group (measured from the moment the previous one was sampled) equals $C^{-1}n/(n-1)$, the mean time taken to sample a third element equals $C^{-1}n/(n-2),\ldots$, and the mean time taken to sample the nth element equals $C^{-1}n$. Averaged over the n elements, the mean sampling time per element can be written as

$$C^{-1}\sum_{i=1}^{n}\tfrac{1}{i}.$$

The mean shifting time per element is s/n. Thus the mean time taken by shifting and sampling is

$$f(n) = \frac{s}{n} + C^{-1}\sum_{i=1}^{n}\tfrac{1}{i} \tag{5.11}$$

per element. If the group size is increased from n to $n+1$ elements, then mean sampling time per element increases, but mean shifting time per element decreases, and the sum of the two means, $f(n)$, shows an increment of

$$f(n+1) - f(n) = \frac{s}{n+1} - \frac{s}{n} + \frac{C^{-1}}{n+1}$$

$$= \frac{nC^{-1} - s}{n(n+1)}.$$

This increment is negative (i.e. time is gained) if $n < Cs$, zero if $n = Cs$, and positive (i.e. time is lost) if $n > Cs$. Hence, to minimize the shifting and sampling time per element in a group, group size n should be equal to Cs or the smallest integer greater than Cs.

with a slope of 29 ms per element, the negative reaction time function was approximately linear with a slope of 67 ms per element, and the positive-to-negative slope ratio was 0.43. In Experiment 2 of Treisman and Gelade (1980), search for a red O among green Os and red Ns yielded a positive reaction time function with a slope constant of 21 ms per element, a negative function with a slope constant of 40 ms per element, and a slope ratio of 0.52. Nearly the same slope constants and a slope ratio of 0.53 were found by Treisman and Gormican (1988) as overall means across 37 conditions of feature search with low target–distractor discriminability.

As described in Section 2.4, the pattern of approximately linear reaction time functions with positive-to-negative slope ratios of about 1: 2 is readily explained by simple serial models of search—serial models in which reallocation of attention between elements is 'blind' in the sense that attention shifting is random with respect to the distinction between target and distractors (Schneider and Shiffrin 1977; Treisman *et al.* 1977; see also Fisher 1982). However, exactly the same predictions can be obtained from a model in which search is carried out in parallel and processing times are distributed exponentially. In this type of model, attention is first distributed evenly among all the N elements in the display, then—when the first element has been sampled—reallocated and distributed evenly among the remaining $N - 1$ elements, then—when a second element has been sampled—reallocated and distributed evenly among the remaining $N - 2$ elements, and so on, until a target has been found or the last element has been sampled. The equivalence between predictions from this model and the previous one was noted by Atkinson *et al.* (1969) and Townsend (1969) (for a thorough discussion, see Townsend and Ashby 1983, Chapter 4).

Finally, as mentioned in Section 2.4.3, rather similar predictions obtain if attention is shifted among small, non-overlapping groups of elements and shifting is random with respect to the distinction between target and distractors. In this case, the total time taken by shifting and sampling should be an approximately linear function of the number of groups processed, and the mean number of groups processed should be approximately linearly related to display size for both positive and negative displays, with a positive-to-negative slope ratio of 1: 2 (Pashler 1987a; Treisman and Gormican 1988). For reasons outlined in the next section, we think this latter model is highly plausible for typical many-view search.

5.3.3 Time course of attentional shifting

Is it reasonable to suppose that attention is reallocated once per element processed, or is it more likely that attention is shifted among non-overlapping groups of elements? Extant data on the time taken to shift attention in response to a visual cue suggest that the process of reallocating attention by changing the pertinence value of a spatial location is fairly slow (Colegate *et al.* 1973; Sperling and Reeves 1980; Tsal 1983; Remington and Pierce 1984; Reeves and Sperling 1986; Weichselgartner and Sperling 1987; Duncan *et al.* 1994; Moore *et al.* 1996; Ward *et al.* 1996; Logan 2005). Some of these data are considered in this section. They lend indirect support to the hypothesis that attention shifting among (largely) non-overlapping groups of elements, not individual objects, normally underlies the pattern of approximately linear reaction time functions with slope ratios of about 1 : 2 commonly observed in difficult search.

Consider the classic study of Colegate *et al.* (1973). Subjects were presented with circular arrays of 8 or 12 letters. Each array was centred on fixation and about 2° of visual angle in diameter. The array was preceded by a bar designating one of the letters for report. As the stimulus–onset asynchrony (SOA) between the bar and the letter array was increased from zero up to about 250 ms, mean reaction time to voice the indicated letter decreased, but with further increase in SOA, the mean reaction time was essentially constant. Apparently, the time taken to prepare for the target by covertly shifting attention to the indicated position (i.e. by ascribing pertinence to the target location) never exceeded 250 ms. Thus the mean time taken to shift attention to the target location in response to the bar should be *at most* 250 ms.

On the other hand, the reduction in mean reaction time obtained by increasing the SOA between the bar and the letter array from zero up to 250 ms was about 80 ms (estimated from Figs 1 and 2 of Colegate *et al.* 1973). Control trials with a neutral warning signal indicated that, when SOA was 250 ms, non-selective 'alerting' effects (cf. Posner and Boies 1971) of the presentation of the bar had vanished at the time the letter array was presented. Apparently, the saving in mean reaction time by having attention shifted to the target location before the presentation of the letter array was 80 ms. If so, then the mean time taken to shift attention to the target location in response to the bar should be *at least* 80 ms. (Deleting a subtask will often decrease the total time taken up by a task, but rarely decreases the total time by more than the time taken to do the subtask.)

According to the suggested analysis of the data of Colegate *et al.* (1973), the mean latency of first selecting an element (the bar) and then reallocating attention by ascribing pertinence to a spatial location near that element (the target location) was somewhere between 80 and 250 ms. From partly the same data, Hoffman (1978, 1979) suggested a mean value of 100 ms. Comparable estimates reported by Tsal (1983) range from 83 to 150 ms, depending upon the visual angle between the fixation point and the target location. Using a model developed by Logan and Bundesen (2003), Logan (2005) obtained separate estimates for the time taken by cue encoding and the time taken by shifting attention from one set of spatial locations to another in response to the cue; the model fits suggested that cue encoding took about 70 ms and attention shifting about 90 ms. Estimates from the paradigms of Sperling and Reeves (1980), Reeves and Sperling (1986), Weichselgartner and Sperling (1987), Duncan *et al.* (1994), and Ward *et al.* (1996) are even greater (but see Moore *et al.* 1996). These data cast doubt on the notion that, in visual search, a process involving selection of an element and subsequent reallocation of attention by a change in pertinence of spatial locations occurs at rates as high as once every 40 ms, as suggested by simple serial models (for further data and arguments, see Pashler and Badgio 1987; see also Pashler 1987*a*). It seems more plausible that attention is typically shifted among groups of elements. The optimal group size may depend on both the time taken to reallocate attention and the total available processing capacity (see Box 5.5).

Box 5.5 Attention shifting between groups of elements

Data such as those of Colegate *et al.* (1973) fit in with the hypothesis that attention shifting among non-overlapping groups of elements underlies the pattern of approximately linear reaction time functions with slope ratios of about 1:2 observed by Treisman and Gelade (1980), Treisman and Gormican (1988), and others. As a numerical illustration, suppose the time taken to shift attention to a group of n elements, s, equals 100 ms, regardless of n. Further suppose that, once attention has been shifted to the group, the total processing capacity, C, distributed over the n elements in the group (i.e. the sum of the v values of the elements) equals 100 elements/s or 0.1 element/ms. By equation 5.11 of Box 5.4, the mean time taken by shifting and sampling is

$$f(n) = \frac{100 \text{ ms}}{n} + (10 \text{ ms}) \sum_{i=1}^{n} \frac{1}{i}$$

per element. The smallest value of $f(n)$ is 39 ms per element. This value is attained if group size n equals the product of C and s, which is 10, or the smallest integer greater than Cs, which is 11. If n is somewhat smaller, $f(n)$ is slightly greater. For instance, $f(7)$ equals 40 ms per element, which

> **Box 5.5 Attention shifting between groups of elements** *(continued)*
>
> corresponds to the highest mean rate of processing observed by Treisman and Gelade (1980, Experiment 2) for shape–colour conjunction search.[3]
>
> If the time taken to shift attention, s, is 100 ms, but the total processing capacity, C, is less than 10 elements/s, then the optimal group size is only 1. Thus, in this case, only one element should be processed at a time (cf. Bricolo *et al.* 2002; see also Woodman and Luck 1999).

5.4 Joint effects of numbers of targets and distractors

In the experiments on divided attention reviewed in Chapter 4, no distractors were displayed. In the experiments on focused attention reviewed previously in this chapter, the stimulus displays contained no more than one target. As argued by Duncan (1980, 1983, 1985) and Thornton and Gilden (2007), among others, stronger empirical constraints on theories of visual attention can be found by studying performance as a joint function of the numbers of targets and distractors in the stimulus. The partial report experiments of Bundesen *et al.* (1984, 1985) and Shibuya and Bundesen (1988) seem to have been the first studies in which numbers of targets and distractors were varied independently. The studies were reviewed in Chapter 3, and the results form a weighty portion of the data accounted for by TVA.

Estes and Taylor (1965, Experiment 2) investigated the effects of multiple, redundant targets in their detection paradigm. Each stimulus display consisted

---

[3] In the suggested account of many-view search, every element that is selected from the display is supposed to be tested in order to determine whether the element is a target. In a complete model of many-view search, the testing process must be specified. We have considered models in which (1) elements in the short-term store are tested one by one in order of arrival; and (2) when an element has been tested, that element is deleted from the short-term store. Neither sampling nor reallocation of attention is supposed to be affected by testing, but (3) sampling is ineffective (new samples are lost) whenever the short-term store is filled up with elements. Finally, (4) attention is supposed to be shifted among non-overlapping groups of elements, so that the expected time taken by shifting and sampling is minimized. Once probability distributions of the time taken to test an element and the time taken to shift attention are specified, computer simulations are feasible but, due to the added degrees of freedom, proper testing of the models and reliable estimation of the parameters are difficult. However, when the capacity of the short-term store is well above one element, and the time taken by testing is short in relation to the time taken by attentional shifting and sampling, the effect of testing is largely to add a constant (viz., the mean time to test a single element) to the mean reaction time. In this case, predictions by equation 5.11 can be compared directly against search rates estimated from slopes of reaction time functions.

of 16 consonant letters. It included one or more Bs or one or more Fs, but not both. The number of targets (Bs or Fs) per display was either one, two, or four, and the task was to report the type of target (B versus F) that appeared in the display, and to disregard the accompanying distractor letters. In other respects, the method was similar to that of Estes and Taylor (1964; see Section 5.1). The observed proportions of correct detections by individual subjects are shown in Table 5.1. As can be seen, individual differences were notable (compare, especially, Subjects 2 and 6).

For each subject, the predicted proportions of correct detections given in Table 5.1 represent a least squares fit to the data. The fit was based on the same assumptions as those used in fitting the data of Estes and Taylor (1964; see Section 5.1), so detection (via non-guessing) was assumed to occur if, and only if, one or more targets were among the elements selected from the display. The assumptions leave three parameters: the short-term storage capacity K, the processing parameter $C(\tau + \mu)$, and the ratio of the attentional weight of a distractor to the attentional weight of a target, α. Fixing the three parameters at the values estimated from the group data of Estes and Taylor (1964) would yield predicted proportions of 0.75, 0.87, and 0.96 for one, two, and four targets, respectively. The predictions for individual subjects given in Table 5.1 were generated by fixing K at the value estimated from the group

Table 5.1 Observed (Obs.) and theoretical (Th.) proportions of correct detections in relation to number of targets per display in Experiment 2 of Estes and Taylor (1965)

| | Parameter | | Number of targets | | | | | |
| | | | 1 | | 2 | | 4 | |
Subject	$C(\tau+\mu)$	α	Obs.	Th.	Obs.	Th.	Obs.	Th.
1	4.63	0.20	0.85	0.83	0.88	0.92	1.00	0.97
2	18.81	0.30	0.81	0.83	0.96	0.94	1.00	0.99
3	3.39	0.55	0.64	0.65	0.76	0.75	0.85	0.86
4	4.88	0.32	0.75	0.76	0.90	0.88	0.94	0.96
5	2.56	0.08	0.85	0.85	0.90	0.91	0.94	0.94
6	0.71	1.00	0.52	0.52	0.51	0.54	0.60	0.58
7	30.95	0.89	0.61	0.66	0.80	0.78	0.93	0.91
8	9.15	0.36	0.79	0.79	0.91	0.91	0.98	0.98
Mean	9.39	0.46	0.73	0.74	0.83	0.83	0.90	0.90

C = processing capacity (elements per unit of time); τ = exposure duration; μ = time constant for decay of information; α = ratio of the attentional weight of a distractor to the attentional weight of a target. Parameter K (storage capacity) was kept constant at a value of 4.70 elements. The observed data are taken from Table 5 of Estes and Taylor (1965).

data of Estes and Taylor (1964) and treating $C(\tau + \mu)$ and α as free parameters. (Formulas for calculating the theoretical proportion of correct detections as a joint function of the numbers of targets and distractors for any values of the three parameters are given in Appendix D.)

5.5 Delay of selection cue

Effects of delay of selection cue have been investigated in a number of partial report experiments (for a review see, for example, Coltheart 1980). Consider the studies of Sperling (1960, Experiments 3 and 4). On each trial, the subject was presented with a matrix of letters and required to report a single row of the matrix. Exposure duration was 50 ms and pre- and postexposure fields were dark. The row to be reported was indicated by one of several tones, each tone corresponding to one row of the matrix. The SOA between the selection cue (the tone) and the stimulus display varied from −50 ms (prestimulus cuing) to 1050 ms (poststimulus cuing). The partial report data were compared with whole report scores obtained with the same subjects (in Experiment 1 of Sperling 1960; see Section 4.2.1). To facilitate the comparison, the proportion of letters reported correctly from a cued row was multiplied by the total number of letters in the matrix, to get an estimate of 'the number of letters available' from the whole display (e.g. 2 out of 4 correct from the cued row in a matrix of 3×4 elements corresponds to $3 \times 4 \times 2/4 = 6$ available elements).

Following Rumelhart (1970), TVA was applied to the partial report experiments of Sperling by assuming that 'at the time the tone sounds the subject immediately assigns weights of zero to all but the indicated row of the matrix' (p. 196). Note that when the cue is given, substantial processing of the display (with more equally distributed attentional weights) may already have occurred. Therefore, the earlier the tone sounds, the more likely it is that items from the target row are among the ones encoded into the limited VSTM store. The assumption of immediate reassignment of attentional weights is strong, but it is broadly consistent with findings by Weichselgartner and Sperling (1987) on visual attention shifts in response to auditory signals.[4] From the new assumption, and the assumptions made previously in fitting the whole report data of Sperling (1960, Experiment 1), theoretical predictions of the

---

[4] Note that, depending upon the relative speed of auditory versus visual processing, an auditory stimulus may have completed processing before perceptual testing of a visual stimulus is begun, even if the auditory stimulus is presented simultaneously with, or later than, the visual one.

number of letters available from an $m \times n$ matrix can be calculated as a function of exposure duration, delay of selection cue, short-term storage capacity K, processing capacity C, and time constant μ. (Formulas for the calculations are given in Appendix E.)

Figure 5.6 shows observed and predicted values of the number of letters available as functions of display size for partial and whole report procedures with each of Sperling's five subjects. The lower curve in a panel shows the mean number of letters correct in whole report. The upper curve shows the mean number of letters available when a selection cue was presented at display offset (SOA = 50 ms). The jagged shape of the upper curve reflects the construction of the displays used by Sperling (matrices with 6, 8, 9, and 12 elements were of orders 2×3, 2×4, 3×3, and 3×4, respectively).

Figure 5.7 yields a more comprehensive picture of the results for Subject ROR. In addition to the whole report scores, observed and predicted values of

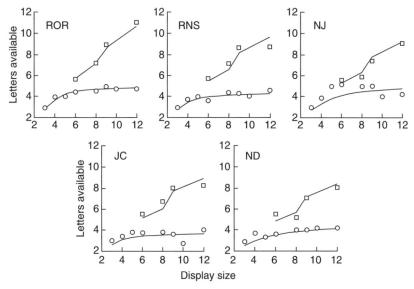

Fig. 5.6 Mean numbers of 'letters available' for whole and partial report as functions of display size in Experiments 1 and 3 of Sperling (1960). Individual data for five subjects. Whole report data are shown by circles, partial report data by squares. Theoretical fits by TVA are indicated by solid curves. The observed data are read from Fig. 3 of Sperling (1960). The information available in brief visual presentations. *Psychological Monographs,* **74** (11, Whole No. 498). Copyright 1960 by the American Psychological Association. Adapted with permission. The use of APA information does not imply endorsement by APA.

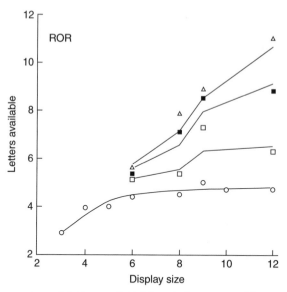

Fig. 5.7 Mean numbers of 'letters available' for whole report and for partial report with various delays of the selection cue as functions of display size in Experiments 1, 3, and 4 of Sperling (1960). Data are for Subject ROR. Delay of the selection cue in partial report was 50 ms (triangles), 200 ms (solid squares), or 550 ms (open squares). Whole report data are shown by circles. A theoretical fit by TVA is indicated by solid curves. The observed data are read from Figs 3 and 9 of Sperling (1960). The information available in brief visual presentations. *Psychological Monographs*, **74** (11, Whole No. 498). Copyright 1960 by the American Psychological Association. Adapted with permission. The use of APA information does not imply endorsement by APA.

the number of letters available are shown as functions of display size, with delay of selection cue (SOA = 50, 200, or 550 ms) as the parameter.

The effect of delay of selection cue on the number of letters available is further illustrated in Figs 5.8 (for 12-element displays) and 5.9 (for 9-element displays). As shown for each subject, observed and predicted values of the number of letters available gradually decline with increasing delay of the selection cue. At the longest delay (SOA = 1050 ms), the number of letters available is approximately the same as the number of letters correct in whole report.

The theoretical functions depicted in Figs 5.6–5.9 were computed from the (least squares) parameter estimates given in Table 5.2. Across the five subjects, estimates for the parameters averaged 4.86 elements for storage capacity K, 16.2 elements/s for processing capacity C, and 533 ms for time constant μ.

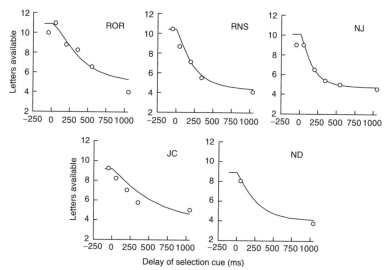

Fig. 5.8 Mean numbers of 'letters available' for partial report as functions of delay of selection cue for 12-element displays in Experiment 4 of Sperling (1960). Individual data for five subjects. Theoretical fits by TVA are indicated by solid curves. The observed data are read from Fig. 7 (graphs in left column on p. 11) of Sperling (1960). The information available in brief visual presentations. *Psychological Monographs*, **74** (11, Whole No. 498). Copyright 1960 by the American Psychological Association. Adapted with permission. The use of APA information does not imply endorsement by APA.

5.6 **Consistent practice**

In almost any task, performance improves with practice, but the amount of improvement depends upon the nature of the task. Schneider and Shiffrin (1977) and Shiffrin and Schneider (1977) investigated effects of extended practice in visual search and detection tasks with either consistent or varied mapping of stimuli to responses. In *consistent mapping* conditions, each stimulus that required a response consistently required the same response whenever it appeared. Specifically, if a stimulus was a target in some trial, it never appeared as a distractor. In such conditions, performance improved dramatically with practice. With extended practice, effects of display size nearly vanished. In *varied mapping* conditions, stimuli that were targets in some trials appeared as distractors in other trials, and vice versa. In such conditions, performance showed little improvement even after thousands of trials. Effects of display size were virtually constant over time.

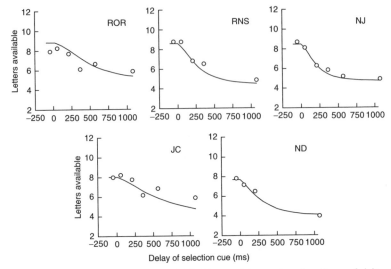

Fig. 5.9 Mean numbers of 'letters available' for partial report as functions of delay of selection cue for 9-element displays in Experiment 4 of Sperling (1960). Individual data for five subjects. Theoretical fits by TVA are indicated by solid curves. The observed data are read from Fig. 8 (graphs in right column on p. 11) of Sperling (1960). The information available in brief visual presentations. *Psychological Monographs*, **74** (11, Whole No. 498). Copyright 1960 by the American Psychological Association. Adapted with permission. The use of APA information does not imply endorsement by APA.

What is learned during consistent practice in search and detection tasks? Dumais (cited in Shiffrin and Dumais 1981; see also Shiffrin *et al.* 1981; Schneider *et al.* 1984) provided evidence that subjects learn both to attend to the targets and to ignore the distractors. After consistent practice in a visual search task, she found strong positive transfer to a new search task, both when

Table 5.2 Estimates of parameters for Sperling's (1960) subjects

Subject	Parameter		
	K	**C**	**μ**
ROR	4.89	11.8	776
RNS	4.43	16.3	456
NJ	5.42	29.4	197
JC	3.93	5.9	983
ND	5.65	17.7	253

K = storage capacity (number of elements); C = processing capacity (elements/s); μ = time constant for decay of information (ms).

the new task used the old targets together with a new set of distractors and when the new task used new targets together with the old set of distractors.

Consistent practice in the search for particular targets can yield negative rather than positive transfer, such that performance is impaired in subsequent experiments. Shiffrin and Schneider gave several impressive demonstrations. In one experiment (Shiffrin and Schneider 1977, Experiment 1), target and distractor sets were reversed after 2100 trials of consistent practice. Just after reversal, the hit rate fell to a level well below that seen at the start of training when the subjects were completely unpractised. Gradually thereafter performance recovered, but it took about 2400 trials of reversed practice to reach a level similar to that seen after only 1200 trials of original practice.

In another experiment (Shiffrin and Schneider 1977, Experiment 4d), subjects who had previously been trained to search for digits among letters (consistent mapping conditions) were instructed to search one diagonal of a 2 × 2 matrix of characters for letter targets among letter distractors in varied mapping conditions. The other diagonal was to be ignored. However, when digits appeared on the diagonal to be ignored, detection of simultaneous letter targets on the diagonal to be attended deteriorated. Apparently, although known to be irrelevant and presented in irrelevant display locations, the previous targets (the digits) 'automatically' attracted attention. This basic finding has been replicated in a series of experiments by Kyllingsbæk et al. (2001).

To account for effects of practice in visual search, Shiffrin and Dumais (1981) and Shiffrin et al. (1981) suggested that the 'attention strength' (attentional weight) of individual stimuli is altered during training, so that stimuli gradually gain in strength when serving as targets and lose in strength when serving as distractors. At a qualitative level, the suggested hypothesis yields a simple account for the results reviewed above. A quantitative model based on TVA is presented in Box 5.6 (for early related work, see Schneider 1985;

Box 5.6 Schneider and Fisk (1982)

Detection (via non-guessing) occurs if, and only if, the target is sampled from the frame in which it appears. The probability of this event is

$$P = 1 - \exp\left(-\frac{C\tau}{1 + \alpha D}\right),$$

where C is the processing capacity, τ is the effective exposure duration of the target letter, D is the number of distractors in the frame containing the

Box 5.6 Schneider and Fisk (1982) *(continued)*

target (i.e. $D = 3$), and α is the ratio of the attentional weight of a distractor to the attentional weight of a target.

The attentional weight of a (target or distractor) letter x of type i is a sum of two components. One component is $\eta(x, i)\pi_i$, where $\eta(x, i)$ is the strength of the sensory evidence that x is a token of type i, and π_i is the current pertinence value of type i. The other component is a constant, w^*, independent of whether x is a target or a distractor.

For any values of x and i, $\eta(x, i)$ equals a positive constant η_0 from time 0 until time τ (i.e. for the effective exposure duration). What changes with practice is the pertinence of letter types. Let $\pi_i(k)$ be the pertinence of letter type i on trial k. For any type i, the initial pertinence value $\pi_i(1)$ equals a positive constant π_0. But for each trial, the type of the letter serving as a target gains in pertinence, and the types of the letters serving as distractors lose in pertinence. Specifically, for any i,

$$\pi_i(k + 1) = h\, \pi_i(k),$$

where h is a constant greater than one, if a letter of type i is a target in trial k, whereas

$$\pi_i(k + 1) = c\, \pi_i(k),$$

where c is a positive constant smaller than one, if a letter of type i is a distractor in trial k. In sum, after having appeared as a target in m trials and as a distractor in n trials, letter x has an attentional weight of

$$w_x = \eta_0 h^m c^n \pi_0 + w^*,$$

which can be rewritten as

$$w_x = \eta_0 \pi_0 \left(h^m c^n + \frac{w^*}{\eta_0 \pi_0} \right).$$

The model has only four free parameters: the product $C\tau$, the two multiplicative constants h and c, and the ratio $w^*/(\eta_0\pi_0)$ between the constant component of attentional weights and the initial value of the variable component. The least squares fit to the data in Fig. 5.11 was obtained with $C\tau$ at about 2.94 elements, h at about 1.004, c at about 0.998, and $w^*/(\eta_0\pi_0)$ at about 5.95.

Shiffrin and Czerwinski 1988). The model is based on a detailed study by Schneider and Fisk (1982) on the effects of practice with varying degrees of consistency.

In each trial in Experiment 1 of Schneider and Fisk (1982), the subject was presented with a sequence of 12 frames in rapid succession. Each frame consisted of a 2×2 matrix of letters presented for 80 ms, followed by pattern masks presented for 30 ms (see Fig. 5.10). One of the frames contained a predesignated target letter, and the task was to indicate the spatial location (the quadrant) of the target, guessing whenever unsure. For a given trial, a set of only four distractor letters was used for all 12 frames, so that, with the exception of the target frame, the same four letters appeared in different locations on each of the 12 frames. The target and distractor letters were selected from a set of nine consonants representing five degrees of consistency: 10/0 (i.e. letter appearing as a target in 10 trials per training block and as a distractor in 0 trials), 10/5, 10/10, 10/20, and 9/61. Subjects received six cycles of (a) 12 training blocks (85 trials each) and (b) one test block of 100 trials (20 for each degree of consistency). In the test blocks, only letters assigned to the 9/61 condition appeared as distractors.

Accuracy of detection is shown in Fig. 5.11 as a function of degree of consistency, with level of practice as the parameter. The data are from test blocks, and they are corrected for guessing. A fairly close theoretical fit is indicated by unmarked points connected with straight lines. The basic idea of the fit is that

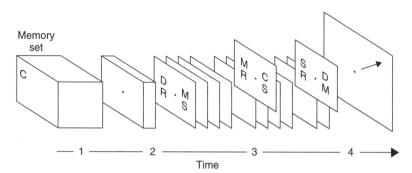

Fig. 5.10 Experimental procedure of Schneider and Fisk (1982). Trial sequence: (1) memory set, (2) fixation dot, (3) 12 frames presented, with a target (the letter C) on frame 5, (4) after a correct response a mark spun off the screen from the target position. Adapted with permission from Schneider and Fisk (1982). Degree of consistent training: improvements in search performance and automatic process development. *Perception & Psychophysics*, **31**, 160–168. Copyright 1982 by the Psychonomic Society.

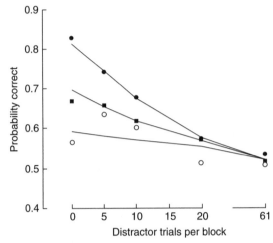

Fig. 5.11 Probability of detecting a letter (on test blocks) as a function of degree of consistency [indicated by the number of trials (per training block) in which the letter appears as a distractor], with level of practice as the parameter, in Experiment 1 of Schneider and Fisk (1982). Group data for nine subjects. Every twelfth training block was followed by a test block. Three levels of training were distinguished: Tests 1 and 2 (open circles), Tests 3 and 4 (squares), and Tests 5 and 6 (solid circles). A theoretical fit by TVA is indicated by unmarked points connected with straight lines. The observed data are read from Fig. 3 of Schneider and Fisk (1982). Degree of consistent training: improvements in search performance and automatic process development. *Perception & Psychophysics*, **31**, 160–168. Copyright 1982 by the Psychonomic Society. Adapted with permission.

for each trial performed, the pertinence of the type of letter used as the target is increased by multiplication with a constant greater than 1, whereas the pertinence values of the types of letters displayed as distractors are decreased by multiplication with a positive constant less than 1 (see Box 5.6 for details). This way attentional weights of targets increase slightly for every trial, while weights of distractors decrease (*negative priming*; cf. Section 2.6.2). Obviously, the overall effect of these modulations depends on the consistency of the target–distractor mapping across many trials. The sensory discriminability of the items (η values) and the perceptual biases (β values) are not assumed to be affected by practice. (For a different view, see Section 5.7 on the instance theory of attention and memory proposed by Logan 2002*a*.)

5.7 Extensions

TVA has been extended in a number of ways. Logan (1996) proposed an extension of TVA, the CODE theory of visual attention (CTVA), which combines TVA with the COntour DEtector theory of perceptual grouping by proximity (van Oeffelen and Vos 1982, 1983). CTVA explains a wide range of findings of effects of perceptual grouping and spatial distance between items on reaction times and error rates in visual attention tasks (see Logan 1996; Logan and Bundesen 1996; see also Bundesen 1998a,b). The findings include effects of grouping (Prinzmetal 1981) and distance between items (Cohen and Ivry 1989) on occurrence of illusory conjunctions; effects of grouping (Banks and Prinzmetal 1976) and distance between items (Cohen and Ivry 1991) in visual search; and effects of distance between target and distractors in the flankers task (B. A. Eriksen and C. W. Eriksen 1974; see Section 2.6.1). In order to account for both mean reaction times and error rates in the flankers task, Logan (1996) configured TVA as a counter model (cf. Section 3.5.5 on trading speed for accuracy). There were two counters, one for each of two alternative targets, and the counting process finished when one of the counters accumulated its criterion number of counts. Thus, by raising the criteria for both counters, the increase in error rate with decreasing spatial distance between the target and response-incompatible flankers could be converted to an increase in mean reaction time as the distance of the response-incompatible flankers from the target was decreased.

Logan and Gordon (2001) extended CTVA into a theory of executive control in dual-task situations. The theory, executive control of TVA (ECTVA), accounts for central effects in this research area: set-switching costs (the costs of switching set from one task to another), crosstalk (informational interference between one communication channel and another), and concurrence costs (the costs of doing two things at once). ECTVA assumes that executive processes control subordinate processes by manipulating their parameters. TVA is used as the theory of subordinate processes, so a task set is defined as a set of TVA control parameters (in particular, βs and πs) that is sufficient to configure TVA to perform a task. Set switching is viewed as a change in one or more of these parameters, and the time taken to change a task set is assumed to depend on the number of parameters to be changed. Specifically, Logan and Gordon (2001) accounted for set-switching times by assuming that (1) the time taken to transmit a control parameter to TVA is distributed exponentially (with the same exponential rate parameter for all control parameters); and (2) the control parameters are transmitted in parallel and independently by a process with unlimited capacity (i.e. such that the time taken to transmit a parameter is independent of the number of other parameters being transmitted). (For related analyses of the conditions inducing switching of task sets, see Logan and Bundesen 2003, 2004; Monsell and Mizon 2006; Logan *et al.* 2007.)

Logan (2002*a*) proposed an instance theory of attention and memory (ITAM) that combines ECTVA with the exemplar-based random-walk model of categorization (Nosofsky and Palmeri 1997). The exemplar-based random-walk model is itself a combination of Nosofsky's (1986) generalized context model of categorization and Logan's (1988) instance theory of automaticity. In ITAM, as in Logan's instance theory of automaticity, a category is represented as a set of instances (individual examples or members of the category). Learning of categories consists of accumulation of more and more instances with practice. Each encounter with an object is represented separately as an instance. It is encoded separately, stored separately in long-term memory, and retrieved separately. When a stimulus object x is presented, it is compared against all instances stored in memory, and each comparison process produces an η value representing the degree of similarity between the stimulus and the instance in question. The TVA parameter $\eta(x, i)$, which represents the strength of the sensory evidence that object x belongs to category i, is given by the sum of all η values representing similarities of x to stored instances of category i. Thus, the more instances representing the category, the stronger the sensory evidence can be.

As in Nosofsky's (1986) generalized context model of categorization (also see Shepard 1957), similarity is represented geometrically in ITAM: objects are represented as points in a multidimensional feature space, and the similarity between two objects (e.g. a stimulus object and an instance of a certain category) is represented by the distance between the corresponding points. Specifically, as the distance is increased from zero toward infinity, the similarity (η value) decays exponentially from one toward zero. All distances in a certain feature dimension (e.g. colour) can be scaled up or down (i.e. multiplied by a constant) by manipulating an attentional weight associated with the dimension. The overall distance between two points (i.e. the similarity of two objects) is a function of the distances in each of the feature dimensions. Both the usual, Euclidian distance function and the so-called city-block metric have been used in applications (see, for example, Nosofsky 1984). By the city-block metric, the overall distance equals the sum of the distances in each of the feature dimensions. Thus, from the generalized context model of categorization, ITAM has adopted both an attentional mechanism for transformation of η values by scaling of psychological distances in particular feature dimensions and a strong theory of geometrical relationships among η values.

The selection of categorizations of the form 'object x belongs to category i' is determined by a race driven by similarities between display objects and memory representations of category exemplars, biased by control parameters (βs and πs) in accordance with the rate and weight equations of TVA.

The categorizations are accumulated in response counters, and there is one counter for each response. Response selection is made by a decision rule that refers to the values in the counters. There are three distinct decision rules, corresponding to a race model, a counter model, and a random-walk model (cf. Section 3.5.5). The random-walk model is the preferred decision rule in ITAM, and the random-walk version of ITAM is similar to the exemplar-based random-walk model of categorization proposed by Nosofsky and Palmeri (1997).

Logan (2002*a*) summarized ITAM in a small set of equations and showed how previous theories—TVA, CTVA (Logan 1996), instance theory (Logan 1988), the generalized context model (Nosofsky 1986), and the exemplar-based random-walk model of categorization (Nosofsky and Palmeri 1997)— could be regarded as special cases of ITAM in a strict mathematical sense. Because the previous theories were special cases of ITAM, the new theory was born with the capability of accounting for a huge body of established findings on attention, categorization, and memory. By integrating such important research areas, the development of ITAM seems to be an important step toward a unified account of visual cognition.

5.8 Summary

In this chapter TVA has been applied to research findings on focused attention from a wide range of experimental paradigms. TVA formed the basis of special models for analysing effects of selection criterion and number of distractors. The detection paradigm of Estes and Taylor (1964, 1965) was readily analysed. A deadline model of one-view search (search without reallocation of attention) fitted data on efficient feature search (Treisman and Gelade 1980) and data on efficient search with perceptual grouping (Bundesen and Pedersen 1983). Data on inefficient feature (Treisman and Gormican 1988) and conjunction (Treisman and Gelade 1980) search were explained by attention shifting among groups of display elements (many-view search). In this way findings on the time taken to reallocate attention (e.g. Colegate *et al.* 1973; Logan 2005) were accommodated. Effects of delay of selection cue were explained in an analysis of Sperling's (1960) experiments on partial report with poststimulus cuing. Furthermore, TVA proved useful in understanding the effects of practice in visual search. It formed the basis of a simple model that accounted for data on effects of practice with varying degrees of consistency in the mapping of stimuli to responses (Schneider and Fisk 1982). Finally, TVA has formed the foundation of a comprehensive account of spatial effects in visual attention (CTVA; Logan 1996), a theory of executive control of visual attention in dual-task situations (ECTVA; Logan and Gordon 2001), and an integrated theory of attention, categorization, and memory (ITAM; Logan 2002*a*) that seems to be an important step toward a unified account of visual cognition.

In conclusion, Chapters 4 and 5 have demonstrated that TVA has very substantial explanatory power. Using a simple set of concepts, the theory organizes a large body of established findings on human performance in visual recognition and attention tasks. Further, TVA is not only consistent with these findings in a general, qualitative way, but includes a set of mathematical specifications that allows for detailed, quantitative modelling of each set of empirical data. In Chapters 4 and 5 we have sought to illustrate the TVA approach in relation to some of the classic studies in the field, but, given the flexibility of the model, many other studies could also have been analysed. We hope that interested readers have been encouraged to take up this challenge.

Part 2

The neurophysiology of visual attention

6

Effects of visual attention in single neurons

Many studies show that changes in the attentional state of the organism are directly reflected in the activity of individual neurons. Single-cell research thus offers a unique view of attentional function at the nervous system's most basic processing level. In this chapter we review the attentional mechanisms that have been uncovered in this field as well as some of the most influential theoretical models. However, first we need to clarify which kind of system is being modulated and take a look at some fundamental properties of neural activity (see Section 6.1). Next, the strengths and disadvantages of doing attention research at the single-cell level are discussed (Section 6.2). Section 6.3 describes the four main types of attentional effects that have been found in this line of work: (1) strong changes in firing activity when multiple stimuli are competing for the neuron's response, (2) more modest effects when only one stimulus is presented to the cell, (3) increases in baseline activity when a stimulus is expected but has not yet occurred, and (4) increased synchronization between firings of neurons that respond to an attended stimulus. Two general types of models have been proposed to account for these findings: attention as gain control (Section 6.4) and biased competition (Section 6.5). Although both types of models can explain important results, none of them accounts for the whole range of effects found in the neurophysiological literature.

6.1 Basics of single-cell behaviour

Neurons are highly specialized cells that can produce electrical pulses and transmit these to other cells (see, for example, Bear *et al.* 2006). The electrical pulses are made in response to chemical inputs (mainly from other neurons), which are picked up by the cell in a branching, tree-like structure of receptors, so-called *dendrites*, or from stimulation to other parts of the cell. In this way, chemical inputs from many different sources influence the cell and push its electrical charge in a positive or negative direction. If the membrane potential of the cell reaches a critical threshold, typically −70 mV compared to the extracellular fluid, the cell fires a single electrical pulse (an *action potential*) and is then unresponsive for several milliseconds. The action potential is propagated down the cell's *axon*, a long nerve fibre, which in turn influences the chemical state of other cells in contact with the axon. Thus the basic signal unit of the nervous system is a distinct, all-or-none pulse of electrical activity: a *spike*.

Each neuron typically sends off many such signals per second, but at highly variable intervals (Fig. 6.1). To a first approximation, the firing activity of a single cell in response to a constant sensory stimulus is a so-called homogeneous stochastic process of Poisson type. The homogeneous Poisson process is completely characterized by the mean rate of firing; given the mean rate, the precise timing of the spikes is entirely random and carries no further information. Accordingly most models of neural information processing focus on the mean firing rate. However, the issue is controversial and the importance of synchronous firing between neurons has also been emphasized. Apparently, when a neuron receives simultaneous signals, the effect on its firing rate is stronger than if the same signals occur interspaced in time (Salinas and Sejnowski 2000). Thus, the precise timing of signals may also be critical for neural processing.

Considered more closely, the firing activity of a single cell in response to a constant stimulus is not strictly homogeneous (i.e. the mean firing rate is not strictly constant over time). The most important systematic change is *adaptation*: the cell's response to a constant stimulus decays over time. This is the neural correlate of sensory adaptation effects at the psychophysical level.

Individual neurons respond only to a very restricted part of the information available to the whole organism. In the visual system there are two main types of limitations. First, a typical visual neuron responds only to stimulation in

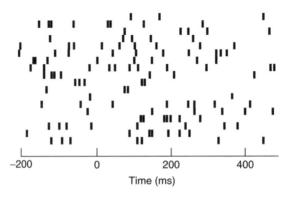

Fig. 6.1 Example of spiking activity in a population of neurons. Each row shows the firing activity of a single cell over the course of about half a second (from $t = -200$ ms to $t = 500$ ms). Each tick mark represents one spike by the cell.

a particular part of the visual field: it has a spatially limited *receptive field*. The limitation varies from smaller than one degree of visual angle in the primary visual cortex to much larger receptive fields in the high-level visual areas of temporal and parietal cortex. A second, stronger limitation is that individual neurons respond only to particular sensory attributes, which often represent very specific aspects of the stimulus. The selectivity concerns not only a particular feature dimension, but also specific values of that feature. An example could be a particular orientation of line segments in visual objects, as found in the classical studies by Hubel and Wiesel (1959, 1962, 1968) of cells in the primary visual cortex. The selectivity for feature values can be more or less broad, corresponding to the width of *tuning curves* for a feature dimension (see Fig. 6.2). Stimuli that elicit a high firing rate are called *preferred* for the cell; stimuli that do not drive the neuron much above its baseline activity are called *non-preferred*.

6.2 Single-cell studies of psychological functions

Psychophysical research on single-cell activity is a difficult and time-consuming process, in which microelectrodes are repeatedly probed into a specific brain area. In each probe the electrode must be positioned near enough to a particular cell to record changes in the extracellular electrical field when the cell

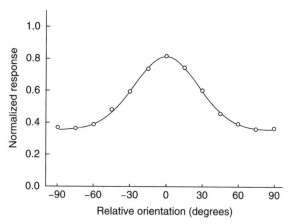

Fig. 6.2 Normalized tuning curves from a population of 262 orientation-selective cells. To compare tuning curves across individual cells, the preferred orientation of each cell was normalized to a value of 0°. Responses were also normalized to the same scale. Adapted with permission from McAdams and Maunsell (1999). Effects of attention on orientation-tuning functions of single neurons in macaque cortical area V4. *Journal of Neuroscience*, **19**, 431–441. Copyright 1999 by the Society for Neuroscience.

generates an action potential. Further, the electrode must be maintained in this position for a long period of time (a considerable technical challenge) in order to characterize the neuron's response to various experimental manipulations at the psychological level. This procedure is typically repeated for hundreds of cells to gather enough data for a study. Due to their invasive nature, single-cell studies are performed only in animals (except for very rare cases of human neurosurgery); typically, macaque monkeys that can be trained to do simple attentional tasks such as visual detection, search, or match-to-sample.

Single-cell recordings provide the highest available spatial and temporal resolution for any measurement of brain activity, but also have important limitations. Besides being invasive, a major constraint is that only a tiny proportion of the neurons in a given brain area are investigated, representing an extremely small part of the total neural processing from stimulus to response. One would not think that reliable correlations with the behaviour of the whole organism could be derived from such small samples, but many studies have proved this assumption wrong. However, this is only due to very carefully designed studies, in particular the use of highly selected behavioural paradigms. Many experimental paradigms used in cognitive psychology are not appropriate for single-cell research. For one thing, the laboratory animal must be able to learn the task, which rules out many of the more complex designs. In addition, stimuli must be used that can fit into the receptive field of the recorded cell and must be tailored to the cell's particular feature selectivity—both of which are more or less unknown each time a new cell is probed. In spite of these strong methodological constraints, single-cell studies of attention have produced some remarkably systematic results, to which we now turn.

6.3 **Attentional modulation of single-cell activity**

Decades of neurophysiological research have revealed several distinct effects of attention in visual neurons. The strongest attentional changes of a cell's firing rate occur when multiple objects are present within its receptive field. Under these conditions, when attention is shifted from one object to another the cell's firing rate can change dramatically, as if the receptive field contracts around the attended object and the cell responds only to the properties of this object. The classical demonstration of such *dynamic remapping of receptive fields* was made by Moran and Desimone (1985). Moran and Desimone presented macaque monkeys with stimuli at two locations. The monkeys were trained to attend only to stimuli presented at one of the locations and to ignore any stimuli shown at the other location (Fig. 6.3). The task was match-to-sample: The monkeys should encode a sample stimulus shown at the attended

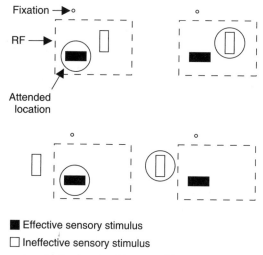

■ Effective sensory stimulus
□ Ineffective sensory stimulus

Fig. 6.3 Four examples of stimulus conditions used by Moran and Desimone (1985). In each condition, the monkey attended to stimuli presented at one location (encircled in this figure) and ignored stimuli presented at another location. The task was to indicate whether or not a sample and a test stimulus that followed each other at the location to be attended were identical to each other. Upper panels: both the stimulus to be attended and the stimulus to be ignored were presented inside the receptive field (RF) of the recorded neuron. The stimulus to be attended was either an effective sensory stimulus (preferred by the recorded neuron; upper left panel) or an ineffective sensory stimulus (upper right panel). Lower left panel: only the stimuli to be attended were inside the RF of the recorded neuron. Lower right panel: only the stimuli to be ignored were inside the RF of the recorded neuron. Adapted with permission from Moran and Desimone (1985). Selective attention gates visual processing in the extrastriate cortex. *Science*, **229**, 782–784. Copyright 1985 by *Science*.

location, retain it for a brief delay period, and then match it to a test stimulus shown at the same location. During many trials with this task, Moran and Desimone recorded from individual neurons in visual area V4 and the inferotemporal cortex. The stimuli in the display were selected so that they elicited either a strong response from the neuron (i.e. were preferred) or a weak response (non-preferred). When both the distractor and the target stimulus were located within the receptive field of the recorded neuron, its firing rate was little affected by the distractor: The cell's firing rate was driven either up or down, depending on whether the target stimulus was a preferred or non-preferred stimulus for the cell. It was as if the cell responded only to the target stimulus, even though the distractor was also present in its receptive field. However, when only a single stimulus was located within the neuron's receptive field (and the other stimulus was in a different part of the visual field), attention had no measurable effect on the firing rate. Thus the response modulation depended on competition between visual objects within the same receptive field. The findings of Moran and Desimone were later replicated and extended to other cortical areas, as described in detail in Section 8.1.

The task used by Moran and Desimone can be described as location-based selection of objects, but dynamic remapping of receptive fields has also been shown in tasks that require selection based on features other than location. Chelazzi *et al.* (1998) measured activity of high-level visual cells in the anterior inferotemporal cortex while monkeys performed a visual search task. First the monkeys were shown an object (the cue) at fixation. The object should be remembered while the screen went blank. Next, two objects were shown at other (non-foveal) locations than the cue, and the monkey had to make a saccade to the target object (Fig. 6.4). Thus selection was based on object identity (i.e. a particular set of features), and the target location was not

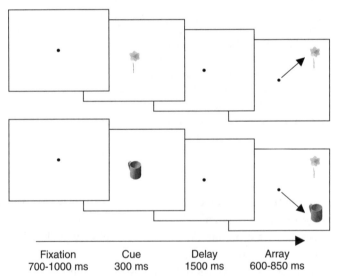

Fixation	Cue	Delay	Array
700-1000 ms	300 ms	1500 ms	600-850 ms

Fig. 6.4 Experimental procedure of Chelazzi *et al.* (1998). A cue stimulus was presented at the start of the trial, followed by a delay, and then an array of stimuli. In target-present trials the array contained a target matching the cue and the monkey was rewarded for making a saccade to it. In some trials the cue-target was a good stimulus for the cell (top row) and in other trials it was a poor stimulus for the cell (bottom row). Adapted with permission from Chelazzi, Duncan, Miller and Desimone (1998). Responses of neurons in inferior temporal cortex during memory-guided visual search. *Journal of Neurophysiology*, **80**, 2918–2940. Copyright 1998 by the American Physiological Society.

known in advance. The receptive fields of the recorded inferotemporal neurons were so large that both the target and distractor stimuli were included, so both could potentially influence the response of the cell. As in the study of Moran and Desimone, Chelazzi *et al.* used (preferred versus non-preferred) stimuli that in isolation elicited clearly different responses from the recorded neuron, to provide a clear index of which object the cell was responding to. After an initial period of about 200 ms in which attention did not have a measurable effect, Chelazzi *et al.* found that the cell's response was strongly dominated by the target stimulus. As in the study of Moran and Desimone, the cell's firing rate went up if the target was a preferred stimulus, and down if it was non-preferred, whereas the status of the distractor object mattered little. Thus dynamic remapping of receptive fields can also occur with selection based on features other than location. Indeed, dynamic remapping seems to be a general mechanism for attentional selection when multiple objects are present within a cell's receptive field.

When the cell's receptive field includes only one object, attentional effects are generally much smaller and less consistent. Some studies have found no effect of attention under these conditions (Moran and Desimone 1985; Luck *et al.* 1997), whereas others have reported moderate enhancements of firing rates (Motter 1994a,b; Connor *et al.* 1997; McAdams and Maunsell 1999a,b; Reynolds *et al.* 1999, 2000; Treue and Martinez-Trujillo 1999; Martinez-Trujillo and Treue 2004), and one study has even found negative effects of attention (Motter 1993). Attentional effects with one receptive field stimulus may depend on a number of factors, including the cognitive task, the visual area studied, and the sensory properties of the stimuli (e.g. low versus high luminance contrast).

A study by Treue and Martinez-Trujillo (1999) illustrates some typical effects of attention with one stimulus in the receptive field. Treue and Martinez-Trujillo recorded from visual area MT, which contains cells that are selective to the direction of motion, while monkeys were shown two patterns of moving dots. The dots of each pattern moved in a coherent fashion and thus had a dominant direction of motion (Fig. 6.5). Before the patterns appeared, the attention of the monkey was directed to the location of one of them. The monkeys were trained to react when a small change occurred in the speed or direction of the cued pattern. In the first experiment of Treue and Martinez-Trujillo, the two patterns moved in the same direction. The receptive field of the recorded neuron contained either the attended or unattended pattern. When attention was directed at the pattern in the receptive field, the firing rate of the cell was on average about 10% higher than when attention was directed at the other pattern (outside the receptive field). The increase in

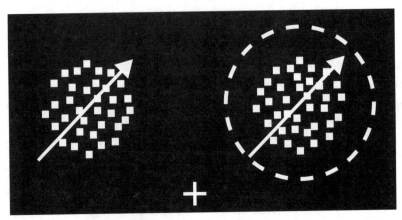

Fig. 6.5 Stimuli used by Treue and Martinez-Trujillo (1999). One random dot pattern (RDP) was presented inside the receptive field (dashed circle) while the other was presented about the same distance from the fixation point in the opposite hemifield. In a given trial, both RDPs moved in the same of 12 possible directions. Adapted with permission from Treue and Martinez-Trujillo (1999). Feature-based attention influences motion processing gain in macaque visual cortex. *Nature*, **399**, 575–579. Copyright 1999 by Macmillan Publishers Ltd.

activation occurred without any sharpening of the tuning curve around the attended direction: Attention to the object in the receptive field simply seemed to scale the neuron's activation up by a constant factor, across variations in the stimulus: *multiplicative modulation*. Multiplicative modulation has also been shown in other studies using single stimuli in the receptive field, notably those by McAdams and Maunsell (1999*a,b*; Fig. 6.6).

In their second experiment, Treue and Martinez-Trujillo showed a similar scaling-up effect when a particular feature value, in contrast to an object at a particular location, was attended. In this experiment the receptive field of the neuron was stimulated by a dot pattern moving in the direction preferred by the cell; however, the monkey was not cued to attend this pattern. Outside the receptive field, a second dot pattern was displayed that moved either in the same or opposite direction, and when the monkey attended this dot pattern the response of the recorded neuron varied with the direction of movement being attended: if the attended direction was the direction preferred by the recorded cell, its firing rate was high, but if the attended direction was the opposite, the firing rate was low. The modulation of the firing rate occurred

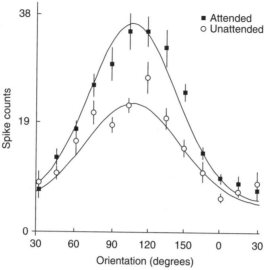

Fig. 6.6 Multiplicative modulation of tuning curve by attention. The tuning curves in response to a single stimulus in the receptive field are shown for an orientation-selective neuron (preferred orientation: around 110°) when attended (closed squares) and unattended (open circles). Each data point is a mean spike count with the standard error indicated by bars. The illustrated cell has a 73% increase in the amplitude of its tuning function by attention. Adapted with permission from McAdams and Maunsell (1999). Effects of attention on the reliability of individual neurons in monkey visual cortex. *Neuron*, **23**, 765–773. Copyright 1999 by Elsevier.

even though the object in the cell's receptive field was unattended in both conditions, which shows that attention to particular features can alter firing rates to stimuli across the visual field. A later study by Martinez-Trujillo and Treue (2004) showed that this attentional mechanism also works by multiplicative modulation, such that the general response of the neuron (across the tuning curve) is scaled up or down by a constant factor.

A third main effect of attention in single cells is an increase of the neuron's spontaneous activity when a target stimulus is expected to appear in its receptive field: a *baseline shift*. This effect was found, for example, in the study by Chelazzi *et al.* (1998) mentioned above. Recall that in this study, monkeys were shown a visual object and then had to remember the object for a period of time while the screen went blank. Even though there was no sensory stimulation during this period, the baseline firing rate went up if the object held in memory was a preferred stimulus for the recorded cell. Baseline shifts have also been demonstrated in many other studies (e.g. Miller *et al.* 1993, 1996; Luck *et al.* 1997; Chelazzi *et al.* 2001; see Section 8.3).

In recent years a fourth type of attentional effect has been discovered: attention to an object may lead to increased synchronization of the activity of neurons with the attended object in their receptive fields. An important demonstration of this effect was made by Fries *et al.* (2001), who recorded both local field potentials and spikes from small clusters of V4 neurons (multi-unit activity) simultaneously at several sites with overlapping receptive fields, while monkeys performed an attentional task. Two stimuli were presented, one inside and one outside the receptive fields of the recorded neurons, and in each trial the monkey's attention was cued to the location of one of the objects. The firing rates in individual neurons showed little effect of attention to the stimulus in their receptive fields. However, gamma-frequency synchronization (between 35 and 90 Hz) between the neurons was increased, while low-frequency synchronization (below 17 Hz) was reduced. Synchronization in the gamma band may have important effects at the next stage of processing (i.e. in neurons that receive projections from the synchronously firing cells), by driving up the firing rate of these neurons (Salinas and Sejnowski 2000). Attention-induced gamma-band synchronization may also have direct behavioural correlates, such as faster reaction times (Womelsdorf *et al.* 2006). However, due to the correlative nature of the evidence, it is unclear whether the observed synchronization reflects a cause rather than an effect of attentional selection.

The size of attentional effects varies considerably between cortical areas. A general finding is that the modulating effect of attention on firing rates becomes stronger as one moves up in the cortical processing hierarchy, from V1 over V2 and V4 to the inferotemporal cortex (see Section 9.2 for an introductory overview of cortical visual areas). An explanation for this effect is the increasingly larger receptive fields at higher processing levels, which implies that stimuli processed by separate neurons at lower levels compete for the same receptive fields higher in the system. As noted above, attention has its most powerful effect when it leads to dynamic remapping of a receptive field that contains more than one object. Therefore the potential for changes in firing rates is much greater in high-level neurons with large receptive fields.

6.4 **Attention as gain control**

As early as the 1920s, the English physiologist Adrian noted that when the sensory intensity of a stimulus (e.g. its luminance contrast) was increased, the firing rate went up in cells that were responsive to the stimulus. An influential class of models claim that attention has a similar effect on neural activity and acts as an amplification mechanism for sensory signals. The notion of attentional *gain control* was originally proposed in the 1950s and 1960s, inspired by electroencephalogram (EEG) studies showing that the amplitude of sensory evoked potentials increased when attention was directed to an object (cf. Hillyard *et al.* 1999; see Section 9.2). Analogous effects were later found in positron emission tomography (PET) and functional magnetic resonance imaging (fMRI) studies (e.g. Corbetta *et al.* 1990, discussed in Section 9.2; see Section 9.1 for an introduction to methods of functional brain imaging). The notion of gain control fits well with psychological 'spotlight' theories, in which attention acts as an amplifier for stimulation in a single, spatially defined focus (Posner and Driver 1992; see Section 2.8.2). Spotlight models provide a simple explanation for the increase in firing rates that is often seen when attention is directed at a solitary stimulus in the cell's receptive field (e.g. McAdams and Maunsell 1999; Treue and Martinez-Trujillo 1999).

There is no general agreement on the details of the amplification mechanism, perhaps apart from the common finding that it seems to work in a multiplicative way. That is, the tuning curves of individual neurons are not changed qualitatively (for example, sharpened around the preferred feature) but simply scaled up by a constant factor in response to both preferred and non-preferred stimuli (McAdams and Maunsell 1999*a,b*; Martinez-Trujillo and Treue 2004; cf. Fig. 6.6). One of the most elaborate hypotheses regarding this amplification mechanism has been put forward by Reynolds (2005) (see also Reynolds and Chelazzi 2004). In his *contrast gain* model, Reynolds suggested that attention works by exploiting the same neural mechanisms that are involved in the processing of luminance contrast. Attention should then, simply, act to increase the effective contrast of stimuli. The main support for this idea comes from the fact that changes in luminance contrast lead to multiplicative modulation of firing rates (Sclar and Freeman 1982), similar to the effect of attention. Also, attention may change the response to a faint, low-contrast stimulus in a way that corresponds to an increase in the effective contrast of the stimulus (Reynolds *et al.* 2000) (but see Section 8.2.2.1 for a different interpretation of these results). Further, when two stimuli compete within the same receptive field, changes in attention and changes in sensory contrast seem to have interchangeable effects on the probability of the neuron selecting one or the other stimulus for its response (Reynolds and Desimone 2003).

A weak point of the contrast gain model is that it predicts no attentional effects with high-contrast stimuli, where the neural response is saturated with respect to effective contrast. However, many studies have found attentional effects, even quite large ones, under these conditions (e.g. Moran and Desimone 1985; Reynolds *et al.* 1999). Another effect unexplained by the contrast gain model is baseline shifts in firing rates when a stimulus is anticipated, but not yet present, in the receptive field. In this case there is no stimulus to modulate the effective contrast of, yet a change in firing rates occurs with attention. Thus the hypothesis of contrast gain, although bold and interesting, is not sufficient to account for attentional effects at the single-cell level in general.

The notion of attention as gain control has also been applied to attentional selection of non-spatial features. Treue and Martinez-Trujillo (1999) (see also Martinez-Trujillo and Treue 2005) have proposed a *feature similarity gain model* that assumes similar response modulation when attention is directed to locations and features. According to this model, a neuron's firing rate is up- or down-scaled in accordance with the similarity of the currently attended feature and the sensory selectivity of the neuron. For example, if the neuron happens to be selective for a particular direction of motion (as in the study of MT neurons by Treue and Martinez-Trujillo 1999), its firing rate is generally increased if this direction is attended. Conversely, the firing rate is down-scaled if the opposite direction of motion is attended. The feature similarity gain model assumes that the attended feature can also be a location, which seems to put effects of spatial attention within the scope of the model. In this case, the 'sensory selectivity' of the neuron (with respect to spatial features) is simply interpreted as the location of its receptive field. However, a major problem for this conjecture is the lack of a distinction between selection *based on* spatial features and attention *to* spatial features. There is a critical difference between, on the one hand, attending to an object at a particular location for the sake of determining, say, its colour, and on the other hand, attending to the spatial position *per se*, for example trying to make a precise localization of the object. The distinction is simple and fundamental in the theory of visual attention (TVA), where it corresponds to the difference between filtering based on location and pigeonholing with respect to location, but the distinction is missing in the feature similarity gain model's concept of spatial attention.

All variations of the idea that attention equals sensory gain control share a fundamental problem. In order to behave effectively, any organism must be able to distinguish external changes in stimuli from internal modulations of sensory representations. However, when attention is equated with sensory gain control, it is not clear how this distinction can be made. For example in Reynold's contrast gain model, the observer has no way of determining whether a change in perceived contrast is due to changes in physical lighting conditions or to attention. Whereas psychophysical studies show that subjects sometimes fail to disentangle these two effects reliably (e.g. Carrasco *et al.* 2004), this cannot generally be the case. Perception must be veridical in order to be useful, and sensory and attentional effects, although related, should also be separable. Any complete theory of attention must show how sensory and attentional effects can be separated.

6.5 **Attention as biased competition**

A major alternative to gain control models of attention is the *biased competition model* of Desimone and Duncan (1995). The notion of biased competition is already familiar from TVA (Bundesen 1990): in TVA, all possible visual categorizations ascribing features to objects *compete* (race) to become encoded into visual short-term memory (VSTM) before the store is filled up. Each possible categorization is supported by the sensory evidence that the categorization is true. However, the competition is *biased* by attentional weights and perceptual biases. The way sensory evidence and attentional biases interact is specified in the rate and weight equations of TVA.

TVA is a cognitive theory describing functional mechanisms of biased competition at an abstract level. The biased competition model presented by Desimone and Duncan (1995), Desimone (1999), and Duncan (1996) is a more concrete, neurobiological model. In this model, attentional selection is an emergent effect of competition between neural representations in multiple brain systems.

Generally speaking, the biased competition model has strong ties to parallel processing models in cognitive psychology, and in several ways stands in opposition to gain control models, which are traditionally related to serial processing. Another main difference is that the biased competition model emphasizes the importance of inhibition (between competing representations) rather than signal enhancement, although not ruling out the latter mechanism.

At the single-cell level, the biased competition model relates most clearly to two effects. First, the notion of competition between object representations fits nicely with dynamic remapping of receptive fields: When two or more stimuli compete for the response of the same neuron, a well-established effect of attention is to modulate the process by remapping the receptive field (in favour of the attended stimulus). Second, the notion of bias signals from higher-level cortical areas may explain the baseline shifts in firing rate that occur when a stimulus is expected to appear in a neuron's receptive field. The biased competition model assumes that the baseline shift sensitizes the neuron to upcoming sensory stimuli. This should increase the cell's response when an object appears, leading to an advantage ('bias') for the object in the further competition process. This sensitization mechanism is, in some ways, similar to gain control, although the (inhibitory) competition for receptive fields remains the primary means for attentional selection in the biased competition model.

The biased competition model is formulated in quite general terms, which has allowed for several computational and neurophysiological interpretations of the details of the selection process. In particular, the mechanisms underlying dynamic remapping of receptive fields are not clear. One possibility is that the remapping is due to synchronized firing for attended objects at lower levels in the visual system (Fries and Desimone 2005). This may drive higher-level neurons more effectively for the attended object, and thus may explain the remapping process even in the absence of changes in mean firing rates at lower levels. Another possibility is that additive or multiplicative (linear) gain control mechanisms at lower levels of the visual system lead to (non-linear) remapping effects at higher levels (Maunsell and McAdams 2001; Reynolds 2005). This idea has been implemented in several computational network models (Reynolds *et al.* 1999; Corchs and Deco 2002; Spratling and Johnson 2004), which show that small changes in the input from a lower-level neuron can strongly influence ('bias') the competition process at higher levels. A third possible explanation is that a gating signal from a structure outside the cortical processing hierarchy (e.g. the thalamus) controls the remapping process. In comparison with the gain control hypothesis outlined before, the gating model has the advantage that signals from lower levels are selected without being transformed: For one thing, the firing rates of lower-level neurons (which, from the perspective of higher-level neurons, represent sensory input) are not changed in the gating model. Thus the original information signal from each neuron is preserved. Second, the gating mechanism can ensure that signals from only one object at a time reach the upper-level neuron. This avoids the possibly intractable computational problem of disentangling information about several stimuli from the activity of one higher-level neuron. Both of these points suggest that perception can be more veridical by use of a gating process for dynamic remapping, but the issue still awaits direct empirical investigation. Figure 6.7 illustrates the three proposed mechanisms behind remapping of receptive fields.

6.6 **Summary**

Decades of single-cell research have provided fairly direct evidence on the basic mechanisms of attentional selection. A number of distinct effects have been identified. By far the strongest effect of attention occurs when more than one stimuli are present within the cell's receptive field. In this situation, attention to one of the objects seems to effectively shrink the receptive field, such that the cell responds exclusively to the attended object, irrespective of whether the object corresponds to the cell's feature specialization (i.e. has a preferred feature) or is ineffective at driving the neuron. This mechanism implies that attention can change the neuron's firing rate in both a positive and a negative direction. A smaller, and less consistent, effect of attention has

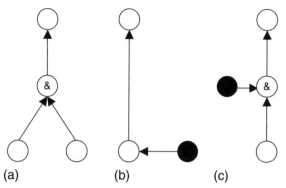

Fig. 6.7 Schematic illustration of three possible mechanisms underlying remapping of receptive fields. (a) Driving a higher-level neuron may require synchronized (simultaneous) firing among neurons at lower levels of the visual system. (b) Activity in a selected lower-level neuron may be boosted by a control unit (solid circle). (c) A selected communication line may be opened by a control unit (solid circle).

been found in studies with only one stimulus in the receptive field of the recorded neuron. In such conditions, attention may cause moderate increases in firing rates. This seems to occur multiplicatively across the cell's tuning curve, such that the activation of the cell is scaled by nearly the same factor irrespective of the stimulus to which it responds. A third reliable finding in the literature is a change in the neuron's baseline rate of firing when no stimulus is present within the receptive field, but a target stimulus is expected to appear. Finally, attentional selection has been linked more recently to synchronous firing, which perhaps has the effect of driving downstream neurons more effectively. However, synchronization may be an effect rather than a cause of attentional selection.

Two main types of models have been proposed to account for these findings, each of them with close parallels in cognitive psychology. In the first type of model, attention is viewed as a sensory gain control mechanism that scales up the signal from attended locations or features. Gain control models account well for enhancement of firing rates with attention to a single stimulus in the receptive field, but have trouble explaining dynamic remapping of receptive fields, where attention may sometimes reduce the firing rate of a neuron (when an ineffective stimulus is selected). More fundamentally, the gain control models have a problem explaining how the organism distinguishes sensory changes from attentional effects, a central computational issue. In the second main type of model, parallel biased competition, the inhibitory aspects of attention are emphasized and dynamic remapping of receptive fields is seen as the main mechanism. Accordingly, biased competition models account well for this type of attentional effect. They are less clear about the enhancement of responses observed with single receptive field stimuli. In both types of model, baseline shifts are interpreted as top-down signals that sensitize the neuron to the upcoming stimulus. However, whereas baseline shifts in themselves are a well-established finding, their effect on subsequent processing (stimulus-driven firing rates) is unclear. A fourth effect of attention that does not directly concern the firing rates of neurons, synchronization, is also beginning to be incorporated in current models.

Overall, although much progress has been made, no model described so far has succeeded in explaining all the main attentional mechanisms identified in the literature regarding single-cell studies. In the next chapter we present a model that aims to do just that, a model that is essentially a direct interpretation of the central TVA equations at the single-cell level.

7

A neural theory of visual attention (NTVA)

In this chapter we present a theory that applies the computational principles of TVA to attentional effects at the single-cell level: a *neural* theory of visual attention, NTVA. The basic idea of NTVA is that the two selection mechanisms of TVA—pigeonholing and filtering—are directly reflected in the activity of individual neurons: pigeonholing changes the *activity level* of individual neurons that signal particular categorizations, whereas filtering changes the *number of neurons* that respond to particular objects. In combination these two mechanisms control the total activity level in each population of neurons that signals a particular categorization of an object. In competition with other cell populations in the visual system, which support other categorizations, each population's level of activity determines whether the categorization it supports will enter visual short-term memory (VSTM). Encoding into visual short-term memory implies that the activity of the cell population is sustained in a positive feedback loop with functionally central parts of the visual system. This way, changes of activity at the microscopic cellular level add up to produce macroscopic selection effects at the psychological level. NTVA fleshes out these simple ideas by network models showing how the computations can be carried out, while remaining completely consistent with the original TVA equations. In the following we describe each of the elements of NTVA and elaborate on many of the implications and details of the model (for a more condensed and mathematically stringent presentation of NTVA, see the original article by Bundesen *et al.* 2005). In the next chapter we follow up by showing how the model can account for a very large part of the empirical literature.

Section 7.1 presents the basic assumptions of NTVA regarding the representation of information by typical visual neurons: each neuron represents the properties of only one object at a time, it is specialized to signal only one perceptual feature, and the information transmitted by the neuron is represented by its rate of activation. Following these simple assumptions, Section 7.2 shows how the rate equation of TVA can be given a direct interpretation at the single-cell level: perceptual processing is organized in two separate stages (see Section 7.3)—an unselective stage, where attentional weights are computed in accordance with the weight equation, and a selective stage, where different categorizations compete in a race for conscious recognition in accordance with the rate equation. The outcome of the race is determined by the first categorizations capturing slots in a VSTM map of locations, which establishes positive feedback loops that keep the visual representations active beyond the immediate stimulation of the eyes (Section 7.4). The attentional processes described in NTVA can be implemented by a set of simple networks that produce information selection according to the equations of TVA (see Section 7.5). Our analysis of possible implementations suggests an interesting reconceptualization of visual processing (Section 7.6), which leads to a generalization of the rate equation (Section 7.7).

7.1 **Basic assumptions**

NTVA defines the *activation* of a neuron (at a certain point in time), by a stimulus in its receptive field, as the increase in firing rate (spikes per second) above a baseline rate representing the undriven activity of the neuron. If the baseline rate is zero, the activation is just the firing rate.

In NTVA, η values (strengths of sensory evidence) are represented by activations in cortical neurons. In neurons representing η values, the instantaneous rate of firing (i.e. current activation) signals the strength of the sensory evidence that a given object x (the object represented by the neuron) has a certain feature i (the feature represented by the neuron). Each neuron is specialized to represent a specific feature. This assumption relates to a long research tradition that has explored the often remarkably selective response properties of visual neurons (e.g. Hubel and Wiesel 1959, 1962, 1968; Tanaka 1996, 2003; see also Section 6.1). The specialization of the neuron need not be for a simple 'physical' feature, say a particular shade of yellow, but can also be for a 'microfeature' in a representation distributed across several neurons, in line with classical parallel distributed processing (PDP) network models (see Hinton *et al.* 1986; for a 'localist' view on cognitive representation, see also Page 2000). Also, the neuron need not be so sharply tuned to a particular feature that it is unresponsive to other, similar features: its tuning curve can be more or less broad. However, simple or complex, specific or general, the feature selectivity of the neuron cannot be modulated directly by attentional processes. Changes in feature specialization happen only as a result of learning and development, possibly by modification of synaptic connections or other relatively slow physiological mechanisms for memory formation. So, learning and development aside, at different times a given neuron may 'look' at different objects in its receptive field, but it always 'looks' for the same feature in the objects. Note, however, that such fixed specialization is characteristic mainly of neurons in sensory (e.g. visual) regions of the brain. Neurons in the frontal and parietal cortex may exhibit much more flexible responses (cf. the adaptive coding theory of Duncan 2001; see Section 9.3).

Each neuron is regarded as representing the properties of only one object at a time. The object represented by the neuron varies not only with the stimuli in its receptive field but also with the state of attention. If both stimulus objects x and y are present in the receptive field of the neuron, the neuron may represent object x, the neuron may represent object y, or the neuron may represent the pair of objects consisting of x and y as a single unit (a group of objects forming a higher-order object). If x is a target and y a distractor, the neuron tends to represent object x but not object y. The view that a given neuron represents just one object at a time was motivated both by findings such as those of Moran and Desimone (1985) (described in Section 6.3) and by considerations of information transfer: if a neuron represented more than one object at a time, later stages of processing would need a system for disentangling the contribution of each object from the cell's unitary response. This is a complex computational problem and, even in principle, it is not clear how it could be solved. However, if the neuron represents the properties of only one object at a time, its output can be read off directly at the next stage of processing.

A *feature-i neuron* can be defined as a neuron that is specialized for representing feature i. In NTVA, some feature-i neurons signal η values independent of pertinence settings (π values) and perceptual decision biases (β values). Other feature-i neurons receive the η values as input and compute either products of η and π values in accordance with the weight equation of TVA or products of η and β values in accordance with the rate equation.

7.2 Neural interpretation of the rate equation of TVA

According to NTVA, the activation of a visual neuron may depend on three factors: first, the sensory evidence that the object in the neuron's (effective) receptive field has the feature the neuron is specialized for. The stronger the sensory evidence that the object has the feature preferred by the neuron, the higher the firing rate. Of course the 'sensory evidence' depends on the information available to the neuron, which can be degraded if the stimulus has low luminance contrast, if it occurs in a part of the visual field where acuity is weak, or by other conditions external to the observer. Unlike this more objective, sensory factor, the two remaining factors depend on the motivational state of the observer, so they are more subjective and attentional in nature. The second factor that may influence the neuron's activity is the perceptual bias in the visual system for making the categorization the neuron is specialized for. The more the system is primed to make this type of categorization, the more the neuron's firing rate is increased—to *any* stimulus in its receptive field. Thus the perceptual bias amplifies the response of the neuron, whatever the neuron is processing, and increases the likelihood that the observer makes the type of categorization for which the neuron is specialized. The third factor relates to the situation where there are several objects present in the neuron's receptive field, which is practically always the case under natural circumstances for high-level neurons with large receptive fields. The probability that the cell responds to the properties of one object rather than another depends on the general setting of attentional weights: the cell is more likely to respond to an object that has high attentional weights in the visual system as a whole.

Each of these three factors corresponds directly to one of the factors in the rate equation of the original TVA model, and NTVA assumes that they are related in the same way at the neural and psychological levels, namely by simple multiplication:

$$v(x,i) = \eta(x,i)\beta_i \frac{w_x}{\sum\limits_{z \in S} w_z}.$$

Let's take a look at the rate equation from the viewpoint of the nervous system. In the neural interpretation of the rate equation, the v-value on the left-hand side represents the total activation of the population of neurons that represent a particular categorization (namely, 'object x has feature i'). In other words, the v-value equals the summed activation of all those neurons that (1) respond to object x and (2) are specialized to signal feature i. The total activation in this population of neurons determines the probability that the categorization 'x has feature i' will be encoded into visual short-term memory, rather than some other categorization. The populations of neurons described by the v-values are located at a stage of processing where their output directly influences the VSTM system. This will typically be a high-level area in the visual system, such as inferotemporal (IT) or prefrontal cortex (see Sections 7.6 and 7.7 for a more general hypothesis), where cells have very large receptive fields. NTVA assumes that the receptive fields of these neurons simply cover the entire visual field, so the competition at this point essentially corresponds to the selection process of the whole perceptual system. In Sections 7.3 and 7.4 we explain how the race towards VSTM occurs in the nervous system, and how the magnitudes of the v-values are critical in this process.

Turning to the right-hand side of the equation, three factors in combination determine the magnitude of the v value. The first factor, $\eta(x,i)$, equals the total activation when every feature-i neuron represents object x and the perceptual bias for making categorizations of type i is maximal. Both β_i and $w_x \big/ \sum_{z \in S} w_z$ range between 0 and 1 (see below), so when both of these factors are maximal (i.e. 1) for a particular categorization, $\eta(x,i)$ becomes equal to $v(x,i)$. In this way $\eta(x,i)$ represents the upper limit for $v(x,i)$. In turn, the maximum value of $\eta(x,i)$ is constrained by the total number of feature-i neurons in the brain and the physiologically maximal firing rate (ceiling response) for each of these neurons. In general, $\eta(x,i)$ reflects the goodness of the sensory match between the features of object x and the specialization of the feature-i neurons.

The second factor, β_i, represents the perceptual bias for making categorizations of type i. This is a simple scaling factor and following the original TVA theory it ranges between 0 and 1. β_i specifically affects the firing rate of cells that are specialized to signal the presence of feature i, while leaving neurons with other specializations unaffected. The β_i factor multiplies the activation of each feature-i neuron by the same constant regardless of which object the cell is responding to. Thus, the activation of the whole population of feature-i neurons, which do not necessarily process the same object, is scaled up or down in accordance with the value of β_i.

In the typical situation where several objects are present in the visual field, different neurons will be responding to different objects. The third factor of the rate equation, $w_x \big/ \sum_{z \in S} w_z$, represents the probability that a given neuron, at the stage of processing where receptive fields cover the entire visual field, responds to object x rather than other objects. The probability is given directly by the relative attentional weight of the object, as defined in the original TVA theory. As the factor applies to each individual neuron at this stage of processing, the probability effectively determines the proportion of all neurons (i.e. the number) that respond to object x.

When β values for certain categories are altered, the cell populations that signal the corresponding categorizations fire more or less strongly. This affects the probability that certain categorizations rather than others are encoded into VSTM, irrespective of which objects are being processed: pigeonholing. Complementary to this, the value of $w_x \big/ \sum_{z \in S} w_z$ determines the number of neurons that respond to particular objects, regardless of the feature preferences of these neurons: filtering. This way, the rate equation describes the combined effects of filtering and pigeonholing on the high-level visual neurons that directly influence the content of VSTM. In essence, the rate equation reduces to the simple statement that the total activation supporting the perceptual categorization that 'object x has feature i' is directly proportional to the product of (1) the number of feature-i cells representing object x (which is proportional to the relative attentional weight of object x) and (2) the level of activation of the individual feature-i cells representing object x (which is proportional to β_i).

7.3 Unselective and selective waves of processing

In line with the original TVA theory and many other models of attention (e.g. the guided search model), NTVA assumes that visual perception is organized in two separate processing stages. First, a preliminary stage whose primary purpose is to locate potentially interesting objects for further analysis. The information computed from this process is stored in a *priority map* of the visual field and utilized in the second, selective stage of processing. Here, the attentional settings of the system critically influence the activity of each cell, so that the most important objects tend to be processed all the way to conscious recognition, while less important ones remain unconscious. As NTVA conceptualizes the processing, one might use the metaphor of 'two waves of processing' in the sense that the same cortical neurons are engaged successively in two different rounds of information processing.

Immediately after a new visual scene stimulates the eyes (e.g. following a saccade), the cortical system has yet to localize its most interesting parts. In neural terms, this implies that the receptive fields of neurons processing the visual input contract randomly around different locations. With respect to the filtering mechanism, their processing is therefore *unselective* and occurs independently of what is currently important for the observer. However, the neurons still signal information about objects according to their feature selectivity, and this information is used for computing attentional weights. The sensory neurons are assumed to project to a priority map (which may possibly be located in the thalamic pulvinar nucleus, see Section 9.5). Here, the input from all the different sensory neurons is summed up in accordance with the weight equation of TVA,

$$w_x = \sum_{j \in R} \eta\,(x, j)\,\pi_j,$$

and produce differential activations at the different locations of the map, corresponding to specific objects. This way, the priority map comes to represent the combined influence of bottom-up and top-down factors on object relevance. Depending on the complexity of the computation, this process will typically be completed within 100–200 ms.

The rate equation of TVA describes the situation after attentional weights have been computed and applied in the visual system: the *selective* wave of processing. At this point the priority map has been used for remapping the receptive fields of the neurons. As a result, cells are now more likely to respond to objects with high attentional weights, which means that more neurons are allocated to process the features of these objects. So, at this moment a situation exists with millions of cells firing. The firing is organized such that more cells respond to objects with high attentional weights, and the neurons fire more vigorously if they have feature specializations that correspond to the current perceptual bias of the whole visual system (Fig. 7.1). In effect, a state of competition exists between populations of neurons, each of which supports a particular categorization of an object. Sooner or later—in any case, within a fraction of a second—one of these cell populations (most probably one with a large number of highly activated cells) sends off a signal that makes a critical difference: It captures one of the few slots of the VSTM system.

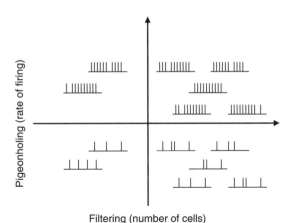

Filtering (number of cells)

Fig. 7.1 Attentional selection in NTVA: combined effects of filtering (selection of objects) and pigeonholing (selection of features) on the set of cortical spike trains representing a particular visual categorization of the form 'object *x* has feature *i*'. The four conditions (quadrants) correspond to the factorial combinations of two levels of filtering (weak versus strong support to object *x*) by two levels of pigeonholing (weak versus strong support to feature *i*). Filtering changes the number of cortical neurons in which an object is represented. Pigeonholing changes the rate of firing of cortical neurons coding for a particular feature. Adapted with permission from Bundesen, Habekost, and Kyllingsbæk (2005). A neural theory of visual attention: bridging cognition and neurophysiology. *Psychological Review*, **112**, 291–328. Copyright 2005 by the American Psychological Association. The use of APA information does not imply endorsement by APA.

7.4 **The VSTM system**

A main purpose of the VSTM system is to keep visual information available for cognitive processing—further perceptual analysis, thinking, or permanent storage—after the immediate sensory stimulation has vanished. In modelling VSTM, NTVA follows a general idea by Hebb (1949), who suggested that short-term memory implies that the activity of neurons representing the selected information is sustained in a positive feedback loop. This way the representation is kept active in a reverberating circuit beyond the duration of the original sensory impression. Hebb's notion of short-term memory has now gained wide popularity in cognitive neuroscience. The feedback mechanism is often assumed to depend on interactions between prefrontal and posterior cortical areas (Goldman-Rakic 1995; Fuster 1997) but thalamo-cortical interaction is also a main candidate; in Section 9.5 we take a closer look at the possible anatomical localization of the VSTM system.

In NTVA the short-term memory mechanism depends on a topographically organized map of the objects in the visual field. The map does not in itself represent the features of the selected objects, but rather functions as a pointer to their locations. Neurons representing features of objects at the pointed-to locations are kept active by reciprocal connections to the corresponding parts of the VSTM map (see Section 7.5 for details of the network architecture). Thus VSTM is constituted by a feedback interaction between sensory neurons and the VSTM map of locations, which makes it possible for visual representations to outlast the original sensory stimulation.

The process of encoding into VSTM starts when the map is initialized (i.e. cleared of previous activity). This is assumed to happen immediately after attentional weights have been computed for a new sensory impression, when the visual system is optimally tuned to select the most relevant information. The selection process functions in a winner-take-all manner, in which the first activated object representations in the VSTM map block later ones from entering. The suggested type of winner-take-all networks are described in detail in Section 7.5, but briefly, all nodes in such a network excite themselves (when triggered) while inhibiting the other nodes. Thus, once a node has been triggered by external stimulation, its activity will sustain itself while inhibiting the other nodes to the point where they cannot be activated by external signals. In the VSTM map the inhibitory connections are configured such that when fewer than K objects are active, an external signal can still overcome the inhibition from the encoded objects. However, when K units are active, external stimulation can no longer activate a new object node ('K-winners-take-all network'). This mechanism explains the limited storage capacity of VSTM, where only K objects can be active at the same time. Note that the limitation applies to the number of objects (or corresponding locations) in the VSTM map, but not to the number of features related to each of the selected objects: Once an object has established itself in VSTM, many categorizations can be attached to it.

What does it take to capture a slot in the VSTM map? It is not currently clear what the effective signal unit is. The simplest possibility is the very first spike from one of the many sensory neurons projecting to the map. If neural processing is viewed as inherently noisy, this may seem like an unreliable mechanism, but there is evidence to suggest that single spikes can have profound effects on cognitive processing (Parker and Newsome 1998). Alternatively, a stronger signal from multiple neurons may be needed, perhaps a volley of at least n synchronized spikes, n being a number substantially greater than one. However the effective signal is defined, NTVA assumes that the VSTM system can be configured so that the first such impulse to the VSTM map activates the winner-take-all network. Together with the assumption that different signals occur independently of one another, this is equivalent to an exponential race model—that is, a model assuming that the selection is determined by a parallel race in which processing times for individual categorizations are mutually independent, exponentially distributed random variables. Of course, this is completely in line with the original TVA model (see Sections 3.3 and 3.4). Suppose the baseline rates of the neurons are negligibly small. If the first spike arriving at a given unit in the VSTM map of objects after the map has been cleared suffices to activate the unit (until K units have been activated), then the processing rate of the categorization that object x has feature i [defined as $v(x, i)$ in TVA] equals the sum of the activations of the neurons that represent this categorization [defined as $v(x, i)$ in NTVA]. If a volley of n or more synchronized spikes are needed for activating a VSTM unit, where $n > 1$, then the observer's rate of making categorizations will be slower but the selection process should still conform to an exponential race model.

The description so far applies to the simple case in which the first categorization arriving in VSTM of a given object is used directly by the cognitive system (*immediate perception*). However, sometimes mutually contradicting categorizations of the same object are encoded into VSTM. For example, this may be the case under poor lighting conditions, where the colour of an object is not obvious: if the η value for 'x is red' is not substantially different from the η value for 'x is yellow', both categorizations may end up in VSTM. In situations like this, decisional procedures are required (*mediate perception*; see Section 3.5.5). Two possible mechanisms for mediate perception have been suggested within the TVA framework, both based on accumulation of evidence: counter procedures and random-walk models. In a counter procedure, a decision is made when one of the categorizations has been repeated (confirmed) a certain number of times. In a random-walk procedure, the decision depends on relative differences between the numbers of alternative categorizations: The "winning" categorization must occur a certain number of times *more* than its closest competitor. These models can both be given a mathematically exact form (see Appendix B of Bundesen *et al.* 2005), but still await conclusive empirical testing.

Representations in VSTM can be relatively concrete and 'pictorial' or relatively abstract, 'schematic', and 'conceptual'. The more concrete and pictorial representations are often named *mental images*. Following Hume (1739/1896), among many others, simple mental images may be regarded as *faint copies* of sense impressions. A suggested implication of this sensory nature is that a mental image specifies the position of the represented object in the visual field, although localization may be less precise than with real sense impressions. Neurophysiologically, mental images should activate a subset of the same neurons that are implicated in the corresponding sensory impressions, but the activity in these neurons should be weaker (hence the 'faintness' of the representation). An observable effect in single-cell activity should be a moderate increase in the firing rate of some neurons when a mental image is positioned in their receptive fields (and no external stimuli are present): a *baseline shift* (cf. Section 6.3).

7.5 Computational networks

In this section we present some simple networks for performing the attentional operations of NTVA. We show how the computations of the networks correspond to the rate and weight equations of TVA, and we hint at where such networks may be localized in the primate brain (hypotheses that are elaborated in Section 9.5). However, NTVA is a fairly general neurophysiological interpretation of TVA, and it does not depend critically on a specific anatomical localization of the proposed operations. The particular networks we present may be regarded as merely proofs of the existence of simple and biologically plausible neural networks implementing the attentional operations of NTVA.

A basic functional element for both dynamic remapping of receptive fields and encoding into VSTM is the winner-take-all network. NTVA uses a simple type proposed by Grossberg (1976, 1980), which is illustrated in Fig. 7.2. As shown in the figure, it consists of a set of units (populations of cells) where each unit excites itself and inhibits all other units in the cluster. When the cluster is initialized (i.e. cleared of previous activity), an external signal of a certain strength is sufficient to trigger one of the units. Once the unit has been triggered, it keeps firing because of its self-excitation. If the other units are inhibited so

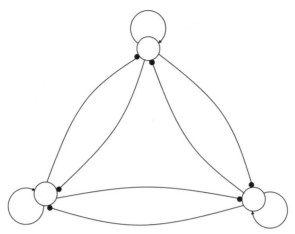

Fig. 7.2 Winner-take-all network with three units. Excitatory connections are shown by arrows. Inhibitory connections are shown by lines ending in solid circles. Adapted with permission from Bundesen, Habekost, and Kyllingsbæk (2005). A neural theory of visual attention: bridging cognition and neurophysiology. *Psychological Review*, **112**, 291–328. Copyright 2005 by the American Psychological Association. The use of APA information does not imply endorsement by APA.

strongly by the unit's activity that they can no longer be activated by external signals, one can read from the state of the cluster which of the units received the first above-threshold trigger signal after the cluster was initialized. In this way, the cluster can serve as a device for recording the winner of a race.

Using the Grossberg winner-take-all network as a building block, dynamic remapping of receptive fields can be carried out in a simple hierarchical network. In this network, processing capacity (neurons) can be distributed among stimuli by opening and closing of gates that control communication from lower to higher levels in the system. The gates can be controlled by attentional weight signals, such that the expected number of cells that represent a particular object at the highest level of the visual system (which projects to VSTM) becomes proportional to the relative attentional weight of the object. The hierarchical network is shown in Fig. 7.3. Three processing levels are shown (named V2/V3, V4, and IT), with gates between the levels. Figure 7.4 shows one of these gates in close-up. It consists of a winner-take-all cluster of units (one unit for each line through the gate), logical AND units (one on each line through the gate) and a logical OR unit (which collects information from the AND units). The winner-take-all cluster records the first occurring signal to one of the two units in the cluster. Thus, if the upper unit receives a signal before the lower unit does, the upper unit will be excited, the lower unit will be inhibited, and only the upper line through the gate will be open. External signals to units

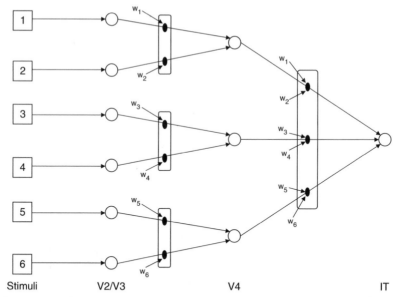

Fig. 7.3 Hierarchic network with processing units at three levels: V2/V3, V4, and IT. Each V2/V3 unit has one stimulus in its classical receptive field, each V4 unit has two stimuli in its classical receptive field, and the IT unit has all of the six stimuli in its classical receptive field. By attentional gating, the effective receptive fields of V4 and IT units are contracted so that each of the effective receptive fields contains only one object: the symbol ⦂ stands for a gate which is open on only the upper or the lower line, and ⦂ stands for a gate which is open on only one of the three lines. The gates are set by competing attentional weight signals. For $i = 1, \ldots, 6$, w_i is the attentional weight of Stimulus i. Adapted with permission from Bundesen, Habekost, and Kyllingsbæk (2005). A neural theory of visual attention: bridging cognition and neurophysiology. *Psychological Review*, **112**, 291–328. Copyright 2005 by the American Psychological Association. The use of APA information does not imply endorsement by APA.

in the winner-take-all clusters come from the priority map and represent attentional weights at particular locations. As indicated in Fig. 7.3, a winner-take-all cluster that gates responses from cells at a lower level to a cell at a higher level receives one attentional weight signal for every object within the classical receptive field of the higher level cell. Attentional weight signals for objects within the receptive field of the lower-level cell go to that unit in the winner-take-all cluster that supports communication from the lower-level cell to the higher-level cell. Attentional weight signals for objects outside the receptive field of the lower-level cell (but within the receptive field of the higher-level cell) go to other, competing units in the winner-take-all cluster. As shown in Box 7.1, this network can perform selection according to the TVA equations.

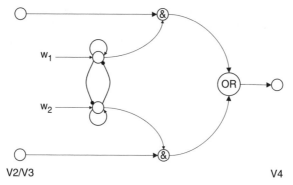

Fig. 7.4 Close-up of the uppermost gate in Fig. 7.3. The gate consists of a winner-take-all network with two units (each controlling one of the two lines through the gate), a logical AND (&) unit on each line, and a logical OR unit transmitting information from either AND unit. For $i = 1, 2$, w_i is the attentional weight of Stimulus i. The signal representing the weight of a given stimulus comes from the representation of the stimulus in a topographic priority map. Adapted with permission from Bundesen, Habekost, and Kyllingsbæk (2005). A neural theory of visual attention: bridging cognition and neurophysiology. *Psychological Review*, **112**, 291–328. Copyright 2005 by the American Psychological Association. The use of APA information does not imply endorsement by APA.

Box 7.1 Selection of objects in NTVA

Consider the probability that the receptive field of the IT unit in the network described contracts around Object 1 rather around one of the other objects. This equals the probability that both the upper one of the gates from V2/V3 to V4 and the gate from V4 to IT open on their upper lines. To estimate the probability, we make some simple assumptions. Let arrival times of attentional weight signals for an object x be exponentially distributed with a rate parameter equal to the attentional weight of x, w_x. Let attentional weight signals for different objects be stochastically independent. Finally, let attentional weight signals that represent the same object x but go to different gates be stochastically independent. On these assumptions, the probability that the upper of the gates from V2/V3 to V4 opens on its upper line is $w_1/(w_1 + w_2)$. The probability that the gate from V4 to IT opens on its upper line is $(w_1 + w_2)/\Sigma w_i$, where the summation extends over Objects 1–6. The probability of both events equals the product of the two probabilities, which is $w_1/\Sigma w_i$. Next, consider a population of IT units, each of which is similar to the one we have considered so far. Each unit has Objects 1–6 and no other objects within its classical receptive field. If there

> **Box 7.1 Selection of objects in NTVA** *(continued)*
>
> are N units in the population, the expected number of IT units representing Object 1 equals $Nw_1/\Sigma w_i$, the expected number of IT units representing Object 2 equals $Nw_2/\Sigma w_i$, and so on. In general, the expected number of IT units representing a particular object should be proportional to the relative attentional weight of the object. In this way, the network converts activity representing attentional weights in the priority map into number of IT cells working on the corresponding objects.

An essential property of both the priority map and the VSTM map is precision in spatial representation. Apart from passing on reliable information to motor processes, for example, this is critical for allocating categorizations to the right objects ('keeping things separate'). Spatial precision presents a challenge, because exact location information seems to be lost in higher-level neurons with very large receptive fields. However, dynamic remapping of receptive fields of high-level neurons should dramatically increase their spatial resolution. In the network model outlined above, the effective receptive field of an IT neuron is coded by the way that the gates in the network are set. The code formed by the gate settings can be used for directing signals from an IT cell, whose effective receptive field is contracted around an object at a particular location, to a unit (a neuron or a population of neurons) representing the object at the selected location. In particular, the code formed by the gate settings can be used for directing signals to the place in a topographic map (such as the priority or VSTM maps) that corresponds to the location of the stimulus object. A simple network for this operation is shown in Fig. 7.5.

Consider a cell in a winner-take-all cluster in one of the gates on the left-hand side of the figure. The cell has an excitatory connection to an AND unit on a particular input line on the route to the IT unit. The cell also has an excitatory connection to an AND unit on a corresponding output line from the IT unit to a topographic map of objects. By this arrangement, the pattern of open and closed lines on the left-hand side of the figure is duplicated on the right-hand side of the figure. As a result, signals from the IT unit are directed to an appropriate place in the topographic map of objects. In the depicted state of the network, the effective receptive field of the IT unit equals the receptive field of the upper V2/V3 unit, and output from the IT unit is directed to a place in the topographic map of objects that corresponds to this location.

The topographic map of objects may be located at a high level of the visual system such as the prefrontal cortex. In this particular case, the dashed lines in

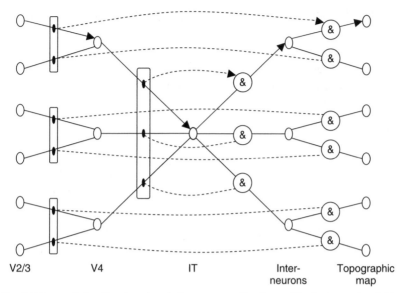

V2/3   V4   IT   Inter-   Topographic
neurons   map

Fig. 7.5 Network for directing signals from an IT cell, whose effective receptive field is contracted around an object at a particular location, to a unit representing the object at the given location in a topographic map. The network on the left-hand side of the figure is similar to the network in Fig. 7.3, but each cell in a winner-take-all cluster in one of the gates on the left-hand side of the figure controls not only an input line on the route to the IT unit but also a corresponding output line from the IT unit to the topographic map. In the depicted state of the network, the effective receptive field of the IT unit equals the receptive field of the upper V2/V3 unit, and output from the IT unit is directed to a place in the topographic map of objects that corresponds to the receptive field of the upper V2/V3 unit. Adapted with permission from Bundesen, Habekost, and Kyllingsbæk (2005). A neural theory of visual attention: bridging cognition and neurophysiology. *Psychological Review*, **112**, 291–328. Copyright 2005 by the American Psychological Association. The use of APA information does not imply endorsement by APA.

Fig. 7.5 symbolize long-ranging connections from cells in gates controlling the flow of information from the retina to the IT (gates on the left-hand side of the figure) to cells controlling the flow of information from IT to the pre-frontal cortex (AND units on the right-hand side of the figure). However, as proposed in Section 9.5, another possibility is that the topographic map is found at a low level of the visual system such as the thalamus. By this hypothesis, the right-hand side of Fig. 7.5 depicts a flow of information from the IT unit back towards the retina: a gate and an AND unit connected by a dashed line are located at the same level of the visual system, and the connections symbolized by the dashed lines are quite short. The hypothesis is illustrated in

Fig. 7.6, which shows a gate in close-up. The figure is an extension of Fig. 7.4, and the dashed lines correspond to dashed lines in Fig. 7.5. The figure illustrates how the same gates routing information from a particular location on the retina to a certain cell at a higher level of the visual system can be used for routing information back from the high-level cell to a corresponding place in a map of objects found at a low level of the visual system.

Visual pathways are generally found in pairs so that a pathway from area A to area B is accompanied by a pathway from B to A (see, for example, Zeki 1993). From an engineering point of view, it seems easy to design the visual system so that the two pathways in a pair open and close at the same time (bidirectional opening and closing). Thus, from an engineering point of view,

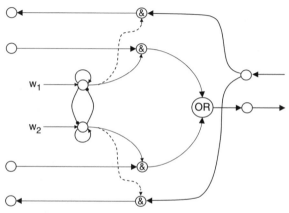

Fig. 7.6 Close-up of the uppermost gate in Fig. 7.5. The figure is an extension of Fig. 7.4, and the dashed lines correspond to dashed lines in Fig. 7.5. The figure illustrates how the same gates routing signals along a particular pathway from lower-level to higher-level cells in the visual system can be used for routing signals along a parallel pathway in the opposite direction. The gate is bistable. In one state, both upper lines through the gate are open and both lower lines are closed; in the other state, both lower lines are open and both upper lines are closed. When the upper lines are open, signals are directed from the retinal location corresponding to the pair of cells in the upper left-hand corner through the ascending pathway originating in the lower member of the rightmost pair of cells. In this state, signals arriving through the descending pathway to the upper member of the rightmost pair of cells are directed back towards the retinal location corresponding to the pair of cells in the upper left-hand corner rather than the retinal location corresponding to the pair of cells in the lower left-hand corner. Adapted with permission from Bundesen, Habekost, and Kyllingsbæk (2005). A neural theory of visual attention: bridging cognition and neurophysiology. *Psychological Review*, **112**, 291–328. Copyright 2005 by the American Psychological Association. The use of APA information does not imply endorsement by APA.

it seems simple to design the system so that information about an object at a particular location in the visual field is processed at high levels of the visual system, but routed back to the right place in a topographic map of objects at a low level of the system (cf. Schneider 1995). Evolution may have chosen this simple solution.

NTVA also provides network models of the two topographic maps: the priority map and the VSTM map. A possible implementation of the priority map is illustrated in Fig. 7.7. Computation of attentional weights occurs at many different levels of the cortical visual system, perhaps all the way from primary visual cortex (V1) up to IT cortex. The network in Fig. 7.7 computes attentional weights by summing up input (activations measured in spikes per second) to a unit (a neuron or a population of neurons) in a topographically organized priority map (tentatively located in the pulvinar nucleus). The input is generated by cortical units specialized to represent different features, based on visual signals from the lateral geniculate nucleus (LGN). Each input to the unit for

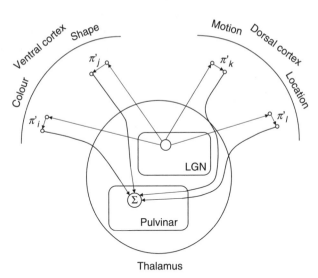

Fig. 7.7 Network for computing attentional weights. Signals from the lateral genicu-late nucleus (LGN) are transmitted to striate and extrastriate cortical areas where η values (strengths of evidence that objects at particular scales and positions have particular features) are computed. The η values are multiplied by π (pertinence) values, and the products are transmitted from the cortex to the pulvinar nucleus of the thal-amus, where the products are summed up as attentional weights of the stimulus objects. Adapted with permission from Bundesen, Habekost, and Kyllingsbæk (2005). A neural theory of visual attention: bridging cognition and neurophysiology. *Psychological Review*, **112**, 291–328. Copyright 2005 by the American Psychological Association. The use of APA information does not imply endorsement by APA.

object x in the priority map is a product of a level of activation of a cortical neuron representing the strength of the sensory evidence that x has some feature, j, and a pertinence factor, π'_j. The products are summed up for each object location in the priority map to produce a topographic distribution of attentional weights, according to the weight equation (for mathematical details, see Appendix A of Bundesen *et al.* 2005).

Following the idea of Hebb (1949), a visual categorization should be encoded in VSTM if (and only if) the categorization is embedded in a positive feedback loop gated by a unit in the VSTM map of objects. Two feedback loops of this type are illustrated in Fig. 7.8. As shown in the figure, impulses routed to a unit that represents an object at a certain location in the topographic VSTM map of objects are fed back to the feature units from which they originated, provided that the VSTM unit is activated. If the VSTM unit is inactive, impulses to the unit are not fed back. Thus, for each feature-i neuron representing object x, activation of the neuron is sustained by feedback when the unit representing object x in the topographic VSTM map of objects is activated.

Figure 7.9 shows how the circuits illustrated in Fig. 7.8 might be implemented as thalamo-cortical feedback loops. In Fig. 7.9, feature i is a shape feature of an object x, and feature j is a motion feature of the same object x. Feature-i neurons

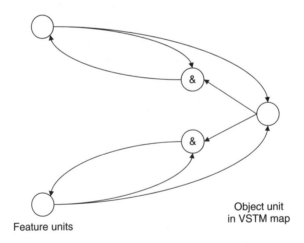

Feature units

Object unit
in VSTM map

Fig. 7.8 Two feedback loops gated by the same unit in the VSTM map of objects. Activation of either feature unit is sustained by positive feedback if, and only if, the object unit is activated. Adapted with permission from Bundesen, Habekost, and Kyllingsbæk (2005). A neural theory of visual attention: bridging cognition and neurophysiology. *Psychological Review*, **112**, 291–328. Copyright 2005 by the American Psychological Association. The use of APA information does not imply endorsement by APA.

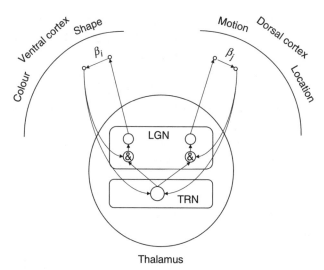

Thalamus

Fig. 7.9 Possible implementation of the circuits illustrated in Fig. 7.8 as thalamo-cortical feedback loops. The feature units are located in different cortical areas, where η values (strengths of evidence that objects at particular scales and positions have particular features) are computed. The η values are multiplied by β (bias) values and the products are projected back to the thalamus as rates of activation. The VSTM map of objects is located in the thalamic reticular nucleus (TRN), which lies like a thin shield between the thalamus and the cortex. When the VSTM map is initialized, objects in the visual field effectively start a race to become encoded into VSTM. In this race, each object is represented by all possible categorizations of the object, and each possible categorization participates with a firing rate (v value) proportional to the product of the corresponding η and β (bias) values. For the winners of the race, the TRN gates activation representing a particular categorization back to some of those cells in LGN whose activation supported the categorization. Thus activity in neurons representing winners of the race is sustained by positive feedback. Adapted with permission from Bundesen, Habekost, and Kyllingsbæk (2005). A neural theory of visual attention: bridging cognition and neurophysiology. *Psychological Review*, **112**, 291–328. Copyright 2005 by the American Psychological Association. The use of APA information does not imply endorsement by APA.

are found in a high-level cortical area in the ventral stream of visual process-ing (see Ungerleider and Mishkin 1982; Milner and Goodale 1995), where their rates of activation are modulated by multiplication with the perceptual decision bias β_i. Feature-j neurons are found in a high-level cortical area in the dorsal stream of visual processing (cf. Ungerleider and Mishkin 1982; Milner and Goodale 1995), where their rates of activation are modulated by multipli-cation with the perceptual decision bias β_j. The rates of activation of both the feature-i and the feature-j neurons allocated to object x are projected back to the thalamus. The top-down impulses representing the categorization that 'object x has feature i' are routed to some of those cells in the LGN whose bottom-up activation supported this categorization, and the top-down impulses representing the categorization that 'object x has feature j' are routed to some of those cells in the LGN whose bottom-up activation supported that categorization. In either case, the feedback occurs through an AND unit, which is located tentatively in the LGN near the cells that are targeted by the feedback. To make the feedback effective, the AND gates must be open, which means that the AND units must receive input from a unit representing object x in the topographic VSTM map of objects found in the thalamic reticular nucleus (TRN). Effectively, the feedback loops with information about features of object x are complete if the TRN unit representing object x in the VSTM map of objects is active. An obvious way of activating the TRN unit is illustrated in the figure: both impulses representing the categorization that 'object x has feature i' and impulses representing the categorization that 'object x has feature j' are projected back, not only whence they came in the LGN, but also to the unit representing object x in the TRN. If, for any reason, the TRN unit representing object x is and remains inactive, impulses from the cortex representing object x are not transmitted beyond the AND units in the LGN.

7.6 A new perspective on visual processing

The rate equation of TVA applies to processing at a cortical level where objects compete for entrance into VSTM. To explain the rate equation, we have assumed that at the cortical level where objects compete for entrance into VSTM, the classical receptive fields of neurons are so large that each one covers the entire visual field (cf. Section 7.2). Now, consider the possibility that not only information represented by neurons with large receptive fields but also information represented by neurons with small receptive fields may become encoded in VSTM—say, the possibility that both neurons with large and neurons with small receptive fields may become embedded in positive feedback loops gated by units in the VSTM map. This possibility suggests an interesting reconceptualization of visual processing.

The suggested reconceptualization is illustrated in Fig. 7.10. As in the more traditional view presented in Chapter 3 on the original TVA model (see Section 3.5), visual processing of stimulus objects begins with registration of retinal images, and the initial, sensory processing consists in extraction of low-level, 'sensory' features. The later, perceptual processing consists of: (1) extraction of higher-level, 'conceptual' features; and (2) representation of objects by feature binding. The binding includes both sensory and conceptual features

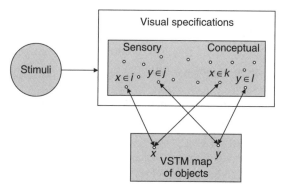

Fig. 7.10 Revised conceptualization of visual processing. Sensory processing is extraction of sensory features (e.g. 'x is red'). This is followed by perceptual processing, which is (1) extraction of conceptual features (e.g. 'x is a car') and (2) representation of objects by feature binding (e.g. binding of sensory and conceptual features). Both visual recognition and attentional selection consist of making visual specifications of the form 'x belongs to *i*'. A (sensory or conceptual) visual specification is *made* if and when it enters VSTM. When a sensory specification enters VSTM, it becomes represented as a *mental image*. When a conceptual specification enters VSTM, it becomes represented as a *perceptual identification*. However, the demarcation between sensory and conceptual features may not be sharp.

and, in particular, binding of both sensory and conceptual features to the same object-representing units (nodes) in VSTM. Specifically, encoding of the specification 'object x has sensory feature i' into VSTM consists of forming a bond (in NTVA, a positive feedback loop) between a sensory cortical unit representing the sensory specification and a unit in VSTM representing object x. Encoding of the specification 'object x has conceptual feature k' into VSTM consists of forming a bond (a positive feedback loop) between the same VSTM unit representing object x and a cortical unit representing the conceptual specification. If and when both the sensory and the conceptual specifications are bound to the same object unit in VSTM, then sensory feature i and conceptual feature k are indirectly bound to each other: VSTM contains a representation of object x as an object with both the sensory and the conceptual feature.

As before, both explicit visual recognition and attentional selection consist in making visual categorizations of the form 'object x has feature i'. Also as before, a visual categorization is said to be *made* when the categorization is encoded into VSTM. Some visual categorizations are low-level, 'raw sensory' specifications, others are high-level, 'conceptual' specifications, and still others are intermediate. When a low-level, sensory specification enters VSTM, it becomes represented as a *mental image* (a relatively concrete, pictorial representation). When a high-level, conceptual specification enters VSTM, it becomes represented as a *perceptual identification* (a more abstract, conceptual representation). As illustrated in Fig. 7.10, there is no sharp boundary between sensory and conceptual specifications; rather, a continuum from very concrete to very abstract visual representations.

In the conceptualization of Bundesen (1990), a visual impression of a stimulus must be formed, and the stimulus must be segregated as a separate perceptual unit, x, before $\eta\,(x, i)$ can be computed (by comparing the visual impression of x with a template for category i). In the suggested new conceptualization, $\eta\,(x, i)$ can be computed not only for a real object x but also for a *potential object x* specified by a spatial location (an extended part of space that may be occupied by a real object). In this view, computation of $\eta\,(x, i)$ presupposes neither that x has been segregated as a separate perceptual unit, nor that a visual impression of x has been formed. On the contrary, the initial extraction of sensory features from a newly presented display consists in computation of η values for all possible sensory features of potential objects at a huge set of spatial locations. The visual impression of the display is defined by these sensory η values, and the visual categorizations supported by the η values may eventually become encoded into VSTM. As before, attentional selection is determined by a processing race among (potential) objects to become encoded into VSTM. The race is started whenever VSTM is initialized, and both sensory and conceptual specifications take part in the race. An element is encoded in VSTM when any visual categorization of the element is encoded in VSTM, so each potential object x is represented in the race by a comprehensive set of possible visual categorizations. In general, however, η values for visual categorizations of real objects will be higher than η values for categorizations of unreal things, so real objects will tend to win the race and become encoded into VSTM.

7.7 Generalization of the rate equation

The revised conceptualization of visual processing requires revision of the rate equation of TVA. The rate equation specifies the rate of processing at a cortical level where objects compete for entrance into VSTM. The traditional rate equation (Equation 3.8) presupposes that, at this level of processing, the classical receptive fields of neurons are so large that each one covers the entire visual field. We generalize the rate equation by lifting this constraint (see Box 7.2). The generalized rate equation (equation 7.1) should hold for neurons with all possible receptive field sizes. It reduces to the rate equation of TVA for neurons with sufficiently large receptive fields.

Box 7.2 A generalized rate equation

Consider the set of all those feature-i neurons that (1) are modulated by the perceptual decision bias β_i and (2) contain object x in their classical receptive fields. Let the neurons in the set be numbered from 1 up to $c(x, i)$, let $n_k(x, i)$ be the kth neuron in the set ($1 \leq k \leq c[x, i]$), and let $\eta_k(x, i)$ be the activation of neuron $n_k(x, i)$ when the neuron represents object x (i.e. the effective receptive field is contracted around x) and the perceptual decision bias in favour of feature i is maximal. The activation of $n_k(x, i)$ equals $\eta_k(x, i)\beta_i$ when the neuron represents object x and the featural bias in favour of i equals β_i.

The total activation of the population of neurons that represent the categorization that 'object x has feature i' equals the sum of the activations of those feature-i neurons that represent object x. The contribution to this sum from neuron $n_k(x, i)$ (the kth of those feature-i neurons in whose classical receptive fields object x is present) equals $\eta_k(x, i)\beta_i$ if the neuron represents object x, but 0 if the neuron represents any other object. The probability that $n_k(x, i)$ represents object x equals the attentional weight of object x divided by the sum of the attentional weights of all those objects that are present in the classical receptive field of neuron $n_k(x, i)$, that is,

$$\frac{w_x}{\sum\limits_{z \in RF[n_k(x,i)]} w_z},$$

where $RF[n_k(x, i)]$ is the set of objects within the receptive field of neuron $n_k(x, i)$. Accordingly, the expected contribution from neuron $n_k(x, i)$ to the sum of the activations of those feature-i neurons that represent object x equals

$$\eta_k(x,i)\beta_i \frac{w_x}{\sum\limits_{z \in RF[n_k(x,i)]} w_z}.$$

Hence, the expected value of the sum, $v(x, i)$, is given by

$$v(x,i) = \sum_{k=1}^{c(x,i)} \eta_k(x,i)\beta_i \frac{w_x}{\sum\limits_{z \in RF[n_k(x,i)]} w_z}, \qquad (7.1)$$

where the outer summation covers the set of all those feature-i neurons in whose classical receptive fields object x is present, whereas the inner

A generalized rate equation *(continued)*

summation covers the attentional weights of all objects within the receptive field of the kth of those feature-i neurons across which the outer summation runs.

Equation 7.1 is a generalization of the rate equation of TVA. In the special case in which the receptive field of every feature-i neuron covers the whole visual field, the number of feature-i neurons containing x in their classical receptive fields, $c(x, i)$, becomes identical to the total number of feature-i neurons, $c(i)$, and the set of objects within the receptive field of neuron $n_k(x, i)$ (i.e. $RF[n_k(x, i)]$) becomes identical to the set of all objects in the visual field (S), so equation 7.1 reduces to

$$v(x,i) = \sum_{k=1}^{c(i)} n_k(x,i)\beta_i \frac{w_x}{\sum_{z \in S} w_z}. \tag{7.2}$$

By defining

$$\eta(x,i) = \sum_{k=1}^{c(i)} n_k(x,i),$$

equation 7.2 reduces to the rate equation of TVA. Thus, the generalized rate equation reduces to the rate equation of TVA for feature-i neurons with sufficiently large receptive fields.

7.8 Summary

In this chapter we have presented an interpretation of TVA at the single-cell level, the NTVA model. NTVA makes a number of simple assumptions about how typical neurons in the visual system represent information: each neuron represents the properties of only one object at a time, it is specialized to signal only one perceptual feature, and the information transmitted by the neuron is represented by its rate of activation. Following these simple assumptions, the rate equation of TVA can be given a direct interpretation at the single-cell level: the rate of processing for a particular visual categorization depends on the total activation of all neurons that support the categorization. This activation depends on three factors, which are related by simple multiplication: (1) the sensory evidence that the object has the feature in question; (2) the general bias in the visual system for making this type of categorization; and (3) the relative attentional weight of the object. Factors 2 and 3 can be manipulated by the subject. At the neurophysiological level, the general perceptual bias is set by multiplying (up- or down-scaling) the activation of each cell that signals a particular categorization (pigeonholing). Conversely, the attentional weight of a particular object corresponds to the number of neurons responding to the object (filtering). This way, pigeonholing changes the *activation* of neurons that signal particular categorizations, whereas filtering changes the *number* of neurons that respond to particular objects. This simple hypothesis is at the heart of NTVA.

In NTVA, perceptual processing is typically organized in two separate stages: an unselective stage where attentional weights are computed and stored in a priority map (according to the weight equation), and a selective stage where different categorizations compete in a race for conscious recognition (according to the rate equation). The outcome of the race is determined by the first categorizations capturing slots in a VSTM map of locations, which establishes reverberating circuits that keep the visual representations active beyond the immediate stimulation of the eyes.

We have presented a set of neural networks and shown how the computations of the networks implement the attentional operations described in the rate and weight equations of TVA. We have also suggested possible anatomical locations for central parts of the networks (in particular, the priority map and the VSTM map); these suggestions are developed further in Section 9.5. However, NTVA is a fairly general neurophysiological interpretation of TVA, and it does not depend critically on a particular anatomical localization of the proposed operations. The networks we have presented may be regarded merely as proofs of the existence of simple and biologically plausible neural networks implementing the attentional operations of NTVA. In Chapter 8 we show how NTVA accounts for empirical findings across the single-cell attention literature.

8

Explaining attentional effects in single neurons by NTVA

The neural theory of visual attention (NTVA) interprets attentional selection at the level of individual neurons. The interpretation was suggested by studies of single-cell activity in monkeys, and in the following we show how NTVA accounts for a very large part of the findings in this field. Since the original presentation of the model by Bundesen *et al.* (2005) important new studies have been published and these are considered along with the older studies. The empirical review in this chapter includes more than 20 central studies and covers all major effects reported in the single-cell attention literature. To illustrate the precision of NTVA we present detailed mathematical fits to a few studies. For the remaining studies we give more general accounts of all key findings.

As described in Chapter 6, neurophysiological research has revealed several distinct types of attentional effects in single cells. By far the strongest changes of a cell's firing rate can occur when multiple objects are present in the classical receptive field. Under these conditions a general finding is that attention to one of the objects modulates the firing rate either up or down, depending on the cell's preference for the attended object. As described in Section 8.1, this effect is readily explained by NTVA's concept of filtering based on attentional weights. A second frequently observed effect of attention is a modest change in firing rates with a single stimulus in the receptive field. In Section 8.2 this finding is explained by the pigeonholing mechanism or by the presence in the receptive field of stimuli other than the one defined by the experimenter: even though an experiment is designed to include only one stimulus in the receptive field, the cell may still respond to only a part of the experimental stimulus or to internally generated random noise. In both cases attentional weighting effects are potentially important. A third common effect of attention is an increase in a cell's baseline firing rate when a target object is expected to appear in its receptive field. In Section 8.3 we explain this *baseline shift* as the neural correlate of encoding a representation of the anticipated stimulus in visual short-term memory (VSTM). Finally, in Section 8.4 we show how

NTVA accounts for findings that attention can lead to increased synchronization of neural activity: Attention increases synchronization between neurons with the attended object in their receptive fields by increasing the likelihood that the neurons are driven by (i.e. take their inputs from) the same cells.

8.1 Attentional effects with multiple stimuli in the receptive field

If multiple stimuli are presented at the same time within the receptive field of a cell, NTVA assumes that the firing rate of the cell is determined by just one of the stimuli. The probability that the cell's receptive field effectively becomes adjusted to a particular stimulus depends on the activation pattern of the central priority map of attentional weights. If the subject is precued about which location to attend, the priority map can be configured before stimulus exposure (see Section 8.1.1). In this case, selective processing of targets may be seen briefly after the presentation of the stimuli. On the other hand, if the subject is precued about target-defining features but not the location of the target, a substantial period of time occurs after the stimulus has been presented before the priority map is appropriately configured. In this case, unselective responses typically proceed until 150–200 ms after display onset; a clear demonstration of the first wave of processing in NTVA (see Section 8.1.2). Further, by the weight equation of the theory of visual attention (TVA), the attentional weight of an object depends jointly on strengths of sensory evidence and pertinence settings. The dependence on strengths of sensory evidence explains why the probability that a cell responds to a particular object changes systematically with the luminance contrast of the stimulus (see Section 8.1.3).

8.1.1 Filtering by location

In typical single-cell experiments that require filtering by location the monkey is given a cue prior to presentation of the stimulus that directs attention to one location among several possible. To measure the effect of directing attention to one object in the receptive field rather than the other, stimuli are chosen so that they elicit clearly different firing rates from the neuron when shown in isolation (effective versus ineffective stimuli). In the studies reviewed in this section, the monkey's task was either (1) to encode, retain and compare stimuli appearing at the cued location (match-to-sample; Moran and Desimone 1985) or (2) to monitor a rapid sequence of displays for the appearance of a target at the cued location (Luck *et al.* 1997; Reynolds *et al.* 1999). The findings from the two experimental paradigms are similar.

8.1.1.1 Moran and Desimone (1985)

NTVA's concept of attentional filtering was originally inspired by a study of Moran and Desimone (1985). As mentioned in Section 6.3, Moran and Desimone presented macaque monkeys with stimuli at two locations. The monkeys were trained to attend only to stimuli presented at one of the locations in the display and to ignore stimuli shown at the other location. The monkeys performed a match-to-sample task in which they encoded a sample stimulus that was shown at the attended location, memorized it during a brief delay period, and then matched it to a test stimulus shown at the same location (cf. Fig. 6.3). During the presentation of both the sample and test displays, Moran and Desimone recorded the responses of single neurons to the stimuli. In visual areas V4 and IT they found that, when the target and distractor stimuli were both within the receptive field of a cell, the rate of firing in the cell showed little effect of the distractor. For example, Moran and Desimone recorded the response of a cell to a pair of stimuli consisting of (1) an object that elicited a high rate of firing in the cell when it was presented alone (i.e. an effective sensory stimulus) and (2) an object that had little or no effect on the rate of firing in the cell when it was presented alone (i.e. an ineffective sensory stimulus). On trials in which the effective sensory stimulus was the target and the ineffective sensory stimulus was the distractor, the cell showed a high rate of firing. However, on trials in which the ineffective sensory stimulus was the target and the effective sensory stimulus was a distractor, the cell showed a low rate of firing. Moran and Desimone remarked that the typical cell responded 'as if the receptive field had contracted around the attended stimulus' (Moran and Desimone 1985, p. 783).

The effect only occurred when both the target and the distractor objects were located within the recorded neuron's receptive field. In IT the receptive fields were very large, covering at least the central 12° of both the left and right visual fields. For these neurons both of the displayed stimuli were always located inside the receptive field. On the contrary, in V1 only one stimulus could be fitted into each neuron's small receptive field. In this case no significant effects of attention were found. Also, for cells in V4 no effect of attention was found when only a single stimulus was placed in the receptive field. These negative findings fit nicely with the predictions of NTVA: if the cell can respond to no more than one stimulus, the only effect of attention should occur when pigeonholing is varied (or if the experimental stimulus is faint or complex, see Section 8.2), which was not the case in the study of Moran and Desimone (1985). Overall, the results of this study clearly support NTVA's notion of filtering; no wonder, because they suggested the interpretation in the first place. The filtering effect was replicated by Luck *et al.* (1997)

(see Section 8.3.3), who displayed two stimuli within the receptive field of V4 neurons. Similar to the findings of Moran and Desimone, the typical neuron tended to respond to the stimulus at the attended location while being relatively unaffected by the distractor stimulus. Extending the findings of Moran and Desimone,, Luck *et al.* also showed the effect in V2 neurons that had receptive fields large enough to include two stimuli at the same time.

Whereas the studies of Moran and Desimone (1985) and Luck *et al.* (1997) demonstrate the existence of an attentional filtering mechanism with more than one stimulus present within the receptive field, the reported data do not allow for testing of a specific hypothesis about the effect: NTVA predicts that the average response to a pair of stimuli within the receptive field is given by a weighted average of the responses to each of the stimuli presented alone. The next study in our review supplies the required information to test this hypothesis.

8.1.1.2 Reynolds *et al.* (1999)

Reynolds *et al.* (1999) recorded from neurons in visual areas V2 and V4. In their first experiment they characterized the response to a pair of stimuli in the receptive field when attention was not involved (i.e. the monkey was trained to fixate a point outside the receptive field passively). In each trial of this experiment, the stimuli were drawn randomly from a set of 16 bar stimuli that covered a range of selectivity from ineffective to effective stimuli. The stimuli could appear at two different locations in the receptive field. In each recording session, a *reference* stimulus was chosen to be shown at one of the locations. In one condition of the experiment, the reference stimulus was shown by itself. In another condition, the reference stimulus was accompanied by one of the 16 bar stimuli (a *probe*) at the second location. In the third condition of the experiment, the probe stimulus was shown in isolation. Reynolds *et al.* systematically varied the combinations of reference and probe stimuli. The results showed that the mean firing rate of a cell to a pair of stimuli in the receptive field was approximately equal to a weighted average of the firing rates to each of the stimuli in the pair when presented alone. For example, for one cell tested with the 16 different probes, the pair response equalled approximately 67% of the response to the (isolated) probe plus 33% of the response to the (isolated) reference stimulus.

In their second experiment, Reynolds *et al.* studied how attention to one of the objects in a pair influenced this basic pattern of responses. The monkey's task was now to monitor a target location in a rapid sequence of displays and react when a diamond-shaped object appeared (see Fig. 8.1). Stimuli could also appear at other locations, but this was irrelevant to the task. Before the

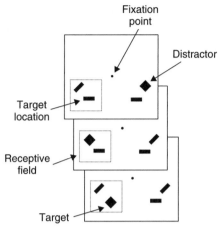

Fig. 8.1 Structure of a trial in Experiment 2 of Reynolds *et al.* (1999). The monkey's task was to monitor a target location in a sequence of displays, responding when a diamond-shaped target object was shown. In the illustrated trial, the target location was the lower one of the two possible locations inside the receptive field (dotted square) of the recorded neuron. Stimuli appearing at other locations should be ignored. Before the target appeared, the monkey was presented with one to six brief displays, each of which contained one or two distractors in the receptive field. Adapted with permission from Reynolds, Chelazzi and Desimone (1999). Competitive mechanisms subserve attention in macaque areas V2 and V4. *Journal of Neuroscience,* **19**, 1738. Copyright 1999 by the Society for Neuroscience.

target appeared, the monkey was presented with 1–6 displays, each of which contained either one or two objects in the receptive field. The objects were drawn from the same set of oriented bars that was used in the first experiment and were also arranged in terms of reference and probe stimuli. The responses to these stimuli, not the response to the less frequent target displays, formed the basis of the analysis.

The stimuli could appear at four different locations: two within the receptive field and two outside. In the *attend-away* condition of the experiment, the monkey attended to one of the two locations outside the receptive field, and in the *attend-receptive-field-stimulus* condition, attention was directed to one of the locations inside the receptive field. The attend-away condition was in effect a replication of the first experiment. The (pre-target) displays in this condition consisted of either (1) a reference stimulus, (2) a probe stimulus, or (3) both a reference and a probe stimulus in the (unattended) receptive field. Reynolds *et al.* found the same basic pattern as in the first experiment, with the cell's response to a pair being a weighted average of the responses to the individual stimuli. The weight of each stimulus (reference or probe) in the pair was on average about equal, consistent with the fact that no attentional selection was required of the monkey in this part of the visual field.

In the attend-receptive-field-stimulus condition, Reynolds *et al.* could study the effect of attention on the pair response. When the monkey's attention was directed to the location of one of the stimuli in the pair, this increased the weight on the stimulus in the target location so that the mean response of the neuron was driven (up or down) toward the response elicited when the stimulus was presented alone. This response pattern was found in both V2 and V4. In V2, when attention was drawn to the probe stimulus, the response was a weighted average approximating 69% of the response to the probe plus 31% of the response to the reference stimulus. In V4, the same weight estimates were 83% and 17%, respectively. With attention to the reference stimulus, the strength of the weight relation was reversed, so that the pair response was given by 76% (in V2) or 79% (in V4) of the response to the reference stimulus plus 24% (in V2) or 21% (in V4) of the response to the probe.

The results of Reynolds *et al.* are consistent with the two hypotheses that (1) at any given time, a typical cell was driven by only one of the stimuli in its receptive field, and (2) the probability that the cell was driven by any given stimulus (i.e. the probability that the cell represented the stimulus) was proportional to the current attentional weight of the stimulus. This is exactly what is predicted by NTVA.

Another important finding by Reynolds *et al.* (1999) was an increase in the baseline firing rate (before the stimulus was presented) of many neurons when attention was directed to a location within the receptive field. This type of finding is discussed in Section 8.3.

8.1.2 Filtering by non-spatial categories

In experiments that require filtering by a non-spatial category the monkey is cued to attend to a target stimulus defined by one or more features (e.g. a particular colour or form) but is not given prior information about where the target is located. Therefore, the activation of the priority map must be configured after the onset of the display, often resulting in a long initial period of unselective processing in the visual neurons. Only after attentional weights have been computed and applied, selective processing takes effect. This two-stage mechanism of selection was clearly demonstrated in studies by Chelazzi and collaborators (1998, 2001).

8.1.2.1 Chelazzi *et al.* (1998)

As mentioned in Section 6.3, Chelazzi *et al.* (1998; see also Chelazzi *et al.* 1993) studied the response of single neurons in anterior inferotemporal (IT) cortex during a visual search experiment. In the basic task, a cue stimulus was first presented at fixation (cf. Fig. 6.4). The cue showed the target to be searched for (e.g. a cup). Following the cue, the screen went blank for 1500 ms while the monkey kept fixating centrally. After this delay, two stimuli were displayed in the peripheral visual field. If one of them matched the cue, the monkey was rewarded for making an eye movement towards that stimulus. If the target was absent from the display, the monkey should just maintain fixation until a third, matching stimulus appeared. The two stimuli in the search display were both located within the large receptive field of the recorded IT neuron, so that both stimuli could potentially influence the cell's response. All stimuli were drawn from a set consisting of a 'good', a 'neutral', and a 'poor' stimulus for the cell. When presented alone, the 'good' and the 'poor' stimuli elicited strong and weak responses, respectively.

When a target was present in the search display and the display was presented in the visual field opposite (*contralaterally*) to the cerebral hemisphere containing the recorded neuron, strong effects of attention were found. Most importantly, the effects followed a characteristic time course. During the first 150–200 ms after stimulus onset, the response of the IT neuron was the same regardless of whether the 'good' or the 'poor' stimulus was the cued target. In terms of NTVA, this period corresponds to the wave of unselective processing before attentional weights had been computed and applied. After this initial activation, a dramatic change occurred in the firing pattern of the neuron. The response was rapidly driven towards the firing rate observed when the target stimulus was presented in isolation; either up in case of the 'good' stimulus or down in case of the 'poor' stimulus (see Fig. 8.2). The effect can be explained by the hypothesis that a large majority of the recorded IT neurons contracted their receptive fields around the attended stimulus, responding only to its properties, following the application of attentional weights. The effect of attention only occurred with several competing stimuli in the receptive field. In a variation of the experiment in which just a single stimulus was shown in the 'search' display, the neuron's response was almost unaffected by whether the stimulus equalled the cued target or not; this corresponds to the null findings described in Section 8.1.1. The attentional effect was also replicated with a different response (manual lever press), suggesting that the mechanism was not specific to the motor response, but reflected basic perceptual processing.

8.1.2.2 Chelazzi *et al.* (2001)

Using a variation of the experimental design described in the last section (and the same monkeys), Chelazzi *et al.* (2001) extended the investigation to V4 neurons. The results were similar to the previous investigation of IT neurons,

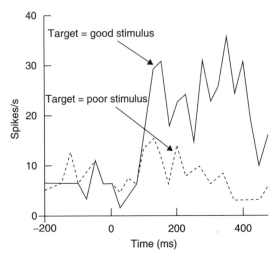

Fig. 8.2 Responses of a form-selective neuron in the inferotemporal cortex during the visual search task of Chelazzi *et al.* (1998). Shortly after the search array was presented (at time = 0 ms), the cell responded well regardless of which stimulus was the target. However, by about 170 ms after stimulus onset, responses diverged dramatically depending on whether the target was the good or the poor stimulus for the cell. Adapted with permission from Chelazzi, Duncan, Miller and Desimone (1998). Responses of neurons in inferior temporal cortex during memory-guided visual search. *Journal of Neurophysiology*, **80**, 2918–2940. Copyright 1998 by the American Physiological Society.

with a few notable exceptions. First, with two stimuli in the receptive field, the wave of selective processing appeared to begin after approximately 150 ms. This was a little earlier than in IT, but several factors may explain the difference in timing: the monkeys had more training than in the previous study, and the stimuli were positioned closer to each other. Second, in contrast to the study of IT neurons, the V4 neurons showed no increase in baseline activity with attention. This interesting discrepancy is discussed in Section 8.3.5.

8.1.3 **Filtering of stimuli with different contrast**

By the weight equation, the attentional weight of an object depends jointly on the sensory evidence (η values) that the object has certain features and the behavioural relevance (π values) of these features. A study by Reynolds and Desimone (2003) demonstrated the complementary influence of these two factors on attentional filtering. The strength of sensory evidence was manipulated by varying the luminance contrast of the displayed objects. When two distractor objects were shown at different levels of contrast in the receptive field of a V4 neuron, Reynolds and Desimone found that the neuron's response was determined primarily by the most visible stimulus. However, the selection could be reversed if attention was directed to the fainter stimulus. Similar results were obtained by Martinez-Trujillo and Treue (2002) in the dorsal stream of visual processing (area MT).

8.1.3.1 Reynolds and Desimone (2003)

Reynolds and Desimone (2003) studied responses of V4 neurons to stimuli at various levels of luminance contrast. The monkey's task was to monitor a rapid sequence of displays, reacting when a target stimulus (a diamond) appeared at a cued location (similar to the task used by Reynolds *et al.* 1999). The target and distractor stimuli could appear at four locations, two inside and two outside the recorded neuron's receptive field (see Fig. 8.3). For each neuron, a pair of distractor stimuli (i.e. objects that appeared earlier in the display sequence than the target) was chosen, which formed the basis of the response analysis. One of these stimuli, the *reference*, remained at a fixed, high contrast throughout the experiment, whereas the contrast of the other stimulus, the *probe*, was varied systematically.

In the *attend-outside-receptive-field* condition, the response (mean rate of firing) to the reference stimulus alone was compared with the response to a pair consisting of reference plus probe. When the probe was less effective at driving the neuron than was the reference stimulus, the addition of the probe to the display typically caused a reduction in response (cf. Reynolds *et al.* 1999). However, the influence of the probe depended on its level of luminance contrast. If the probe had very low contrast, the neuron's response to the pair was approximately equal to the response to the reference stimulus alone. In this case it seemed as if the probe was simply not present in the receptive field. As the contrast of the probe was increased, the neuron's response became more and more suppressed, reflecting stronger influence of the (ineffective) probe stimulus. In other words, the attentional weight of the probe seemed to increase with its visibility (i.e. η values).

In the *attend-inside-receptive-field* condition, the monkey's attention was directed at the probe stimulus in the receptive field by cuing the location of the probe. Presumably, the effect of cuing the location of the probe was to increase the pertinence (π value) of this location and, accordingly, the attentional weight of the probe. The manipulation caused the pair response (mean rate of firing to the pair consisting of the probe and the reference) to move towards the response to the probe alone, even when the probe was shown at lower contrast than the reference stimulus. Thus, the response to the pair could be driven towards the response to the probe, both by (1) increasing the contrast of the probe and (2) increasing the pertinence of the probe's location.

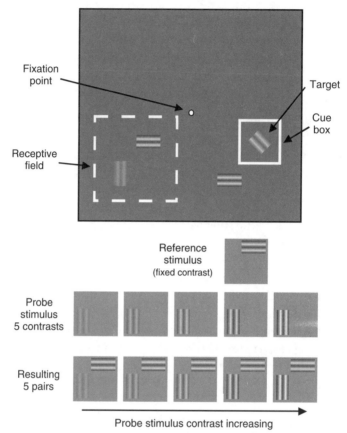

Fig. 8.3 Stimuli and task used by Reynolds and Desimone (2003). Monkeys fixated a small spot at the centre of the display. Stimuli appeared at up to four positions: two inside the receptive field (dashed box, upper panel) and two at mirror-symmetric positions across the vertical meridian. At the beginning of a block of trials, a cue box (solid square in upper panel) appeared, which indicated where the monkey was to attend throughout that block of trials. The cue box was removed after a few instruction trials, and the monkey continued to perform the task at that location without the cue. The task was to detect a diamond-shaped target stimulus that appeared at the cued location after a variable length sequence of non-target stimuli, while ignoring distracter targets that occasionally appeared at the other three locations. The three rows of panels show the combinations of non-target stimuli that appeared within the receptive field: (1) a reference stimulus, which appeared at a fixed, high contrast (single panel in first row); (2) a single probe stimulus, which varied in contrast (second row); or (3) a fixed-contrast reference stimulus and a variable-contrast probe stimulus (third row). Adapted with permission from Reynolds and Desimone (2003). Interacting roles of attention and visual salience in V4. *Neuron*, **37**, 853–863. Copyright 2003 by Elsevier.

In accordance with the weight equation, both manipulations (which cause changes in η and π values, respectively) should increase the attentional weight of the probe. Indeed, both manipulations drove the mean rate of firing to the pair towards the response to the probe when this was presented alone.

8.1.3.2 Martinez-Trujillo and Treue (2002)

Martinez-Trujillo and Treue (2002) recorded from the middle temporal visual area (MT), which contains cells that are specialized to signal direction of motion. They presented monkeys with patterns of coherently moving, random dots. Four random dot patterns were shown: a pair inside the receptive field and a pair outside (Fig. 8.4). The two pairs were identical, either one consisting of (1) a pattern moving in the preferred direction of the recorded neuron (i.e. an effective sensory stimulus) and (2) a pattern moving in the opposite, null direction (i.e. eliciting a response close to baseline). Before each trial, the monkey

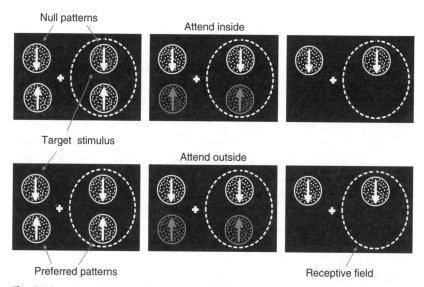

Fig. 8.4 Experimental design for a cell preferring upward motion in the experiment of Martinez-Trujillo and Treue (2002). Each stimulus display showed two pairs of random dot patterns, one pair inside and the other outside the receptive field (dashed oval) of the recorded cell. Each pair consisted of one preferred and one null pattern. In the attend-inside condition (top row), the monkeys attended to the null pattern inside the receptive field. In the attend-outside condition (bottom row), the monkeys attended to the null pattern outside the receptive field. From left to right, the panels show decreasing contrast of the preferred patterns. Adapted with permission from Martinez-Trujillo and Treue (2002). Attentional modulation strength in cortical area MT depends on stimulus contrast. *Neuron*, **35**, 365–370. Copyright 2002 by Elsevier.

was cued to attend the null pattern either in the receptive field or at the other location. The task was to detect small changes in the movement of the cued pattern while ignoring changes in the other patterns. Martinez-Trujillo and Treue varied the luminance contrast of the unattended pattern in the receptive field to see how this changed the neuron's response, depending on whether the monkey was attending inside or outside the receptive field. The attended (null) pattern was always displayed at high contrast.

Given this experimental design, NTVA predicts the following response pattern. With a probe pattern of very low contrast, the neuron's response should be almost entirely determined by the (high contrast) null stimulus, regardless of whether the monkey is attending inside or outside the receptive field. As the null pattern is effectively the only visible stimulus for the cell, a response close to baseline should occur regardless of whether the null pattern is attended or not. As the contrast of the preferred stimulus is increased, its probability of being selected should also increase (cf. the η factor in the weight equation), driving the neuron's average response up. However, the increase should be weaker in the attend-inside-receptive-field condition, because in this case, the behavioural relevance of the attended null pattern should counter the influence of the preferred pattern and reduce its probability of being selected (represented) by the cell (cf. Reynolds and Desimone 2003). At maximum contrast (i.e. when the preferred and null patterns are equally visible), the probability of selecting the preferred pattern should reach a ceiling of about 50% in the attend-out-side-receptive-field condition. However, in the attend-inside-receptive-field condition, the probability should remain below 50% because of attention to the null pattern. Thus NTVA predicts a difference between the responses in the attend-inside-receptive-field and the attend-outside-receptive-field conditions, even at maximum contrast. As detailed in Box 8.1, this account closely matches the data reported by Martinez-Trujillo and Treue.

Box 8.1 Martinez-Trujillo and Treue (2002)

Figure 8.5 displays a quantitative fit to the data of Martinez-Trujillo and Treue (2002, Fig. 5B) based on NTVA. The abscissa shows the contrast index (contrast – C50)/(contrast + C50), where C50 is the contrast generating a response in the attend-outside-receptive-field condition half as strong as the response obtained with the maximum contrast. The maximum firing rate varied between MT neurons, but for each of the tested neurons in each of the two attention conditions, the activations of the neuron (i.e. the firing rates of the neuron minus the neuron's baseline rate) were normalized by

Box 8.1 Martinez-Trujillo and Treue (2002) *(continued)*

being expressed as proportions of the neuron's maximum activation in the attend-outside-receptive-field condition. The normalized activations for each condition were binned by the contrast index, averaged across neurons within the bins, and plotted along the ordinate in Fig. 8.5.

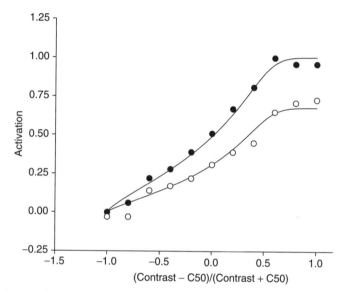

Fig. 8.5 Effect of attention in the experiment of Martinez-Trujillo and Treue (2002). The normalized activation is shown as a function of an index of the stimulus contrast when the monkey was attending to a stimulus inside the receptive field (open circles) and when the monkey was attending to a stimulus outside the receptive field (solid circles). A theoretical fit based on NTVA is indicated by smooth curves. Data are from Martinez-Trujillo and Treue (2002). Attentional modulation strength in cortical area MT depends on stimulus contrast. *Neuron*, **35**, 365–370. Copyright 2002 by Elsevier. Adapted with permission.

The smooth curves in the figure show a fit based on the following assumptions. First, for the investigated neurons, the mean firing rate of a cell is a sum of a baseline rate (undriven activity) and a mean activation (stimulus-driven activity). As explained in Box 7.2, the mean activation of the cell (say, the kth feature-i neuron) can be written as

$$v_{ki} = \eta_k(x,i)\beta_i \frac{w_x}{w_x + w_z}, \tag{8.1}$$

Box 8.1 Martinez-Trujillo and Treue (2002) *(continued)*

where x is the preferred pattern inside the cell's receptive field, z is the null pattern inside the cell's receptive field, and w_x and w_z are the attentional weights of x and z; β_i is the featural bias in favour of i, $\eta_k(x, i)\beta_i$ is the activation of the (kth feature-i) neuron when it responds to the preferred pattern (x) with the given featural bias (β_i), and $w_x/(w_x + w_z)$ equals the probability that the cell responds to the preferred pattern rather than the null pattern.

Second, all η values for features of pattern x increase with the contrast of pattern x. Let c be the natural logarithm of the stimulus contrast. For simplicity we assume that all η values for task-relevant features of pattern x increase by the same sigmoid contrast response function,

$$f_{lsa}(c) = \{1 + \exp[-2 (c - l)/s]\}^{-a}, \tag{8.2}$$

which implies that for all k and i,

$$\eta_k(x, i) = \eta_k^*(x, i) f_{lsa}(c), \tag{8.3}$$

where $\eta_k^*(x, i)$ is the value of $\eta_k(x, i)$ at maximum contrast [theoretically, the asymptotic value of $\eta_k(x, i)$ as c approaches infinity]. Similarly, for all η (x, j) values contributing to the attentional weight of pattern x [w_x given by $\Sigma_{j \in R} \eta(x, j) \pi_j$],

$$\eta (x, j) = \eta^*(x, j) f_{lsa}(c), \tag{8.4}$$

where $\eta^*(x, j)$ is the value of $\eta (x, j)$ at maximum contrast.

For $l = 0$, $s = 1$, and $a = 1$, $f_{lsa}(c)$ is the standard logistic function of the logarithm of the contrast, c. The standard logistic function is rotationally symmetric about the point $(0, 1/2)$, approaches 1 as c approaches infinity, and approaches 0 as c approaches minus infinity. Parameter l determines the location of the contrast response function $f_{lsa}(c)$ along the c axis, scale parameter s determines the steepness of the function, and parameter a determines the degree of rotational asymmetry of the function. Examples of theoretical contrast response functions $f_{lsa}(c)$ with different values of parameters l, s, and a are shown in Fig. 8.6.

By equation 8.4 and the weight equation, the attentional weight of pattern x also increases by the contrast response function $f_{lsa}(c)$, that is,

$$w_x = w_x^* f_{lsa}(c), \tag{8.5}$$

Box 8.1 Martinez-Trujillo and Treue (2002) *(continued)*

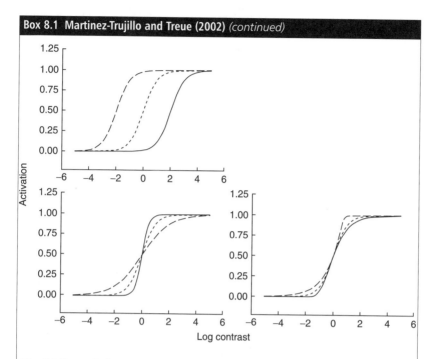

Fig. 8.6 Theoretical contrast response functions $f_{lsa}(c)$ with different values of location parameter l, scale parameter s, and asymmetry parameter a. Upper panel: $s = 1$; $a = 1$; $l = -2$ (dashed), 0 (dotted), or 2 (solid). Lower left panel: $l = 0$; $a = 1$; $s = 0.5$ (solid), 1 (dotted), or 2 (dashed). Lower right panel: $l = 0.693$, $s = 0.2$, and $a = 0.1$ (dashed); $l = 0$, $s = 1$, and $a = 1$ (dotted); or $l = -4.55$, $s = 1.5$, and $a = 300$ (solid). Adapted with permission from Bundesen, Habekost, and Kyllingsbæk (2005). A neural theory of visual attention: bridging cognition and neurophysiology. *Psychological Review*, **112**, 291–328. Copyright 2005 by the American Psychological Association. The use of APA information does not imply endorsement by APA.

where

$$w_x^* = \Sigma_{j \in R} \, \eta^*(x, j) \, \pi_j$$

is the value of w_x at maximum contrast. By equations 8.1, 8.3, and 8.5, the mean activation of the kth feature-i neuron is

$$v_{ki} = m f_{lsa}(c) \frac{f_{lsa}(c)}{f_{lsa}(c) + w_{\text{ratio}}}, \tag{8.6}$$

where $m = \eta_k^*(x, i) \, \beta_i$ and $w_{\text{ratio}} = w_z/w_x^*$. Note that at maximum contrast, equation 8.6 reduces to

$$\max\{v_{ki}\} = \frac{m}{1 + w_{\text{ratio}}} = m \frac{w_x^*}{w_x^* + w_z}.$$

Box 8.1 Martinez-Trujillo and Treue (2002) *(continued)*

In the attend-outside-receptive-field condition, both the null pattern and the preferred pattern inside the neuron's receptive field were distractors, so attentional weights w_z and w_x^* should be about the same, whence w_{ratio} should be about 1. In the attend-inside-receptive-field condition, the null pattern was the target, so w_{ratio} should be greater than 1. The fit by equation 8.6, shown in Fig. 8.5, was obtained with w_{ratio} kept constant at a value of 1 in the attend-outside-receptive-field condition. The fit was found with w_{ratio} at 1.96 in the attend-inside-receptive-field condition, normalized maximum activation, m, at 2.01, and a contrast response function, f_{lsa}, with location parameter, l, at 1.11 log units of contrast, scale parameter, s, at 0.52, and asymmetry parameter, a, at 0.11.

The fit shown in Fig. 8.5 is close. Note, in particular, that in both the observed data and the fitted functions, the relative effect of attention [measured, for example, by (response attending outside receptive field − response attending inside receptive field) / (response attending outside receptive field + response attending inside receptive field)] was greatest in the mid-contrast range. Thus, the main findings of Martinez-Trujillo and Treue (2002) can be explained by equation 8.1 on the assumption that η values, and therefore attentional weights, are sigmoid functions of stimulus contrast.

8.2 Attentional effects with a single stimulus in the receptive field

Experiments with multiple stimuli in the receptive field have consistently shown strong effects of attention. In studies with only one experimental stimulus in the receptive field, effects of attention have generally been much smaller and less consistent. Moran and Desimone (1985) and Luck *et al.* (1997) found no measurable effect of attention when only a single stimulus was presented in the receptive field of the recorded neuron. Other investigators have reported minor, but statistically significant enhancements of firing rates with attention (Motter 1994*a,b*; Connor *et al.* 1997; McAdams and Maunsell 1999*a,b*, 2000; Reynolds *et al.* 1999, 2000; Treue and Martinez-Trujillo 1999; Martinez-Trujillo and Treue 2004; Williford and Maunsell 2006), whereas Motter (1993) found both positive and negative modulations of firing rates.

When only a single object x appears in the receptive field of a given feature-i neuron, NTVA implies that the neuron responds to object x. The resultant activation of the kth feature-i neuron equals $\eta_k(x, i)\, \beta_i$, where $\eta_k(x, i)$ is independent of the attentional state of the organism whereas β_i is the current perceptual bias in favour of feature i. Hence, an effect of attention should be found if, and only if, the perceptual bias in favour of feature i is varied (pigeonholing). Further, the effect of varying the bias (β_i) should be a multiplicative scaling (up or down) of the activations of all feature-i neurons.

When a single experimental stimulus appears in the receptive field of a recorded neuron, the stimulus may be the only noteworthy object for the cell; but this need not be the case. Even when an experiment is designed to include only one stimulus in the receptive field, the neuron may respond to an individual part of the experimental stimulus as a separate object, or the neuron may respond to a 'ghost' object formed by internally generated random noise. Effects of individual parts of an experimental stimulus should primarily occur in experiments with a complex stimulus in the receptive field. For example, if the experimental stimulus is a cloud of dots moving within the receptive field of a recorded neuron (Treue and Martinez-Trujillo 1999), the neuron may sometimes respond to the whole pattern, but at other times respond to a sub-pattern or even a single dot. Effects of internally generated random noise should occur primarily in experiments with a faint stimulus in the receptive field. In this case, the neuron must solve a classical problem of signal detection (cf. Green and Swets 1966; see Section 2.2.1): discrimination of a weak signal (the experimental stimulus) from pure noise (the ghost object formed by internal random noise).

In general, a neuron presented with a single stimulus may perform a filtering operation and respond to either the experimental stimulus (as a whole) or one out of a possibly very large set of noise objects. The set of possible noise objects includes individual parts of the experimental stimulus as well as ghost objects formed by internally generated random noise. In accordance with the rate equation, the probability that the neuron responds to a particular object equals the attentional weight of the object divided by the sum of the attentional weights of all objects in the receptive field. Thus, the neuron's response can be regarded as a probability mixture of its response to the experimental stimulus and its responses to the noise objects. This implies that the neuron's mean response can be computed as a weighted average of its response to the experimental stimulus object and its mean responses to each of the noise objects.

Studies of attentional effects with a single, complex stimulus in the receptive field are discussed in Section 8.2.1. Studies of attentional effects with a single, faint stimulus in the receptive field of the recorded neuron are discussed in Section 8.2.2, and attentional studies with a single, relatively simple and strong stimulus in the receptive field are discussed in Section 8.2.3.

8.2.1 Effects with a complex stimulus

With a single, complex experimental stimulus in the receptive field of a recorded neuron, NTVA assumes that there is a substantial probability that the neuron responds to an individual part of the stimulus rather than the whole pattern. This probability should depend on the monkey's general state of attention. If the monkey is trained to treat the complex stimulus as a target, this should increase the attentional weight on the complex stimulus and, therefore, increase the probability that the recorded neuron responds to the whole pattern rather than responding to a noise object such as a smaller part of the stimulus. Assuming that the experimental stimulus object is a more effective stimulus for the cell than are any of the noise objects, attention should increase the firing rate of the cell. As detailed in the following sections, this filtering mechanism explains cases in which *spatial attention* enhanced the response to a cloud of moving dots (Treue and Martinez-Trujillo 1999) or a Gabor pattern (McAdams and Maunsell 1999*a,b*, 2000).

In addition to providing evidence of filtering with a single complex stimulus in the receptive field, the studies by Treue and Martinez-Trujillo (1999) and McAdams and Maunsell (2000), as well as a more recent study by Martinez-Trujillo and Treue (2004), have shown effects of pigeonholing at the cellular level: a *feature-based* mechanism of attention that selects a group of neurons with a given stimulus preference for increased activation. The evidence consists mainly of data showing that attention to a preferred feature of a neuron (e.g. a certain direction of motion) enhances the response of the neuron, even though the stimulus to be attended is located outside the receptive field. Thus feature-based attention seems to generalize across the visual field and influence the processing of objects even when they were not in the spatial focus of attention.

McAdams and Maunsell (1999*a*), Treue and Martinez-Trujillo (1999), and Martinez-Trujillo and Treue (2004) also found evidence of *multiplicative scaling* of neural tuning curves with attention. More precisely, attention was found to increase a neuron's activation (firing rate above baseline) by the same factor for all objects across a feature dimension (e.g. orientation). NTVA directly predicts such an effect from pigeonholing by the multiplicative effect of the β factor in the rate equation. NTVA also predicts multiplicative scaling of the tuning curve when the attentional weight of the experimental stimulus versus noise objects is varied, provided that activations caused by noise objects are either zero or else proportional to the activation caused by the experimental stimulus (Box 8.2).

Box 8.2 Multiplicative scaling of firing rates

Consider the orientation tuning of a neuron whose mean activation, $v(\theta)$, is a function of the stimulus orientation, θ. Let w_x be the attentional weight of the stimulus, and let w_z be the attentional weight of the noise (i.e. the sum of the attentional weights of all noise objects). The probability p that the neuron responds to the experimental stimulus is given by

$$p = \frac{w_x}{w_x + w_z}.$$

The mean activation of the neuron is a weighted average of the mean activation, $v_x(\theta)$, when the neuron responds to the experimental stimulus (which happens with probability p) and the mean activation, $v_z(\theta)$, when the neuron responds to a noise object (which happens with probability $1 - p$):

$$v(\theta) = p\, v_x(\theta) + (1 - p)\, v_z(\theta).$$

If activations caused by noise objects are zero [i.e. $v_z(\theta) = 0$], we get

$$v(\theta) = p\, v_x(\theta),$$

which implies multiplicative scaling of the tuning curve: as the relative attentional weight (p) of the experimental stimulus is varied, the mean activation of the neuron is scaled by the same factor (p) for all stimulus orientations (θ).

A similar argument applies if the mean activation when the neuron responds to a noise object is proportional to the mean activation when the neuron responds to the experimental stimulus [i.e. $v_z(\theta) = k\, v_x(\theta)$, where k is a constant independent of θ]. In this case we get

$$v(\theta) = p\, v_x(\theta) + (1 - p)\, k\, v_x(\theta)$$

$$= [p + (1 - p)\, k]\, v_x(\theta)$$

$$= q\, v_x(\theta),$$

where

$$q = p + (1 - p)\, k,$$

which also implies multiplicative scaling of the tuning curve: As the relative attentional weight (p) of the experimental stimulus is varied, the mean activation of the neuron is scaled by the same factor (q) for all stimulus orientations (θ).

Activations at zero (baseline firing rate) should result from ghost objects formed by internal random noise. Activations proportional to the activation caused by the experimental stimulus would be expected from noise objects that are parts of the experimental stimulus, if the parts have the same value as the whole stimulus on the feature dimension along which the tuning curve is defined (e.g. the same orientation if this is the dimension along which tuning is being measured). As explained in the next sections, this condition appears to have been satisfied by the stimuli used by McAdams and Maunsell (1999*a,b*) and Treue and Martinez-Trujillo (1999).

8.2.1.1 McAdams and Maunsell (1999*a,b*)

McAdams and Maunsell (1999*a*) studied the effect of attention on the orientation tuning curves of V4 neurons. They aimed to test whether attention changes the stimulus selectivity of the neurons or, more specifically, whether attention sharpens the tuning curves around the preferred orientation (as suggested by Haenny and Schiller 1988; Spitzer *et al.* 1988). The monkeys were trained to carry out a delayed match-to-sample task. They were shown two sample stimuli for 500 ms, one of them at a cued location. The monkeys had to remember the cued stimulus for a delay period of 500 ms and then match it to a test stimulus appearing at the same location (while ignoring the test stimulus at the other location). The stimuli used in the experimental task were either Gabor patterns (constructed by multiplying a sinusoidal grating and a two-dimensional Gaussian) or coloured Gaussians (isoluminant coloured patches whose saturation varied with a two-dimensional Gaussian profile) (Fig. 8.7). The stimuli were always located so that the Gabor pattern was in the receptive field of the neuron being recorded, whereas the coloured Gaussian was presented outside. If the location of the Gabor stimulus was cued, the monkey should indicate whether the orientation of the (Gabor) test stimulus matched the orientation of the sample stimulus. If the Gaussian was cued, the monkey should indicate whether the colour of the (Gaussian) test stimulus matched the sample colour. For each neuron recorded, McAdams and Maunsell systematically varied the orientation of the Gabor stimulus in the receptive field, to obtain an orientation tuning curve and to see whether attention to the object would change the shape of the curve.

The attended and unattended stimuli thus differed in both spatial location and relevant feature dimension (orientation versus colour). McAdams and Maunsell chose this design to increase the chances of demonstrating attentional modulations in area V4. In terms of NTVA, both filtering and pigeonholing should be expected in such a task. Consider, first, the effect of filtering. The Gabor stimulus for each recorded cell was adjusted in spatial frequency,

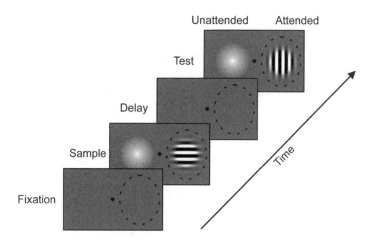

Fig. 8.7 Experimental procedure of McAdams and Maunsell (1999*a*). Gabor stimuli were shown within the receptive field (dashed circle) and coloured Gaussians were presented outside. The illustration shows the experimental condition where the Gabor stimulus was cued (attended) and the test (Gabor) stimulus did not match the sample stimulus. Adapted with permission from McAdams and Maunsell (1999). Effects of attention on orientation-tuning functions of single neurons in macaque cortical area V4. *Journal of Neuroscience*, **19**, 431–441. Copyright 1999 by the Society for Neuroscience.

colour, and size to generate the strongest possible response in the match-to-sample task. We assume (a) that the optimized Gabor stimulus for a given cell was a more effective stimulus object than were possible noise objects, including individual parts (such as individual bars) of the Gabor stimulus. We also assume (b) that activations in response to noise objects were either zero (namely, responses at baseline caused by ghost objects formed by internal random noise) or else approximately proportional to the activation caused by the experimental stimulus as a whole (responses caused by individual parts of the Gabor pattern with the same orientation as the whole pattern). Finally, we assume (c) that the task of responding to the Gabor stimulus increased the attentional weight of the experimental stimulus (the Gabor pattern as a whole) relative to the attentional weights of noise objects. By Assumptions a and c, the task of responding to the Gabor stimulus should enhance the activation of the cell; by Assumption b, the enhancement should be a multiplicative scaling of the activation (cf. Box 8.2).

Consider, second, the effect of pigeonholing. The requirement to report orientation instead of colour should increase the general perceptual bias in favour of categorizing objects with respect to orientation instead of categorizing objects with respect to colour. Thus, β values should be high for orientations and low for colours. Following McAdams and Maunsell we assume that the recorded V4 neurons were predominantly selective for orientation so that the activation of a neuron scaled with the attentional emphasis (β value) on orientation rather than the emphasis on colour. Accordingly, the pigeonholing due to the requirement to report orientation rather than colour should also cause a multiplicative enhancement of the activation (multiplication by the β value for the orientation preferred by the cell regardless of the orientation of the stimulus). Finally, given that both filtering and pigeonholing scaled the activation of a recorded neuron multiplicatively (with the same factor for all stimulus orientations), the combined effect of the two attentional mechanisms should also be a multiplicative scaling of the activation of the neuron to stimuli in all orientations.

For each recorded neuron, McAdams and Maunsell fitted the mean rates of firing at the tested orientations by a theoretical tuning curve that was the sum of a one-dimensional Gaussian and two constants, one at the level of the baseline firing of the neuron (i.e. the undriven activity found when the receptive field was empty) and one representing the activation caused by a Gabor stimulus in the least preferred orientation. For those neurons that yielded satisfactory fits to this simple model, the standard deviation of the Gaussian function was interpreted as the tuning curve's width, and the mean of the function as the neuron's preferred orientation. The normalized population-tuning curves for all V4 neurons are shown in Fig. 8.8a. As can be seen, the responses to the Gabor patterns were substantially enhanced by attention at all possible stimulus orientations. Specifically, the amplitude of the tuning curve and the activation caused by stimuli in the least preferred orientation were both increased by attention; but the width of the tuning curve and the (undriven) baseline firing were unaffected by attention. Based on the same data, Fig. 8.8b shows a plot of the attended response against the unattended response at each of the 12 tested orientations. A strikingly good fit is provided by a straight line with a slope of 1.32 through the point representing the baseline firing rate (undriven activity) in both experimental conditions. The goodness of fit strongly suggests that the effect of attention on the mean rate of firing of a recorded V4 neuron was simply a linear scaling (multiplicative enhancement by a factor of about 1.32) of the activation of the neuron (the firing rate minus the baseline rate) to stimuli in all orientations.

McAdams and Maunsell (1999b) presented further analyses of the same data set. They tested the hypothesis that attention modulates the signal-to-noise ratio in the neuron's firing by decreasing the noise component.

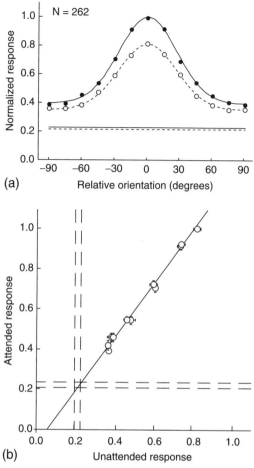

Fig. 8.8 Effects of attention on mean rates of firing in the experiment of McAdams and Maunsell (1999*a*). (a) Normalized population tuning curves for all V4 neurons. Solid circles fitted by a solid Gaussian curve show the normalized response as a function of the angular deviation between the stimulus and the preferred orientation when the monkey was attending to the stimulus inside the receptive field. The solid horizontal line represents the undriven activity, measured as the mean firing rate during the fixation period before stimulus presentation in the same attention condition. Corresponding data for the condition in which the monkey was attending to the stimulus outside the receptive field are shown by open circles, the dotted Gaussian curve, and the dotted horizontal line. (b) The attended response versus the unattended response for each of the tested orientations. The results are fitted by a least-squares line with a slope of 1.32. The pairs of dashed lines show undriven activity ±1 SE. The strikingly close fit and the finding that the line very nearly passes through the point where attended response = unattended response = undriven activity show that attention very nearly effected a multiplicative scaling of the activation (the total firing rate minus the level of undriven activity). Adapted with permission from McAdams and Maunsell (1999). Effects of attention on orientation-tuning functions of single neurons in macaque cortical area V4. *Journal of Neuroscience*, **19**, 431–441. Copyright 1999 by the Society for Neuroscience.

Specifically, when the firing rate is scaled up by attention, the variability in the neuron's response (i.e. the noise) might be reduced relative to the mean response (i.e. the signal). Such an increase in the reliability of the neuron's response would improve stimulus discrimination. However, McAdams and Maunsell found no systematic change in the relation between response magnitude and response variance when attention was directed at the stimulus. Instead, McAdams and Maunsell pointed out that higher firing rates by themselves produce a better signal-to-noise ratio, even with a constant mean-variance ratio. When the firing rate (signal) is increased, the variance tends to increase proportionately. However, the standard deviation, being only the square root of the variance, increases less rapidly. Therefore, when the noise is measured by the standard deviation, the signal-to-noise ratio generally increases when the firing rate is scaled up.

McAdams and Maunsell (1999*b*) also tested the hypothesis that attention affects the temporal pattern of firing. In particular, attention might make neurons more likely to fire in bursts, which is generally more effective at driving other neurons and might therefore increase the information transmitted by a neuron. However, attention changed neither the rate of bursting, the number of spikes within each burst, nor the length of each burst (when corrected for the increase in firing rate, which decreases the average interspike interval). Overall, McAdams and Maunsell concluded that the only systematic effect of attention in their study was a general upscaling of the activation (firing rate minus baseline). The qualitative pattern of firing did not change systematically, neither by narrowing of the tuning curve nor by a decrease in the variability of responses. All of these findings are in agreement with NTVA.

8.2.1.2 McAdams and Maunsell (2000)

McAdams and Maunsell (2000) followed up on their previous study by modifying the experimental design to separate effects of 'spatial attention' (filtering) from effects of 'feature-based attention' (pigeonholing). One experimental condition was similar to the experiment of McAdams and Maunsell (1999*a*): the stimuli outside the receptive field of the recorded neuron were Gaussians, the stimuli inside the receptive field were Gabor patterns, and either the Gaussians outside the receptive field or the Gabors inside the receptive field should be attended (cf. Fig. 8.7). In this combined location-and-feature-based attention task (filtering by spatial locations inside or outside the receptive field combined with pigeonholing by orientation or colour), the raw firing rates were 54% higher (median across neurons) when the monkey attended to the orientation of the Gabor in the receptive field than when it attended to the colour of the Gaussian outside the receptive field. This effect replicated the previous results of McAdams and Maunsell (1999*a*).

The other experimental condition used in the new study was similar, but now the stimuli inside the receptive field and the stimuli outside the receptive field were both Gabors. In this location-based attention task with no pigeon-holing component, firing rates were only 31% higher when the monkey attended to the orientation of the Gabor in the receptive field than when attending to the orientation of the Gabor outside the receptive field. A direct measure of the effect of pigeonholing (by orientation versus colour) could thus be obtained by comparing firing rates to the Gabor in the receptive field when the monkey attended the orientation (of a Gabor) outside the receptive field (Experiment 2) against firing rates when the monkey attended the colour (of a Gaussian) outside the receptive field (Experiment 1). By this compari-son, pigeonholing by orientation rather than colour increased the firing rates by 11% on average. Thus feature-based attention (pigeonholing) seemed to have a separate, enhancing effect on the firing rate, beyond the effect of location-based attention (filtering). More direct evidence on the pigeonholing mecha-nism was provided in the next study of our review.

8.2.1.3 Treue and Martinez-Trujillo (1999)

Treue and Martinez-Trujillo recorded from visual area MT, which contains cells that are selective to direction of motion. Although the MT area is located in the dorsal visual stream, the effects of attention were similar to those found in studies of ventral areas such as V4 (McAdams and Maunsell 1999*a*,*b*, 2000). In their basic task Treue and Martinez-Trujillo presented monkeys with two coherently moving random dot patterns (RDPs), one placed inside the recep-tive field of the neuron being recorded and the other one located in the oppo-site visual hemifield (Fig. 8.9a). At the start of each trial, the monkey was shown a cue at one of the stimulus locations. Following this, the RDPs appeared and the monkey was required to detect small changes in the speed or direction of the moving pattern at the cued location. These changes occurred after a random delay, which ranged between 270 and 4000 ms.

Experiment 1 of Treue and Martinez-Trujillo showed an effect of filtering based on spatial location ('spatial attention'). In this experiment, the two RDPs were moving in the same direction on any given trial (12 different direc-tional pairs were used to obtain a tuning curve for the neuron). When atten-tion was directed at the RDP in the receptive field of the recorded cell, the cell's mean activation (i.e. its response above baseline) was about 10% higher than when attention was directed at the stimulus outside the receptive field. As in the study of McAdams and Maunsell (1999*a*), the increase in activation occurred without any sharpening of the tuning curve around the preferred direction. On the contrary, the relative increase with attention was approxi-mately the same across all orientations (i.e. *multiplicative modulation*).

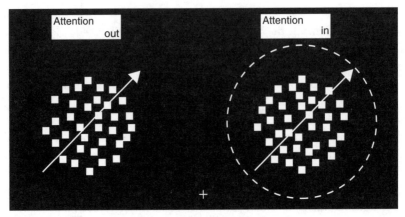

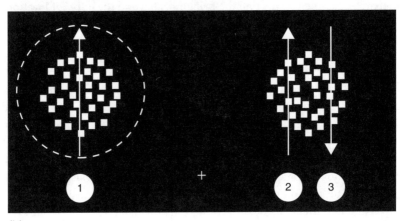

Fig. 8.9 Stimuli used by Treue and Martinez-Trujillo (1999). (a) One random dot pattern (RDP) was presented inside the receptive field (dashed circle) while the other was presented about the same distance from the fixation point in the opposite hemifield. In a given trial, both RDPs moved in the same of 12 possible directions. Attention was cued randomly to either the RDP within or outside the receptive field. (b) The RDP inside the receptive field always moved in the cell's preferred direction (upward pointing arrow, 1); the stimulus outside moved in either the same (2) or the opposite direction (3). Trials in which the animal was instructed to attend to (1), (2), and (3) were presented in an interleaved fashion. Adapted with permission from Treue and Martinez-Trujillo (1999). Feature-based attention influences motion processing gain in macaque visual cortex. *Nature*, **399**, 575–579. Copyright 1999 by Macmillan Publishers Ltd.

Following NTVA, the results can be explained by assuming that the probability of selecting the whole RDP versus a smaller part of the pattern differed between the two experimental conditions. The stimulus used by Treue and Martinez-Trujillo, a cloud of moving random dots, was so complex that there should be a substantial probability that the recorded cell responded to only a part of the pattern. In the attended condition, the monkey most likely treated the complex stimulus in the receptive field of the recorded neuron as the target, which should increase the probability that the neuron responded to the whole RDP pattern rather than smaller parts of it. Furthermore, the whole RDP should elicit a stronger response than parts consisting of only one or a few moving dots (presumably Treue and Martinez-Trujillo chose the cloud stimulus because it was more effective at driving the cell than individual dots). Taken together, these two assumptions can explain why activations were stronger in the attended condition. Furthermore all dots were moving coherently, so selection of smaller parts of the RDP should elicit activations that were approximately proportional to, but smaller than, the activation elicited by the whole RDP. Given this, attentional modulation should be multiplicative across the tuning curve.

Experiment 2 of Treue and Martinez-Trujillo showed an effect of pigeonholing ('feature-based attention') with respect to a given categorization, namely the attended direction of movement; probably the first direct demonstration of pigeonholing in the single-cell literature. In this experiment, the recorded neuron's receptive field was stimulated by an RDP moving in the direction preferred by the neuron. Outside the receptive field, another RDP was presented that moved either in the same direction or in the opposite direction (Fig. 8.9b). When the monkey attended to the RDP outside the receptive field, the response of the recorded neuron varied with the direction of movement being attended. Depending on whether the direction in the attended pattern was the same as or opposite to that preferred by the cell being recorded, the firing rate went up or down, respectively. The attentional modulation of the neuron's response occurred although the spatial location of the attended pattern was unchanged between the two conditions; only the attended feature was varied. Thus a non-spatial, feature-based mechanism of attention seemed to be at work.

NTVA can explain the result readily by the hypothesis that β values for particular directions of movement differed between the two conditions of the experiment. Because the monkey was monitoring the pattern for hundreds to thousands of milliseconds, there should be plenty of time to adjust the β values in accordance with the display within each trial. Consider the situation in which the preferred movement of the recorded neuron was upwards but the monkey attended to movement in the opposite direction (downwards), trying to detect a small change in the speed or direction of movement of the RDP outside the receptive field. Since the monkey had learned that only small changes in the direction of movement of the target stimulus would occur, β_{upwards} should be low (perceptual bias should generally reflect expectations). Because the activation of the recorded cell should be proportional to β_{upwards} (the cell was specialized to represent upward motion) the recorded activation should also be low. In contrast, when the monkey attended to movement in the preferred direction of the recorded cell, β values should be high for upwards and similar directions. In this case, β_{upwards} being high, the activation of the recorded neuron should also be high.

Treue and Martinez-Trujillo also studied the combined effects of filtering ('spatial attention') and pigeonholing ('feature-based attention') by compar-ing (a) trials in which the animal was attending the anti-preferred direction outside the receptive field with (b) trials in which attention was directed inside the receptive field to a stimulus moving in the preferred direction. The total increase in activation due to filtering and pigeonholing was about 25%. This corresponds to a 10% increase in activation due to change in the relative attentional weight of the complex stimulus within the receptive field [i.e. increase in $w_x/(w_x + w_z)$, where w_x is the weight of the complex stimulus and w_z is the sum of the weights of the noise objects in the receptive field] combined with a 13% increase in the perceptual bias (β value) for the preferred direction of the recorded neuron. Following the rate equation of TVA, these two effects interact multiplicatively to produce the observed effect (i.e. 110% × 113% ≈ 125%).

8.2.1.4 Martinez-Trujillo and Treue (2004)

The study by Treue and Martinez-Trujillo (1999) provided the first direct evi-dence of pigeonholing at the single-cell level, but left several questions open. First, the results of their Experiment 2 might also be explained in another way than by the β factor of NTVA: besides matching the *preferred feature* of the recorded cell, the receptive field stimuli used in Experiment 2 of Treue and Martinez-Trujillo (1999) also matched the *feature of the target object* (outside the receptive field) in the condition where response enhancement was observed (see Fig. 8.9b). Therefore, the increase in firing rates could also be due to a 'feature-matching' mechanism (Motter 1994a,b) in which response enhancement occurs when a cell is responding to a stimulus with the same feature as that of a target object. Unlike NTVA, the feature-matching hypothe-sis predicts that response enhancement occurs even for features that are non-preferred for the recorded cell, provided that the target object has these features. Non-preferred stimuli in the receptive field were not used in Experiment 2 by Treue and Martinez-Trujillo (1999), so both interpretations of their results are possible. Second, Treue and Martinez-Trujillo demonstrated multiplicative modulation of firing rates only in their spatial attention task (Experiment 1), but it was unclear whether the feature-based attention mechanism (i.e. pigeonholing) in Experiment 2 was also characterized by multiplicative modulation, as predicted by NTVA.

A more recent study by Martinez-Trujillo and Treue (2004) has given clear answers to these questions, and the results support NTVA. Martinez-Trujillo and Treue recorded from 135 direction-selective neurons in cortical area MT. As in their previous study, the response of each cell to an unattended RDP was recorded while the monkey attended to another RDP in the opposite hemifield. This time, however, the RDP in the receptive field of the recorded neuron could move either in the preferred or the anti-preferred direction for the cell, independently of whether the other (attended) RDP moved in the same or the opposite direction. Contrary to the predictions of the feature-matching model, the response to an anti-preferred stimulus was not increased when the attended object had the same feature (see the lower right data point in Fig. 8.10). Instead it was reduced, compared with the condition in which the monkey was attending a motion direction that was preferred by the recorded cell but different from the direction of the RDP in the receptive field of the recorded cell (see the lower left data point in Fig. 8.10). The results fit the explanation by NTVA that the β value multiplying the response of a cell depends on the similarity between the feature to be attended and the preferred feature of the cell. The results of Martinez-Trujillo and Treue also provided evidence that pigeonholing is a multiplicative operation: for both the preferred and anti-preferred stimulus in the receptive field, attention to the preferred (versus the anti-preferred) feature led to response enhancement by nearly the same factor (12–13% on the average; cf. the 'modulation ratio' illustrated in Fig. 8.10), suggesting that the activation of the cell was scaled up by essentially the same constant across the tuning curve. This is also as predicted by the rate equation.

Another important finding of Martinez-Trujillo and Treue (2004) was that the effect of feature-based attention (pigeonholing) on the firing rate of a neuron varied systematically with the degree of similarity between the attended feature and the preferred feature of the neuron: The β value multiplying the response of a cell appeared to be a monotonically increasing function of the similarity between the attended feature and the preferred feature of the cell. Thus, in the second experiment of Martinez-Trujillo and Treue (2004), responses to RDPs with 12 different motion directions were recorded while the monkey was attending another RDP moving in the same direction. In this

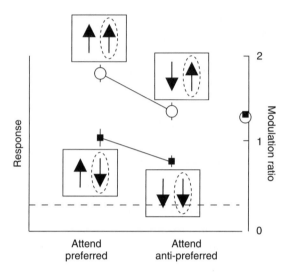

Fig. 8.10 The pigeonholing effect in the study of Martinez-Trujillo and Treue (2004). Average responses of an MT neuron are shown to stimuli moving in the preferred (open circles) and anti-preferred (filled squares) directions of the cell. The monkey was simultaneously attending the same or opposite direction in a second stimulus pattern outside the receptive field. The abscissa represents the attentional condition, the ordinate on the left represents the magnitude of neuronal responses, and the ordinate on the right displays the modulation ratio between the responses in the two attentional conditions for the preferred (open circle) and anti-preferred (filled square) directions in the receptive field, respectively. Unlike the feature-matching model, NTVA predicts both solid lines to show a downward slope from left to right. The two points plotted on the right ordinate indicate the ratios between the responses of the data connected by solid lines. The similarity of the two ratios also supports NTVA. Adapted with permission from Martinez-Trujillo and Treue (2004). Feature-based attention increases the selectivity of population responses in primate visual cortex. *Current Biology*, **14**, 744–751. Copyright 2004 by Elsevier.

way β values were always set high for the direction of the RDP in the receptive field, but the direction of the RDP varied systematically between being preferred and anti-preferred for the cell. The response of the cell was compared with its response in a neutral condition, in which the monkey monitored a small square at fixation for luminance changes. Assume β values for different directions of motion were the same (β_{neutral}) in the neutral condition, and let β_v be the beta value multiplying the response of a cell whose preferred direction of motion deviated from the direction of the target by an angular difference of v in the attention-to-motion condition. The results of the experiment appeared to show that β_v decreased as v was increased from 0° up to 180° (Fig. 8.11). Apparently, when the attended direction was equal to the

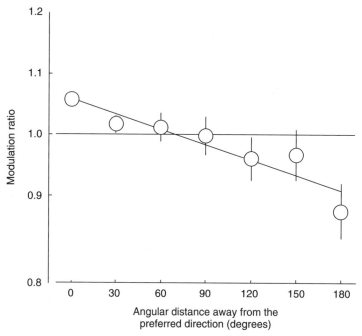

Fig. 8.11 The effect of pigeonholing may vary systematically with the similarity between the attended and the preferred feature of a cell. The figure shows data supporting this hypothesis from the study of Martinez-Trujillo and Treue (2004). Modulation ratios between the response of an MT neuron when the monkey was attending an RDP with a particular direction of motion (outside the receptive field) versus a neutral condition are plotted as a function of the angular distance between the direction of the RDPs and the cell's preferred direction. The bars represent standard errors. Note that the 12 directions tested were collapsed into seven data points because directions that were angled clockwise and counterclockwise by the same angular distance from the preferred direction have been pooled and averaged. The line represents the best linear model fitted to the data. Adapted with permission from Martinez-Trujillo and Treue (2004). Feature-based attention increases the selectivity of population responses in primate visual cortex. *Current Biology*, **14**, 744–751. Copyright 2004 by Elsevier.

cell's preferred direction, attention increased the response by about 7%, so the ratio $\beta_{0\ degrees} / \beta_{neutral}$ was about 1.07. When the attended direction was orthogonal to the cell's preferred direction, attention had little or no effect, so $\beta_{90\ degrees}$ was nearly the same as $\beta_{neutral}$. When the attended direction was opposite to the cell's preferred direction, attention decreased the response by about 12%, so $\beta_{180\ degrees} / \beta_{neutral}$ was about 0.88. Of course, the finding of opposite effects of attention for opposite directions of motion may be limited in generality. It would seem useful for an organism to be able to manipulate β values independently, and the capacity for doing this may show up in other tasks or cortical areas.

8.2.2 Effects with a faint stimulus

With a single, faint experimental stimulus in its receptive field, a neuron is faced with a classical problem of signal detection: discrimination of a weak signal (the stimulus) from pure noise (ghost objects formed by internally generated random noise). In this condition NTVA assumes that there is a substantial probability that the neuron responds to noise instead of responding to the faint stimulus. Studies by Reynolds *et al.* (2000) and Williford and Maunsell (2006) have provided intricate patterns of data on the way attentional effects depend upon stimulus contrast (and thus, visibility). In the following we show how these data can be accounted for by NTVA.

8.2.2.1 Reynolds *et al.* (2000)

Reynolds *et al.* (2000) studied responses of V4 neurons to single stimuli presented in the receptive field by a method adapted from Luck *et al.* (1997) and Reynolds *et al.* (1999). First, the monkey fixated a small dot at the centre of a computer screen. Sequences of oriented, bar-shaped patches of grating were then simultaneously presented at two locations, one inside the receptive field of the recorded V4 neuron and the other at an equally eccentric position in the opposite hemifield (Fig. 8.12). At the beginning of a block of trials, a cue indicated which of the two sequences should be attended. In each trial, stimulus sequences of variable length were presented simultaneously at the two locations. The monkey's task was to release a bar when a target stimulus (a rotated square patch of grating) appeared at the cued location.

For each neuron Reynolds *et al.* selected five contrasts that were spaced at equal logarithmic intervals of contrast (typically by doubling the next lower contrast) so that they spanned the dynamic response range of the cell. The contrast of the stimuli (including targets) varied randomly among the five values from presentation to presentation. The orientation and spatial frequency of the stimuli were selected to be non-optimal for the cell, so that not even the one with highest contrast elicited the strongest possible response from the neuron. For this reason, a lack of attentional enhancement of responses to the brightest stimuli could not be due to a physiological saturation of the cell's firing rate.

All analyses were based on the neurons' responses to nontarget stimuli. Figure 8.13 shows the mean firing rate of 84 tested neurons as a function of the stimulus contrast (in logarithmic units) with attention condition (attend-inside-receptive-field versus attend-outside-receptive-field) as the parameter. Values of the contrast along the abscissa have been normalized so that for each

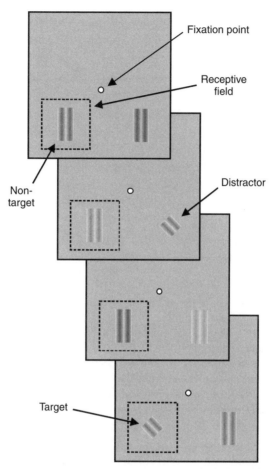

Fig. 8.12 Experimental procedure of Reynolds *et al.* (2000). Sequences of oriented, bar-shaped patches of grating were presented simultaneously at two locations: one in the receptive field (indicated by a dashed black square) and the other at an equally eccentric position in the opposite hemifield. In each trial the length of the sequence was chosen at random to be from one to six stimuli. The contrast of each stimulus was also chosen at random. Adapted with permission from Reynolds, Pasternak and Desimone (2000). Attention increases sensitivity of V4 neurons. *Neuron*, **26**, 703–714. Copyright 2000 by Elsevier.

neuron, the five selected contrasts are found at 1, 2, 3, 4, and 5 log units, respectively. As can be seen, the mean firing rate increased with the contrast of the stimulus grating, and at all levels of stimulus contrast, the firing rate was higher to attended than to ignored stimuli (i.e. higher in the attend-inside-receptive-field condition than in the attend-outside-receptive-field condition). The close fits to the data by NTVA shown by the smooth curves in Figs 8.13 and 8.14 are explained in Box 8.3.

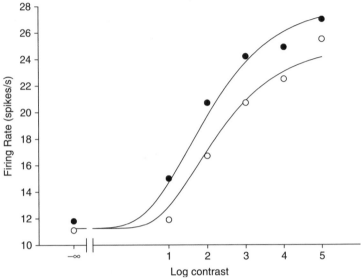

Fig. 8.13 Effect of attention in the experiment of Reynolds *et al.* (2000). The mean firing rate is shown as a function of the logarithm of the stimulus contrast when the monkey attended to a stimulus inside the receptive field (solid circles) and when the monkey attended to a stimulus outside the receptive field (open circles). A theoretical fit based on NTVA with the same contrast response function for all features is indicated by smooth curves. Data are from Reynolds, Pasternak and Desimone (2000). Attention increases sensitivity of V4 neurons. *Neuron*, **26**, 703–714. Copyright 2000 by Elsevier. Adapted with permission.

Box 8.3 Reynolds *et al.* (2000)

The smooth curves in Fig. 8.13 show a fit based on the hypothesis that when only a faint stimulus is present inside the classical receptive field of a V4 neuron, there is a substantial probability that the neuron responds to internal random noise rather than responding to the faint stimulus. We further assumed that when the neuron responds to internal random noise, the firing rate of the neuron equals the baseline rate (undriven activity) of the neuron, b. When the neuron responds to the stimulus, x, the firing rate of the neuron (say, the kth feature-i neuron) equals $b + \eta_k(x, i)\, \beta_i$, where β_i is the featural bias in favour of i. The probability that the neuron responds to the stimulus (x) rather than the noise (z) equals $w_x/(w_x + w_z)$, where w_x is the attentional weight of the stimulus, and w_z is the attentional weight of the noise. Hence the mean rate of firing when stimulus x is the

Box 8.3 Reynolds et al. (2000) *(continued)*

only real stimulus in the receptive field can be written as $b + v_{ki}$, where v_{ki} is given by

$$v_{ki} = \eta_k(x,i)\beta_i \frac{w_x}{w_x + w_z}.$$

As when fitting the data of Martinez-Trujillo and Treue (2002), we assumed that all η values for features of the stimulus grating increase with the contrast of the grating in accordance with the same contrast response function $f_{lsa}(c)$ (given by equation 8.2) so that (by equations 8.3–8.6)

$$v_{ki} = m f_{lsa}(c) \frac{f_{lsa}(c)}{f_{lsa}(c) + w_{ratio}},$$

where $m = \eta_k^*(x, i)\beta_i$ (the activation of an average feature-i neuron when it responds to stimulus x rather than responding to noise and x is presented at maximum contrast) and $w_{ratio} = w_z/w_x^*$ (the ratio between the attentional weight of the noise and the attentional weight of the stimulus grating at maximum contrast).

In the attend-inside-receptive-field condition, stimuli inside the receptive field should be attended, but noise should be ignored, so w_{ratio} should be as small as possible. The fit shown in Fig. 8.13 was obtained with $w_{ratio} = 0$ in the attend-inside-receptive-field condition but $w_{ratio} = 0.22$ in the attend-outside-receptive-field condition. In both conditions, baseline rate b was 11.2 spikes/s, parameter m was 16.9 spikes/s, and the contrast response function had a location parameter l at −5.25 log units of contrast, scale parameter s at 2.39, and asymmetry parameter a at 296.

The fit shown in Fig. 8.13 is based on very simple assumptions and it is close. In this fit, the relative effect of attention [measured, for example, by (response attending inside receptive field − response attending outside receptive field) / (response attending inside receptive field + response attending outside receptive field)] is greatest in the mid-contrast range, but the absolute effect of attention [i.e. (response attending inside receptive field − response attending outside receptive field)] increases monotonically as the contrast is increased. There is a trend in the observed data that not only the relative but also the absolute effect of attention is greatest in the mid-contrast range. This trend may be captured in the fit by relaxing the assumption that all η values for features of the stimulus grating increase with the contrast of the grating in accordance with the same contrast response function $f_{lsa}(c)$. Figure 8.14 shows a very close fit to the data, which was obtained with two different contrast

Box 8.3 Reynolds *et al.* (2000) *(continued)*

response functions of the form $f_{lsa}(c)$. For both contrast response functions, parameter a was fixed at a value of 1. The contrast response function for $\eta_k(x, i)$ had location parameter l and scale parameter s, so

$$\eta_k(x, i) = \eta_k^*(x, i) f_{ls1}(c),$$

where $\eta_k^*(x, i)$ is the value of $\eta_k(x, i)$ at maximum contrast. The contrast response function for η values contributing to the attentional weight of x had location parameter l' and scale parameter s', so

$$w_x = w_x^* f_{l's'1}(c),$$

where w_x^* is the value of w_x at maximum contrast. The fit was obtained with $w_{ratio} = 0.004$ in the attend-inside-receptive-field condition and $w_{ratio} = 0.014$ in the attend-outside-receptive-field condition. Baseline rate b was 11.3 spikes/s and parameter m was 15.9 spikes/s. The contrast response function for $\eta_k(x, i)$ had a location parameter l at 1.02 log units of contrast and a scale parameter s at 0.72, whereas the contrast response function for w_x had a location parameter l' at 7.68 log units of contrast and a scale parameter s' at 2.33.

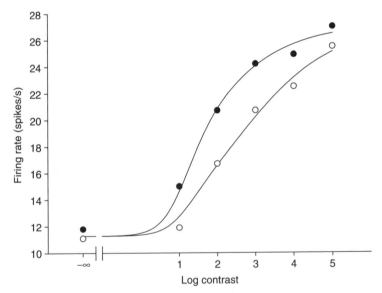

Fig. 8.14 Alternative fit to the effect of attention in the experiment of Reynolds *et al.* (2000). The empirical data are the same as those shown in Fig. 8.13. A theoretical fit based on NTVA with different contrast response functions for different features is indicated by smooth curves. Data are from Reynolds, Pasternak and Desimone (2000). Attention increases sensitivity of V4 neurons. *Neuron*, **26**, 703–714. Copyright 2000 by Elsevier. Adapted with permission.

8.2.2.2 Williford and Maunsell (2006)

Reynolds *et al.* (2000) interpreted their results in terms of a 'contrast gain' mechanism (see Section 6.4) in which attention effectively adds contrast to a stimulus. However, other studies (McAdams and Maunsell 1999*a*; Treue and Martinez-Trujillo 1999) have reported attentional modulations of the response to a single receptive field stimulus that instead suggest that the effect of attention is an 'activity gain' (i.e. a multiplicative modulation of the total firing rate) or a 'response gain' (i.e. a multiplicative modulation of the rate of activation, which is the firing rate minus the baseline rate). The latter mechanism corresponds to NTVA's explanation of the studies of McAdams and Maunsell (1999*a*) and Treue and Martinez-Trujillo (1999) (see Section 8.2.1). The three different types of models are illustrated in Fig. 8.15.

Williford and Maunsell (2006) aimed to test these three models against each other by studying the effects of attention to stimuli of different contrasts. They recorded from 131 individual V4 neurons during a spatial attention task. In this task, stimuli were presented at two locations—one within and one outside the receptive field of the recorded neuron—and the monkey was cued to monitor one of the two locations. On each trial, a consecutive series of Gabor patterns that were mutually identical but varied in contrast was presented at the target location (while another series was presented at the distractor location) and the monkey was rewarded for reacting (by making a saccade to the target location) when a Gabor pattern with a different orientation appeared. Whereas the contrast of each Gabor was varied systematically within each trial (cf. Reynolds *et al.* 2000), the orientation was varied only between trials. Consistent with the findings of McAdams and Maunsell (1999*a*) (see Section 8.2.1.1), attention to the receptive field stimulus scaled responses similarly to preferred and non-preferred orientations, suggesting multiplicative modulation of the tuning curve. However, the effect on the contrast response function was less clear. The sensory response of the cells followed the usual sigmoid pattern as a function of the logarithmic contrast (cf. Fig. 8.6). Attention to the stimulus in the receptive field generally increased responses, but the specific effect on each cell's contrast response function was not perfectly consistent with any of the three models, although it tended to favour the activity gain or response gain models over the contrast gain model. In particular, clear effects of attention were found even at the highest levels of contrast (see Fig. 8.16), which is inconsistent with the contrast gain model. Clear effects of attention also were found at zero contrast (i.e. on baseline firing). Effects on baseline firing are inconsistent with both the contrast gain and the response gain models, and the effects on baseline firing were larger than predicted by the activity gain model. The close fits by NTVA shown by the smooth curves in Fig. 8.16a, b are explained in Box 8.4.

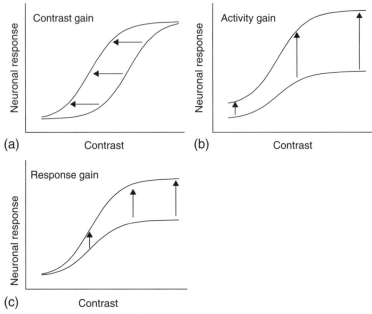

Fig. 8.15 Alternative models of the effects of attention on visual responses in single cells. (a) Effect of contrast gain on a contrast response function. The effect is a shift along the contrast axis. (b) Effect of activity gain on a contrast response function. The effect is a multiplicative modulation of the total activity, which is the overall firing rate. (c) Effect of response gain on a contrast response function. The effect is a multiplicative modulation of the rate of activation, which is the firing rate minus the baseline rate. Adapted with permission from Williford and Maunsell (2006). Effects of spatial attention on contrast response functions in macaque area V4. *Journal of Neurophysiology*, **96**, 40–54. Copyright 2006 by the American Physiological Society.

Box 8.4 Williford and Maunsell (2006)

Figure 8.16a shows the normalized firing rate, averaged across the 48 neurons that showed significant modulation by attention, as a function of the stimulus contrast with attention condition (attend-inside-receptive-field versus attend-outside-receptive-field) and stimulus orientation (preferred orientation versus null orientation) as parameters. The smooth curves show a fit based on the same assumptions as the fit to the data of Reynolds *et al.* (2000) shown in Fig. 8.13. The fit in Fig. 8.16a was obtained with

Box 8.4 Williford and Maunsell (2006) *(continued)*

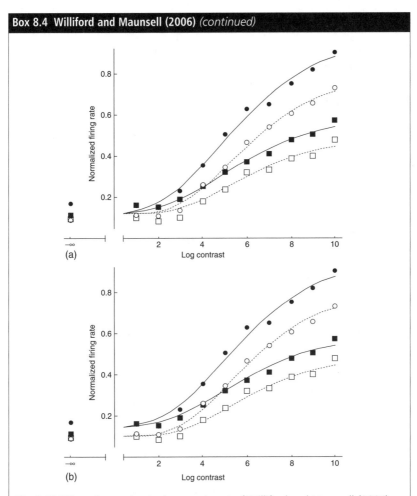

Fig. 8.16 Effect of attention in the experiment of Williford and Maunsell (2006). (a) Normalized firing rate as a function of the logarithm of the stimulus contrast with attention condition and stimulus orientation as parameters. Attention was either inside the receptive field (solid symbols) or outside the receptive field (open symbols) of the recorded cell. Stimulus orientation was either the preferred orientation (circles) or the null orientation (squares) for the cell. A theoretical fit based on NTVA with the same baseline firing rate in the two attention conditions is indicated by smooth curves (solid for attend-inside-receptive-field conditions, dotted for attend-outside-receptive-field conditions). (b) Alternative fit to the same empirical data. The fit was based on NTVA with different baselines for the two attention conditions. Data are from Williford and Maunsell (2006). Effects of spatial attention on contrast response functions in macaque area V4. *Journal of Neurophysiology*, **96**, 40–54. Copyright 2006 by the American Physiological Society. Adapted with permission.

Box 8.4 Williford and Maunsell (2006) *(continued)*

$w_{ratio} = 0$ in the attend-inside-receptive-field condition but $w_{ratio} = 0.24$ in the attend-outside-receptive-field condition. In both attention conditions, baseline rate b was 0.118 (i.e. 11.8% of the neuron's strongest response); the maximum activation m was 0.866 and 0.477 when the stimulus was presented in the preferred and the null orientations, respectively; and the contrast response function had a location parameter l at -2.05 log units of contrast, scale parameter s at 5.05, and asymmetry parameter a at 14.9.

The fit shown in Fig. 8.16a is fairly close but not perfect. It captures the pattern of the data except for the notable effect of attention on baseline firing. As suggested by Williford and Maunsell (2006, p. 52), 'it is as if attention to the receptive field location added a few spikes per second of activity on top of a multiplicative effect on driven activity'. The suggestion fits in with the NTVA hypothesis about baseline shifts as reflections of representations in VSTM (see Section 8.3). It seems plausible that the monkeys performed the task by retaining the first stimulus presented at the target location as a mental image, matching the image against each of the succeeding stimuli at the target location, and responding by a saccade to the target location as soon as a mismatch in orientation was detected. Consistent with this hypothesis, Fig. 8.16b shows a nearly perfect fit to the data obtained by letting baseline rate b differ between the two attention conditions. The fit was found with $w_{ratio} = 0$ and $b = 0.144$ in the attend-inside-receptive-field condition but $w_{ratio} = 0.15$ and $b = 0.100$ in the attend-outside-receptive-field condition. In both attention conditions, the maximum activation m was 0.835 and 0.455 when the stimulus was presented in the preferred and the null orientations, respectively, and the contrast response function had a location parameter l at -1.95 log units of contrast, scale parameter s at 5.03, and asymmetry parameter a at 15.2.

8.2.3 **Effects with a relatively simple and strong stimulus**

Single-cell studies with one experimental stimulus in the receptive field of the recorded neuron have shown relatively small but consistent effects of attention for stimuli that are complex (cf. Section 8.2.1) or faint (cf. Section 8.2.2). Results from studies that have used a single, relatively simple and strong stimulus in the receptive field are less consistent. Some studies have reported no effects of attention. Using 200-ms exposures of bars of various colours, orientations, and sizes, Moran and Desimone (1985) found no effect of attention when only one stimulus was present in the receptive field of a recorded neuron in area V1 or V4. Similarly, using 50-ms presentations of bars (rectangles) followed by blank intervals of at least 300 ms, Luck *et al.* (1997) found essentially no effect of attention when only one stimulus was present in the receptive field of neurons in area V1, V2, or V4. Such null effects of attention are readily explained by NTVA by assuming that the attentional weights of noise objects were negligibly small relative to the attentional weight of the experimental stimulus: the weight of the experimental stimulus should be much higher than the weight of 'ghost' objects formed by internal random noise, because the experimental stimulus was high in contrast; and the weight of the experimental stimulus should be much higher than the weight of any of its individual parts, because the stimulus was too simple to have any noteworthy parts.

However, other studies with a single, relatively simple and strong stimulus in the receptive field have shown significant effects of attention. With bars as stimuli, Motter (1993) found both positive and negative effects of spatial attention on the firing rates of neurons in V1, V2, and V4; Motter (1994*a,b*) found attentional enhancement of firing rates of V4 neurons in a task that required filtering by a non-spatial category (cf. Chelazzi *et al.* 1998, 2001); and Connor *et al.* (1997) found evidence of dynamic remapping of receptive fields in V4 neurons when spatial attention was varied. These findings are analysed in the following sections. The main findings may be accounted for in terms of NTVA if we assume that although the experimental stimuli were relatively simple and strong, attentional weights of noise objects were noticeable relative to the weight of the experimental stimulus.

8.2.3.1 Motter (1993)

Motter (1993) showed that spatial attention can modulate the responses of neurons as early in the (macaque) visual system as V1, as well as in V2 and V4. Most important in the present context, Motter's results also suggested that such modulation (with only one stimulus in the receptive field) can be both positive and negative. In Motter's experiment, the monkey's attention was cued to a specific location on the display screen. The cuing procedure was as follows (see Fig. 8.17). First the monkey was shown an array of small dots located on the circumference of an imaginary circle centred at fixation. After a variable interval (400–1000 ms), all but one of these dots disappeared. The remaining (cue) dot stayed on the screen for 200–400 ms at the location at which the target stimulus would appear. The location thus cued was either inside or outside the receptive field of the neuron being recorded. Immediately after the cue stimulus disappeared, 3–8 bars with different orientations were shown, only one of them located in the receptive field. Thus the stimulus in the receptive field was sometimes attended and sometimes unattended. The monkey's task was to make a discrimination of the orientation of the bar at the cued location. More than one-third of the recorded neurons in each

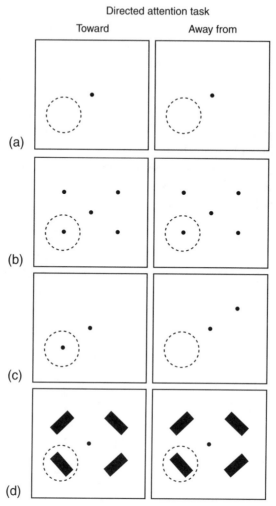

Fig. 8.17 The experimental procedure of Motter (1993). Each frame represents a field of view with a fixation dot in the centre and the neuron's receptive field indicated by a dotted circle. After establishing fixation (a), an array of cues appeared designating all possible stimulus locations for the trial (b). After a random interval (400–1000 ms) all but one cue was turned off (c). The remaining single cue marked the location of the stimulus (appearing in d) for which the monkey had to make a discriminative response. The task is shown under two conditions: when attention was directed *toward* and *away from* the cell's receptive field. Adapted with permission from Motter (1993). Focal attention produces spatially selective processing in visual cortical areas V1, V2 and V4 in the presence of competing stimuli. *Journal of Neurophysiology*, **70**, 909–919. Copyright 1993 by the American Physiological Society.

cortical area (V1, V2, and V4) showed significant differences between firing rates in the attended and unattended conditions. Remarkably, a substantial portion of these neurons had *lower* firing rates when the object in the receptive field was cued compared to when it was unattended. This was the case for 30% of the neurons in V1 and V2 and for about half of the neurons in V4.

Motter's (1993) findings of both significant increases and decreases in mean firing rates when attention was directed at a receptive field stimulus are reminiscent of the findings obtained in studies with multiple stimuli in the receptive field. When both an effective and an ineffective sensory stimulus are present in the receptive field of a neuron, the firing rate increases when attention is directed to the effective sensory stimulus, but decreases when attention is directed to the ineffective sensory stimulus (e.g. Moran and Desimone 1985). The findings of Motter (1993) can be explained by assuming that although his experimental stimuli were relatively simple and strong, there were noise objects with appreciable attentional weights that stimulated some of the recorded neurons more effectively than did the experimental stimuli (Schneider 1995). Although a bar is a relatively simple object, it does have individual parts, such as edges, and it is possible to attend to a particular edge rather than attending to the bar as a whole. Thus, it seems possible that individual edges have appreciable attentional weights. It also seems plausible that for some neurons (e.g. 'bar detectors' in V1), the bar was a more effective sensory stimulus than was an individual edge of the bar, but for other neurons (e.g. 'edge detectors' in V1), a particular edge of the bar was a more effective stimulus than was the bar as a whole. Hence, when the attentional weight of the bar in the receptive field of the recorded neuron was increased in relation to the weights of individual edges of the bar (as should occur in the *attended* condition), the expected firing rate increased in some neurons (e.g. bar detectors in V1) but decreased in others (e.g. edge detectors in V1, responding strongly to a particular edge but weakly to any other objects).

8.2.3.2 Motter (1994*a,b*)

Motter (1994*a,b*) modified the experimental design used in his previous study to investigate attentional selection (filtering) by colour. He recorded from neurons in cortical area V4, most of which were selective to both orientation and colour. The monkey's task was to select a bar stimulus on the basis of colour (or luminance) and report its orientation. The procedure was as follows (see Fig. 8.18). First the monkey fixated a cue stimulus that showed the target colour of the trial. Then the monkey was presented with an array of 4–6 coloured bars, only one of them located in the receptive field of the neuron being recorded. Initially there were several possible targets (i.e. objects

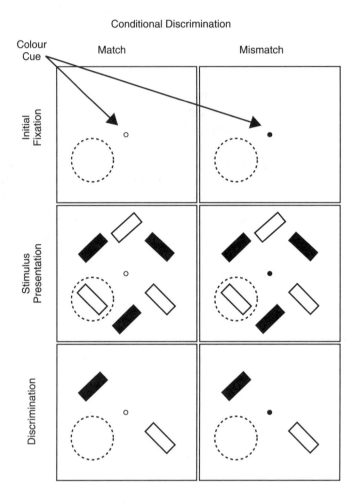

Fig. 8.18 The experimental procedure of Motter (1994a). Each frame represents a field of view with a fixation dot in the centre and the neuron's receptive field indicated by a dotted circle. The monkey initially fixated the central dot and was then presented with an array of stimuli. The monkey had to remember the colour of the fixation dot so that, when the array was reduced to two stimuli, the monkey could discriminate the orientation of the bar stimulus whose colour matched that of the fixation point. The task is shown under two conditions: when the target colour matched the stimulus in the receptive field, and when it did not match. Adapted with permission from Motter (1994). Neural correlates of attentive selection for color or luminance in extrastriate area V4. *Journal of Neuroscience*, **14**, 2178–2189. Copyright 1994 by the American Physiological Society.

matching the colour cue) in the display. At this stage, the monkey's attention was presumably uniformly distributed across all the objects with colours matching the cue, once attentional weights had been computed and applied (cf. Section 8.1.2). Finally, after a period of 1500–2700 ms, all possible targets but one were deleted from the screen, and the monkey reported the orientation of the remaining target stimulus.

During the stimulus presentation, a large majority of the recorded V4 neurons showed significantly stronger responses to the object in their receptive field when the cued colour matched the colour of the object. A relative increase of the response in case of mismatch was not seen in any neuron. Thus, whereas Motter (1993) found both increases and decreases in firing rates of V4 neurons with attention to the receptive field stimulus, Motter (1994*a,b*) found only increases. The cause of this discrepancy is not clear. However, the fact that attentional modulations did occur in both studies can be explained by assuming that although the experimental stimuli were relatively simple and strong, weights of noise objects were not negligible, so the probability that a V4 neuron responded to the bar in its receptive field instead of responding to noise objects increased with the attentional weight of the bar in the receptive field.

Motter reported that the difference in response to matching and mismatching stimuli began 150–200 ms after stimulus onset, continued to rise until 500 ms, and was stable for the remainder of the trial. Thus, as in the study by Chelazzi *et al.* (1998), the wave of unselective processing (before attentional weights had been computed and applied) seemed to take about 150–200 ms, which is 2-3 times the standard latency of responses to visual stimuli in area V4 (Motter 1994*b*, p. 2195). If the cue that showed the target colour was changed during the trial, the attentional effect on firing rates could be reversed over the course of 150–300 ms (Motter 1994*b*) (cf. Section 5.3.3 on the time course of attentional shifting).

8.2.3.3 Connor *et al.* (1997)

In a study of V4 neurons, Connor *et al.* (1997; see also Connor *et al.* 1996) found an interesting effect of spatial attention. In their own interpretation, the results suggested that attentional enhancement of neural responses spreads from the attended object to behaviourally irrelevant objects at nearby locations, as if the attended object was illuminated by a diffuse *spotlight of attention* (see Section 2.8.2). The basic task was as follows. First the monkey was shown a fixation point and an array of ring stimuli. After fixation was achieved the animal depressed a lever, and 500 ms later a target ring appeared. The delayed onset indicated that this was the target object. The monkey had to monitor the target ring for up to 4500 ms and respond to the disappearance of a 90° section anywhere along the ring's circumference. Changes in the other, distractor rings were to be ignored. The target ring was always placed slightly outside the receptive field of the neuron being recorded. At the same time, bar stimuli (with optimal values of colour, orientation, and width for the cell's response) irrelevant to the task were flashed inside the receptive field. The bars were displayed one at a time, and the first appeared 1000 ms after the target ring (by which time spatial attention should long have taken effect). The bar stimuli were displayed for 150 ms each, and a new stimulus appeared every 1000 ms until completion of the trial. Crucially, the bars were shown at varying distance from the attended ring. For example in the *4 ring/5 bar* experiment, five locations were probed (Fig. 8.19).

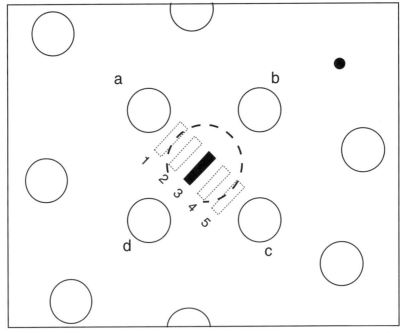

Fig. 8.19 The stimulus display used by Connor *et al.* (1997). The dot in the top right represents the fixation point and the dashed circle represents the receptive field. The monkey monitored one of four rings surrounding the receptive field at positions a–d. The rest of the screen was filled with distractor rings. Bars were presented (individually) at positions 1–5, which spanned the receptive field along the axis perpendicular of orientation. Adapted with permission from Connor, Preddie, Gallant, and van Essen (1997). Spatial attention effects in macaque area V4. *Journal of Neuroscience*, **17**, 3201–3214. Copyright 1997 by the American Physiological Society.

The mean rate of firing in response to a bar at a given location typically increased if the attended ring was placed close to the bar. No cells showed the opposite effect. For example in the *4 ring/5 bar* experiment, the average cell shifted 16% of its total response profile from one-half of the receptive field to the other as attention was directed from one side to the other. Analysed in another way, the receptive field position in which the mean response was strongest shifted 0.1 receptive field diameters on average, depending on the position of the attended ring. In a variation of the experiment (*2 ring/7 bar*), even larger response shifts were found. In general, it seemed that the receptive field was dynamically remapped such that the most responsive part (the *hot spot*) moved towards the attended object.

The finding can be explained in NTVA by assuming that although any bar flashed in the receptive field of the recorded neuron was a relatively strong stimulus, the weight of ghost objects (pure noise) in the receptive field was noticeable compared with the weight of the bar. As the monkey's task was to monitor the target ring for deletion of a section anywhere along the ring's circumference, the monkey presumably ascribed attentional weights so that objects in the immediate vicinity of the target ring got high attentional weights. (For optimal performance, the location being monitored should probably be a ring-shaped area extending somewhat beyond the edges of the target ring.) Because the target ring was close to the border of the receptive field of the recorded neuron, bars flashed inside the receptive field got higher attentional weight the closer they were to the target ring. Hence, when the target ring was moved closer to the bar flashed in the receptive field, the probability that the recorded neuron responded to the bar instead of responding to a noise object increased, and so the mean rate of firing also increased.

Like the analyses of the studies by Motter (1993, 1994*a,b*), our explanation of the study by Connor *et al.* (1997) shows that the main findings can be accounted for in terms of NTVA if we assume that although the experimental stimuli were relatively simple and strong, attentional weights of noise objects were noticeable relative to the weight of the experimental stimuli. It is not clear why effects of noise stimuli were negligibly small in the studies of Moran and Desimone (1985) and Luck *et al.* (1997) but noticeable in the studies of Motter (1993, 1994*a,b*) and Connor *et al.* (1997). However, it does seem clear that when only one stimulus is present in the receptive field of a recorded neuron, attentional effects are much smaller than when multiple stimuli are present. It also seems clear that the effects depend upon the complexity and the visibility of the receptive field stimulus. Studies with a single stimulus in the receptive field have shown consistent effects of attention for stimuli that are complex (see Section 8.2.1) or faint (see Section 8.2.2). With a single, relatively simple and strong stimulus in the receptive field, effects of attention have been less consistent (sometimes noticeable and significant, sometimes not). When effects of attention have been found, they generally conform to predictions from NTVA.

8.3 **Attentional effects on baseline firing**

With no stimulus in its receptive field, a neuron fires at baseline level. However, the baseline firing rate is not fixed, but has been found to depend on the attentional state of the organism. Many studies have reported that when a target is expected to appear inside a recorded cell's receptive field, the baseline firing rate is increased (Miyashita and Chang 1988; Fuster 1990; Miller *et al.* 1993, 1996; Luck *et al.* 1997; Chelazzi *et al.* 1998; Rainer *et al.* 1999; Reynolds *et al.* 1999, 2000; Williford and Maunsell 2006). The *baseline shift* is usually interpreted as being due to top-down signals that prepare the organism for processing an upcoming stimulus (e.g. Desimone 1999). Here we assume that the baseline shift reflects that a visual representation, such as a mental image, is held in VSTM (cf. Section 7.4), so that inner-driven activity is added to the undriven activity. Use of a more or less schematic mental image of the target seems plausible in tasks like delayed match-to-sample (Miller *et al.* 1993, 1996; McAdams and Maunsell 1999*a*), detection of a target in a sequence of displays (Luck *et al.* 1997; Reynolds *et al.* 1999, 2000), or standard visual search (Chelazzi *et al.* 1998, 2001). The mental image may be generated bottom-up (from a recent stimulus presentation) or top-down (from long-term memory).

8.3.1 **Miller et al. (1993)**

Miller *et al.* (1993) recorded from single neurons in the anterior inferotemporal (IT) cortex while monkeys performed a delayed match-to-sample task. Consistent with previous studies of IT neurons (Miyashita and Chang 1988, Fuster 1990), Miller *et al.* found increased baseline activity during the retention interval following the sample display (*delay activity*). The baseline shifts were stimulus-specific: a neuron fired more strongly if the target object was a preferred stimulus. The findings are readily interpreted as reflecting a mental image of the sample stimulus. Miller *et al.* now tested the effect of presenting several intervening stimuli between the sample and the probe stimulus. This procedure revealed that the stimulus-specific baseline shift was eliminated after the first intervening (mismatching) stimulus was shown on the screen. Therefore, the baseline shift in IT cells could not be representing the memory of the sample stimulus throughout the trial. Instead, as the monkey was still able to carry out the task, this memory must be represented in a different part of the brain: the following study points to the prefrontal cortex.

8.3.2 Miller *et al.* (1996)

Miller *et al.* (1996) extended the investigation of baseline shifts to neurons in the prefrontal (PF) cortex. They also used a match-to-sample task with multiple items intervening between the sample and the probe. Unlike IT neurons (which were also tested in this study) the PF neurons continued to respond with stimulus-specific delay activity across several intervening objects. One way to interpret this finding is to assume that immediately after the presentation of the sample stimulus, the sample was represented in the visual system by a comparatively concrete mental image (in PF, IT, and possibly lower visual areas), but later on, only representations of relatively abstract features of the sample were kept active (in PF). This more abstract representation might help in setting attentional parameters after the sample presentation, but free the visual system (up to IT) to process the stimuli later in the sequence.

In a further exploration of baseline shifts in PF, Rainer *et al.* (1999) showed that neurons can code for an anticipated stimulus that is different from the presented sample (i.e. generate a representation in VSTM top-down from long-term memory). They used a task in which the sample should be matched not with an identical stimulus but with a different, paired stimulus that the monkey had been trained to associate with it. Initially, after presentation of the sample stimulus, the baseline shift in PF reflected the sample, but soon it changed to reflect the features of the paired associate.

8.3.3 Luck *et al.* (1997)

Luck *et al.* (1997) studied the response of V1, V2, and V4 neurons when attention was directed to a specific location. The design was similar to that used by Reynolds *et al.* (1999, Experiment 2; 2000) (see Fig. 8.1). The monkey's task was to monitor a target location in a sequence of displays, reacting when a target object was shown. Attention was directed to the target location by means of instruction trials, and the monkey then had to remember the location for a whole block of trials. Stimuli could also appear at another location, but this was irrelevant to the task. The target object, a square, was the same throughout the whole study. Before the target appeared, the monkey was presented with 1–6 brief displays, each containing either one or two distractors in the attended or the unattended location. The stimuli were rectangles of different orientations and colours, some effective, some ineffective at driving the cell.

We have already mentioned one main result of Luck *et al.*'s study: a confirmation of the filtering mechanism discovered by Moran and Desimone (1985; see Section 8.1.1.1). A second important finding was a change in the baseline firing rates with attention. Luck *et al.* found that 54% of the recorded V4 neurons had significantly higher firing rates during the last 100 ms before stimulus exposure when attention was directed to stimuli inside their receptive fields rather than being directed to stimuli outside their receptive fields; 75% of V2 neurons showed the same pattern, whereas V1 neurons were generally unaffected. The increase in baseline firing rate was quite large, about 30–40%. The effect was also found when location marker boxes were removed from the display, so the effect could not be due to a sustained sensory response to these background stimuli. Instead, the increase in baseline firing appeared to be due to top-down input to the recorded cells.

Luck *et al.* dismissed the idea that the top-down input reflected an internal template or mental image of the target stimulus. They argued that if this was the case, the baseline shift should be found only when the target stimulus was an effective stimulus for the cell, but not when it was an ineffective stimulus (cf. Miller *et al.* 1993). Only eight cells were tested for this effect, but their responses generally pointed to an increase in baseline firing rate independent of whether the target stimulus was a preferred stimulus for the cell or not. Luck *et al.* instead suggested that it was the direction of attention into the receptive field *per se* that caused the shift in baseline firing, but also mentioned the possibility that the baseline shift might reflect 'a memory that specifies only the location of the target' (p. 36).

Within the framework of NTVA, the hypothesis that the baseline shift in the study by Luck *et al.* manifested a VSTM representation of just the target location seems very plausible. Presumably, stimulus selection (filtering) was based mainly on spatial location, and the main components of the attentional weights were based on η values computed by matching the stimuli against a neural representation of the target location. It seems plausible that this neural representation of the target location was kept in VSTM. The fact that the target object (square) was kept constant throughout the entire study presumably eliminated any need to keep specifications of the colour and shape of the target in VSTM (cf. Li *et al.* 1993; Miller *et al.* 1993).

Using similar experimental paradigms, Reynolds *et al.* (1999, 2000) also reported baseline shifts when attention was directed into the receptive field. The effects were not further characterized in these studies, but can presumably be explained in the same way as the data of Luck *et al.*

8.3.4 McAdams and Maunsell (1999*a*)

In the match-to-sample task of McAdams and Maunsell (1999*a*) (cf. Section 8.2.1.1), no shift in the baseline activity of V4 neurons was observed when attention was directed to a location in their receptive fields. However, McAdams and Maunsell only measured the neural response before the sample was presented. It is thus possible that the monkey used a mental image in the delay interval after sample presentation, as preparation for the upcoming matching task with the probe stimulus. As pointed out by Williford and Maunsell (2006), the absence of a baseline shift before sample presentation can also be regarded as an artefact of the task design: the stimuli were presented for relatively long periods (500 ms) and with perfectly predictable timing, so the animal had no motivation to direct attention to the location of the receptive field (producing a baseline shift) until after a stimulus appeared.

8.3.5 Chelazzi *et al.* (1998 versus 2001)

Recall from Section 8.1.2 that Chelazzi *et al.* (1998, 2001) found a baseline shift in IT neurons but not in V4 neurons, although using very similar experiments and testing the same monkeys. The baseline shift in IT was stimulus specific: a cell fired more strongly if the target object was a preferred stimulus for the cell (cf. Miller *et al.* 1993). This happened even though the target's location was not known in advance. The target was only expected to fall somewhere inside the receptive field. However, if the monkey used a mental image to remember the cue stimulus, it presumably imagined the target at a particular location (cf. Section 7.4) inside the large receptive field of the IT neuron, most plausibly at the central location where the cue stimulus had been shown. This may explain why Chelazzi *et al.* (2001) found no baseline effect in V4: in this case, the central location of the cue stimulus fell outside the small receptive fields of the recorded neurons. The same should be the case for the cue stimulus in Motter's (1994*a*) study of V4 neurons, which also failed to show a cue-specific baseline shift.

Note that, by a generalization of the argument presented above, attentional effects on baseline firing rates should be more widespread at higher than at lower levels of the visual system. Because receptive fields are larger at higher levels, the likelihood that an imagined object is located in the receptive field of a randomly chosen neuron is simply greater. Therefore, imagining an object at a specific position in the visual field is likely to involve a higher proportion of the cells at higher than at lower levels of the visual system.

The fact that the two studies by Chelazzi *et al.* showed similar effects of attention in the recorded cells in V4 and IT, but only the IT neurons showed baseline shifts, speaks against the notion that baseline shifts reflect 'bias signals' needed for controlling the competition between stimuli in the receptive field (cf. Desimone 1999). Instead, baseline shifts or representations kept in VSTM seem to have more indirect influences on the competition between stimuli for neural representation. In particular, the competition can be 'biased' by attentional weighting based on η values computed by matching the stimuli against a mental image of a particular type of target object.

8.4 **Attentional effects on neural synchronization**

In recent years another main type of attentional effect has been discovered: attention to an object may lead to increased synchronization of the activity in neurons with the attended object in their receptive fields (Fries *et al.* 2001). Moreover, the neural synchronization seems to be correlated with behavioural effects such as faster reaction times (Womelsdorf *et al.* 2006).

The general finding that neural synchronization is modulated by selective visual attention may be explained by the following line of reasoning based on NTVA. Other things equal, synchronized inputs of the same polarity (excitatory versus inhibitory) to two neurons tend to synchronize their firing. When two neurons are driven by the same cell, the inputs from the cell to the neurons are closely synchronized and also have the same polarity, so the two neurons tend to synchronize their firing. Common input that synchronizes two neurons may, for example, be feedback signals from VSTM structures or top-down signals setting attentional parameters (bias and pertinence values). The common input may also come from lower levels of processing: when a particular object must be attended, the receptive fields of relevant neurons are remapped so that a higher proportion of the cells with the target object in their receptive fields respond to the target. This means that, to an increasing degree, the neurons receive input from the lower-level cells that represent the target object, rather than other lower-level cells representing distractors or noise objects in the classical receptive field. Thus, a higher proportion of the neurons are driven by the same lower-level cells rather than being driven by different lower-level cells, leading to increased synchronization of their firing (simultaneous spiking).

Attention may lead to increased synchronization of oscillations in one frequency band while decreasing synchronization in another frequency band. NTVA makes no assumption that the activity of cells representing a particular object shows rhythmic oscillations. However, in circumstances in which a common input to two neurons from a certain lower-level cell shows oscillations at a particular frequency, both neurons should tend to oscillate at the same frequency, and the oscillations between the two neurons should tend to be synchronized in phase. As an example, let both neurons have Stimuli 1 and 2 in their classical receptive fields, and assume that input from lower-level cells representing Stimulus 1 shows oscillations at Frequency 1, whereas input from lower-level cells representing Stimulus 2 shows oscillations at Frequency 2. First, let the stimuli be distractors, with comparable attentional weights. In this case there is a substantial probability that one of the neurons responds to Stimulus 1 while the other neuron responds to Stimulus 2, but there is also a substantial probability that both neurons are driven by Stimulus 1 and a substantial probability that both neurons are driven by Stimulus 2. Hence, the two neurons will tend to show phase synchronization at Frequencies 1 and 2. Now, let Stimulus 1 become a target, such that the neurons almost always represent Stimulus 1 rather than Stimulus 2. If so, then attention to the target will lead to increased synchronization at Frequency 1 while decreasing synchronization at Frequency 2.

8.4.1 Fries *et al.* (2001)

Fries *et al.* (2001) recorded both spikes from small clusters of V4 neurons (multi-unit activity) and local field potentials (LFPs) simultaneously at several sites with overlapping receptive fields while monkeys performed a change detection task. At the start of each trial, the monkey's attention was cued to one of two locations, one inside and one outside the receptive fields of the recorded V4 neurons. After a brief delay period, objects appeared at each of these two locations. The monkey was rewarded for detecting a subtle colour change in the object at the cued location, which occurred after a variable time interval. Mean firing rates were not significantly increased by attention to the receptive field stimulus until very late in sensory processing, more than 450 ms after stimulus onset (this late effect might be explained as an effect of VSTM encoding). However, attention affected neural synchronization. Fries *et al.* found rhythmic oscillations in both the firing patterns of the recorded neurons and the local field potentials, analysed the phase synchronization between spikes and local field potentials (recorded from separate electrodes) at different frequencies, and found that attention to the stimulus in the receptive fields of the recorded neurons increased synchronization in the gamma frequency band (between 35 and 90 Hz) but decreased low-frequency (below 17 Hz) synchronization. The effect could be observed very early in the sensory response (e.g. in the period from 50 to 150 ms after stimulus onset). In the anticipatory delay period before stimulus onset, there was little power in the gamma band, but attention decreased synchronization in the low-frequency band.

The results of Fries *et al.* (2001) could not have been predicted in detail by NTVA but the results are consistent with the type of explanation suggested before. To see this, consider the possible effects of three types of stimuli: the experimenter-defined stimuli (circular patches of grating), individual parts of these (e.g. individual bars), and grey background. Assume that (1) input to the recorded V4 cells from lower-level (V1 or V2) cells representing grey background showed oscillations at low frequencies; (2) input from lower-level cells representing the experimenter-defined stimuli showed oscillations in the gamma band; and (3) input from lower-level cells representing certain individual parts of the experimenter-defined stimuli showed oscillations at low frequencies, whereas input from lower-level cells representing other parts of the experimenter-defined stimuli showed oscillations in the gamma band. First, consider the delay period before stimulus exposure. It seems plausible that, in the unattended condition, almost all of the lower-level cells providing input to the recorded V4 cells represented grey background, yielding fairly strong synchronization at the low frequencies. In the attended condition, a substantial proportion of the lower-level cells providing input to the V4 cells during the anticipatory delay period may have represented the anticipated stimulus (as constituents of a mental image of the stimulus). This may explain why attention caused desynchronization in the low-frequency band during the delay period.

Second, consider the effects found during stimulus presentation. In the unattended condition, some of the recorded V4 cells responded to the experimenter-defined stimuli, others responded to individual parts of these. In the attended condition, almost all of the recorded V4 cells responded to the experimenter-defined stimuli. Presumably, low-frequency synchronization decreased with attention because fewer V4 cells were driven by lower-level cells showing low-frequency oscillations. Gamma-band synchronization increased with attention because more V4 cells were driven by lower-level cells showing gamma-band oscillations and, in particular, because more of the V4 cells driven by lower-level cells showing gamma-band oscillations received inputs from the same lower-level cells.

8.4.2 **Womelsdorf *et al.* (2006)**

Reanalysing the data of Fries *et al.* (2001) trial by trial, Womelsdorf *et al.* (2006) showed that the monkey's speed of response was positively correlated with the strength of gamma-band synchronization among neurons with the attended object in their receptive fields. For distractors the effect was reversed: mean reaction times to the target were slower when synchronization was high among the neurons processing the distractor object. Thus, the relation between synchronization and reaction time was quite specific and could not be explained by a general increase in cortical arousal.

The correlations reported by Womelsdorf *et al.* (2006) should be expected whether (a) synchronization led to increased firing rates at later stages of processing, or (b) synchronization was merely a side-effect of attentional selection (an epiphenomenon) with no effect on mean rates of firing at later stages of processing. By Assumption a, when V4 neurons processing the same object fired in synchrony, their impact on downstream (e.g. IT) neurons increased. Hence, at higher levels in the visual system, neurons processing the relevant object increased their firing rate, which led to higher v values (cf. the rate equation), faster encoding into VSTM, and faster responses. However, fast reaction times should co-occur with strong synchronization even if the synchronization had no effect on firing rates at later processing stages (Assumption b). Consider the effect of random variations from trial to trial in the relative attentional weight of the target. For trials in which the relative attentional weight of the target was comparatively high, a higher proportion of the cells with the target in their receptive fields responded to the target rather than responding to noise objects. One effect of the target being represented in a higher proportion of the cells (and, therefore, in a greater number of cells) was faster processing of the target and faster reaction times. Another effect of the target being represented in a higher proportion of the cells with the target in their receptive fields was that more of these cells were being driven by the same lower-level cells, which increased their synchronization. Thus, faster reaction times and increased synchronization should co-occur whether or not the speed-up in reaction times was caused by the increase in synchronization.

8.5 **Summary**

We have tested the explanatory power of NTVA against more than 20 central studies in the single-cell visual attention literature. Using the filtering mechanism of NTVA, it was straightforward to explain the strongest and most consistent effect in the literature: the change in firing rate when attention is reallocated across multiple stimuli in the same receptive field (see Section 8.1). The finding of linear weighting of mean responses to individual receptive field stimuli (e.g. Reynolds *et al.* 1999) followed readily from the rate equation. The long unselective processing stage in experiments requiring non-spatial selection also fits the model's predictions (Section 8.1.2) and effects of varying the luminance contrast of receptive field stimuli accorded closely with the weight equation (Section 8.1.3).

The filtering mechanism of NTVA further accounted for many findings with a single experimental stimulus in the receptive field (Section 8.2). NTVA explained why filtering has relatively little or no effect when the stimulus is sufficiently simple and strong. NTVA also explained how filtering becomes effective when the stimulus is complex (so that individual parts of the stimulus must be considered) or faint (so that internally generated random noise must be considered). In experimental conditions in which attention was directed to a particular feature across spatial locations, the pigeonholing mechanism of NTVA could explain the modulation of firing rates.

Both mechanisms described were compatible with the common finding of multiplicative modulation of neural activation (across a stimulus dimension) with attention.

Extant findings on shifts in baseline firing rates with attention (see Section 8.3) also seemed in general agreement with NTVA's notion of representations in VSTM (in particular, mental images). Among other findings, NTVA explained why baseline shifts are more widespread at higher than lower levels of the cortical visual system.

Finally, NTVA accounted for findings that attention can lead to increased synchronization in firing activity across neurons (Section 8.4). When a group of neurons receive a common input, the coherence of their spiking activity should increase. The common input may be generated bottom-up, as a result of dynamic remapping of receptive fields in favour of target objects, or top-down, due to VSTM encoding or attentional parameter setting. At the behavioural level, synchronization should co-occur with faster reaction times for target objects, even if the coherence is an effect rather than a cause of attentional selection.

In conclusion, NTVA provides a simple theoretical frame that explains findings across the whole single-cell literature on visual attention, while being completely consistent with its counterpart in cognitive psychology, the TVA model.

Part 3

The anatomy of visual attention

9

Brain imaging of visual attention

The anatomical localization of mental functions has always been a central question in neuropsychology. Historically the discussion has shifted from the extremes of phrenology (Gall and Spurzheim 1808), which claimed that highly complex functions (e.g. 'poetical talent') were located in specific parts of the cortex, to theories of the brain as a largely undifferentiated, 'equipotent' organ (Lashley 1950). Today, the dominating notion is that of functional networks (Fuster 2003): complex mental activities are not viewed as the product of single centres (although tendencies towards 'neo-phrenology' are still with us; see Uttal 2001) nor of the brain in general. Rather, such functions are thought to depend on the integrated activity of widely distributed anatomical networks in which each component delivers a specific contribution. The mapping of these systems has been boosted enormously by the advent of brain imaging methods such as positron emission tomography (PET) and functional magnetic resonance imaging (fMRI), which enable *in vivo* measurements of the activity of the whole network during a given cognitive task. The relatively high anatomical resolution of PET and fMRI has been complemented by electrophysiological recordings of event related potentials (ERPs) and magnetoencephalography (MEG), which can measure the time course of neural processes with millisecond precision.

In relation to anatomical networks for visual attention a distinction is often made between *source* and *target* areas. The source areas are presumed to transmit attentional control signals to target areas in the visual system, where they modulate the basic sensory processing that goes on in these areas. The distinction between source and target areas is not clear-cut, but is nonetheless useful as an organizing principle for most findings in the field. Functional brain imaging has, in particular, elucidated the source of attentional signals, but also confirmed and elaborated findings from single-cell research on attentional effects in (target) visual areas.

In this chapter we provide an overview of attention research within this relatively young, but highly expansive field. We explain the main methods of functional brain imaging (Section 9.1), describe central findings on attentional processing in both target (Section 9.2) and source (Section 9.3) areas of the brain, and discuss some of the most influential anatomical models of visual attention (Section 9.4). On the basis of this and other research, we go on to suggest how the processes described in the NTVA model may be distributed in the brain (Section 9.5).

9.1 **Methods of functional brain imaging**

Currently several methods are available for imaging the brain's activity during cognitive processing, each with their strengths and weaknesses. One main type of method measures changes in the blood flow of the brain while experimental subjects are doing cognitive tasks in a scanner. This type of research rests on the assumption that a local increase in blood flow (or related metabolic activity) in a given area of the brain can be taken as an indirect measure of increased neural activity in that area. The existence of a link between the *haemodynamic response* and neural activity is firmly established, but the specific physiological mechanisms behind the coupling are less well understood. Although the vascular response is traditionally taken as an indication of increases in spiking activity of the cells in a given area, it may instead reflect changes in the area's synaptic input or its intrinsic processing, which might be both excitatory and inhibitory (Logothetis *et al.* 2001; Logothetis 2003). Findings of 'neural activation' in blood flow studies should therefore be interpreted with some caution. Another critical property of the haemodynamic response is its spatial and temporal precision. Although the change in blood flow occurs in a larger area than the neurally active area (as if to 'water the whole garden for the sake of one flower'), its precision is still within millimetre range. This allows for quite specific anatomical localization in this line of research, at least theoretically. The temporal precision of the link between vascular response and neural activity is, however, inherently limited. Whereas changes in neural activity occur within tens of milliseconds, the vascular response is sluggish and blurred: it is delayed for seconds and only washes out slowly before a new measurement can be made.

The nature of the vascular response imposes significant constraints for this kind of neuropsychological research. However, many ingenious experimental designs have been devised to get around these limitations, sometimes rewarded by spectacular results, as we shall see in the next sections. In the classical design for cognitive brain mapping, relative differences in regional cerebral blood flow (rCBF) between two psychological tasks are measured. Ideally, the two tasks are so tightly matched that they differ only with respect to one cognitive operation, namely the one of interest to the study (e.g. setting attentional weights for a particular location). By subtracting the rCBF measured during the first task from the other, all other task-related activity should be cancelled out and only the one elicited by the targeted cognitive operation should be left; an experimental logic that dates back to the cognitive *subtraction method* of Donders (1869). However, it is difficult to match two cognitive tasks so tightly, and in practice the subtractive design may not work out so simply. For better experimental control, more complex set-ups are possible (especially for fMRI, as explained later); for example, factorial designs where more combinations of cognitive states are contrasted, or correlational studies where the amount of activity is related to the *degree* of cognitive manipulation (see Owen *et al.* 2003). In the newest development, spontaneous fluctuations of blood flow are measured in the absence of a cognitive task (Fox *et al.* 2005, 2006): *resting-state fMRI.* Correlations in activity between different brain areas under these circumstances supposedly reveal anatomical networks that are in operation without external stimulation.

The first method to tap effectively into the relation between blood flow and cognition was positron emission tomography (PET). The technology of PET imaging was pioneered in the 1970s and developed through the 1980s, by which time it became the dominant method for functional brain imaging until fMRI assumed this position in the late 1990s. PET measures the concentration of positron-emitting (radioactive) compounds of molecules in the blood, such as glucose and oxygen, which serve as indicators for the amount of blood flow in an area. Different chemical isotopes can be used, giving PET high flexibility for biochemical investigations, for example in relation to pharmacological effects. The spatial resolution of PET is about a centimetre, which is so high that it revolutionized brain imaging in the 1980s. However, the temporal resolution is quite poor: to obtain enough data for statistical analysis, all activity occurring in a window of about 1 min must be integrated. Therefore cognitive activity must be kept constant across many trials (*blocked design*), and processes occurring within a single trial are far beyond the reach of PET. Another important constraint is that, for health reasons, studies of the same individual must be limited in extent because of the injection of a radioactive tracer before each testing session. Therefore, typically, brain activity has to be averaged across many subjects, creating a challenge with correcting the results for individual anatomical variation (the *normalization problem*). Normalization of brain images implies that individual patterns of activation are to some extent 'smeared out' in the analysis, limiting the anatomical precision of the investigation.

At the beginning of the 1990s it was discovered that haemodynamic processes in the brain can be measured non-invasively using functional magnetic resonance imaging (fMRI). Magnetic resonance imaging exploits the fact that different kinds of tissue (e.g. grey and white matter) have different magnetic properties. In the extremely strong and coherent magnetic field of an MR scanner these differences can be localized very precisely. In this way a high-resolution map of tissue contrasts in the brain can be produced. The MR scanner can be calibrated to measure many tissue contrasts, but for cognitive brain imaging the so-called blood oxygen level dependent (BOLD) signal has been used most extensively. The BOLD signal is based on magnetic differences between oxygenated and deoxygenated blood. When more blood flows into a brain area as a result of increased neural activity, oxygen consumption is increased, though not enough to use up the extra oxygen provided by the larger blood flow. The result is that blood oxygenation is locally increased, creating a stronger BOLD signal that can be taken as a marker for neural activity. Being a vascular signal, BOLD lags 4–8 seconds behind the original neural activity, which limits the temporal resolution of fMRI. However, compared with PET, fMRI has great advantages for experimental design. As mentioned, the method is non-invasive and it is therefore possible to test individuals extensively to improve the signal-to-noise ratio of each measurement or to set up more experimental conditions (e.g. complex factorial designs). In addition, the temporal resolution of functional MRI is still good enough to isolate the BOLD response for individual trials of an experiment. In contrast to the minute-long experimental blocks of PET studies, this opens up the possibility of so-called *event-related designs*, where conditions can be varied from trial to trial in a randomized manner and analysis can be made depending on performance in each trial (e.g. contrasting occasions where a stimulus was perceived versus missed). The spatial resolution of fMRI is also good; in theory, it is on the order of millimetres, close to the precision of the vascular response itself. However, such high resolution can only be obtained in single subjects. When comparing activations between individuals the normalization problem also applies to fMRI, which substantially reduces the anatomical resolution of the method.

Whereas PET and functional MRI provide efficient ways of mapping the anatomical networks involved in cognitive tasks, another technology is better suited for studying the time course of neuropsychological processes. In the 1930s it was discovered that fluctuations in electrical voltage recorded at the scalp (electroencephalograms; EEGs) correlate with general activation states such as alertness or sleep. The EEG signal typically arises from simultaneous stimulation of the dendrites (input receivers) in large populations of similarly oriented neurons, thus producing coherent electrical activity (Luck and Girelli 1998). The EEG as a whole reflects global properties of brain activity, but it is possible to isolate a small portion of the signal linked to a particular stimulation. This can be done by repeating exactly the same, time-locked stimulation ('event') many times and averaging the measurements. Because the large background EEG signal is unrelated to the experimental stimulation and fluctuates randomly, it is averaged out, while the remaining small signal specifically reflects the studied event. This analysis is the basis of the event-related potential (ERP) technique, which has been in use for about 30 years. ERP recordings have excellent temporal resolution—on the order of milliseconds—and so potentially offer real-time measurement of the cognitive processes occurring in the brain between stimulus and response. The main drawback of ERP is that the anatomical source of the measured signals cannot be localized very well. This is in part due to strong deflection of the electrical signal when passing through the skull. A powerful, but expensive variation of the ERP technique, magnetoencephalography (MEG), utilizes magnetic recordings that are not nearly as vulnerable to this disturbance. However, a more fundamental challenge for localization is the so-called *inverse problem*: it is not mathematically possible to compute exactly which set of generators has caused a given surface potential; the problem always has multiple solutions. By making some simplifying assumptions it is still possible to localize roughly the anatomical source of ERP and MEG signals, but more reliable evidence is obtained by combining the results with analogous experiments conducted by PET or fMRI.

A limitation shared by all methods of functional brain imaging is that measurements are inherently correlational and cannot demonstrate causal mechanisms. Functional imaging shows brain activity while a given psychological task is carried out. However, activation of a brain area during a given task does not imply that the area is functionally critical, that is, *necessary* to carry out the task. It is conceivable that the activation of the area is merely secondary to critical neural processing in other brain regions. To derive conclusions about which areas are causally related to some psychological process, one needs a more direct experimental intervention: to study what happens if the neural function of the area of interest is altered. This is the rationale behind lesion studies and other manipulations of brain activity such as transcranial magnetic stimulation (TMS), which are discussed in Chapter 10.

Another limitation of functional brain imaging, which is of particular relevance to the neural theory of visual attention (NTVA), should also be noted. Increased activity in a brain area does not specify whether a higher number of neurons have become active and/or the average activity in each neuron has increased. In fact, increases in blood flow might be caused by changes in the synaptic input or intrinsic processing of an area, rather than alterations of spiking activity. Also, in the case of ERP and MEG a stronger signal cannot be ascribed simply to changes in spiking rates. This creates a need for converging evidence obtained from single-cell studies, which can address these different possibilities more directly.

9.2 Effects of attention in the visual system

Largely thanks to studies of non-human primates, the anatomy and physiology of the visual system is among the best described in the brain. Neurophysiological mappings have revealed an intricate network of over 30 separate visual modules in the monkey cortex (Fig. 9.1). Though probably not organized in exactly the same way, the human visual cortex is hardly less complex. The visual modules have been identified in a number of ways, most commonly by a unique pattern of input–output connections and/or special histological features (Felleman and van Essen 1991). Also, about half of the modules contain their own (more or less precise) topographic representation of the visual field. Functionally it is interesting that many areas have been shown to exhibit specialized response properties. For example, cells in area MT respond specifically to speed and direction of motion, whereas cells in IT areas are selective for complex form properties.

The anatomical connectivity of the visual system is highly complex (as should be evident from Fig. 9.1), but also shows important regularities. A large proportion of all connections are *reciprocal*, suggesting extensive feedback interactions. Also, although the system is generally organized in a highly parallel manner, it is also characterized by several distinct levels, forming a *hierarchy* of the visual areas. The hierarchy shown in Fig. 9.1 is grounded on anatomical criteria such as a given area's connectivity to/from particular cortical layers. However, this anatomically defined hierarchy corresponds well with functional properties such as receptive field size and response complexity, both of which increase at higher levels in the system.

In terms of overall function, the design of the visual system is also relatively well understood. A generally accepted organizing principle has been found in Ungerleider and Mishkin's (1982) distinction between two cortical processing streams: a *ventral* occipito-temporal route for object recognition and a *dorsal* occipito-parietal route for spatial cognition (or visuomotor control, as suggested by Milner and Goodale 1995; see Rossetti *et al.* 2003 for a critical discussion of this hypothesis). Of course, these two visual processing streams interact, but also, to large extent, they operate independently. Still, despite its highly parallel and complex design, the visual system works in a very integrated and efficient manner. A main reason for this efficiency may be the selective influence brought about by attention, which serves to focus activity on the most important parts of the visual input (see, for example, Schneider 1995; Schneider and Deubel 2002).

The visual system in the posterior cortex may be regarded roughly as the *target* for visual attention, the site where selective modulations take effect. As we

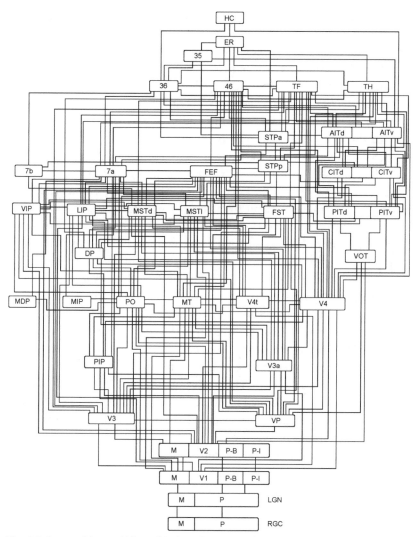

Fig. 9.1 Connectivity and hierarchical organization of visual areas in the primate cortex. The boxes represent individual visual modules (labelled) and the lines between boxes signify direct axonal linkages (most of which have been shown to be reciprocal). Subcortical structures (retinal ganglion cells, RGC; lateral geniculate nucleus, LGN) are shown at the bottom of the figure together with the magnocellular (M) and parvocellular (P) pathways to the visual cortex. To illustrate the hierarchical organization of the visual system, modules at the same anatomical level are located in the same horizontal row. From Felleman and van Essen (1991) Distributed hierarchical processing in the primate cerebral cortex. *Cerebral Cortex*, **1**, 1–47. Copyright 1991 by Oxford University Press.

know from previous chapters, attention may lead to a number of changes in the activity of individual visual cells, and functional imaging studies have shown parallels to many of these effects at the macroscopic level. Some of the most direct parallels have been provided in fMRI experiments by Sabine Kastner and collaborators. As described in Chapters 6 and 8, the strongest effects of attention at the single-cell level occur when more than one stimulus is present in the receptive field (e.g. Reynolds *et al.* 1999). Kastner *et al.* (1998) studied this competitive effect in an ingenious fMRI experiment. Subjects were shown complex visual patterns at four locations, either sequentially (one pattern at a time for 250 ms each with no blank interval between them) or simultaneously (all four at the same time for 250 ms followed by a blank period of 750 ms). Integrated over time, the physical stimulation was thus the same in the two conditions. However, competitive interactions between stimuli should occur only in the simultaneous condition and only in areas where the receptive fields of cells were large enough to contain several stimuli. In accordance with this, Kastner *et al.* found significantly weaker activations of visual areas during the simultaneous presentations. There was no effect in V1, but a clear effect in V4, and an even stronger effect in the temporal cortex (area TEO), suggesting that the strength of the effect depended on receptive field size. This observation was followed up in a study by Kastner *et al.* (2001), who used the same experimental design to estimate directly the size of receptive fields in the visual system. The crucial question was how far the competing stimuli should be separated from each other to eliminate the suppressive effect in a given visual area. The results were strikingly similar to predictions from single-cell studies of receptive field sizes: less than 2° in V1, between 2° and 4° in V2, between 4° and 6° in V4, more than 7° (but still confined to one quadrant) in TEO, and more than 6° (confined to one quadrant) in area V3A. These closely parallel results strongly suggest that the same competitive mechanism was reflected in Kastner *et al.*'s macroscopic fMRI studies and the previous single-cell investigations.

Another major single-cell effect investigated by Kastner *et al.* is the shift in baseline activity that is often observed when a target object is expected to occur in a cell's receptive field. Kastner *et al.* (1999) instructed subjects to direct their attention covertly to a peripheral location where a prespecified target stimulus would appear and 'to expect the occurrence' of the stimulus presentation. During the expectation period before the stimulus was presented, Kastner *et al.* found significant activations of those parts of extrastriate areas V2, V4, and TEO that process information from the attended location. Similar effects have been found in a number of other fMRI studies (e.g. Chawla *et al.* 1999; Shulman *et al.* 1999). These activations seem analogous to the baseline shift seen in individual neurons during comparable cognitive tasks. Like the results of the single-cell studies, the results of Kastner *et al.* (1999) and others may be explained by assuming that the subjects generated a mental image of the target object in visual short-term memory (VSTM) (cf. Section 8.3).

A common result in the functional imaging literature is that attention to an object changes activity in visual areas processing information from the object. This occurs even for stimuli that are relatively free from competition with other objects, and when pigeonholing is not a factor. For example, in an ERP study by Mangun *et al.* (1993), rectangles were flashed one at a time to the four visual quadrants (in random order) while subjects attended covertly to stimuli in one of the quadrants. Attention increased the amplitude of a characteristic component in the visual evoked potential, the so-called P1 pattern, in the hemisphere contralateral to the attended object (cf. Fig. 9.2). In a similar study that combined ERP with PET measurements, Heinze *et al.* (1994) showed two stimuli, one in each hemifield. When covert attention was directed at one stimulus rather than the other, PET showed a larger blood flow in the extrastriate areas of the corresponding (i.e. contralateral) hemisphere. ERP measurements during the same experiment showed the usual enhancement of the P1 component in the corresponding side of the brain. As elaborated in Chapters 6 and 8, similar effects of attention have been found in firing rates of single cells with a single experimenter-defined stimulus in the receptive field.

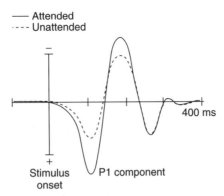

Fig. 9.2 Event-related potential (ERP) responses to attended stimuli typically have greater amplitude than responses to unattended stimuli. The figure shows a schematic example of this effect. Activations are shown in the right lateral occipital area, which responds to stimuli in the left visual field and is maximally activated in the P1 component range. Note the difference in amplitude between responses to left (attended) and right (unattended) events.

However, it should be noted that the observed ERP and blood flow changes may reflect neural mechanisms other than increased spiking activity to sensory stimulation. In the case of the ERP modulation, more synchronized input to an area should lead to a stronger electrophysiological signal even in the absence of higher firing rates in individual neurons, and increased synchronization between the cells in a visual area may be expected when they receive a common input from a high-level attentional control structure (cf. Section 8.4). The changes in blood flow, on the other hand, might be due to VSTM encoding rather than the initial sensory response to the stimuli. Due to the sluggish nature of the vascular response, PET and fMRI measurements cannot differentiate reliably between these two possibilities.

An fMRI study by Brefczynski and DeYoe (1999) showed that the effect of spatial attention exhibits considerable retinotopic precision. In this study, the covert attention of subjects was shifted within a dense array of objects. The brain areas activated by attending to a particular object in the array closely matched the retinotopic activation when the object was perceived in isolation. Thus spatial attention seems to modulate sensory processing with an anatomical precision that approaches the fine-grained topographic organization of the visual system. Like other fMRI studies, Brefzynski and DeYoe (1999) found changes with attention not only in extrastriate cortex, but also in primary visual cortex (V1). Recent fMRI studies have pointed to attentional effects at an even lower level of the visual system, the lateral geniculate nucleus (LGN) in the thalamus (O'Connor et al. 2002).

The results of Brefczynski and DeYoe (1999) and O'Connor et al. (2002) bear on the *locus of selection* debate in cognitive psychology (see Sections 2.6.3 and 3.1) and challenge the traditional notion that attention does not affect the earliest stages of visual processing. Even strong proponents of 'early selection' (e.g. Broadbent 1958) assume that the initial sensory processing is unaffected by attention, a view that might seem to be undermined by these fMRI results. However, 'early' in terms of anatomical location in the visual processing hierarchy is not necessarily equal to 'early' in the time course of processing. The temporal resolution of fMRI is quite coarse and it is possible that the observed activations of V1 and LGN occur late in processing, as a result of feedback from high-level visual areas (cf. Schneider 1995; Bundesen et al. 2002). This possibility is supported by ERP studies, which have the necessary temporal resolution to address this issue. In a series of studies, Steven Hillyard and colleagues have studied how spatial attention influences stimulus evoked potentials to visual stimuli (e.g. Hillyard and Muente 1984; Mangun et al. 1993; Hillyard and Anllo-Vento 1998). As mentioned before, a typical result is that attention to an object increases the amplitude of the P1 component, which occurs with a latency of 80–100 ms. However, an earlier visual component, the C1, occurring 50–60 ms after stimulation, has not been found to be influenced by attention. Localization analysis of the ERP signal indicates that the P1 component is caused by extrastriate activity, whereas the C1 is generated in V1 (Martínez and Hillyard 2005). Thus, the data are consistent with the possibility that although attentional modulation can set in quite early in visual processing, its effects at levels at or below V1 are delayed and reflect a feedback-induced reactivation (perhaps occurring in V1 as late as 150–250 ms after stimulus onset; Martínez et al. 1999).

Most functional imaging studies have examined the effect of filtering (typically location-based), but there are also studies addressing pigeonholing. In one of the classic studies in the PET literature, Corbetta et al. (1990) showed that when observers were discriminating different visual attributes (colour, motion, or form) of the same object, areas in visual cortex specialized for the attended feature were activated (e.g. MT and MST were activated for motion, V4 for colour). This is a clear parallel to the upscaling effect of β values for attended features at the single-cell level. A study by Saenz et al. (2002) showed that the effect of pigeonholing generalizes to unattended objects across the visual field, analogously to the single-cell findings of Treue and Martinez-Trujillo (1999; see Chapters 6 and 8) and consistently with NTVA.

9.3 The source of attentional control

There is now general agreement that attentional modulation of visual processing depends on structures outside the visual system, a fact that has been driven home mainly by functional brain imaging. Specifically, a network of areas in the frontal and parietal cortex has been found to be activated consistently in tasks that require voluntary control of attention. Activations often centre on the posterior parietal cortex and the lateral prefrontal cortex (Fig. 9.3). In a typical experimental design of this type, subjects are endogenously cued to attend to a particular location or feature, after which the visual stimulus appears. Early PET studies found reliable fronto-parietal activation under such circumstances, compared to passive fixation or exogenous capture of attention (e.g. Corbetta et al. 1993). However, due to the low temporal resolution of PET, these studies could not differentiate the activity elicited by the cue from that of the visual stimulus. Thus it was possible that the fronto-parietal activation reflected a part of the visual processing, rather than a separate control signal. This confound was addressed in later fMRI studies, where Kastner et al. (1998) and Hopfinger et al. (2000) demonstrated that the fronto-parietal activity was present before visual stimulation occurred. It thus seemed to reflect a pure control signal.

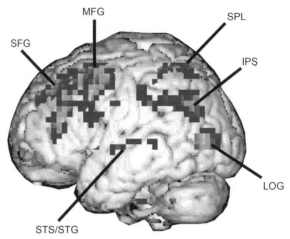

Fig. 9.3 Example of brain activity related to control of spatial attention in an fMRI experiment by Hopfinger *et al.* (2000). The figure shows statistically significant activations (labelled) in the left hemisphere when attention was cued to the right visual field. SFG, superior frontal gyrus; MFG, middle frontal gyrus; SPL, superior parietal lobe; IPS, intraparietal sulcus; STS, superior temporal sulcus; STG, superior temporal gyrus; LOG, lateral occipital gyrus. Adapted with permission from Hopfinger, Buonocore, and Mangun (2000). The neural mechanisms of top-down attentional control. *Nature Neuroscience*, **3**, 284–291. Copyright 2000 by Macmillan Publishers Ltd.

Fronto-parietal activations were initially demonstrated for spatial orienting, but have now been found across a range of attentional control tasks, including both spatial and non-spatial tasks, suggesting a general-purpose system for attentional control (Wojciulik and Kanwisher 1999). For example, fronto-parietal areas are activated in such diverse tasks as paying attention to particular time intervals (Coull and Nobre 1998), monitoring a stream of rapid visual presentations (Marois *et al.* 2000), feature-based filtering (Giesbrecht *et al.* 2003), and sustaining attention during monotonous tasks (Sturm *et al.* 1999). Such general functions of the fronto-parietal networks fit with the biased competition theory of Desimone and Duncan (1995), according to which attentional selection is the product of a distributed competition between object representations at many levels in the cortex, in which spatial attention has no special status. In this view there is no specialized system controlling the (spatial) focus of attention, but rather an interaction between many bottom-up and top-down influences on selection. A main source of top-down influences on attentional competition should derive from structures implicated in working memory, specifically the prefrontal cortex (Desimone 1999). This top-down bias can take many forms, and the non-specialized nature of pre-frontal neurons has been emphasized in Duncan's (2001) *adaptive coding* theory, which claims that individual cells in the prefrontal cortex can adjust their function according to the requirements of the current task. Main support for this hypothesis comes from single-cell studies that show flexible response properties in prefrontal neurons as the task of the organism is varied (e.g. Freedman *et al.* 2001; Everling *et al.* 2006). The adaptive coding theory also rests on findings from functional imaging, where a large meta-analysis has shown activations in the same prefrontal area across a wide range of attentional, working memory, and cognitive control tasks (Duncan and Owen 2000). These findings question the view that particular areas in the prefrontal cortex are specialized for specific cognitive operations or types of information.

However, anatomical differences in activations between attentional tasks have also been found, and lately the possible functional subdivisions within the fronto-parietal system have received much interest. For example, it has been claimed that there are two fronto-parietal networks, which are specialized for endogenous (top-down) and exogenous (bottom-up) shifts of attention, respectively (Corbetta et al. 2002). The proposed ('dorsal') system for endoge-nous shifts includes the superior frontal cortex and the intraparietal sulcus in both hemispheres, whereas exogenous shifting should depend on more inferi-orly located (ventral) areas in the right temporo-parietal junction and right inferior frontal gyrus. Besides traditional functional imaging experiments, this theory has received support from the new method of resting state fMRI, where spontaneous fluctuations of blood flow are observed in the absence of a cogni-tive task or sensory stimulation. In such a study, Fox *et al.* (2006) found corre-lations in spontaneous neural activity between areas in the proposed dorsal network as well as a separate correlation between areas in the right lateralized ventral network. Fox *et al.* also found a region in the prefrontal cortex where activity correlated with both systems and suggested that this area might medi-ate the functional interaction between the two systems.

While supported by some studies, theories of specialized fronto-parietal networks such as the one mentioned above have trouble accounting for the full range of findings in the field. A possible reason for this is that functional specialization in high-level cortical areas may be relative rather than absolute (Haxby *et al.* 2000; Duncan 2001; Hampshire *et al.* 2007). According to this view, there is a broad distribution of cells in frontal and parietal cortex that can represent a given type of control information. Consider for example location-based filtering. Cells in certain areas—say, particular parts of the superior frontal gyrus—should be maximally involved in such attentional settings, but cells in surrounding areas should also have the potential to support the process to some degree. For a different kind of control information (e.g. feature-based filtering), the peak 'specialization' could be in a different region—say, in the middle frontal gyrus—but the distributions of cells sensitive to the two control operations should overlap, so that the same cells are able to support different attentional processes depending on the current task. This statistical notion of functional specialization represents a plausible compromise between findings on response flexibility versus anatomical segregation within the fronto-parietal cortex.

Even though combined activity in frontal and parietal areas has consistently been found in tasks that require top-down control of attention, one should keep in mind a fundamental limitation of functional imaging studies: these methods cannot demonstrate causal relationships. For evidence on the extent to which fronto-parietal areas are truly necessary for attentional control, as opposed to just activated secondarily, one must turn to lesion studies or other direct manipulations of brain activity (see Chapter 10).

9.4 Anatomical models of visual attention

Based on functional neuroimaging (as well as evidence from lesion studies, see Chapter 10), several anatomical network models for visual attention have been proposed. In line with the popular view in cognitive psychology that visual attention is inherently spatial, many models describe visual attention as controlled by spatial orienting structures, typically located in frontal and parietal areas. A classic, and still influential, example of this type of model was presented by Mesulam (1981, 1990, 2000). Mesulam's network model includes three main anatomical nodes: the posterior parietal cortex, the frontal eye fields, and the cingulate gyrus (Fig. 9.4). The parietal component, which is centred at the intraparietal sulcus, creates spatial maps of perceptual saliency (priority) and computes provisional plans for shifting (spatial) attention between significant objects. The frontal component, centred at the frontal eye fields, converts these plans into specific motor sequences. The cingulate component influences object saliency by motivational and emotional factors. The three main centres are strongly connected to each other, as well as to supplementary areas in the striatum, pulvinar, and superior colliculus. The concerted activity of this network provides a 'vector' function that determines the direction of attention in space. fMRI studies have confirmed that these structures are jointly activated in spatial attention tasks (Gitelman et al. 1999).

There is a lateralization built into Mesulam's model, such that the left hemisphere directs attention predominantly to the right side of space, whereas the right hemisphere directs attention to both sides. This hypothesis is consistent

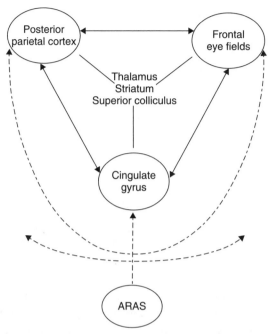

Fig. 9.4 Mesulam's anatomical model of visual attention. Three cortical nodes (posterior parietal cortex, frontal eye fields, cingulate gyrus) direct spatial attention, supported by activity in subcortical structures (thalamus, striatum, superior colliculus). The whole attentional network depends on the subcortical ascending reticular activating system (ARAS) to maintain a sufficient amount of general arousal. From Mesulam (2002). Functional anatomy of attention and neglect: from neurons to networks. In: Karnath, Milner, and Vallar (eds), *The cognitive and neural bases of spatial neglect*, pp. 33–45. Oxford: Oxford University Press. Copyright 2002 by Oxford University Press.

with the common notion that the perceptual style of the right hemisphere is relatively 'global' versus a 'local' bias of the left hemisphere (Robertson *et al.* 1988). It also explains why severe inattention to the contralateral part of space ('neglect'; see Section 10.2.1) occurs much more frequently after lesions in the right side of the brain: in this case, there is no 'back-up' representation of contralateral space in the other hemisphere. In addition, several functional imaging studies have confirmed that the right hemisphere is involved in attention to both sides of space (Nobre *et al.* 1997; Gitelman *et al.* 1999; Kim *et al.* 1999). However, the general evidence on this issue is mixed. Fink *et al.* (1997) reported largely symmetrical activations under spatial shifts of attention, and others have reported that cortical activity was indifferent to the direction of attention (although generally stronger in the right hemisphere; Vandenberghe *et al.* 1997).

These varied findings suggest that the right hemisphere is dominant only for some aspects of spatial attention. One possibility is that voluntary (endogenous) shifts of spatial attention recruit activity bilaterally, but that the right hemisphere contains a specialized system for stimulus-driven (exogenous) reorienting of attention, as suggested by Corbetta and Shulman (2002). However, this simple dichotomy between exogenous and endogenous selection does not capture the fundamental interactions between bottom-up and top-down factors that are evident from the cognitive literature (see Section 2.7.1) and described in the rate and weight equations of the theory of visual attention (TVA) (see Section 5.2.3).

Mesulam's model also includes a different kind of component, which is shared by many other theories. Independent of where attention is directed, a certain level of cortical arousal should be necessary for the attentional system to work (see also Luria 1973; Heilman 1979). According to Mesulam, the general level of arousal depends on the *ascending reticular activating system* (ARAS), which includes a number of brainstem nuclei (first described by Moruzzi and Magoun 1949) that project to widespread regions in the cortex by way of the intralaminar thalamic nuclei (Fig. 9.5). Recent research has shown that the ARAS system involves multiple transmitter-specific pathways (Marocco and Davidson 1998) and so should probably be theoretically fractionated. Judging from ERP and galvanic skin response studies of patients

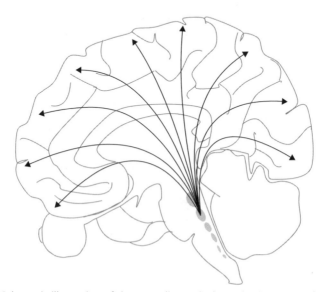

Fig. 9.5 Schematic illustration of the ascending reticular activating system (ARAS).

with unilateral brain damage, the right side of the brain seems most critical for bottom-up influences on arousal (Heilman *et al.* 2003). The general level of arousal is also modulated top-down from limbic and frontal areas. These structures represent motivational and volitional factors necessary for sustaining attention during monotonous tasks that do not automatically engage the arousal system. As with the bottom-up component, Mesulam (2000) assumes that the top-down modulation of arousal is lateralized to the right hemisphere. Both imaging and lesion studies confirm that the right prefrontal cortex and inferior parietal lobe are important for sustaining attention (Coull *et al.* 1996; Robertson and Manly 1999; Sturm *et al.* 1999).

Another highly influential model of attention was proposed by Posner and Petersen (1990). This model includes three semi-independent networks that mediate different aspects of attention. The first is the posterior network, which is critical for orienting the (spatial) focus of attention. The posterior network consists of structures in the posterior parietal lobe, the superior colliculus, and the pulvinar. These structures are supposed to perform the operations of disengaging, moving, and engaging (spatial) attention, respectively. This part of the theory is based mainly on spatial cuing studies of patients with selective lesions in one of the mentioned areas, who showed different types of impairment in the cuing task, depending on their lesion (Posner *et al.* 1984, 1987; but see also Bundesen 1998*b*). Whereas the posterior network operates relatively automatically in response to external stimulation, the anterior network is responsible for executive control of attention and response preparation. This system was specified in less anatomical detail by Posner and Petersen, but the cingulate gyrus and the supplementary motor cortex were assumed to be central. However, as mentioned in the previous section, later studies of endogenous orienting of attention have instead pointed to the superior frontal lobe (e.g. Hopfinger *et al.* 2000), probably in close interaction with the intraparietal sulcus (Corbetta *et al.* 2000). The third network in Posner and Petersen's model is responsible for general alertness. The network is assumed to depend mainly on the right hemisphere and, in general, seems similar to the ARAS system described in relation to Mesulam's model. Posner and Petersen's three-network model has recently been supported by the development of a simple test battery (the ANT; Fan *et al.* 2002), which provides separate measures of the functions of the three networks.

The models of Mesulam (1981, 1990, 2000) and Posner and Petersen (1990) are based on some of the major findings in the literature, and in many ways represent useful frameworks for thinking about the anatomy of visual attention. However, these models also have important limitations. One is that attention is conceived in a rather narrow way, as a spatial focus that is shifted around in the visual field. As discussed in Chapter 2, this notion of a serial orienting process seems inadequate to account for many findings in the cognitive literature. Another limitation is that the time-course of attentional processing is not described, mainly because these models do not incorporate evidence from electrophysiological measures such as ERP and single-cell recordings. For a full understanding of the functional anatomy of visual attention, temporal aspects of processing must also be considered. In the next section we present an anatomical model of visual attention, grounded in NTVA theory, which tries to take these elements into account.

9.5 The functional anatomy of NTVA

NTVA does not depend on any specific anatomical localization of the computations described in the theory. In this sense it is a fairly general neurophysiological interpretation of the original TVA equations. Still, the issue of anatomical localization is important, and it is interesting to consider how the computations of NTVA may be distributed across the brain. One such possibility, the *thalamic model* of NTVA, is illustrated in Fig. 9.6 and explained below.

The initial sensory analysis is uncontroversial. In the first, unselective wave of processing, visual information is picked up at the retina and transmitted via the optic nerve to the lateral geniculate nucleus (LGN) of the thalamus and then on to the striate cortex. A small part of the visual information bypasses the geniculo-striate pathway, which may lead to blindsight and related phenomena (Weiskrantz 1997). Such phenomena are not modelled in NTVA. The geniculo-striate input provides the raw sensory information for specialized neurons in the occipital, temporal, and parietal cortex that compute η values for many different features of the objects in the visual field. The different η values are multiplied by corresponding pertinence values (projected from higher-level brain areas, see later in this section) in closely adjacent interneurons. The resulting activity is transmitted to the priority map, where the input is summed up to produce attentional weights of objects in accordance with the weight equation of TVA.

The anatomical location of the priority map is not obvious. In previous research a number of different brain areas have been linked to processing of visual relevance: the pulvinar nucleus of the thalamus (e.g. Robinson and Petersen 1992; Robinson and Cowie 1997; see also Olshausen *et al.* 1993), the inferior parietal lobe (Bushnell *et al.* 1981; cf. also Mesulam's network model), the lateral intraparietal area (Colby and Goldberg 1999; Gottlieb 2007), and the frontal eye fields (Schall and Thompson 1999). Perhaps the pulvinar is the most obvious candidate for a priority map. Several lines of evidence support

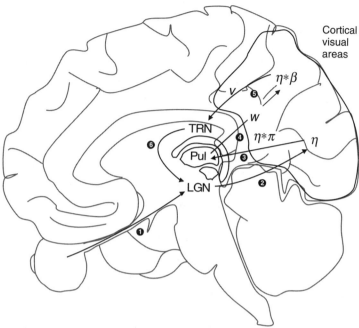

Fig. 9.6 The thalamic model of NTVA. Visual information from the eye enters the lateral geniculate nucleus (LGN) of the thalamus (1) and is transmitted to striate and extrastriate cortical areas where η values (strengths of evidence that objects at particular scales and positions have particular features) are computed (2). The η values are multiplied by π (pertinence) values, and the products are transmitted from the cortex to a priority map in the pulvinar (Pul) nucleus of the thalamus, where the products are summed up as attentional weights of the stimulus objects (3). After the first (unselective) wave of processing, cortical processing capacity is redistributed by means of attentional weight signals (w) from the pulvinar to the cortex, so that during the second (selective) wave of processing, objects with high attentional weights are processed by many neurons (4). The resulting η values are multiplied by β (bias) values, and the products are transmitted from the cortex to a multiscale VSTM map of locations, which is tentatively localized in the thalamic reticular nucleus (TRN) (5). When the VSTM map is initialized, objects in the visual field effectively start a race to become encoded into VSTM. In this race, each object is represented by all possible categorizations of the object, and each possible categorization participates with a firing rate (v value) proportional to the corresponding η value multiplied by the corresponding β value. For the winners of the race, the TRN gates activation representing a categorization back to some of those cells in LGN whose activation supported the categorization (6). Thus activity in neurons representing winners of the race is sustained by positive feedback. Adapted with permission from Bundesen, Habekost, and Kyllingsbæk (2005). A neural theory of visual attention: bridging cognition and neurophysiology. *Psychological Review*, **112**, 291–328. Copyright 2005 by the American Psychological Association. The use of APA information does not imply endorsement by APA.

this notion. One has to do with anatomical connectivity: the (lateral) pulvinar nucleus is interconnected with all areas in the occipito-temporal pathway and large parts of the posterior parietal cortex. The nucleus should therefore be in a good position to collect attentional weight components from across the visual system and widely influence cortical responses in turn. In line with this, functional imaging studies have often found pulvinar activations during attentional processing (e.g. LaBerge and Buchsbaum 1990; Kastner *et al.* 2004). More direct support comes from single-cell studies in monkeys. Petersen *et al.* (1985) recorded from cells in various parts of the pulvinar. Nearly all cells increased their firing rate in response to visual stimuli, but few were selective for stimulus features such as orientation, colour, or direction of movement. In a dorsomedial portion of the lateral pulvinar (Pdm) with a crude retinotopic organization, about half of the tested cells showed visual responses whose strength reflected the behavioural relevance of the stimulus in their receptive field. The enhancement was unrelated to specific motor responses and thus seemed to reflect pure visual relevance. In a further study, Petersen *et al.* (1987) injected bicuculline (a γ-aminobutyric acid antagonist) or muscimol (a γ-aminobutyric acid agonist) into the Pdm. As measured by reaction times in a Posner cuing task (cf. Sections 2.8.1 and 4.3.1), injection of bicuculline increased attentional weights of stimuli contralateral to the injection, whereas injection of muscimol depressed attentional weights of contralateral stimuli. The finding suggests that the priority representation in the pulvinar is anatomically lateralized, so that each side of the nucleus represents the contralateral visual field. This is supported by lesion studies of humans, in which damage to one side of the pulvinar caused asymmetry in attentional weighting (neglect or extinction disturbances; Karnath *et al.* 2002a; Habekost and Rostrup 2006; see Chapters 10 and 11).

In the second, selective wave of processing, attentional capacity is distributed by means of weight signals from the priority map to cortical visual areas, so that the receptive fields of individual neurons are more likely to contract around objects with high attentional weights. Again, η values for objects are computed across the many visual areas in the posterior cortex. Using interneurons these η values are multiplied by β values (transmitted from higher-level regions, as described later) and the products of these two factors are projected towards the VSTM map of locations.

As with the priority map, the anatomical location of the VSTM map is not very clear. An interesting possibility is that the map is contained within the thalamic reticular nucleus (TRN). Like the pulvinar, the TRN has a functionally central anatomical location: the TRN lies like a thin shield around the thalamus, so all fibres between the thalamus and the cortex pass through the TRN.

Many of the fibres that traverse the TRN have side branches with excitatory synapses to cells in the nucleus. In turn, the TRN sends inhibitory impulses to the thalamus, including the LGN. The TRN contains at least one topographically ordered representation of the visual field (Guillery *et al.* 1998), which should make it capable of representing specific parts of the visual field. Further, all cells in the TRN are inhibitory and the nucleus is widely interconnected, so the nucleus should be well suited to function as a *K*-winners-take-all network (cf. Sections 7.4–7.5). TRN activity should be able to sustain responses in the LGN (and indirectly, the visual cortex) by way of *feedforward disinhibition* (Sherman and Guillery 2001): suppose two neurons representing corresponding locations in topographic maps within the LGN and the TRN, respectively, receive excitatory input from the same cortical neuron signalling a particular visual feature. If the activated TRN cell inhibits other neurons in the LGN that excite TRN cells projecting directly to the LGN cell, the LGN cell should be released from inhibition. This would sustain the activity of the LGN cell and thereby close a positive feedback loop between the thalamus and the cortex (cf. Fig. 7.9). In this way the visual representation is kept active in a reverberating circuit, in line with Hebb's notion of short-term memory.

The functional anatomy suggested in the previous paragraphs represents a predominantly thalamo-cortical model of NTVA. Another possibility is that the functionally central systems—the priority map and the VSTM map—are located in high-level areas in parietal or frontal cortex. Micro-stimulation of cells in the frontal eye fields increases the firing rate of sensory (V4) neurons for stimuli at particular locations (namely, potential targets for saccades; Moore and Armstrong 2003) and also seems to influence object selection in the sensory neurons (Armstrong *et al.* 2006). This suggests that the frontal eye fields are (also) central to the representation of visual relevance. In addition, functional imaging studies have tentatively identified regions implicated in VSTM in posterior parts of the superior frontal sulcus and the middle and inferior frontal gyri (Courtney *et al.* 1998; see also Bundesen *et al.* 2002) as well as the intraparietal sulcus (Todd and Marois 2004; Xu and Chun 2006). A way to integrate such findings with the thalamic model of NTVA is to assume that frontal and parietal areas function as higher-order control structures for attention—needed, for example, to protect against sensory masking or to maintain attentional focus under distraction—rather than constituting the basic topographic maps of priority and visual short-term memory. One main reason for locating the basic maps at relatively low levels in the visual system is the clear retinotopic organization found in these parts of the brain. Another reason is the unimodal (visual) specialization of these areas. In contrast, the frontal eye fields are deeply involved in oculomotor functions, whereas high-level areas in parietal and frontal cortex often respond to inputs from several sensory modalities and change their response patterns according to the current task, as pointed out in the adaptive coding theory of Duncan (2001).

Top-down settings of attention—bias and pertinence values—are not generated within the visual system. A long research tradition, involving functional imaging (see Section 9.3), lesion studies, and other direct manipulations of brain activity (see Chapter 10), suggests that attentional control settings are transmitted 'on-line' via long-range projections from higher-level ('executive') areas in the frontal and parietal cortex. The activity in these fronto-parietal networks is typically influenced by motivational factors, which also makes emotional processing structures, such as the orbitofrontal cortex and the amygdala, relevant. However, in addition to bias (β) and pertinence (π) values, attentional selection depends on measures of the strength of sensory evidence for particular categorizations (η values), and these measures are modulated in ways that depend on intrinsic properties of the visual system. The modulations become manifest when attention is captured by a stimulus; for example, when a suddenly appearing object attracts attention, overruling voluntary control signals generated in the fronto-parietal networks (cf. Section 5.2.3).

9.6 **Summary**

Functional brain imaging studies, especially using the PET and fMRI methods, have now firmly established that the neural basis of visual attention comprises large-scale anatomical networks. There is disagreement on the exact structure and functional organization of these networks, but some general features are widely accepted. A basic condition for attentional function is a sufficient amount of cortical arousal, and most theories relate this function to a cortico-subcortical system in which the brainstem, thalamus, and frontal/limbic structures are central, in combination with transmitter-specific biochemical pathways. Both bottom-up and top-down regulation of this system seem to depend mainly on the right side of the brain. There is also wide consensus on the importance of fronto-parietal structures for the control of attentional selection. Anatomical models of visual attention typically also include subcortical structures, especially the superior colliculus, the striatum, and the pulvinar nucleus, but the specific contributions of these areas are not well established. An interesting possibility is that the pulvinar contains a priority map, as suggested in the 'thalamic model' of NTVA, but attentional weights might also be represented in other areas such as the frontal eye fields. Another suggestion of the thalamic model of NTVA is that the reticular nucleus establishes the feedback loops that support the VSTM system, but this hypothesis also awaits further investigation.

Corresponding to the wide variety of attentional functions described in cognitive psychology, these large cortico-subcortical networks seem to be involved in many different aspects of visual attention. It is unclear to which extent the different operations are mediated by anatomically distinct circuits, for example a 'dorsal' and a 'ventral' set of connections between the frontal and the parietal lobe, or rather by more general-purpose ('adaptive coding') networks. Probably, functional specialization in fronto-parietal areas is relative rather than absolute.

The 'source' networks for attentional selection transmit control signals that modulate the sensory processing in 'target' areas in the large visual regions of the posterior cortex. Contrary to the high-level areas in frontal and parietal cortex, the functional specialization in different parts of the visual system is much more obvious. As shown by many brain imaging studies, visual attention generally has the effect of increasing the local activity of cortical areas that process information related to the attended object or feature. ERP studies have been especially informative on the time course of these processes, shedding new light on the 'locus of selection' debate in cognitive psychology.

Overall, due to converging evidence from both single-cell and functional imaging studies, we now have an elaborate understanding of the nature and location of attentional effects in the human brain. The NTVA model offers a theoretical framework for integrating this large pool of knowledge.

10

Disturbances of visual attention

A powerful way to understand how a system works is to observe what happens if one of its parts is damaged. This is the simple idea underlying research on brain disturbances, one of the main areas of cognitive neuroscience. In this chapter we explain the basic methodology of this field, the lesion method (Section 10.1). Visual attention can be disturbed in many ways after damage to different parts of the brain. As described in Section 10.2, these functional deficits can be classified broadly as lateralized (i.e. confined to one side of the visual field) or non-lateralized (i.e. general). In recent years the classic study of naturally occurring brain damage has been supplemented by *transcranial magnetic stimulation* (TMS), in which normal brain activity is temporarily disturbed following magnetic stimulation (Section 10.3). Although still a fairly new method, TMS has clear methodological advantages that promise much for future research.

10.1 **The lesion method**

Historically, studies of brain damage have been the main way to obtain knowledge about mind–brain relationships. The first observations date back hundreds, or perhaps thousands, of years, when it was noted that damage to one side of the brain leads to problems with sensing and moving the opposite side of the body. As a scientific field, studies of brain damage took off in the nineteenth century, using a combination of systematic behaviour observations and post-mortem examinations of patients with damage in circumscribed parts of the brain. Major discoveries were made, such as Broca's (1861) demonstration of the importance of the left frontal lobe for speech production and Wernicke's (1874) analogous finding on the left temporal cortex and language comprehension. Indeed, the latter decades of the nineteenth century are often referred to as 'the golden age' of neurology. However, the cognitive models proposed to account for these path-breaking findings were often simplistic and speculative, and by the turn of the century the neurological approach to psychological studies fell into disfavour. During the long reign of behaviourism in the first part of the twentieth century, the brain (and cognitive processing) was largely treated as a 'black box' outside proper scientific enquiry. However, in the 1960s the lesion approach was revived, paralleling the rapid development of cognitive psychology ('the cognitive revolution') described in Chapter 2. The Russian neuropsychologist Alexander Luria was a leading figure in this enterprise, which aimed to integrate patient studies with the recent theoretical progress in psychology. Neuropsychology was further boosted in the 1970s, when computer-aided tomography (CT) scanning made it possible to examine lesions *in vivo*, opening the door to much more systematic neuroanatomical studies than previously. This development was further facilitated in the 1980s when magnetic resonance imaging provided an even more powerful investigation method (see Fig. 10.1 for an example). Today, the lesion method has found its place alongside other main research tools in cognitive

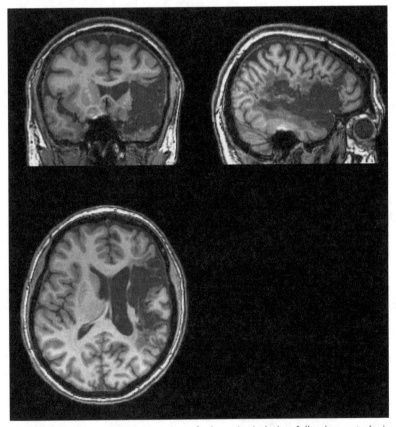

Fig. 10.1 Magnetic resonance scanning of a large brain lesion following a stroke in the right hemisphere. Beginning at the upper left corner and proceeding clockwise, the lesion is shown in two-dimensional sections, viewed from behind ('coronal section'), from the side ('sagittal section'), and from above ('transversal section').

neuroscience and, like these other methods, it is characterized by a unique set of strengths and weaknesses.

The basic aim of the lesion method is to demonstrate a correlation between damage in a well-defined brain region and changes in some experimentally controlled psychological variable. In relation to a given theory of psychological processing in the normal brain, the lesion (ideally) makes it possible to test the theory's assumptions about how a particular aspect of cognition is implemented neurally. By measuring whether lesions in a specific brain area make a functional difference or not, one can determine whether the area is *necessary* for the psychological process of interest. This causal dimension sets lesion studies fundamentally apart from functional imaging, which can only show how neural activity co-occurs with psychological behaviour, but not whether the measured activity is functionally critical. However, the lesion method also has its weaknesses. Naturally occurring brain damage is rarely confined to a particular area, but typically involves several regions. In practice this often makes it difficult to relate an observed cognitive deficit to damage in a specific structure. Recent studies featuring statistical lesion analysis of large groups of patients (e.g. Karnath *et al.* 2004) have improved on this traditional limitation, but the typical anatomical resolution of brain-damage studies remains considerably below that of PET or fMRI. In animal studies (e.g. of rats) the location of the lesion is under direct experimental control and thus very precise, but this advantage is countered by the difficulty of translating the findings to the more complex human brain. A further complication for the lesion method is that damage in a brain area often leads to disturbances of activity in anatomically connected, but structurally intact brain areas. Such effects are not visible in the structural imaging of the lesion, but can be taken into account by including measurements of blood flow, which is typically reduced in the indirectly affected areas (*diaschisis;* e.g. Hillis *et al.* 2005). However, brain damage can have another indirect effect that is more difficult to control for. The brain is a plastic organ and following damage the organism will seek to compensate for the loss of function. This might occur either by reorganizing cognitive processing so that a given task is solved by a different set of computations than before (viz., computations that can be carried out by the intact brain structures) or, more radically, by alteration of the neural specialization of the remaining tissue. Either way, significant functional compensation and reorganization after brain damage can make it difficult to infer how the normal brain is organized.

Another challenge for lesion studies relates to individual variability. The variation in the extent and location of naturally occurring lesions implies that any group of brain-damaged individuals will be more or less heterogeneous, and no two patients will exhibit exactly the same pattern of deficits. Instead of trying to average out these differences in group comparisons, some researchers have advocated the use of in-depth single-case studies (Coltheart 2003). In order to describe the individual patient's function in as much detail as possible, case studies use customized experiments that systematically test hypotheses about the nature of the patient's impairment. In this line of *cognitive neuropsychology*, the ideal finding is the *double dissociation*: two patients where one has a deficit in cognitive function A but not B, while the other is impaired at B but not A. Such a dissociation is strong evidence that A and B are implemented in different parts of the brain and represent independent cognitive components. Whereas this line of research is appropriate for testing hypotheses of cognitive psychology, the single-case design is not well suited for making general inferences on the relationship between lesion location and deficit. For this, one must turn to (preferably large) group studies of 'reasonably similar' patients, bearing in mind the problems of cognitive and anatomical heterogeneity. Often, pioneering studies of single patients serve to generate hypotheses that can be tested reliably in larger groups of patients.

In spite of the difficulties outlined, the lesion method remains one of the most important tools of cognitive neuroscience, often providing information that cannot be obtained in any other way. One should also keep in mind that studies of brain damage serve another purpose than that of basic cognitive neuroscience research, namely to inform the clinical treatment of patients. In this endeavour, the issue of functional brain mapping is secondary to understanding the effects of particular types of brain damage (e.g. Parkinson's disease) on psychological function. Given the high frequency of brain damage in the general population, *clinical neuropsychology* is, of course, a research field of great importance.

In recent years the classical approach to lesion studies has been supplemented by a new experimental technology, which seems to bypass some of the limitations of studying naturally occurring brain damage. In *transcranial magnetic stimulation* (TMS) a temporary 'virtual lesion' is created by applying a brief magnetic pulse above the scalp. In the underlying cortex the changing magnetic field induces a current that stimulates neural activity. The magnetic stimulation can be applied either in a single pulse or as a repeated train of pulses (*repetitive TMS*; rTMS) at rates of up to 50 Hz and continued for seconds or even minutes (Walsh and Rushworth 1999). Whereas the former procedure seems to be completely harmless, rTMS must be carried out following strict safety guidelines to avoid the risk of inducing a seizure. The precise effects of TMS in the neural tissue are not well characterized. Both excitatory and inhibitory activity can be produced, but in any case TMS should interfere with the function of the tissue by adding neural noise to the normal information processing. In this way, the effect of TMS can be considered a 'lesion'. Single-pulse TMS can be given at very precise points in time and disrupts cortical activity only briefly, probably for between 20 and 200 ms (Pascual-Leone *et al.* 2000); it is therefore well suited to study different stages in the time course of processing. However, the impact of single-pulse TMS on cognitive processing is typically slight, and it is often necessary to use the stronger manipulation of rTMS to demonstrate significant effects. Depending on the amount of stimu-lation, rTMS can have a much longer-lasting impact on brain processing; indeed, rTMS has even been proposed as a treatment for psychiatric disorders (George *et al.* 1999). This also means that cognitive function can be probed at a later time than the actual magnetic stimulation (*off-line TMS*). Concerning the spatial resolution of TMS, although the precise cortical depth and exten-sion of the stimulation is unclear, different cognitive effects can be produced by stimulating scalp sites about 1 cm apart, which is a very good resolution compared to brain-damage studies. However, a serious complication is that the induced activity tends to spread along the axonal connections of the tar-geted cortical area, often activating widespread anatomical networks rather than localized brain modules. The extent of these effects can be studied by combining TMS with functional imaging, to detect changes in blood flow (Paus 1999; Ruff *et al.* 2006), or ERP activity (Fuggetta *et al.* 2006) in brain areas remote from the stimulation site.

Compared to brain damage, TMS has several advantages for experimentation. The 'lesioned' brain is not given much opportunity to reorganize, so the observed behaviour after TMS should reflect a relatively pure disturbance of normal activity. Another strength is the reversibility of the cognitive disturbance, which allows for direct comparisons in each individual between performance under baseline and TMS conditions; in brain-damage studies the patient's premorbid level of function must be inferred indirectly from control participants. In addition, the high temporal resolution of single-pulse TMS creates unique possibilities for probing the time course of cognitive processing, although in practice it is often difficult to elicit robust effects. rTMS is a more powerful method for disturbing neural activity, but its impact is, of course, less than with real damage. Logically this should limit the statistical power of TMS compared to 'real' lesion studies, although the method's higher level of experimental control may compensate. Further, as noted above, the spatial resolution of TMS should be superior to that of brain-damage studies, but is complicated by activation spreading to anatomically connected areas. However, studies of brain damage share a similar confound, because a lesion can disturb the activity of structurally intact areas. Overall, TMS is an experimental technique with great potential, but with limitations that still seem to be less well charted than those for studies of conventional brain lesions.

10.2 Deficits in visual attention after brain damage

Defined broadly, disturbances of visual attention are very common after brain damage. As a consequence, research on visual attention deficits is a large and heterogeneous field, ranging from the effects of traumatic brain injury to developmental disorders, stroke, and dementia. A useful organizing principle can found in the distinction between lateralized and non-lateralized deficits. Lateralized deficits are confined to one side of the visual field, typically opposite a *unilateral* lesion (i.e. confined to one hemisphere). Classified under the syndromes of neglect and extinction, lateralized deficits have been much studied and their relation to lesion anatomy is fairly well described (see Section 10.2.1). In contrast, non-lateralized (general) deficits of visual attention have traditionally been studied with less refined testing measures, often after diffuse brain damage, and clear relations to specific lesion sites are lacking (see Section 10.2.2).

10.2.1 Lateralized deficits in visual attention

By far the most studied disturbance of attention is the *neglect* syndrome, with hundreds of articles published over the past decades. Neglect can be defined as a failure to report, respond, or orient to novel or meaningful stimuli presented to the side opposite a brain lesion (*contralesionally*), when this failure cannot be attributed to either sensory or motor defects (Heilman 1979). A typical example of neglect behaviour is when a patient systematically fails to locate left-side targets in a visual search task (Fig. 10.2), even when allowed free viewing and unlimited scanning time. In daily life such a patient may bump into things, not groom or dress herself on one side of the body, and fail to notice when people are approaching her from the affected side. It is not hard to understand why research on this topic is popular. Neglect is a fascinating, paradoxical condition where patients remain unaware of stimuli even though their basic perceptual apparatus is often intact. It is arguably one of the clearest examples in neuropsychology of a selective disturbance of consciousness. In addition, neglect is a very frequent effect of stroke, especially in the acute stage, and therefore holds large clinical interest.

Early accounts described neglect as a sensory deficit (Battersby *et al.* 1956; Sprague *et al.* 1961), but there are now strong reasons to regard the disturbance as primarily attentional. Visual field cuts and neglect occur independently in different patients (doubly dissociable deficits) and are related to damage in different

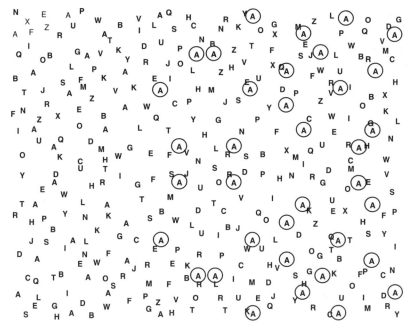

Fig. 10.2 Typical performance of a neglect patient in a visual search task. The task is to locate and encircle all tokens of letter type A. Many items are overlooked on the left side of the test paper.

parts of the brain: primary visual pathways versus higher-level cortical areas, respectively. In addition, neglected stimuli can affect the patient's behaviour implicitly (Halligan and Marshall 1988; Berti 2002) indicating substantial cognitive processing beneath the conscious threshold. Neural correlates of this implicit processing have been found in the form of (relatively weak) cortical activations by the neglected stimuli in functional imaging studies (Vallar *et al.* 1991; Rees *et al.* 2000). Further, neglect is not necessarily defined in retinotopic coordinates, but can be relative to different parts of the patient's body and even to the attended object itself, which is not consistent with a simple sensory deficit. Still, the contemporary emphasis on attentional or 'cognitive' explanations of neglect may have overshadowed basic sensory aspects of the condition (Halligan and Marshall 2002). For example, under conditions where competing stimuli are absent and motor exploration is neutralized, perception of single flashes in the neglected side is still deficient (Smania *et al.* 1998). A recent theory of visual attention (TVA)-based study by Habekost and Rostrup (2006; see Section 11.2.2.2) suggests that similar sensory impairment can be found after many cases of right-side brain damage, even when neglect is weak or absent.

Neglect is a complex disorder that involves many aspects of visuospatial cognition and behaviour (for an overview, see Karnath *et al.* 2002*b*). It is now clear that there is no unitary neglect syndrome but rather a cluster of dissociable symptoms, where each patient is likely to display only a subset. Neglect typically affects perceptual function, but can also relate to motor function, such that patients fail to respond to a stimulus even though they are aware of it (Heilman *et al.* 2003). Although probably rare, studies have also reported neglect confined to stimuli in near (reaching) space (Halligan and Marshall 1991) and far space (Cowey *et al.* 1994). Vertical neglect for stimuli in the lower (Butter *et al.* 1989) or upper visual field (Shelton *et al.* 1990) has also been reported. Neglect is often manifest across sensory modalities and may include personal neglect, where one side of the body is neglected, and auditory neglect. Such generalized impairment is consistent with damage to supramodal representations of personal and extrapersonal space.

Although neglect also occurs after damage in the left side of the brain, evidence from thousands of patients shows that the condition is more frequent, severe, and persisting after right-side damage (Mesulam 2000). Clinically significant neglect after left-side injury seems to be rare beyond the acute stage (Stone *et al.* 1992). Several explanations have been offered for this marked lateralization. As mentioned in Section 9.4, Mesulam (1981) suggested that the left hemisphere directs attention predominately to the right side of space, whereas the right hemisphere directs attention to both sides. This way, left-side lesions should not cause much neglect because the right hemisphere can usually take over, whereas there is no similar 'back-up' for the representation of the left visual field.

Other theories view neglect as a disturbance of the normal competition between the two hemispheres. In his *orientation bias* model, Kinsbourne (1993) hypothesized that each hemisphere directs attention to the opposite end of the visual display, but that these 'opponent processors' keep each other in check by mutual inhibition across the corpus callosum. If the strength of one hemisphere is weakened by a large lesion, the other hemisphere becomes hyperactive and pushes spatial attention in its preferred direction. Kinsbourne explains the relation of neglect to right-side damage by assuming that the left-hemisphere processor is normally more powerful than the right-hemisphere processor, and lesions of the latter system therefore lead to more severe imbalance. Although this hypothesis has not received strong empirical support, the general notion that unilateral brain damage should lead to asymmetrical neural competition fits well with many findings, as well as with the theoretical frameworks of both the neural theory of visual attention (NTVA) and the biased competition model of Desimone and Duncan (1995).

Yet there seems to be more to neglect than attentional imbalance, and general disturbances of arousal and vigilance are increasingly seen as central factors in the syndrome. One of the first to point this out was Robertson (1993), who noted that the frequency of neglect in the acute stage is quite similar after lesions in either side, but that only right-side lesions lead to chronic deficits. Robertson proposed that two conditions are necessary for persisting neglect: damage to an orienting network and to a network for vigilance and arousal (cf. the model of Posner and Petersen 1990; see Section 9.4). Left-side lesions affect only the orienting network, but due to the lateralization of the arousal system right-side lesions lead to chronic disturbance in this system also. Reduced arousal and vigilance have been found repeatedly in neglect patients, and recently neglect has also been associated with other non-lateralized disturbances of attention (Robertson and Manly 1999; Husain and Rorden 2003). These deficits include slow attentional blinks (Husain *et al.* 1997), reduced spatial working memory span (Wojciulik *et al.* 2001), and bilateral deficits in visual processing speed and visual short-term memory (VSTM) capacity (Duncan *et al.* 1999; see Section 11.2.1.1). Thus, non-lateralized deficits have been established as an important part of the neglect syndrome.

Historically, neglect is associated with parietal lesions (Brain 1941; Critchley 1949), later specified to the inferior parietal cortex (Vallar and Perani 1986), which is still widely considered to be the main lesion location for neglect (Mort *et al.* 2003). Recently the traditional association with parietal lobe damage has been challenged by two large patient studies featuring new methods of lesion analysis (Karnath *et al.* 2001, 2004) that point to the superior temporal gyrus as the critical site. This issue is currently the focus of intense debate. However, neglect has also been found after damage to other parts of the brain, though less frequently: the (inferior) frontal cortex (Heilman and Valenstein 1972; Husain and Kennard 1996), the basal ganglia (Damasio *et al.* 1980; Karnath *et al.* 2002*a*), the insula (Manes *et al.* 1999), the thalamus (Watson and Heilman 1979), the cingulate gyrus (Watson *et al.* 1973), and the internal capsule (Vallar and Perani 1986). This diversity of relevant lesions makes sense if neglect is conceived as a 'network syndrome' where damage in multiple parts of an interconnected system for spatial orienting (and perhaps general arousal) leads to similar symptoms. In keeping with this view, disconnection of cortical areas following white-matter damage is recognized increasingly as an important factor behind the neglect syndrome (Bartolomeo 2007).

Neglect patients often show *extinction*, defined as a condition where stimuli presented opposite the side of lesion (contralesionally) are perceived normally when shown in isolation, but missed when accompanied by a stimulus in the same side as the lesion (ipsilesionally). A strong attentional component in extinction is evident from demonstrations that performance can be improved by instructing patients to ignore ipsilesional events (Karnath 1988). The definition of extinction implies a selective disturbance of attentional weights (i.e. an ipsilesional bias), whereas sensory effectiveness should be normal in both sides. However, as with neglect, there is now evidence that perception of isolated contralesional stimuli is often impaired in patients who show clinical extinction, although typically too slight to be detected in standard testing (Marzi *et al.* 2001; Habekost and Rostrup 2006). Extinction is often considered to be a part of the neglect syndrome (Heilman *et al.* 2003), but double dissociations have been found between the two conditions (Cocchini *et al.* 1999) and the lesion anatomy may also be different. Specifically, extinction occurs after a wide range of unilateral lesions (Vallar *et al.* 1994) with simple lesion volume as a major predictor (Peers *et al.* 2005; Habekost and Rostrup 2006), and seems equally frequent after left- and right-side lesions (Rafal 1994). For these reasons the two syndromes may be regarded as partly independent. However, by an extended definition of extinction, in which ipsilesional stimuli interfere with the processing of contralesional stimuli without making them completely invisible, extinction-like perception can probably be found in most patients with neglect (Geeraerts *et al.* 2005). Besides being a common clinical phenomenon, extinction is interesting because it can be viewed as a prototype for disturbed attentional competition. For this reason the extinction effect holds great interest for general theories of visual attention.

10.2.2 General (non-lateralized) deficits in visual attention

A useful distinction for classification of general attentional deficits can be made between *energetic* versus *structural* limitations in attentional capacity. Energetic factors correspond to the neurological concepts of arousal and alertness, and represent phasic or temporary aspects of attentional function. Alertness is often deficient in the early stages after brain injury has occurred, most severely in the acute confusional state where attentional functions are globally impaired (Mesulam 2000). Acute confusion is typically caused by metabolic disturbance and reflects dysfunction in the subcortical arousal system (see Section 9.4) and diffusely in the cortex. The patient is only able to concentrate for short periods of time, is amnesic and disoriented, and often shows psychotic behaviour. Given adequate medical treatment the confusional state usually wears off, but alertness can be disturbed after brain injury in other, more subtle ways. The activation of the subcortical arousal system is top-down modulated by motivational and volitional factors, which depend primarily on limbic structures and the frontal cortex. Whereas subcortical disturbances of arousal lead to general reductions in attentional function, impaired top-down modulation typically leads to larger variability (attentional fluctuations), particularly when the external input is not engaging. Such difficulties with sustaining attention to a task seem to be related to lesions in the right dorsolateral prefrontal cortex (Robertson and Manly 1999), supporting theories of involvement of the right hemisphere in arousal and vigilance (e.g. Posner and Petersen 1990).

If energetic factors are normal, the maximum processing ability of the individual depends on structural limitations in attentional capacity. Similar to the C and the K parameters of TVA, the clinical neuropsychological tradition distinguishes between two main types of deficit: reduced processing speed ('how fast?') and reduced span of attention ('how much?'). The first type of function is usually tested by reaction time tasks, whereas the second type is examined by tests of immediate memory span (Lezak 1995). A tendency towards prolonged reaction time in cognitive tests has been found after nearly all types of brain injury (van Zomeren and Brouwer 1987). The effect is traditionally considered a non-specific effect of brain injury, and research has focused on diffuse lesions such as head trauma or dementia (van Zomeren and Brouwer 1994). Van Zomeren and Brouwer suggest that diffuse affection of the white matter (e.g. fibre shearing after traumatic brain injury) causes slower information transfer between brain centres. This is an interesting hypothesis, but reaction time is a composite measure and processing can be delayed at many stages between stimulus and response, which often makes results difficult to interpret. In vision the relevant variable is the speed of visual processing. Reaction time tasks are generally not adequate for measuring this function because it is difficult to control for the influence of motor processes and other factors. However, as described in Chapter 11, a direct measure of visual processing speed can be obtained by TVA analysis of whole report data. This testing method has provided some of the only evidence available so far on the lesion anatomy of visual processing speed (Peers *et al.* 2005; Habekost and Rostrup 2007) (see Section 11.2.1).

Most neuropsychological tests of 'attentional span' in fact measure auditory storage capacity (e.g. the ability to repeat sentences or strings of digits). Supposedly visual span tests typically examine the memory for sequences of visual events, for example the examiner's tapping of different blocks on a board (the Corsi Block Tapping test; see Lezak 1995). However, a valid test for VSTM capacity requires simultaneous presentation of items, so briefly that verbal recoding during the presentation cannot influence performance. One example is change detection tasks, which have been used for estimating VSTM capacity in normal subjects (Luck and Vogel 1997; Vogel *et al.* 2001) but remain little applied in neuropsychological research. Other studies have used whole report experiments with a single exposure duration of such length (100–200 ms unmasked) that it could be assumed that VSTM was filled up in each trial (Peers *et al.* 2005). However, the most robust way of estimating the visual span limitation includes strict control for the effect of visual processing speed. Whole report experiments with variable exposure durations, combined with TVA analysis, currently seems to be only method for this.

Higher-level aspects of visual attention such as filtering, set switching, and monitoring—in general, attentional control—can also be disturbed selectively after brain damage. For example, as described in Section 9.3, filtering depends on top-down signals from parietal and frontal cortex to visual areas of the posterior cortex. Accordingly, filtering deficits have been reported in single cases of (bilateral) parietal lesions (Friedmann-Hill *et al.* 2003), prefrontal lesions (Gehring and Knight 2002), and selective damage in the occipito-temporal area V4 (Gallant *et al.* 2000). Other investigations have shown no deficits in visual filtering after damage to the parietal or frontal cortex (Duncan *et al.* 1999; Habekost and Bundesen 2003), although some relation to lesion volume has been found in comprehensive patient studies (Peers *et al.* 2005; Habekost and Rostrup 2006). These mixed results are in line with the absence of findings after traumatic brain injury in many studies (van Zomeren and Brouwer 1994) and suggest that top-down control of visual filtering is rather robust to brain damage. An alternative explanation is that there seems to be large normal variability in the efficiency of top-down attentional control, which makes it hard to demonstrate deficits after brain damage. In the face of this interindividual variability, transcranial magnetic stimulation may provide more statistical power, because this method allows for direct comparison of each individual's performance with or without the 'lesion' produced by TMS. A good example of this point is a TVA-based TMS study by Hung *et al.* (2005; see Section 11.2.1.6).

10.3 Attention research using TMS

Although still a relatively young field, attention research using TMS has provided important information on the involvement of specific brain areas, particularly the posterior parietal cortex, in some of the classic attention tasks. These tasks include visual search, Posner's cuing task, and change detection. In other interesting lines of research, TMS has been used to simulate neglect behaviour in normal participants or, paradoxically, to facilitate certain attentional processes.

One of the most studied effects in this field is the role of the right posterior parietal cortex (PPC) in visual search. This issue has been investigated using both single-pulse (Ashbridge *et al.* 1997; Fuggetta *et al.* 2006) and repetitive TMS (Ellison *et al.* 2003; Rosenthal *et al.* 2006). A general finding is that TMS to the right PPC impairs (many-view) conjunction search, but not (one-view) feature search (i.e. effortless 'pop-out' of the target; see Section 2.4). For example, Rosenthal *et al.* (2006) applied rTMS to the right PPC for 500 ms after the onset of a search array that either had high or low target–distractor discriminability. In the case of the most difficult task condition (low target discriminability, large set size), rTMS was also applied at a later stage during processing (500–1000 ms after onset). rTMS to the right PPC increased reaction time selectively for the most difficult displays, indicating that an intact right parietal cortex is necessary only for this type of search. Interestingly, the effective timing of TMS depended on the presence of a target: if a target was present in the display, TMS within the first 500 ms after onset impaired performance, but if the target was absent, the effect was confined to late stimulation (500–1000 ms after onset). This suggests that the right PPC is engaged in both the detection of difficult targets as well as search termination/response selection, but at different points in time.

TMS studies have also shown the involvement of the PPC in many other attentional processes. An interesting lateralization is often found, such that stimulation of the left parietal cortex either has no or the opposite effect on attentional selection compared to right-side TMS. For example, rTMS to the right PPC led to impaired change detection in a study by Beck *et al.* (2006), whereas left-side stimulation had no measurable effect. On the other hand, Mevorach *et al.* (2006) found evidence that TMS to the right PPC disrupted guidance of attention *toward* salient stimuli, but that left-side TMS impaired the ability to direct attention *away* from salient stimuli. Of particular interest in relation to the debate about critical lesions for neglect (see Section 10.2.1), TMS to the right PPC has often been shown to induce neglect-like symptoms in normal participants (Pascual-Leone *et al.* 1994; Fierro *et al.* 2000; Hilgetag *et al.* 2001; Bjoertomt *et al.* 2002; Muggleton *et al.* 2006). For example, Hilgetag *et al.* (2001) applied rTMS at the right intraparietal sulcus for 10 min in normal volunteers. After stimulation was terminated, the ability to detect visual stimuli was tested in either one of the hemifields or simultaneously in both. Compared with performance before TMS, detection of left-side stimuli was impaired, especially if accompanied by a right-side stimulus (extinction behaviour). To the contrary, detection of right-side stimuli was in fact facilitated by TMS.

The study of Hilgetag *et al.* (2001) is not the only example that TMS can enhance some aspects of attentional performance. Oliveri *et al.* (1999) found that the (somatosensory) extinction shown by patients with right-side brain damage was relieved by single-pulse TMS to the left frontal lobe. In normal subjects, Walsh *et al.* (1998) found that when single-pulse TMS was applied to visual area MT, search performance was impaired in a motion 'pop-out' task, but not for the 'pop-out' of a particular form. This was perhaps to be expected due to the well-known involvement of MT in motion perception. However, when motion was present in the display but irrelevant, or when filtering based on colour or form was required, TMS to MT actually improved search performance. The results of both Oliveri *et al.* and Walsh *et al.* can be explained by assuming that TMS decreased the attentional weights of particular stimuli, which in some circumstances were defined as irrelevant for the task, by disturbing their cortical representation.

10.4 Summary

The evidence from disturbances of brain activity—either following brain damage or induced by transcranial magnetic stimulation—has both *confirmed* and *elaborated* the knowledge gained by functional imaging on the anatomy of visual attention. On the one hand, the general notion that visual attention is organized in large-scale anatomical networks, where each area provides a specific contribution to processing, has been confirmed: damage to particular parts of these networks leads to characteristic disturbances of attention, such as visual neglect after lesions in the right posterior parietal cortex or difficulties with sustaining attention after right prefrontal damage. On the other hand, due to the causal logic of the lesion method, studies of brain disturbance enables one to go beyond functional imaging and point to brain areas that are not only activated in relation to a given task, but also *necessary* to carry out the task.

Besides its great clinical importance, the study of brain damage has traditionally been the main way to obtain knowledge about brain–behaviour relationships. Attentional deficits after brain damage can generally be classified as lateralized or non-lateralized. Lateralized deficits typically follow damage to one side of the brain and have been much studied, particularly in the form of the neglect syndrome. Such deficits can generally be considered to be a result of asymmetrical neural competition between the two hemispheres. Non-lateralized deficits in visual attention have been less investigated experimentally, but typically seem to result from disturbances in the subcortical arousal system, generally impaired information transmission due to white-matter damage, or lesions in high-level control structures in parietal or frontal cortex. In addition to these neuropsychological findings, transcranial magnetic stimulation (TMS) is emerging as an important alternative to studies of naturally occurring brain damage. The 'virtual lesions' induced by TMS offer greater experimental control and do not suffer from the complication of brain reorganization after damage. On the other hand, the most robust findings in the field still come from traditional studies of brain damage.

Overall, research on attention disturbances is a large and varied field, where many different investigation methods have been applied. The psychological testing and analysis used to characterize the disturbances is often more closely related to the specific clinical pattern at hand than to general theories of visual attention. However, as explained in Chapter 11, the field can now benefit from a more principled investigation method based on TVA.

11

TVA-based assessment

Inspired by its success in cognitive psychology, the theory of visual attention (TVA) has also been applied to the study of visual attention deficits after brain damage. TVA-based patient assessment depends on a specific combination of experimental testing and data analysis, which was pioneered by John Duncan and Claus Bundesen in the late 1990s (see Section 11.1). The mathematical details of the data analysis have now been generalized and implemented in computer software by Søren Kyllingsbæk (2006). TVA-based assessment holds many advantages compared to conventional clinical tests of visual attention. In Section 11.2 we illustrate the four most important of these advantages in a review of the studies currently published using the method. First, performance is analysed into separable functional components: *specificity* (Section 11.2.1). Second, the method can reveal deficits that are not evident in standard clinical examination: *sensitivity* (Section 11.2.2). Third, the measurement error related to each test result can be quantified directly and in most cases shown to be minor: *reliability* (Section 11.2.3). Fourth, the functional components measured are not specific to the tasks used, but grounded in a general theory of visual attention: *validity* (Section 11.2.4).

11.1 The basic method

Due to its broad coverage of attention research, it is possible to apply TVA analysis to many experimental paradigms, for example Posner's cued detection task, visual search, and rapid serial visual presentation. So far TVA-based patient studies have focused on whole and partial report tasks. As described in Chapter 2, these are two classical methods for investigating divided and focused attention, respectively. Besides having the virtue of a simple design, whole and partial report represent the most direct way to estimate individual values of five central TVA parameters: the visual threshold, t_0, the visual processing speed, C, the visual short-term memory (VSTM) storage capacity, K, the efficiency of top-down control, α, and the spatial bias of attentional weighting, w_{index} [defined as the ratio between attentional weights in the left and right side: $w_{\text{index}} = w_{\text{left}} / (w_{\text{left}} + w_{\text{right}})$]. The exact details of the paradigms vary from study to study, but the basic design is as follows. An array of simple visual objects (typically letters) is shown to the subject (see Fig. 11.1 for an example), so briefly that eye movements are prohibited (i.e. for at most 200 ms). The display is followed by either a set of pattern masks or a blank screen. In *whole report* the task is to report the identity of as many items as possible. The exposure duration is typically varied to cover the range from the individual's perception threshold up to near-ceiling performance. This design enables one to estimate an individual's visual threshold (t_0), processing rate (C), and capacity of VSTM (K). If stimuli are shown simultaneously in both sides of the visual field, the relative attentional weight of left- versus right-side objects (spatial bias w_{index}) can also be measured. In *partial report* only a subset of the stimuli defined by a selection criterion (e.g. a particular colour, location, or alphanumeric class) is to be identified. The selection criterion is usually given in advance of the display and remains constant within a testing block. Partial report tasks enable one to estimate the efficiency of top-down controlled selectivity (α). In both whole and partial report, each display condition is repeated many times to obtain reliable data. The number of repetitions per condition depends on the purpose of the assessment (e.g. clinical or research), but is typically between 25 and 100.

To interpret whole and partial report performance with letter stimuli solely in terms of TVA parameters it must be assumed that other, necessary components of task performance can be neglected (i.e. are normal). In studies of normal cognition, where young university students comprise the usual study population, all of these factors can be taken more or less for granted. However, in case of brain-damage studies, screening and control procedures must be included to ensure that performance is not confounded by any of these deficits. A basic condition is that visual field cuts in the tested areas must be absent. If the patient has field cuts, C values are reduced to zero at certain

Fig. 11.1 Typical stimulus display used in TVA-based assessment.

display locations, which makes testing pointless. Further, visual processing is not measured directly, but through verbal report. Therefore visual-to-verbal recoding should be adequate, and expressive aphasia must be absent. Also visual acuity must be sufficient (i.e. not cause special difficulties for discriminating letters or distinguishing targets from distractors). Participants should be highly trained in recognition of letters (i.e. literate and with an intact letter recognition system in the brain, usually located in the posterior left hemisphere). Verbal short-term storage capacity must be larger than VSTM capacity in order not to confound estimates of the latter. In addition, arousal levels must not be significantly reduced during testing, and participants should be able to understand the instructions. Motor activity is another process that is not modelled by TVA. To eliminate the influence of this factor, report must be unspeeded and stimulation so brief that eye movements are not possible during the presentation (i.e. 200 ms). Central fixation can be controlled by direct observation, video recordings, or special equipment for detection of eye movements.

11.2 **TVA-based patient studies**

Since the field was opened up by a pioneer study of Duncan *et al.* (1999), about a dozen TVA-based patient studies have been published, most of them within the past few years (i.e. 2005–2007). The studies have covered a wide range of attention disturbances, such as neglect, extinction, simultanagnosia, alexia, form perception deficits, distractability, and reduced general capacity. Most studies have investigated stroke patients, but there is an increasing interest in applying the method to neurodegenerative disorders such as Alzheimer's and Huntington's disease, as well as developmental conditions such as ADHD (attention deficit hyperactivity disorder). TMS studies using TVA-based assessment are also beginning to appear. In the following we review the state of this new research field while illustrating the four central strengths of the test method: its specificity, sensitivity, reliability, and validity.

11.2.1 **Specificity**

To be useful, a neuropsychological test should measure relatively pure aspects of the patient's cognitive function. A test score that reflects many different abilities at the same time is difficult to interpret. For example, many clinical tests of visual attention have a complex motor component (e.g. the patient has to move the eyes across a piece of paper and manually cross out target items). Often reaction time is used as the dependent measure, which also obscures measurement of processes at the sensory stage of analysis. More fundamentally, performance in many clinical tests does not relate in a simple way to basic cognitive components, but rather to the particular (often complex) task used for the investigation. TVA-based assessment has much more to offer in this respect. The involvement of motor processes is minimal and performance is directly analysed into the fundamental elements (TVA parameters) of visual attention that have been identified in the general theory. As detailed in this section, many patient studies have already profited from this specificity.

11.2.1.1 Duncan *et al.* (1999)

The first TVA-based patient study was made by Duncan *et al.* (1999), who investigated nine patients with varying degrees of visual neglect after lesions in the right parietal cortex. In their first experiment, Duncan *et al.* presented the patients (and age-matched control participants) with five letters arranged in a vertical column, either to the left or right of fixation (Fig. 11.1). The task was whole report. Six exposure conditions (three durations of stimulus exposure followed by a blank screen or a mask) were individually calibrated to cover the range from near-threshold to ceiling performance. For each participant the total set of scores on individual trials was fitted by TVA analysis. The analysis specified the set of parameter values (for C, K, and t_0) that could have produced the observed scores with the highest likelihood. Given that stimuli were shown either to the left or right of fixation, parameter estimates could be obtained separately for each visual field. Compared to control participants, the patients had bilateral reductions of the visual span (parameter K). The reduction was uniform: no difference was found between mean K values in either side. The patients also had reduced visual processing speed (parameter C) in both hemifields, but especially in the left side. Surprisingly, these results indicated large bilateral deficits in the supposedly lateralized neglect syndrome.

In the second experiment of the study, a partial report task, participants were instructed to report only letters with a specific colour (red or green) and ignore letters with a different colour. They were shown either one target object, two targets, or a target and a distractor. Stimuli could occur at four positions in a 2×2 grid (Fig. 11.2) and exposure duration was calibrated individually so that performance was neither at floor nor ceiling.

The partial report data were fitted by TVA analysis, which produced three parameter estimates for each of the four display positions: sensory effectiveness (the processing speed of a stimulus when presented alone), the attentional weight of a distractor object, and the attentional weight of a target object. When comparing these values across positions, the neglect patients showed low attentional weighting of left-side objects in general (low value of parameter w_{index}, see Fig. 11.3). This result was expected due to the typical association

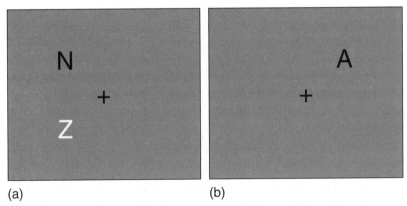

(a)   (b)

Fig. 11.2 Sample displays used by Duncan *et al.* (1999) for partial report by colour. Red and green are represented by black and white, respectively. (a) Target accompanied by distractor; (b) single target condition.

between neglect and extinction (cf. Section 10.2.1). Sensory effectiveness was also lower in the left side, consistent with the whole report measurements of visual processing speed in this side. However, no deficiency in top-down control of filtering (parameter α) could be demonstrated in either visual field. Surprisingly, this aspect of attentional function seemed to be normal even in the 'neglected' left hemifield.

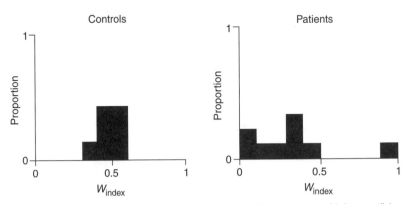

Fig. 11.3 Distributions of w_{index} for controls (left panel) and patients (right panel) in the study by Duncan *et al.* (1999). Adapted with permission from Duncan, Bundesen, Olson, Humphreys, Chavda, and Shibuya (1999). Systematic analysis of deficits in visual attention. *Journal of Experimental Psychology: General*, **128**, 450–478. Copyright 1999 by the American Psychological Association. The use of APA information does not imply endorsement by APA.

Overall, Duncan *et al.*'s mixed findings of preserved, unilaterally deficient, and bilaterally deficient functions went counter to traditional notions of neglect as a general contralesional deficit, and provided a strong first demonstration of the specificity of TVA-based assessment.

11.2.1.2 Duncan *et al.* (2003)

Another example of the specificity of TVA-based assessment is a case study of simultanagnosia by Duncan *et al.* (2003). Simultanagnosia is a severe visual disturbance that typically follows bilateral lesions in the parietal cortex. The most obvious symptom is a profound difficulty in perceiving complex scenes: the patient seems able to grasp only a small part of the surroundings at a time. However, the exact nature of the disturbance has long been controversial. Proposals range from a 'sticky' attentional focus that only allows one object to be processed at a time (Kinsbourne and Warrington 1962) to an extreme slowing of visual processing in general (Luria 1959). According to the latter hypothesis, difficulties should be evident even in single-stimulus situations. Duncan *et al.* (2003) used TVA-based assessment to distinguish between these possibilities in a simultanagnostic patient (G.K.) with bilateral parietal lesions ('dorsal simultanagnosia'). Whole report testing was again used, but this time in versions featuring both single and multiple stimuli. Compared with control participants, patient G.K. showed an extreme, tenfold reduction in visual processing speed in both situations (see Fig. 11.4 for whole report of multiple stimuli). However, G.K. had a much more modest deficit in the visual span, with a K value of 2.5. In other words, G.K. was able to perceive two and occasionally three objects at the same time, but required an extraordinarily long time to do so. The results thus went counter to the hypothesis that the perception span is limited to one object in simultanagnosia. Another theoretical possibility, that the patient focused most of his attentional resources on one location, could also be rejected from the whole report data: Attentional weights were distributed more evenly across objects. Duncan *et al.* found the same deficit pattern in another simultanagnostic patient (M.P.) who had a left occipito-temporal lesion ('ventral simultanagnosia'). The results suggested that, across variations in the syndrome, a specific deficit is at the core of simultanagnosia: a severe reduction of the visual processing rate. However, the generality of this conclusion is questioned by another study (Coslett and Saffran 1991), where a simultanagnostic patient seemed to have a visual span of only one object. Whereas different capacity reductions may underlie simultanagnosia, the study of Duncan *et al.* (2003) showed that TVA-based assessment can distinguish clearly between these deficits in individual patients.

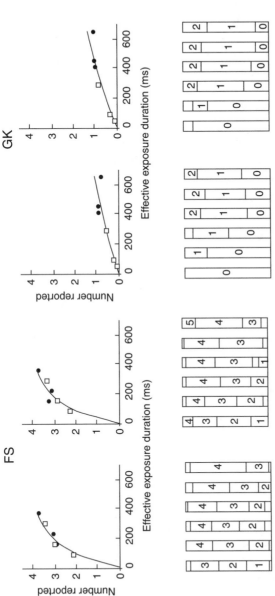

Fig. 11.4 Whole report experiment of Duncan *et al.* (2003). Data for a typical control participant (F.S.) and for patient G.K., separately for left and right visual fields (left and right panels, respectively). Upper panels: mean number of letters reported as a function of effective exposure duration; open squares = masked exposures; solid circles = unmasked exposures; solid line = fit by TVA. Lower panels: proportions of trials with 0, 1,..., 5 letters reported correctly for each effective exposure (increasing duration from left to right); for clarity, proportions below 0.1 are unlabelled. Adapted with permission from Duncan, Bundesen, Olson, Humphreys, Ward, Kyllingsbæk, van Raamsdonk, Rorden, and Chavda (2003). Dorsal and ventral simultanagnosia. *Cognitive Neuropsychology*, **20**, 675–701. Copyright 2003 by Taylor & Francis.

11.2.1.3 Finke *et al.* (2006, 2007)

Finke *et al.* (2006) showed that TVA-based assessment can be used to obtain cognitive biomarkers for the progression of Huntington's disease. Huntington's disease is an inherited neurological disorder that entails a gradual degeneration of neurons in the basal ganglia, eventually also disturbing cortical function and leading to dementia. Symptoms typically emerge at the age of 30–45 years and consist of a triad of motor, psychiatric, and cognitive disturbances. The involuntary movements (*hyperkinesia*) typical of the disease preclude many neuropsychological tests, but not TVA-based assessment with its minimal requirement for motor response. Using the same whole report design as Duncan *et al.* (1999), Finke *et al.* found strong bilateral reductions of both visual processing speed and VSTM capacity in their patient group. The magnitude of these deficits was related to disease progression (as measured by the number of years since disease onset), but not to the individual genetic load for the disease (as measured by the number of cytosine–adenine–guanine repeats on the relevant gene). In a partial report experiment, Finke *et al.* found a pathological attentional bias towards left-side stimuli, probably reflecting stronger neural degeneration in the left side of the brain. However, in contrast to the findings from whole report, these deficits correlated strongly with the individual genetic load (as well as the age of onset), but not with the disease progression (time since onset). Thus, deficits in specific TVA parameters— K and C versus w_{index}—seem linked to the stage of disease progression and the intensity of the pathogenic mechanisms, respectively, in Huntington's disease.

In a follow-up study, Finke *et al.* (2007) found that difficulties with visual identification of overlapping figures under free-viewing conditions, a typical symptom of simultanagnosia, were common in patients with Huntington's disease. Further, this deficit was significantly related to reductions in visual processing speed (cf. Duncan *et al.* 2003), but not to visual short-term storage capacity.

11.2.1.4 Peers *et al.* (2005)

As described in Section 10.2, a general distinction can be made between lateralized and non-lateralized attention deficits. Peers *et al.* (2005) used the specificity of TVA-based assessment to explore the lesion anatomy of these deficit types. They studied 25 patients with focal brain damage in either frontal or parietal cortex. Each patient's lesion was confined to one side of the brain, and the study included equally many patients with left and right hemisphere damage (no relations were found between test performance and side of lesion). In the first part of the study, Peers *et al.* tested patients (and control participants) using whole report. A single letter was presented briefly at fixation, and the exposure duration was varied systematically. The use of single-stimulus displays enabled a relatively pure estimation of parameter C, with no confounding influence of limitations in storage capacity (parameter K). Compared to control participants, no deficits on this test were found in patients with frontal lesions, but patients with parietal lesions were significantly impaired. The generality of this finding was tested using a second set of stimuli: faces. Patients with parietal lesions were also impaired at perceiving these stimuli (Fig. 11.5). Statistical lesion analysis of the patients' structural MR scans indicated that the deficit in visual processing speed was related to damage in the region of the temporo-parietal junction.

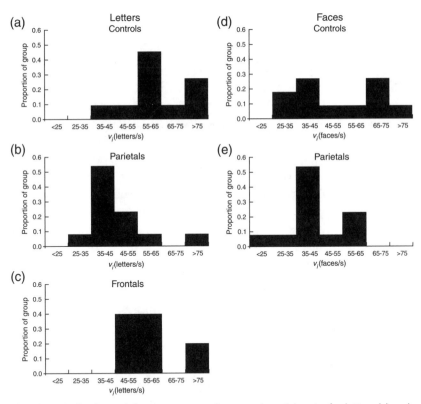

Fig. 11.5 Distributions of the v_i parameter: for control participants, for letters (a) and faces (d); for patients with parietal lesions, for letters (b) and faces (e), and for patients with frontal lobe lesions, for letters (c). Lower values of v_i indicate slower visual processing. From Peers, Ludwig, Rorden, Cusack, Bonfiglioli, Bundesen, Driver, Antoun, and Duncan (2005). Attentional functions of parietal and frontal cortex. *Cerebral Cortex*, **15**, 1469–1484. Copyright 2005 by Oxford University Press.

Peers *et al.* went on to study attentional weighting and storage capacity limitations with multi-element displays. Participants were shown either three or six letters in a relatively long, unmasked exposure. The letters were arranged in vertical columns of three letters each, and appeared either on one side only (three-element displays) or simultaneously in both visual fields (six-element displays). Extinction-like effects, where objects ipsilateral to the brain lesion (left or right) systematically received higher attentional weights, were found in many patients. The deficit did not seem to be related to a particular lesion location, but correlated with total lesion volume. To investigate attentional weighting of targets versus distractors, Peers *et al.* used an experimental condition in which one of the two three-letter columns was coloured differently and should be ignored (partial report). The score reduction in this condition (relative to scores obtained with the three-element displays) provided a measure of the efficiency of top-down control of filtering (parameter α). A modest, but significant correlation was again found between total lesion volume and high (i.e. poor) α values. Thus, only relatively large fronto-parietal lesions seemed to have a disturbing effect on top-down selectivity. Finally, from performance with displays containing six targets (whole report) Peers *et al.* estimated the maximum storage capacity of VSTM, K. Reductions in this parameter seemed to be related to damage in the same area as that for visual processing speed: the area around the temporo-parietal junction. As was the case for visual processing speed, patients with frontal lesions were not significantly impaired on this parameter. Thus general deficits in attentional capacity (both C and K) were related to posterior cortical lesions, in particular the temporo-parietal junction. On the other hand, parameters related to attentional weighting (extinction parameter w_{index} and distractibility parameter α) were predicted by simple lesion size.

11.2.1.5 Habekost and Rostrup (2007)

The lesion anatomy of general deficits in attentional capacity was further explored by Habekost and Rostrup (2007), who studied 22 patients with right hemisphere strokes of widely varying size and location. The patients were tested using a whole report experiment in which five letters were flashed either to the left or right of fixation, and exposure duration was varied systematically. For right-side (ipsilesional) stimuli, the resulting estimates of K and C were normal for most patients, even those with large cortical lesions. Thus, although many patients had lower performance with left-side stimuli (see the study of Habekost and Rostrup 2006, described in Section 11.2.2.2) they showed no general (i.e. bilateral) impairment in attentional capacity. These results suggest that lesions in a large part of the anterior right hemisphere are not critical for the general capacity of visual attention. However, six patients did have capacity reductions in both visual fields. These patients had either very large strokes that extended deep into the cerebral white matter, or 'leukoaraiosis', an age-related condition that selectively damages white-matter tracts (see Fig. 11.6). In this way, the study of Habekost and Rostrup pointed to the importance of white-matter connections for general visual capacity, in terms of both process-ing speed and the ability to perceive multiple items at the same time. The results are in line with previous suggestions that diffuse white-matter damage leads to reduced 'mental speed' (van Zomeren and Brouwer 1994) as meas-ured by (less specific) reaction time tasks.

11.2.1.6 Hung et al. (2005)

In the first study to combine TVA-based assessment with transcranial magnet-ic stimulation, Hung et al. (2005) investigated the role of the posterior parietal cortex (PPC) in top-down selection. Nine healthy subjects were given rTMS over either the right or left PPC, or no TMS, while carrying out the partial report task designed by Duncan et al. (1999; see Fig. 11.2). With no or left-side

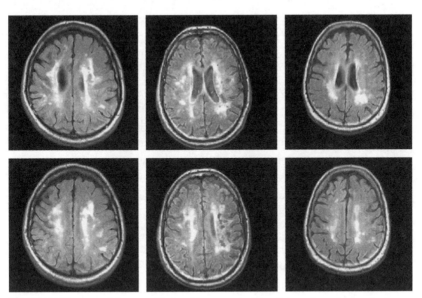

Fig. 11.6 MR scans of three patients with severe leukoaraiois and marked reduction of VSTM capacity. Upper panels: periventricular damage in each of the three patients. Lower panels: centrum semiovale damage in the same patients. Adapted with permission from Habekost and Rostrup (2007). Visual attention capacity after right hemisphere lesions. *Neuropsychologia*, **45**, 1474–1488. Copyright 2007 by Elsevier.

rTMS, selectivity for targets versus distractors was preserved. However, when the right PPC was stimulated, top-down control (α) was impaired in the left hemifield but enhanced in the right hemifield. The results of Hung *et al.* thus demonstrated a causal role of the right posterior parietal cortex for attentional filtering by colour. It is interesting to compare this result with the results of Duncan *et al.* (1999; see Section 11.2.1.1), which did not show significant deficits in α following strokes in the right parietal cortex. Besides the possibility that the strokes affected different parts of the parietal lobe than the ones stimulated by Hung *et al.*, a possible explanation for the discrepant findings is that the TMS procedure allows each participant's α score to be measured both with and without the 'lesion'. In contrast, the α scores of the stroke patients had to be compared with the scores of other individuals (i.e. healthy control participants). Given the typically large normal variability in α scores, as well as the greater statistical problems with estimating this parameter than the other TVA variables (see Section 11.2.3), the TMS method may have provided critically more statistical power.

11.2.1.7 Bublak *et al.* (2006)

Bublak *et al.* (2006) continued the TVA-based studies of neurogenerative diseases of Finke *et al.* (2006), broadening the investigation to include both Huntington's and Alzheimer's disease, as well as patients with mild cognitive impairment (MCI). The study followed the experimental design of Duncan *et al.* (1999). Whereas Duncan *et al.* demonstrated the specificity of TVA-based assessment by showing general deficits (in C and K) in a neurological condition traditionally considered to be a lateralized disorder (visual neglect), Bublak *et al.* found the reverse pattern: lateralized deficits in neurodegenerative diseases that are conventionally associated with general impairments of attention. Besides general reductions of visual processing speed (most pronounced in patients with Huntington's disease; cf. Finke *et al.* 2006), Bublak *et al.* found strong leftward biases of spatial attention, both in patients with Huntington's and with Alzheimer's disease. Thus the study demonstrated a surprising similarity between neglect and these two neurodegenerative diseases: although different in many other ways, both types of disorders involve a characteristic combination of lateralized and non-lateralized deficits in visual attention.

11.2.2 Sensitivity

Sensitivity, the ability to detect subtle functional disturbances, is another critical property of neuropsychological testing. Minor attention deficits can often be demonstrated by TVA-based assessment. The sensitivity of the method has been most clearly shown in studies by Habekost and Bundesen (2003) and Habekost and Rostrup (2006). Many patients with right hemisphere stroke show marked symptoms of visual neglect in the acute stage, but performance in clinical tests is often normalized some months later (cf. Section 10.2.1). Yet patients may still experience visual attention problems in their daily life, suggesting persistent subclinical deficits.

11.2.2.1 Habekost and Bundesen (2003)

Habekost and Bundesen (2003) used whole and partial report experiments to test a patient (G.L.) with haemorrhage in the right basal ganglia and overlying frontal cortex. Patient G.L. was in the stable phase of recovery and showed no neglect in clinical testing. Still she had a subjective experience of slight attentional asymmetry. This impression was confirmed by the TVA assessment and the deficit was specified into several components. The whole report experiment revealed a marked bilateral reduction of the patient's visual memory span (parameter K), whereas processing speed (parameter C) in both visual fields was in the lower normal range, compared to age-matched controls. In addition, patient G.L. had elevated thresholds for conscious perception, with a trend towards higher thresholds in the left side. The possible asymmetry near the perception threshold was explored in a partial report experiment using very brief, post-masked displays. Under these conditions the patient performed clearly worse with unilateral displays in the left side, confirming the hypothesis of a higher visual threshold in this side. Further, testing with bilateral stimulation revealed that the patient had markedly lower attentional weighting (w_{index}) of objects in the left side. However, no impairment of top-down selectivity (α) could be demonstrated in either visual field. Overall, TVA-based assessment was able to confirm the patient's subjective experience of attentional disturbance and to specify it into different functional components.

11.2.2.2 Habekost and Rostrup (2006)

Following this case study, a larger TVA-based patient study showed that subtle visual asymmetries are highly common after right-side stroke, even months and years after the initial insult. Habekost and Rostrup (2006) studied 26 patients with lesions in different parts of the right hemisphere, who generally showed minor or no clinical signs of neglect or extinction. Individual values of the main TVA parameters were determined by whole and partial report experiments. Stimulus presentations were lateralized to test performance separately in the left and right visual fields. The testing revealed two main types of asymmetry in the patient group. One was related to perception of unilateral displays, where a large majority of the patients showed lower processing speeds

(*C* values) for left- versus right-side presentations (Fig. 11.7). By statistical lesion analysis of the patients' MR scans, the deficit was linked to damage in the right putamen area. Surprisingly, the asymmetry in visual processing speed was not exacerbated by additional involvement of large cortical areas: it occurred to an equal extent after both small and large strokes that included the putamen area. The other main finding of Habekost and Rostrup was an asymmetry that occurred selectively with bilateral stimulation: extinction-like attentional weighting in favour of right-side (ipsilesional) stimuli. This deficit was found in most patients with large strokes that included both cortical and subcortical structures. However, the deficit rarely occurred after more focal lesions, which suggested a relation to lesion volume (cf. Peers *et al.* 2005). An important exception to this rule was a patient with a small thalamic lesion, who showed a clear extinction effect. By comparing this patient's lesion with the lesions of three other patients with thalamic damage but normal attentional weighting, it turned out that the extinction effect was related to damage in the pulvinar nucleus. This localization is directly predicted by the thalamic model of the neural theory of visual attention (NTVA) (see Section 9.5), which proposes that a map of attentional weights is located in the thalamic pulvinar nucleus. Damage to one side of this map should lead to the observed asymmetry in attentional weighting.

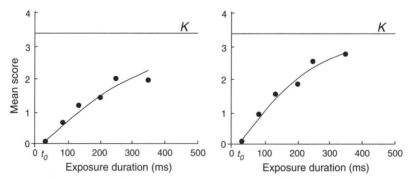

Fig. 11.7 Whole report performance of a representative patient (L4) with a large lesion in the right hemisphere. The mean number of correctly reported letters is shown as a function of exposure duration, separately for the left and right visual fields (left and right panels, respectively). Solid curves represent maximum likelihood fits to the observations by TVA. The estimate of visual short-term memory capacity, K, is marked by a horizontal line, and t_0 denotes the visual threshold. The slope of the curve at $t = t_0$ corresponds to the visual encoding rate, C. Note the different slopes of the two curves, reflecting different C values. Adapted with permission from Habekost and Rostrup (2006). Persisting asymmetries of vision after right side lesions. *Neuropsychologia*, **44**, 876–895. Copyright 2006 by Elsevier.

11.2.3 **Reliability**

Besides specificity and sensitivity, reliability is one of the key features of neuro-psychological assessment. Dependable conclusions about the patient's function are required, but often the reliability of individual test results is largely unknown. One strategy to counter this problem is to perform syndrome analysis. That is, the individual test results in the assessment must fit into a coherent neuropsychological pattern to guide the general conclusion. A classical example of this approach is Luria's system of neuropsychological assessment (Christensen 1975). In TVA-based assessment, this holistic strategy can be complemented by something that is rarely available in neuropsychological assessment: a quantitative estimate of the measurement error related to each individual test result.

To achieve this, TVA analysis can be coupled with statistical *bootstrap* methods (Efron 1979; Efron and Tibshirani 1993). The method works as follows: TVA-based assessment includes many repeated measurements for each testing condition (e.g. a particular spatial arrangement and exposure duration). Even under equal display conditions the number of correctly reported items varies from repetition to repetition. This is a simple empirical fact, but also follows from the stochastic nature of visual encoding assumed in TVA. The question is, how reliable are the TVA parameter estimates or test scores (e.g. the individual value of the C parameter), based on such variable measurements? This question can be answered directly by bootstrap analysis. The bootstrap procedure works by sampling at random, with replacement, from the total set of individual measurements in the test. This results in a 'bootstrap data set', which represents a random but systematic variation of the original data. TVA analysis is now performed on the bootstrap data set to obtain a new set of parameter estimates. This statistical procedure is repeated many times (which can easily be done using a TVA software package; Kyllingsbæk 2006) resulting in a *distribution* of estimates for a given parameter, for example the processing rate in the right visual field (Fig. 11.8). The key idea of bootstrapping is that the variability of this distribution represents the measurement error inherent in the original data set (for a mathematically formal treatment, see Chernick 1999).

In general, the reliability of parameters C and K has been found to be high (Habekost and Bundesen 2003; Habekost and Rostrup 2006), even with the reduced number of repetitions suitable for a clinical examination (Bublak *et al.* 2005; Finke *et al.* 2005). Measurement of the w_{index} parameter (spatial bias) is also generally reliable, but estimates of the α parameter (efficiency of attentional filtering) are often related to substantial measurement error. One possible explanation for the relatively low reliability of α is that the parameter is

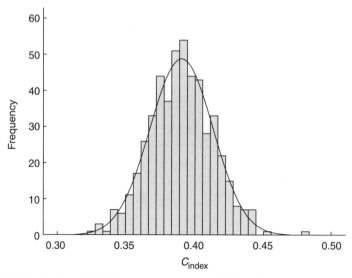

Fig. 11.8 Distribution of 1000 bootstrap estimates of C_{index} for a representative patient (L4) in the study by Habekost and Rostrup (2006). The solid curve indicates a normal distribution. The 95% confidence interval was $0.34 \leq C_{index} \leq 0.43$. Adapted with permission from Habekost and Rostrup (2006). Persisting asymmetries of vision after right side lesions. *Neuropsychologia*, **44**, 876–895. Copyright 2006 by Elsevier.

defined as a ratio between two variables (the attentional weight of a distractor and a target, respectively), a formal property that is known to make mathematical estimation less stable. Another explanation is that VSTM encoding of distractor items, an event of large relevance for α estimation, is not directly visible in the experimental data, because only target items are reported. The example of the α parameter shows that bootstrap analysis can point to specific functional components where interpretation of the test result should be cautious and rely on supplementary measures if possible.

11.2.4 **Validity**

A final aspect of TVA-based assessment concerns the validity of the method: does the test battery measure what it is supposed to measure (i.e. central aspects of visual attention)? Main support for the validity of the TVA approach comes from the fact that the parameters used for data modelling can also account for a wide range of findings from other experimental tasks (as described in Chapters 4 and 5). Thus, unlike most clinical tests, the results of TVA-based assessment are not closely linked to particular tasks. However, the validity of a psychological test potentially has many sides, depending on the kind of inferences that are drawn from it. Besides the relation to other experimental studies, four aspects of the method's validity are: (1) the relation of the stimulus material to visual objects in general; (2) the relation to perception that involves more than a single fixation (i.e. exploratory activity); (3) the relation to other clinical measures of visual attention; and (4) the functional specificity of each TVA parameter. We discuss each of these points in turn.

In TVA-based assessment the usual stimulus materials are letters. There are several reasons for this choice. Letter perception is a precondition for one of our most important visual activities: reading and, as such, an interesting object of study in itself. More importantly, letters are well suited for investigating perception of (simple) visual objects in general. Letters are perhaps the most over-learned visual forms in our environment, and recognition is highly efficient. This means that visual short-term memory can be filled up within a few hundred milliseconds (i.e. a single fixation), which is practical for assessing the limits of this function. TVA-based assessment targets mainly high-level attentional mechanisms, and it would be a confounding factor if the basic recognition of the test stimuli was deficient. Therefore it is also practical that letter perception is quite robust to brain damage, especially if the left posterior cortex is not affected. Another practical property is that the alphabet is so large that many different letters can be presented in the same display with little risk of having the score confounded by guessing, and that the response (verbal report) is straightforward. Also, the individual items are approximately equally difficult to identify (the stimulus set is homogeneous), which simplifies the data analysis. For all these reasons, in previous research letter stimuli have been widely used. This allows results to be compared with many other studies. On the other hand, the empirical basis for generalizing to different stimulus types (e.g. faces or digits) is weaker, and more studies using alternative materials would be useful.

The presentation of stimuli in whole and partial report is limited to fractions of a second (called *tachistoscopic* presentation after the apparatus that was originally used for this experimental procedure). This situation is less artificial than it may seem at first. In our normal visual activities, from reading to perceiving a scene, perception of the surrounding environment is built up through an ongoing cycle of saccades and fixations. This is due to the highly uneven distribution of acuity in the visual field, which makes foveal vision necessary for detailed object recognition. After each saccade the eyes normally remain fixated for only about 200–300 ms, during which time visual information is collected. Information uptake is inhibited during saccades, which, in effect, makes the eye a tachistoscope (Rayner 1998). Thus, the processes measured in whole and partial report experiments can be said to reflect the most basic building block in the visual process: the information uptake of a single fixation. Although the relation to visual exploration in general (oculomotor activity and other orienting movements) is still relatively unexplored, it seems highly plausible that a visual abnormality evident in single fixations should also affect perception in general.

In the absence of a 'gold standard' against which visual attention tasks can be measured (*criterion validity*), the validity of a test depends on the gradual development of converging evidence from related, but non-overlapping measures (*construct validity*). The first systematic attempt to compare TVA-based assessment with clinical attention tests was carried out by Finke *et al.* (2005). In addition to TVA-based assessment, 38 healthy participants were given various standard clinical tests, each of which was selected to correspond (roughly) to a specific TVA parameter (viz., C: a test of phasic alertness; K: a test of visual memory span; w_{index}: a lateralized visual scanning task; α: a version of the Stroop test). Significant correlations were found between all four TVA parameters and their paired clinical test. Equally important, the TVA parameters generally did not correlate with their non-paired tests. Although the TVA parameters do not represent exactly the same functions as the selected clinical tests, the specific correspondences are encouraging.

In principle, the various TVA parameters represent separate aspects of visual processing, and the model does not specify any dependence between their settings. However, in reality it is possible that the different parameters depend on the same abilities to some extent, which would lead to correlations in their values. Finke *et al.* (2005) also examined this issue of *discriminant validity*, and computed correlations between the values of all four TVA parameters. Only K and C were significantly correlated (to a moderate degree: $r = 0.40$). This correlation suggests that individuals vary in a general level of visual capacity that is reflected in both processing speed and VSTM capacity.

11.3 Summary

Since its introduction in 1999, TVA-based assessment of attention has become a firmly established method for neuropsychological research. It has been used to study a broad variety of conditions: visual neglect (Duncan *et al.* 1999), simultanagnosia (Duncan *et al.* 2003), Huntington's disease (Finke *et al.* 2006, 2007), Alzheimer's disease (Bublak *et al.* 2006), and subclinical attention deficits (Habekost and Bundesen 2003; Habekost and Rostrup 2006). TVA-based assessment has also been used to study the lesion anatomy of lateralized and non-lateralized attention deficits (Peers *et al.* 2005; Habekost and Rostrup 2006, 2007). Besides the studies described in this chapter, the method has been applied to investigate deficits in visual shape integration (Gerlach *et al.* 2005), alexia (Habekost and Starrfelt 2006), and several other conditions (currently on-going work): ADHD, dyslexia, depression, schizophrenia, and age-related changes in white matter. TVA-based assessment has even been applied to study the 'virtual lesions' produced by transcranial magnetic stimulation of healthy subjects (Hung *et al.* 2005). Given the method's qualities on four central test parameters—sensitivity, specificity, reliability, and validity—we expect even greater use of TVA-based assessment in the coming years.

Conclusion

A unified theory of visual attention

12.1 Attention in a nutshell

What is visual attention? This question formed the starting point of the book and has been its central motivation. Now it is time to summarize our answer. According to the theory of visual attention we have presented, TVA, cognition of the world consists of making *categorizations of objects*. Compared to the huge amount of information that is typically present in the sensory input, our ability to make perceptual categorizations is very modest. Similarly, our capacity to make visually guided actions is limited to one or a few objects at a time. The limitations in perception and action create a strong need for *selectivity* in the processing of visual information. Visual attention, then, is a selection mechanism that, at the same time, chooses between the different objects in the visual field (*filtering*) and between the categorizations that can be made of these objects (*pigeonholing*). By simultaneously selecting the behaviourally most important objects and the behaviourally most important features of these objects, attention serves both perception and action. TVA is a computational model of how this dual selection comes about in the human mind.

A categorization of an object is selected when it is encoded into *visual short-term memory* (VSTM), a system that sustains the information over time and makes it available for other cognitive processes and behavioural response. The storage capacity of VSTM is strongly limited and its content is determined by a competitive process that, in simple cases, takes the form of a race. Visual recognition takes time, typically hundreds of milliseconds, as it depends on a series of physical processes in the brain. The simple idea behind the race model is that the first object categorizations to be fully processed are the ones chosen by the visual system.

The speed of processing for an individual categorization is given directly by the central equation of TVA, the *rate equation*. According to the rate equation, processing speed depends on three factors. The first factor is purely sensory and represents the strength of evidence in the visual input that the categorization is valid. The two other factors can be manipulated by the subject and may thus be considered attentional rather than sensory in nature. The second factor of the rate equation represents the perceiver's subjective bias for making certain kinds of categorizations. The third factor represents the relative attentional weight given to the object; it results from a prior computation that follows the other main equation of TVA, the *weight equation*. The values of these three factors in combination determine how fast a particular categorization is processed and thus how likely it is to be selected by the visual system. In this way, the rate equation describes a very general mechanism for attentional selection in exact mathematical form. Given adequate information from sensory receptors and top-down settings of attentional priorities, the system provides the most interesting valid categorizations of the most relevant objects in the visual field. In our view, this is essentially how visual attention works.

12.2 **Integrating fields of research**

There is, of course, much more to say about attention besides its defining properties. During the course of this book we have expanded the ideas of TVA across three major research fields: psychology, neurophysiology, and functional neuroanatomy. Our ambition was to establish TVA as a unifying frame for the whole range of attention studies from neuron to behaviour. Regardless of which scientific perspective one takes on attention—information selection on the psychological scale, the activity of the individual cell, or the interplay between brain regions—these are all just different aspects of the same process. This integration in the real world should be mirrored in the scientific understanding of the phenomenon, and we hope to have shown that the concepts of TVA can provide such a bridge between disciplines. The equations and the general model are the same whether one interprets them at the psychological or the biological level. In both cases, they account for a large part of the existing scientific evidence.

Chapter 2 presented a review of half a century of attention studies in cognitive psychology. Much progress has been made, both empirically and theoretically, from the pioneering studies to the complex scientific field of today. Many attentional effects have been characterized and theories have moved from being largely qualitative towards a much higher degree of quantitative precision. Until the mid-1990s serial models dominated attention research, but these models were based on a narrow set of experimental paradigms, such as visual search, and could not account for more recent developments in the field. Instead parallel processing models have become increasingly influential. The most powerful type of model should incorporate both serial and parallel modes of selection, but few models show such flexibility. In addition, the typical attention model relates to a few specific paradigms rather than to the empirical literature as a whole. Chapter 3 described the historical background and basic concepts of TVA, a theory that aims at a general explanation of attentional phenomena and is compatible with both serial and parallel selection. TVA was formed by integrating a number of earlier models into a unified mathematical frame centred on the rate and weight equations. The preceding models were highly successful at describing single stimulus identification (selection of categories) and partial report (selection of objects), respectively, and TVA inherited this explanatory power. However, as detailed in Chapters 4 and 5, the scope of the unified TVA model is much wider and includes many of the central findings in cognitive psychology on divided and focused attention. TVA is not only consistent with these results in a general qualitative way, but includes a set of mathematical specifications that allows for detailed quantitative modelling of each set of empirical data. In this way, the concepts and equations of TVA form an analytical toolbox that can be applied to most of the experimental paradigms used in visual attention research.

Attention has not just been studied psychologically, but also within the field of neurophysiology. Decades of experiments with behaving monkeys have shown that the attentional state of the organism is reflected systematically in the activity of individual neurons. In Chapter 6 we introduced this research area and outlined the main findings. One important effect is that attention to a single stimulus in the cell's receptive field tends to increase its firing activity; this can be explained by models that view attention as a simple gain control mechanism. However, a much stronger effect (dynamic remapping) is found when attention is shifted between multiple stimuli in the receptive field, which may both increase and decrease the cell's activity. This effect fits much better with models assuming that attention works in an inhibitory fashion. Overall, however, none of the models described in Chapter 6 can account for the full range of attentional effects demonstrated in single cells. In Chapter 7 we presented a model that aims for such general coverage, the neural theory of visual attention (NTVA). NTVA is essentially a simple interpretation of the equations of TVA at the single-cell level: the two selection mechanisms of TVA—pigeonholing and filtering—are directly reflected in the activity of individual neurons. Pigeonholing changes the *activity level* of individual neurons that signal particular categorizations, whereas filtering changes the *number of neurons* that respond to particular objects. In appropriately configured networks, these effects at the microscopic level produce the well-known selection behaviour at the psychological scale. Analogous to Chapters 4 and 5, Chapter 8 demonstrated the explanatory power of NTVA in relation to specific data: more than 20 studies covering central findings in the neurophysiological literature were modelled in detail. Thus the scope of the cognitive TVA model has been dramatically expanded to include this very different area of attention research.

There is, of course, a long way from the activity of the individual neuron to the attentional selection of the whole organism. An important mediating level is that described by functional neuroanatomy: the information processing of distinct brain regions and their interaction. In recent decades this scientific field has been revolutionized by the brain imaging methods described in Chapter 9, which have enabled measurements of brain activity with high spatial and temporal resolution. These investigations have firmly established that visual attention depends on integrated activity in a number of widely distributed anatomical networks. These networks modulate the information processing in visual regions of the posterior cortex to produce the selection effects that are also evident in single-cell measurements. To link the micro- and macroscopic levels of description, we went on to suggest how the computations described in the NTVA model may be distributed anatomically, giving thalamo-cortical interaction a central role. Another perspective on functional neuroanatomy is brought about by human lesion studies. Chapter 10 provided an overview of this field, including the classical area of brain damage studies as well as the recent experimental technology of transcranial magnetic stimulation. The results from these investigations have generally confirmed that visual attention depends on networks of specific brain structures, each of which delivers its own contribution which can be disturbed selectively. As described in Chapter 11, this line of research has been closely linked to TVA theory following the recent development of *TVA-based patient assessment*, a powerful method for quantifying attentional function after brain damage. About a dozen studies spanning a wide variety of neurological disturbances have already been published using this new method. Thus clinical neuropsychology has also been integrated into the TVA framework, which completes the book's tour of disciplines in cognitive neuroscience. We hope to have convinced the reader that every area covered fits with our general story about the nature of visual attention.

12.3 Beyond attention: the great puzzle of human cognition

Like cognitive psychology as a whole, the typical model of attention has been more or less *paradigm specific*, accounting well for one or a few types of experiments, but showing little generality to other investigations of the phenomenon. At the other end of the theoretical spectrum, a few bold attempts have been made to model the totality of human psychological function, famous examples being Hull's principles of behaviour (Hull 1943) and Anderson's ACT model (Anderson 1996). Such models have tremendous generality, but tend to be weakly constrained at the level of concrete empirical data. TVA occupies a middle position in this respect, being general enough to apply to a wide range of attentional paradigms, but still able to explain specific experimental findings.

We believe the time has come for models of this intermediate generality in psychology. Instead of the elusive goal of one grand theory of psychology, a more realistic vision may be that successful theories of cognitive subdomains gradually merge like big parts of a puzzle. In fact, TVA fits well into a larger theoretical context of mental functions neighbouring attention. Logan (2002*a*) pointed out that a group of powerful models within quite different research traditions—memory, categorization, attention, and executive control—describe choice behaviour in very similar ways. The compatibility of these models is deep: they share the same computational structure and were, in many cases, developed as direct extensions of one another to cover new cognitive domains. For example, as described in Section 5.7, the original TVA model by Bundesen (1990) has been extended to account for a wide range of spatial effects in visual perception [CODE theory of visual attention (CTVA); Logan 1996], and the executive control over parameter settings in TVA has also been modelled [executive control of TVA (ECTVA); Logan and Gordon 2001]. In Logan's instance theory of attention and memory (ITAM) (Logan 2002*a*) this theoretical 'family' from attention research was brought together with a large group of memory and categorization models to form one unified framework. Theoretical integration on this scale promises much for the future. Emotion research could be the next candidate for a fusion with attention models. In TVA terms, emotional processes should be strongly involved in determining attentional pertinence values; rather than the fronto-parietal networks described in Chapter 9, this kind of attentional control may depend primarily on the amygdala nucleus (see Vuilleumier and Driver 2007).

Besides traditional psychological functions, one may enquire into the nature of experience itself, consciousness. The term *consciousness* has been used in many ways, but a very influential distinction has been made by Block (1996, 2005), among others, between *access consciousness* and *phenomenal consciousness*. Conceived this way, consciousness can be related readily to TVA. In our view, consciousness is a set of storage spaces ('memories'), which include modality-specific short-term stores, such as VSTM, as well as sensory memories, such as iconic memory (Neisser 1967). Basically, visual access consciousness is the same as VSTM. Visual phenomenal consciousness is the storage space for visual sensations, which is essentially the same as iconic memory. TVA and NTVA provide detailed accounts of encoding into VSTM. Once visual categorizations have been encoded in VSTM (i.e. retained in feedback loops of the VSTM system), the categorizations can be accessed and further processed in very many different ways. Depending on the interests of the observer, the contents of VSTM can be further analysed, transformed, elaborated, evaluated, reported, or otherwise responded to. Such general, optional accessibility is the hallmark of material in access consciousness.

Phenomenal consciousness is quite different. After a brief glance at a complex scene, we feel that we have 'seen' much more than we can report (Sperling 1960). What we 'see' in this sense of the word is what is represented by our visual sensations: the contents of visual phenomenal consciousness. What we can report is only what is retained in VSTM: the contents of visual access consciousness. Sensory processing and iconic memory are not capacity-limited in ways that are comparable to those in which perceptual processing and VSTM are limited. With respect to storage capacity, there is no obvious limitation on the number of sensations that can be held at the same time in iconic memory (nothing corresponding to TVA's parameter K). With respect to processing capacity, sensory neurons have small receptive fields—so small that, to a first approximation, effects of filtering may be neglected. Because of the small receptive fields (usually not more than one behaviourally relevant object can be fitted into a single receptive field), the sensory system appears nearly unlimited in processing capacity (nothing corresponding to TVA's parameter C). Accordingly, phenomenal consciousness is not bounded by the strong selection that is characteristic of access consciousness, but forms a rich, though vaguely specified, background to the objects at the centre of our minds.

12.4 **Conclusion**

The nature of attention is one of the oldest and most central problems of psychology. In this book we have presented an overview of attention research within the visual modality, where a huge amount of empirical evidence has been accumulated during the past half century. Although much progress has been made, many still view visual attention research as a fragmented field, dominated by theories and experimental traditions each covering only a very limited part of the phenomenon. We have taken a different position: the many sides of visual attention can be integrated within one theoretical perspective, the TVA model.

Unlike many other psychological models, TVA is formulated in mathematical terms, which perhaps makes it easy to overlook the fact that TVA is basically a way of *thinking* about visual attention: what it is, and how it works. TVA provides a coherent set of concepts—processing speed, attentional weighting, perceptual bias, and so on—that can be applied to almost any situation involving visual selection. The model also describes the very process of attentional selection, as an intelligently configured race (a 'biased competition') for encoding information into visual short-term memory (visual 'access consciousness'). The fact that all elements of TVA can be described quantitatively makes it a powerful scientific instrument, but in our view a more fundamental strength of the model lies in its general conceptualization of visual attention.

Humans are biological creatures and every psychological function depends on physical processes in the brain. As we have detailed in this book, visual attention is no exception. On the contrary, our neural interpretation of TVA suggests that there is a strikingly simple and direct correlate to attentional selection in the spiking activity of individual cells in the visual cortex. Millions of these microscopic cells are organized in large anatomical networks that combine to produce selection of visual information on the psychological level. The neural interpretation closes the circle of the TVA framework: a unified theory of visual attention, linking mind and brain.

Appendices

Appendices

Appendix A

Serial position curves

Referring to Box 4.4 on the experiment of Sperling (1967), let element m be the letter in stimulus location m ($m = 1, 2, \ldots, 5$). The conditional probability density that (the correct categorization of) element m finishes processing at time t, provided that the element has not finished processing before time t, is a constant v_m if $0 < t \leq \tau$, but zero if $t \leq 0$ or $t > \tau$. Hence, for $0 < t \leq \tau$, the unconditional probability density of the event that the element finishes processing at time t is given by

$$f_m(t) = v_m \exp(-v_m t),\tag{A1}$$

and the probability that the element finishes processing at or before time t is given by

$$F_m(t) = 1 - \exp(-v_m t).\tag{A2}$$

If short-term storage capacity, K, is five or more, the probability, P_m, that element m is correctly reported via non-guessing (i.e. the probability that the element enters the short-term store) equals $F_m(\tau)$. If K is less than five, P_m is smaller than $F_m(\tau)$. A procedure for calculating P_1 for $K = 4$ (the value estimated for the data of Sperling 1967) is developed below. Of course, from the formula given for P_1, formulas for P_2 through P_5 can be found by permuting the indices.

For $K = 4$, the event that Element 1 enters the short-term store is equivalent to the event that Element 1 finishes processing at a time t such that $0 < t \leq \tau$ and at least one among Elements 2–5 fails to finish processing at or before time t. Thus, the probability that Element 1 enters the short-term store is

$$P_1 = \int_0^\tau f_1(t)[1 - \prod_{m=2}^{5} F_m(t)]dt.\tag{A3}$$

From equations A1–A3, one finds that

$$P_1 = v_1 \left[g(v_2) + g(v_3) + g(v_4) + g(v_5) \right.$$

$$- g(v_2{+}v_3) - g(v_2{+}v_4) - g(v_2{+}v_5) - g(v_3{+}v_4) - g(v_3{+}v_5) - g(v_4{+}v_5)$$

$$+ g(v_2{+}v_3{+}v_4) + g(v_2{+}v_3{+}v_5) + g(v_2{+}v_4{+}v_5) + g(v_3{+}v_4{+}v_5)$$

$$\left. - g(v_2{+}v_3{+}v_4{+}v_5) \right],$$

where function g is given by

$$g(z) = \frac{1 - \exp[-(v_1 + z)\tau]}{v_1 + z}.$$

Appendix B

Attentional cost and benefit

Referring to Box 4.5 on the experiment of Posner *et al.* (1978), suppose the signal is presented in Location L. If so, then by the rate equation and the stated assumptions, the v value of the categorization that the signal element is a signal equals

$$\eta_1 \beta_1 \frac{w_L}{w_L + w_R},$$

which can be written as wC, where $w = w_L/(w_L + w_R)$ and $C = \eta_1 \beta_1$. Thus, provided that the signal is presented in Location L, the expected reaction time is given by

$$\frac{1}{wC} + b.$$

(Since η_0 is assumed to be vanishingly small in relation to η_1, the v value of the categorization that the noise element in Location R is a signal need not be considered.) By similar reasoning, in the case of the signal being presented in Location R, the expected reaction time equals

$$\frac{1}{(1 - w)C} + b.$$

Therefore, given that the signal is presented in Location L with probability p ($0 < p < 1$) and in Location R with probability $1 - p$, the expected reaction time is

$$E(\text{RT}) = \frac{p}{wC} + \frac{1 - p}{(1 - w)C} + b.$$

By analysing $E(\text{RT})$ as a function of w for $0 < w < 1$, one finds an absolute minimum of $E(\text{RT})$ at a value of w such that

$$\frac{w}{1 - w} = \sqrt{\frac{p}{1 - p}}.$$

Thus, for $p = 0.5$, $E(RT)$ has an absolute minimum at $w = 0.5$. The absolute minimum is given by

$$E(RT \mid \text{neutral}) = \frac{1}{0.5\,C} + b. \tag{B1}$$

For $p = 0.8$, $E(RT)$ has an absolute minimum at $w = 0.67$. This minimum equals

$$0.8\, E(RT \mid \text{valid}) + 0.2\, E(RT \mid \text{invalid}),$$

where

$$E(RT \mid \text{valid}) = \frac{1}{0.67\,C} + b \tag{B2}$$

and

$$E(RT \mid \text{invalid}) = \frac{1}{0.33\,C} + b. \tag{B3}$$

By symmetry, equations B2 and B3 also hold for $p = 0.2$.

Appendix C

Detection scores

Referring to Section 5.1 on the study by Estes and Taylor (1964), consider the theoretical detection score for a display of one target and D distractors with an exposure duration of τ ms. One v value must be considered for each element. The v value for the target is a function of time (t), given by

$$v(t) = \begin{cases} 0 & \text{for } t \leq 0 \\[2ex] \dfrac{C}{(1 + \alpha D)} & \text{for } 0 < t \leq \tau \\[2ex] \dfrac{C}{(1 + \alpha D)} \exp\left(-\dfrac{t - \tau}{\mu}\right) & \text{for } \tau < t, \end{cases}$$

and the v value for a distractor equals

$$u(t) = \alpha \, v(t). \tag{C1}$$

Remember that C stands for $\eta_0 \beta_0$. For any token x of letter type i, the strength of the sensory evidence that x belongs to i is assumed: (1) to be zero until time zero; (2) to equal η_0 from time zero until time τ; and (3) to decay exponentially with time constant μ after time τ. For any letter type i, the perceptual decision bias β_i is assumed to equal β_0.

The probability that (the correct categorization of) the target finishes processing at or before time t $(t \geq 0)$ is given by

$$F(t) = 1 - \exp[-\int_0^t v(s)ds, \tag{C2}$$

and the corresponding density function $dF(t)/dt$ is

$$f(t) = v(t)[1 - F(t)].$$

Similarly, the probability that (the correct categorization of) a particular distractor finishes processing at or before time t is given by

$$G(t) = 1 - \exp[-\int_0^t u(s)ds], \tag{C3}$$

and the corresponding density function $dG(t)/dt$ is

$$g(t) = u(t)[1 - G(t)]. \tag{C4}$$

Consider the probability, P, that the target is *not* selected from the display. P is a sum of two probabilities, P_1 and P_2. P_1 is the probability that the target is not selected and the number of selected distractors is less than the storage capacity, K. It is given by

$$P_1 = (1 - s) \sum_{m=0}^{\min(D, K-1)} \binom{D}{m} r^m (1 - r)^{D-m},$$

where

$$s = 1 - \exp\left[-\int_0^\infty v(t)dt\right] = 1 - \exp\left[-\frac{C(\tau + \mu)}{1 + \alpha D}\right]$$

is the probability that, sooner or later, the target finishes processing, and

$$r = 1 - \exp\left[-\int_0^\infty u(t)dt\right] = 1 - \exp\left[-\frac{C(\tau + \mu)\alpha}{1 + \alpha D}\right]$$

is the probability that, sooner or later, a given distractor finishes processing.

P_2 is the probability that the target is not selected and the number of selected distractors equals K. Clearly, if $D < K$, P_2 is zero. Otherwise,

$$P_2 = \binom{D}{1}\binom{D-1}{K-1}\int_0^\infty [1 - F(t)] G(t)^{K-1}[1 - G(t)]^{D-K} g(t)dt. \tag{C5}$$

A closed-form expression for P_2 is obtained as follows. First substitute from equation C1 into equations C3 and C4 and from equation C3 into equation C4. Then substitute from equations C2, C3, and C4 into equation C5. Simplify the resulting integral by the substitution

$$x = \int_0^t v(s)ds,$$

which yields $dx = v(t)dt$ and

$$P_2 = \binom{D}{1}\binom{D-1}{K-1}\int_0^z \exp(-x)[1 - \exp(-\alpha x)]^{K-1}[\exp(-\alpha x)]^{D-K}\alpha\exp(-\alpha x)dx,$$

(C6)

where

$$z = \frac{C(\tau + \mu)}{1 + \alpha D}.$$

By solving the integral in equation C6, one finds that

$$P_2 = \binom{D}{1}\binom{D-1}{K-1}\alpha\sum_{i=0}^{K-1}\binom{K-1}{i}\frac{(-1)^{K-1-i}}{1+\alpha(D-i)}\left[1 - \exp\left(-\frac{C(\tau+\mu)[1+\alpha(D-i)]}{1+\alpha D}\right)\right].$$

Given the probability P (i.e. $P_1 + P_2$) that the target is not selected from the display, the theoretical 'number of elements processed' is found by multiplying $1 - P$ by the number of elements in the display.

Appendix D

Detection scores with redundant targets

Referring to Section 5.4 on the study by Estes and Taylor (1965), consider the probability, P, that no targets are selected from a display of T targets and D distractors with an exposure duration of τ ms. Formulas for the special case in which $T = 1$ were derived in Appendix C. Formulas for the general case in which T may differ from one can be derived by similar reasoning. P is found to be a sum of two probabilities, P_1 and P_2. P_1 is the probability that no targets are selected and the number of selected distractors is less than the storage capacity K. It is given by

$$P_1 = (1-s)^T \sum_{m=0}^{\min(D,K-1)} \binom{D}{m} r^m (1-r)^{D-m},$$

where

$$s = 1 - \exp\left[-\frac{C(\tau + \mu)}{T + \alpha D}\right]$$

and

$$r = 1 - \exp\left[-\frac{C(\tau + \mu)\alpha}{T + \alpha D}\right].$$

P_2 is the probability that no targets are selected and the number of selected distractors equals K. If $D < K$, P_2 is zero. Otherwise,

$$P_2 = \binom{D}{1}\binom{D-1}{K-1}\alpha \sum_{i=0}^{K-1}\binom{K-1}{i}\frac{(-1)^{K-1-i}}{T+\alpha(D-i)}\left[1 - \exp\left(-\frac{C(\tau+\mu)[T+\alpha(D-i)]}{T+\alpha D}\right)\right].$$

The probability that at least one target is selected from the display is $1 - P$. By a standard correction for guessing, the predicted proportion of correct detections, p_c, is given by

$$p_c = (1 - P) + \frac{P}{2} = 1 - \frac{P_1 + P_2}{2}.$$

Appendix E

Partial report with delayed selection cue

Consider the whole and partial report experiments by Sperling (1960) described in Section 5.5. For both whole report and partial report with prestimulus cuing, the expected number of correctly reported letters is a function of number of targets T, storage capacity K, and the product $C(\tau + \mu)$, where C is the processing capacity (given by $\eta_0\beta_0$), τ is the exposure duration, and μ is the time constant for decay of η and v values. The function is given by equations 4.1–4.4. Note that, for whole report, T equals the total number of letters in the stimulus matrix, whereas for partial report, T equals the number of letters in the cued row.

Consider partial report with poststimulus cuing. Let the stimulus be presented for τ ms, beginning at time 0, and let the cue be presented at time t_c, where $t_c \geq \tau$. The v value for a target (a letter in the cued row) is a function of time given by

$$
v(t) = \begin{cases}
0 & \text{for } t \leq 0 \\[2mm]
\dfrac{C}{T + D} & \text{for } 0 < t \leq \tau \\[3mm]
\dfrac{C}{T + D}\exp\left(-\dfrac{t - \tau}{\mu}\right) & \text{for } \tau < t \leq t_c \\[3mm]
\dfrac{C}{T}\exp\left(-\dfrac{t - \tau}{\mu}\right) & \text{for } t_c < t,
\end{cases}
$$

where T equals the number of letters in the cued row, and D is the number of letters outside the cued row. The v value for a distractor (a letter outside the cued row) is given by

$$
u(t) = \begin{cases}
v(t) & \text{for } t \leq t_c \\
0 & \text{for } t_c < t.
\end{cases}
$$

The probability that (the correct categorization of) a particular target finishes processing at or before time t ($t \geq 0$) is given by

$$F(t) = 1 - \exp[-\int_0^t v(s)ds],$$

where

$$\int_0^t v(s)ds$$

$$= \begin{cases} \dfrac{Ct}{T+D} & \text{for } 0 \leq t \leq \tau \\[3mm] \dfrac{C\tau}{T+D} + \dfrac{C\mu}{T+D}\left[1 - \exp\left(-\dfrac{t-\tau}{\mu}\right)\right] & \text{for } \tau < t \leq t_c \\[3mm] \dfrac{C\tau}{T+D} + \dfrac{C\mu}{T+D}\left[1 - \exp\left(-\dfrac{t_c-\tau}{\mu}\right)\right] + \dfrac{C\mu}{T}\left[\exp\left(-\dfrac{t_c-\tau}{\mu}\right) - \exp\left(-\dfrac{t-\tau}{\mu}\right)\right] & \text{for } t_c < t. \end{cases}$$

The corresponding density function is

$$f(t) = v(t)[1 - F(t)].$$

The probability that (the correct categorization of) a particular distractor finishes processing at or before time t is

$$G(t) = \begin{cases} F(t) & \text{for } 0 \leq t \leq t_c \\ F(t_c) & \text{for } t_c < t, \end{cases}$$

and the corresponding density function is

$$g(t) = \begin{cases} f(t) & \text{for } 0 \leq t \leq t_c \\ 0 & \text{for } t_c < t. \end{cases}$$

Consider the probability $P(j)$ that the number of selected targets equals j, where $0 \leq j \leq \min(T, K)$. Let m be the number of selected distractors. $P(j)$ is a sum of three probabilities, $P_1(j)$, $P_2(j)$, and $P_3(j)$. $P_1(j)$ is the probability that the number of selected targets equals j and the total number of selected letters (i.e. $j + m$) is less than K. If $j = K$, $P_1(j)$ is zero; otherwise,

$$P_1(j) = \binom{T}{j} s^j (1-s)^{T-j} \sum_{m=0}^{\min(D,K-j-1)} \binom{D}{m} r^m (1-r)^{D-m},$$

where

$$s = 1 - \exp\left[-\int_0^\infty v(t)dt\right]$$

$$= 1 - \exp\left\{-C\left[\frac{\tau + \mu}{T + D} + \mu\exp\left(-\frac{t_c - \tau}{\mu}\right)\left(\frac{1}{T} - \frac{1}{T + D}\right)\right]\right\}$$

is the probability that, sooner or later, a given target finishes processing, and

$$r = 1 - \exp\left[-\int_0^\infty u(t)dt\right]$$

$$= 1 - \exp\left\{-C\left[\frac{\tau + \mu}{T + D} - \mu\exp\left(-\frac{t_c - \tau}{\mu}\right)\left(\frac{1}{T + D}\right)\right]\right\}$$

is the probability that, sooner or later, a given distractor finishes processing.

$P_2(j)$ is the probability that the number of selected targets equals j and the total number of selected letters equals K and the Kth letter selected is a target. If $j = 0$ or $j < K - D$, $P_2(j)$ is zero; otherwise,

$$P_2(j) = \binom{T}{1}\binom{T-1}{j-1}\binom{D}{m}\int_0^\infty F(t)^{j-1}[1 - F(t)]^{T-j}G(t)^m[1 - G(t)]^{D-m}f(t)dt,$$

where $m = K - j$.

Finally, $P_3(j)$ is the probability that the number of selected targets equals j and the total number of selected letters equals K and the Kth letter selected is a distractor. If $j = K$ or $j < K - D$, $P_3(j)$ is zero; otherwise,

$$P_3(j) = \binom{D}{1}\binom{D-1}{m-1}\binom{T}{j}\int_0^\infty G(t)^{m-1}[1 - G(t)]^{D-m}F(t)^j[1 - F(t)]^{T-j}g(t)dt,$$

where $m = K - j$.

The expected number of letters correctly reported is

$$E(\text{score}) = \sum_{j=0}^{\min(T,K)} j[P_1(j) + P_2(j) + P_3(j)].$$

The theoretical 'number of letters available' is found by multiplying the $E(\text{score})$ by $(T + D)/T$.

References

Allport, D. A. (1968). The rate of assimilation of visual information. *Psychonomic Science*, **12**, 231–232.

Allport, D. A. (1989). Visual attention. In: M. I. Posner (ed.), *Foundations of cognitive science*, pp. 631–682. Cambridge, MA: MIT Press.

Allport, D. A. (1993). Attention and control: have we been asking the wrong questions? A critical review of twenty-five years. In: D. E. Meyer and S. Kornblum (eds), *Attention and performance XIV: synergies in experimental psychology, artificial intelligence, and cognitive neuroscience*, pp. 183–218. Cambridge, MA: MIT Press.

Alvarez, G. A. and Cavanagh, P. (2004). The capacity of visual short-term memory is set both by visual information load and by number of objects. *Psychological Science*, **15**, 106–111.

Anderson, J. R. (1996). *The architecture of cognition*. Hillsdale, NJ: Lawrence Erlbaum Associates.

Armstrong, K. M., Fitzgerald, J. K., and Moore, T. (2006). Changes in visual receptive fields with microstimulation of frontal cortex. *Neuron*, **50**, 791–798.

Ashbridge, E., Walsh, V., and Cowey, A. (1997). Temporal aspects of visual search studied by transcranial magnetic stimulation. *Neuropsychologia*, **35**, 1121–1131.

Ashby, F. G. and Perrin, N. A. (1988). Toward a unified theory of similarity and recognition. *Psychological Review*, **95**, 124–150.

Ashby, F. G., Prinzmetal, W., Ivry, R., and Maddox, W. T. (1996). A formal theory of feature binding in object perception. *Psychological Review*, **103**, 165–192.

Atkinson, R. C., Holmgren, J. E., and Juola, J. F. (1969). Processing time as influenced by the number of elements in a visual display. *Perception & Psychophysics*, **6**, 321–326.

Awh, E. and Pashler, H. (2000). Evidence for split attentional foci. *Journal of Experimental Psychology: Human Perception and Performance*, **26**, 834–846.

Bacon, W. F. and Egeth, H. E. (1994). Overriding stimulus-driven attentional capture. *Perception & Psychophysics*, **55**, 485–496.

Banks, W. P. and Prinzmetal, W. (1976). Configurational effects in visual information processing. *Perception & Psychophysics*, **19**, 361–367.

Bartolomeo, P. (2007). Visual neglect. *Current Opinion in Neurology*, **20**, 381–386.

Bashinsky, H. S. and Bacharach, V. R. (1980). Enhancement of perceptual sensitivity as the result of selectively attending to spatial locations. *Perception & Psychophysics*, **28**, 241–248.

Battersby, W. S., Bender, M. B., and Pollack, M. (1956). Unilateral spatial agnosia (inattention) in patients with cerebral lesions. *Brain*, **79**, 68–93.

Baylis, G. C. and Driver, J. (1992). Visual parsing and response competition: the effect of grouping factors. *Perception & Psychophysics*, **51**, 145–162.

Bear, M. F., Connors, B. W., and Paradiso, M. A. (2006). *Neuroscience: exploring the brain*, (3 edn). Baltimore: Lippincott Williams & Wilkins.

Beck, D. M., Muggleton, N., Walsh, V., and Lavie, N. (2006). Right parietal cortex plays a critical role in change blindness. *Cerebral Cortex*, **16**, 712–717.

Berti, A. (2002). Unconscious processing in neglect. In: H.-O. Karnath, D. Milner, and G. Vallar (eds), *The cognitive and neural bases of spatial neglect*, pp. 313–326. Oxford, UK: Oxford University Press.

Bichot, N. P., Cave, K. R., and Pashler, H. (1999). Visual selection mediated by location: feature-based selection of non-contiguous locations. *Perception & Psychophysics*, **61**, 403–423.

Biederman, I. and Gerhardstein, P. C. (1995). Viewpoint-dependent mechanisms in visual object recognition: reply to Tarr and Bülthoff (1995). *Journal of Experimental Psychology: Human Perception and Performance*, **21**, 1506–1514.

Bjoertomt, O., Cowey, A., and Walsh, V. (2002). Spatial neglect in near and far space investigated by repetitive transcranial magnetic stimulation. *Brain*, **125**, 2012–2022.

Block, N. (1996). How can we find the neural correlate of consciousness? *Trends in Neurosciences*, **19**, 456–459.

Block, N. (2005). Two neural correlates of consciousness. *Trends in Cognitive Sciences*, **9**, 46–52.

Bouma, H. (1978). Visual search and reading: eye movements and functional visual field: a tutorial review. In: J. Requin (ed.), *Attention and performance VII*, pp. 115–147. Hillsdale, NJ: Lawrence Erlbaum Associates.

Bowman, H. and Wyble, B. (2007). The simultaneous type, serial token model of temporal attention and working memory. *Psychological Review*, **114**, 38–70.

Bradley, R. and Terry, M. (1952). The rank analysis of incomplete block designs. I. The method of paired comparisons. *Biometrika*, **39**, 324–345.

Brain, W. R. (1941). Visual disorientation with special reference to lesions of the right cerebral hemisphere. *Brain*, **64**, 224–272.

Brefczynski, J. A. and DeYoe, E. A. (1999). A physiological correlate of the 'spotlight' of visual attention. *Nature Neuroscience*, **2**, 370–374.

Brehaut, J. C., Enns, J. T., and Di Lollo, V. (1999). Visual masking plays two roles in the attentional blink. *Perception & Psychophysics*, **61**, 1436–1448.

Bricolo, E., Gianesini, T., Fanini, A., Bundesen, C., and Chelazzi, L. (2002). Serial attention mechanisms in visual search: a direct behavioral demonstration. *Journal of Cognitive Neuroscience*, **14**, 980–993.

Broadbent, D. E. (1958). *Perception and communication*. London: Pergamon Press.

Broadbent, D. E. (1971). *Decision and stress*. London: Academic Press.

Broadbent, D. E. (1982). Task combination and selective intake of information. *Acta Psychologica*, **50**, 253–290.

Broadbent, D. E. and Broadbent, M. H. P. (1987). From detection to identification: response to multiple targets in rapid serial visual presentation. *Perception & Psychophysics*, **42**, 105–113.

Broca, P. (1861). Perte de la parole, ramollissement chronique et destruction partielle du lobe antérieur gauche du cerveau. *Bulletin de la Société d'Anthropologie*, **2**, 235–237.

Bruner, J. S., Postman, L., and Mosteller, F. (1950). A note on the measurement of reversals of perspective. *Psychometrika*, **15**, 63–72.

Bublak, P., Finke, K., Krummenacher, J., Preger, R., Kyllingsbæk, S., Müller, H. J., and Schneider, W. X. (2005). Usability of a theory of visual attention (TVA) for parameter-based measurement of attention II: evidence from two patients with frontal or parietal damage. *Journal of the International Neuropsychological Society*, **11**, 843–854.

Bublak, P., Redel, P., and Finke, K. (2006). Spatial and non-spatial attention deficits in neurodegenerative diseases: assessment based on Bundesen's theory of visual attention (TVA). *Restorative Neurology and Neuroscience*, **24**, 287–301.

Bundesen, C. (1982). Item recognition with automatized performance. *Scandinavian Journal of Psychology*, **23**, 173–192.

Bundesen, C. (1987). Visual attention: race models for selection from multielement displays. *Psychological Research*, **49**, 113–121.

Bundesen, C. (1990). A theory of visual attention. *Psychological Review*, **97**, 523–547.

Bundesen, C. (1993). The relationship between independent race models and Luce's choice axiom. *Journal of Mathematical Psychology*, **37**, 446–471.

Bundesen, C. (1996). Formal models of visual attention: a tutorial review. In: A. F. Kramer, M. G. H. Coles, and G. D. Logan (eds), *Converging operations in the study of visual selective attention*, pp. 1–43. Washington, DC: American Psychological Association.

Bundesen, C. (1998*a*). A computational theory of visual attention. *Philosophical Transactions of the Royal Society of London, Series B*, **353**, 1271–1281.

Bundesen, C. (1998*b*). Visual selective attention: outlines of a choice model, a race model, and a computational theory. *Visual Cognition*, **5**, 287–309.

Bundesen, C. and Larsen, A. (1975). Visual transformation of size. *Journal of Experimental Psychology: Human Perception and Performance*, **1**, 214–220.

Bundesen, C. and Pedersen, L. F. (1983). Color segregation and visual search. *Perception & Psychophysics*, **33**, 487–493.

Bundesen, C., Larsen, A., and Farrell, J. E. (1981). Mental transformations of size and orientation. In: J. Long and A. Baddeley (eds), *Attention and performance IX*, pp. 279–294. Hillsdale, NJ: Lawrence Erlbaum Associates.

Bundesen, C., Pedersen, L. F., and Larsen, A. (1984). Measuring efficiency of selection from briefly exposed visual displays: a model for partial report. *Journal of Experimental Psychology: Human Perception and Performance*, **10**, 329–339.

Bundesen, C., Shibuya, H., and Larsen, A. (1985). Visual selection from multielement displays: a model for partial report. In: M. I. Posner and O. S. M. Marin (eds), *Attention and performance XI*, pp. 631–649. Hillsdale, NJ: Lawrence Erlbaum Associates.

Bundesen, C., Larsen, A., Kyllingsbæk, S., Paulson, O. B., and Law, I. (2002). Attentional effects in the visual pathways: a whole-brain PET study. *Experimental Brain Research*, **147**, 394–406.

Bundesen, C., Kyllingsbæk, S., and Larsen, A. (2003). Independent encoding of colors and shapes from two stimuli. *Psychonomic Bulletin & Review*, **10**, 474–479.

Bundesen, C., Habekost, T., and Kyllingsbæk, S. (2005). A neural theory of visual attention: bridging cognition and neurophysiology. *Psychological Review*, **112**, 291–328.

Bushnell, M. C., Goldberg, M. E., and Robinson, D. L. (1981). Behavioral enhancement of visual responses in monkey cerebral cortex: I. Modulation in posterior parietal cortex related to selective visual attention. *Journal of Neurophysiology*, **46**, 755–772.

Butter, C. M., Evans, J., Kirsch, N., and Kewman, D. (1989). Altitudinal neglect following traumatic brain injury: a case report. *Cortex*, **25**, 135–146.

Carrasco, M., Ling, S., and Read, S. (2004). Attention alters appearance. *Nature Neuroscience*, **7**, 308–313.

Cattell, J. M. (1885). Über die Zeit der Erkennung und Benennung von Schriftzeichen, Bildern und Farben. *Philosophische Studien*, **2**, 635–650.

Cave, K. R. and Bichot, N. P. (1999). Visuospatial attention: beyond a spotlight model. *Psychonomic Bulletin & Review*, **6**, 204–223.

Cave, K. R. and Kosslyn, S. M. (1989). Varieties of size-specific visual selection. *Journal of Experimental Psychology: General*, **118**, 148–164.

Cave, K. R. and Wolfe, J. M. (1990). Modeling the role of parallel processing in visual search. *Cognitive Psychology*, **22**, 225–271.

Chawla, D., Rees, G., and Friston, K. J. (1999). The physiological basis of attentional modulation in extrastriate visual areas. *Nature Neuroscience*, **2**, 671–676.

Chelazzi, L., Miller, E. K., Duncan, J., and Desimone, R. (1993). A neural basis for visual search in inferior temporal cortex. *Nature*, **363**, 345–347.

Chelazzi, L., Duncan, J., Miller, E. K., and Desimone, R. (1998). Responses of neurons in inferior temporal cortex during memory-guided visual search. *Journal of Neurophysiology*, **80**, 2918–2940.

Chelazzi, L., Miller, E. K., Duncan, J., and Desimone, R. (2001). Responses of neurons in macaque area V4 during memory-guided visual search. *Cerebral Cortex*, **11**, 761–772.

Chernick, M. R. (1999). *Bootstrap methods. A practitioner's guide*. New York: John Wiley & Sons.

Cherry, E. C. (1953). Some experiments on the recognition of speech, with one and with two ears. *Journal of the Acoustical Society of America*, **25**, 975–979.

Christensen, A.-L. (1975). *Luria's neuropsychological investigation*. New York: Spectrum Publications.

Chun, M. M. and Potter, M. C. (1995). A two-stage model for multiple target detection in rapid serial visual presentation. *Journal of Experimental Psychology: Human Perception and Performance*, **21**, 109–127.

Cocchini, G., Cubelli, R., Della Sala, S., and Beschin, N. (1999). Neglect without extinction. *Cortex*, **35**, 285–313.

Cohen, A. and Ivry, R. (1989). Illusory conjunctions inside and outside the focus of attention. *Journal of Experimental Psychology: Human Perception and Performance*, **15**, 650–663.

Cohen, A. and Ivry, R. (1991). Density effects in conjunction search: evidence for a coarse location mechanism of feature integration. *Journal of Experimental Psychology: Human Perception and Performance*, **17**, 891–901.

Colby, C. L. and Goldberg, M. E. (1999). Space and attention in parietal cortex. *Annual Review of Neuroscience*, **22**, 319–349.

Colegate, R. L., Hoffman, J. E., and Eriksen, C. W. (1973). Selective encoding from multielement visual displays. *Perception & Psychophysics*, **14**, 217–224.

Coltheart, M. (1980). Iconic memory and visible persistence. *Perception & Psychophysics*, **27**, 183–228.

Coltheart, M. (2003). Cognitive neuropsychology. In: H. Pashler and J. Wixted (eds), *Stevens' handbook of experimental psychology: vol. 4. Methodology in experimental psychology*, (3rd edn), pp. 139–174. New York: John Wiley & Sons.

Connor, C. E., Gallant, J. L., Preddie, D. C., and van Essen, D. C. (1996). Responses in area V4 depend on the spatial relationship between stimulus and attention. *Journal of Neurophysiology*, **75**, 1306–1308.

Connor, C. E., Preddie, D. C., Gallant, J. L., and van Essen, D. C. (1997). Spatial attention effects in macaque area V4. *Journal of Neuroscience*, **17**, 3201–3214.

Corbetta, M. and Shulman, G. L. (2002). Control of goal-directed and stimulus-driven attention in the brain. *Nature Reviews Neuroscience*, **3**, 201–215.

Corbetta, M., Miezin, F. M., Dobmeyer, S., Shulman, G. L., and Petersen, S. E. (1990). Attentional modulation of neural processing of shape, color, and velocity in humans. *Science*, **248**, 1556–1559.

Corbetta, M., Miezin, F. M., Shulman, G. L., and Petersen, S. E. (1993). A PET study of visuospatial attention. *Journal of Neuroscience*, **13**, 1202–1226.

Corbetta, M., Kincade, J. M., Ollinger, J. M., McAvoy, M. P., and Shulman, G. L. (2000). Voluntary orienting is dissociated from target detection in human posterior parietal cortex. *Nature Neuroscience*, **3**, 292–297.

Corbetta, M., Kincade, J. M., and Shulman, G. L. (2002). Neural systems for visual orienting and their relationships to spatial working memory. *Journal of Cognitive Neuroscience*, **14**, 508–523.

Corchs, S. and Deco, G. (2002). Large-scale neural model for visual attention: integration of experimental single-cell and fMRI data. *Cerebral Cortex*, **12**, 339–348.

Coslett, H. B. and Saffran, E. (1991). Simultanagnosia: to see but not two see. *Brain*, **114**, 1523–1545.

Coull, J. T. and Nobre, A. C. (1998). Where and when to pay attention: the neural systems for directing attention to spatial locations and to time intervals as revealed by both PET and fMRI. *Journal of Neuroscience*, **18**, 7426–7435.

Coull, J. T., Frith, C. D., Frackowiak, R. S., and Grasby, P. M. (1996). A fronto-parietal network for rapid visual information processing: a PET study of sustained attention and working memory. *Neuropsychologia*, **34**, 1085–1095.

Courtney, S. M., Petit, L., Maisog, J. M., Ungerleider, L. G., and Haxby, J. V. (1998). An area specialized for spatial working memory in human frontal cortex. *Science*, **279**, 1347–1351.

Cowey, A., Small, M., and Ellis, S. (1994). Left visuo-spatial neglect can be worse in far than near space. *Neuropsychologia*, **9**, 1059–1066.

Critchley, M. (1949). The phenomenon of tactile inattention with special reference to parietal lesions. *Brain*, **72**, 538–561.

Czerwinski, M., Lightfoot, N., and Shiffrin, R. M. (1992). Automatization and training in visual search. *American Journal of Psychology*, **105**, 271–315.

Dalrymple-Alford, E. C. and Budayr, B. (1966). Examination of some aspects of the Stroop color-word test. *Perceptual and Motor Skills*, **23**, 1211–1214.

Damasio, A. R., Damasio, H., and Chui, H. C. (1980). Neglect following damage to the frontal lobe or basal ganglia. *Neuropsychologia*, **18**, 123–132.

Deco, G. and Zihl, J. (2001). Top-down selective visual attention: a neurodynamical approach. *Visual Cognition*, **8**, 119–141.

Desimone, R. (1999). Visual attention mediated by biased competition in extrastriate visual cortex. In: G. W. Humphreys, J. Duncan, and A. M. Treisman (eds), *Attention, space, and action*, pp. 13–30. Oxford, UK: Oxford University Press.

Desimone, R. and Duncan, J. (1995). Neural mechanisms of selective visual attention. *Annual Review of Neuroscience*, **18**, 193–222.

Deubel, H. and Schneider, W. X. (1996). Saccade target selection and object recognition: evidence for a common attentional mechanism. *Vision Research*, **36**, 1827–1837.

Deutsch, J. A. and Deutsch, D. (1963). Attention: some theoretical considerations. *Psychological Review*, **70**, 80–90.

Donders, F. C. (1869). On the speed of mental processes. *Acta Psychologica*, **30**, 412–431.

Donk, M. (1999). Illusory conjunctions are an illusion: the effects of target–nontarget similarity on conjunction and feature errors. *Journal of Experimental Psychology: Human Perception and Performance*, **25**, 1207–1233.

Downing, C. J. (1988). Expectancy and visual-spatial attention: effects on perceptual quality. *Journal of Experimental Psychology: Human Perception and Performance*, **14**, 188–202.

Driver, J. and Tipper, S. P. (1989). On the nonselectivity of 'selective' seeing: contrasts between interference and priming in selective attention. *Journal of Experimental Psychology: Human Perception and Performance*, **15**, 304–314.

Duncan, J. (1980). The locus of interference in the perception of simultaneous stimuli. *Psychological Review*, **87**, 272–300.

Duncan, J. (1981). Directing attention in the visual field. *Perception & Psychophysics*, **30**, 90–93.

Duncan, J. (1983). Perceptual selection based on alphanumeric class: evidence from partial reports. *Perception & Psychophysics*, **33**, 533–547.

Duncan, J. (1984). Selective attention and the organization of visual information. *Journal of Experimental Psychology: General*, **113**, 501–517.

Duncan, J. (1985). Visual search and visual attention. In: M. I. Posner and O. S. M. Marin (eds), *Attention and performance XI*, pp. 85–105. Hillsdale, NJ: Lawrence Erlbaum Associates.

Duncan, J. (1996). Cooperating brain systems in selective perception and action. In: T. Inui and J. L. McClelland (eds), *Attention and performance XVI: information integration in perception and communication*, pp. 549–578. Cambridge, MA: MIT Press.

Duncan, J. (2001). An adaptive coding model of neural function in prefrontal cortex. *Nature Reviews Neuroscience*, **2**, 820–829.

Duncan, J. (2006). Brain mechanisms of attention. *Quarterly Journal of Experimental Psychology*, **59**, 2–27.

Duncan, J. and Humphreys, G. W. (1989). Visual search and stimulus similarity. *Psychological Review*, **96**, 433–458.

Duncan, J. and Owen, A. M. (2000). Common regions of the human frontal lobe recruited by diverse cognitive demands. *Trends in Neurosciences*, **23**, 475–483.

Duncan, J., Ward, R., and Shapiro, K. (1994). Direct measurement of attentional dwell time in human vision. *Nature*, **369**, 313–315.

Duncan, J., Bundesen, C., Olson, A., Humphreys, G., Chavda, S., and Shibuya, H. (1999). Systematic analysis of deficits in visual attention. *Journal of Experimental Psychology: General*, **128**, 450–478.

Duncan, J., Bundesen, C., Olson, A., Humphreys, G., Ward, R., Kyllingsbæk, S., *et al.* (2003). Dorsal and ventral simultanagnosia. *Cognitive Neuropsychology*, **20**, 675–701.

Efron, B. (1979). Bootstrap methods: another look at the jackknife. *Annals of Statistics*, **7**, 1–26.

Efron, B. and Tibshirani, R. (1993). *An introduction to the bootstrap*. New York: Chapman & Hall.

Egly, R. and Homa, D. (1984). Sensitization of the visual field. *Journal of Experimental Psychology: Human Perception and Performance*, **10**, 778–793.

Ellison, A., Battelli, L., Cowey, A., and Walsh, V. (2003). The effect of expectation on facilitation of colour/form conjunction tasks by TMS over area V5. *Neuropsychologia*, **41**, 1794–1801.

Eriksen, B. A. and Eriksen, C. W. (1974). Effects of noise letters upon the identification of a target letter in a non-search task. *Perception & Psychophysics*, **16**, 143–149.

Eriksen, C. W. (1966). Independence of successive inputs and uncorrelated error in visual form perception. *Journal of Experimental Psychology*, **72**, 26–35.

Eriksen, C. W. and Eriksen, B. A. (1979). Target redundancy in visual search: do repetitions of the target within the display impair processing? *Perception & Psychophysics*, **26**, 195–205.

Eriksen, C. W. and Hoffman, J. E. (1973). The extent of processing of noise elements during selective encoding from visual displays. *Perception & Psychophysics*, **14**, 155–160.

Eriksen, C. W. and Hoffman, J. E. (1974). Selective attention: noise suppression or signal enhancement? *Bulletin of the Psychonomic Society*, **4**, 587–589.

Eriksen, C. W. and Lappin, J. S. (1965). Internal perceptual system noise and redundancy in simultaneous inputs in form identification. *Psychonomic Science*, **2**, 351–352.

Eriksen, C. W. and Lappin, J. S. (1967). Independence in the perception of simultaneously presented forms at brief durations. *Journal of Experimental Psychology*, **73**, 468–472.

Eriksen, C. W. and Schultz, D. W. (1978). Temporal factors in visual information processing: a tutorial review. In: J. Requin (ed.), *Attention and performance VII*, pp. 3–23. Hillsdale, NJ: Lawrence Erlbaum Associates.

Eriksen, C. W. and Spencer, T. (1969). Rate of information processing in visual perception: some results and methodological considerations. *Journal of Experimental Psychology Monograph*, **79** (2, Pt 2).

Eriksen, C. W. and St. James, J. D. (1986). Visual attention within and around the field of focal attention: a zoom lens model. *Perception & Psychophysics*, **40**, 225–240.

Eriksen, C. W. and Webb, J. M. (1989). Shifting of attentional focus within and about a visual display. *Perception & Psychophysics*, **45**, 175–183.

Eriksen, C. W. and Yeh, Y. (1985). Allocation of attention in the visual field. *Journal of Experimental Psychology: Human Perception and Performance*, **11**, 583–597.

Estes, W. K. and Taylor, H. A. (1964). A detection method and probabilistic models for assessing information processing from brief visual displays. *Proceedings of the National Academy of Sciences USA*, **52** (2), 446–454.

Estes, W. K. and Taylor, H. A. (1965). Visual detection in relation to display size and redundancy of critical elements. *Perception & Psychophysics*, **1**, 9–16.

Everling, S., Tinsley, C. J., Gaffan, D., and Duncan, J. (2006). Selective representation of task-relevant objects and locations in the monkey prefrontal cortex. *European Journal of Neuroscience*, **23**, 2197–2214.

Fan, J., McCandliss, B. D., Sommer, T., Raz, A., and Posner, M. I. (2002). Testing the efficiency and independence of attentional networks. *Journal of Cognitive Neuroscience*, **14**, 340–347.

Farmer, E. W. and Taylor, R. M. (1980). Visual search through color displays: effects of target-background similarity and background uniformity. *Perception & Psychophysics*, **27**, 267–272.

Feldman, J. (2003). What is a visual object? *Trends in Cognitive Sciences*, **7**, 252–256.

Felleman, D. J. and van Essen, D. C. (1991). Distributed hierarchical processing in the primate cerebral cortex. *Cerebral Cortex*, **1**, 1–47.

Feller, W. (1968). *An introduction to probability theory and its applications*, (3rd edn), vol. 1. New York: John Wiley & Sons.

Fierro, B., Brighina, F., Oliveri, M., Piazza, A., La Bua, V., Buffa, D., and Bisiach, E. (2000). Contralateral neglect induced by right posterior parietal rTMS in healthy subjects. *Neuroreport*, 11, 1519–1521.

Fink, G. R., Dolan, R. J., Halligan, P. W., Marshall, J. C., and Frith, C. D. (1997). Space-based and object-based visual attention: shared and specific neural domains. *Brain*, 120, 2013–2028.

Finke, K., Bublak, P., Krummenacher, J., Kyllingsbæk, S., Müller, H. J., and Schneider, W. X. (2005). Usability of a theory of visual attention (TVA) for parameter-based measurement of attention I: evidence from normal subjects. *Journal of the International Neuropsychological Society*, 11, 832–842.

Finke, K., Bublak, P., Dose, M., Müller, H. J., and Schneider, W. X. (2006). Parameter-based assessment of spatial and non-spatial attentional deficits in Huntington's disease. *Brain*, 129, 1137–1151.

Finke, K., Schneider, W. X., Redel, P., Dose, M., Kerkhoff, G., Müller, H. J., and Bublak, P. (2007). The capacity of attention and simultaneous perception of objects: a group study of Huntington's disease patients. *Neuropsychologia*, 45, 3272–3284.

Fisher, D. L. (1982). Limited-channel models of automatic detection: capacity and scanning in visual search. *Psychological Review*, 89, 662–692.

Folk, C. L., Remington, R. W., and Johnston, J. C. (1992). Involuntary covert orienting is contingent on attentional control settings. *Journal of Experimental Psychology: Human Perception and Performance*, 18, 1030–1044.

Folk, C. L., Remington, R. W., and Johnston, J. C. (1993). Contingent attentional capture: a reply to Yantis (1993). *Journal of Experimental Psychology: Human Perception and Performance*, 19, 682–685.

Folk, C. L., Remington, R. W., and Wright, J. H. (1994). The structure of attentional control: contingent attentional capture by apparent motion, abrupt onset, and color. *Journal of Experimental Psychology: Human Perception and Performance*, 20, 317–329.

Fox, E. (1995a). Negative priming from ignored distractors in visual selection: a review. *Psychonomic Bulletin and Review*, 2, 145–173.

Fox, E. (1995b). Pre-cuing target location reduces interference but not negative priming from visual distractors. *Quarterly Journal of Experimental Psychology*, 48A, 26–40.

Fox, M. D., Snyder, A. Z., Vincent, J. L., Corbetta, M., Van Essen, D. C., and Raichle, M. E. (2005). The human brain is intrinsically organized into dynamic, anticorrelated functional networks. *Proceedings of the National Academy of Sciences USA*, 102, 9673–9678.

Fox, M. D., Corbetta, M., Snyder, A. Z., Vincent, J. L., and Raichle, M. E. (2006). Spontaneous neuronal activity distinguishes human dorsal and ventral attention systems. *Proceedings of the National Academy of Sciences USA*, 103, 10046–10051.

Freedman, D. J., Riesenhuber, M., Poggio, T., and Miller, E. K. (2001). Categorical representation of visual stimuli in the primate prefrontal cortex. *Science*, 291, 312–316.

Friedmann-Hill, S. R., Robertson, L. C., Desimone, R., and Ungerleider, L. G. (2003). Posterior parietal cortex and the filtering of distractors. *Proceedings of the National Academy of Sciences USA*, 100, 4263–4268.

Fries, P. and Desimone, R. (2005). Selective visual attention modulates oscillatory neuronal synchronization. In: L. Itti, G. Rees, and J. K. Tsotsos (eds), *Neurobiology of attention*, pp. 520–525. London: Elsevier Academic Press.

Fries, P., Reynolds, J. H., Rorie, A. E., and Desimone, R. (2001). Modulation of oscillatory neuronal synchronization by selective visual attention. *Science*, **291**, 1560–1563.

Fuggetta, G., Pavone, E. F., Walsh, V., Kiss, M., and Eimer, M. (2006). Cortico-cortical interactions in spatial attention: a combined ERP/TMS study. *Journal of Neurophysiology*, **95**, 3277–3280.

Fuster, J. M. (1990). Inferotemporal units in selective visual attention and short-term memory. *Journal of Neurophysiology*, **64**, 681–697.

Fuster, J. M. (1997). *The prefrontal cortex: anatomy, physiology, and neuropsychology of the frontal lobe*. New York and Philadelphia: Lippincott-Raven.

Fuster, J. M. (2003). *Cortex and mind*. Oxford, UK: Oxford University Press.

Gall, F. J. and Spurzheim, J. C. (1808). Recherches sur la systéme nerveux en général, et sur celu du cerveau en particulier. *Academie de Sciences, Paris, Memoirs.*

Gallant, J. L., Schoup, R. E., and Mazer, J. A. (2000). A human extrastriate area functionally homologous to macaque V4. *Neuron*, **27**, 227–235.

Geeraerts, S., Lafosse, C., Vandenbussche, E., and Verfaillie, K. (2005). A psychophysical study of visual extinction: ipsilesional distractor interference with contralesional orientation thresholds in visual hemineglect patients. *Neuropsychologia*, **43**, 530–541.

Gehring, W. J. and Knight, R. T. (2002). Lateral prefrontal damage affects processing selection but not attention switching. *Cognitive Brain Research*, **13**, 267–279.

George, M. S., Lisanby, S. H., and Sackeim, H. A. (1999). Transcranial magnetic stimulation: applications in neuropsychiatry. *Archives of General Psychiatry*, **56**, 300–311.

Gerlach, C., Marstrand, L., Habekost, T., and Gade, A. (2005). A case of impaired shape integration. *Visual Cognition*, **12**, 1409–1443.

Gibson, B. S. and Egeth, H. (1994). Inhibition of return to object-based and environment-based locations. *Perception & Psychophysics*, **55**, 323–339.

Gibson, J. J. (1950). *The perception of the visual world*. Boston: Houghton Mifflin.

Giesbrecht, B., Woldorff, M. G., Song, A. W., and Mangun, G. R. (2003). Neural mechanisms of top-down control during spatial and feature attention. *Neuroimage*, **19**, 496–512.

Gitelman, D. R., Nobre, A. C., Parrish, T. B., LaBar, K. S., Kim, Y. H., Meyer, J. R., and Mesulam. M.-M. (1999). A large-scale distributed network for spatial attention: further anatomical delineation based on stringent behavioural and cognitive controls. *Brain*, **122**, 1093–1106.

Gold, J. I. and Shadlen, M. N. (2001). Neural computations that underlie decisions about sensory stimuli. *Trends in Cognitive Sciences*, **5**, 10–16.

Goldman-Rakic, P. S. (1995). Cellular basis of working memory. Neuron, **14**, 477–485.

Gottlieb, J. (2007). From thought to action: the parietal cortex as a bridge between perception, action, and cognition. *Neuron*, **53**, 9–16.

Graf, M. (2006). Coordinate transformations in object recognition. *Psychological Bulletin*, **132**, 920–945.

Green, D. M. and Swets, J. A. (1966). *Signal detection theory and psychophysics*. New York: John Wiley & Sons.

Grindley, G. C. and Townsend, V. (1968). Voluntary attention in peripheral vision and its effects on acuity and differential thresholds. *Quarterly Journal of Experimental Psychology*, **20**, 11–19.

Grossberg, S. (1976). Adaptive pattern classification and universal recoding: I. Parallel development and coding of neural feature detectors. *Biological Cybernetics*, **23**, 121–134.

Grossberg, S. (1980). How does a brain build a cognitive code? *Psychological Review*, **87**, 1–51.

Guillery, R. W., Feig, S. L., and Lozsádi, D. A. (1998). Paying attention to the thalamic reticulate nucleus. *Trends in Neurosciences*, **21**, 28–32.

Habekost, T. and Bundesen, C. (2003). Patient assessment based on a theory of visual attention (TVA): subtle deficits after a right frontal-subcortical lesion. *Neuropsychologia*, **41**, 1171–1188.

Habekost, T. and Rostrup, E. (2006). Persisting asymmetries of vision after right side lesions. *Neuropsychologia*, **44**, 876–895.

Habekost, T. and Rostrup, E. (2007). Visual attention capacity after right hemisphere lesions. *Neuropsychologia*, **45**, 1474–1488.

Habekost, T. and Starrfelt, R. (2006). Alexia and quadrant-amblyopia. Reading disability after a minor visual field deficit. *Neuropsychologia*, **44**, 2465–2476.

Haenny, P. E. and Schiller, P. H. (1988). State dependent activity in monkey visual cortex: II. Retinal and extraretinal factors in V4. *Experimental Brain Research*, **69**, 225–244.

Halligan, P. W. and Marshall, J. C. (1988). Blindsight and insight in visuo-spatial neglect. *Nature*, **336**, 766–767.

Halligan, P. W. and Marshall, J. C. (1991). Left neglect for near but not far space in man. *Nature*, **350**, 498–500.

Halligan, P. W. and Marshall, J. C. (2002). Primary sensory deficits after right brain damage— an attentional disorder by any other name? In: H.-O. Karnath, D. Milner, and G. Vallar (eds), *The cognitive and neural bases of spatial neglect*, pp. 327–340. Oxford, UK: Oxford University Press.

Hampshire, A., Duncan, J., and Owen, A. M. (2007). Selective tuning of the blood oxygenation level-dependent response during simple target detection dissociates human frontoparietal subregions. *Journal of Neuroscience*, **27**, 6219–6223.

Harms, L. and Bundesen, C. (1983). Color segregation and selective attention in a nonsearch task. *Perception & Psychophysics*, **33**, 11–19.

Haxby, J. V., Petit, L., Ungerleider, L. G., and Courtney, S. M. (2000). Distinguishing the functional roles of multiple regions in distributed neural systems for visual working memory. *Neuroimage*, **11**, 145–156.

Hayward, W. G. and Tarr, M. J. (2005). Visual perception II: high-level vision. In: K. Lamberts and R. L. Goldstone (eds), *The handbook of cognition*, pp. 48–70. London, UK: Sage.

Hebb, D. O. (1949). *Organization of behavior*. New York: John Wiley & Sons.

Heilman, M. (1979). Neglect and related disorders. In: K. M. Heilman and E. Valenstein (eds), *Clinical Neuropsychology*, pp. 268–307. Oxford, UK: Oxford University Press.

Heilman, M. and Valenstein, E. (1972). Frontal lobe neglect in man. *Neurology*, 22, 660–664.

Heilman, K. M., Watson, R. T., and Valenstein, E. (2003). Neglect and related disorders. In: K. M. Heilman and E. Valenstein (eds), *Clinical neuropsychology*, (4th edn), pp. 296–346. Oxford, UK: Oxford University Press.

Heinke, D. and Humphreys, G. W. (2003). Attention, spatial representation, and visual neglect: simulating emergent attention and spatial memory in the selective attention for identification model (SAIM). *Psychological Review*, **110**, 29–87.

Heinze, H. J., Mangun, G. R., Burchert, W., Hinrichs, H., Scholz, M., Münte, T. F., *et al.* (1994). Combined spatial and temporal imaging of brain activity during visual selective attention in humans. *Nature*, **372**, 543–546.

Hilgetag, C. C., Théoret, H., and Pascual-Leone, A. (2001). Enhanced visual spatial attention ipsilateral to rTMS-induced 'virtual lesions' of human parietal cortex. *Nature Neuroscience*, **4**, 953–957.

Hillis, A. E., Newhart, M., Heidler, J., Barker, P. B., Herskovits, E. H., and Degaonkar, M. (2005). Anatomy of spatial attention: insights from perfusion imaging and hemispatial neglect in acute stroke. *Journal of Neuroscience*, **25**, 3161–3167.

Hillstrom, A. P. and Yantis, S. (1994). Visual motion and attentional capture. *Perception & Psychophysics*, **55**, 399–411.

Hillyard, S. A. and Anllo-Vento, L. (1998). Event-related brain potentials in the study of visual selective attention. *Proceedings of the National Academy of Sciences USA*, **95**, 781–787.

Hillyard, S. A. and Muente, T. F. (1984). Selective attention to color and locational cues: an analysis with event-related brain potentials. *Perception & Psychophysics*, **36**, 185–198.

Hillyard, S. A., Vogel, E. K., and Luck, S. J. (1999). Sensory gain control (amplification) as a mechanism of selective attention: electrophysiological and neuroimaging evidence. In: G. W. Humphreys, J. Duncan, and A. M. Treisman (eds), *Attention, space, and action*, pp. 31–53. Oxford, UK: Oxford University Press.

Hinton, G. E., McClelland, J. L., and Rumelhart, D. E. (1986). Distributed representations. In D. E. Rumelhart and J. L. McClelland (eds), *Parallel distributed processing*, vol. 1, pp. 77–109. Cambridge, MA: MIT Press.

Hoffman, J. E. (1978). Search through a sequentially presented visual display. *Perception & Psychophysics*, **23**, 1–11.

Hoffman, J. E. (1979). A two-stage model of visual search. *Perception & Psychophysics*, **25**, 319–327.

Hopfinger, J. B., Buonocore, M. H., and Mangun, G. R. (2000). The neural mechanisms of top-down attentional control. *Nature Neuroscience*, **3**, 284–291.

Horowitz, T. S. and Wolfe, J. M. (1998). Visual search has no memory. *Nature*, **394**, 575–577.

Hubel, D. H. and Wiesel, T. N. (1959). Receptive fields of single neurones in the cat's striate cortex. *Journal of Physiology*, **148**, 574–591.

Hubel, D. H. and Wiesel, T. N. (1962). Receptive fields, binocular interaction, and functional architecture in the cat's visual cortex. *Journal of Physiology*, **160**, 106–154.

Hubel, D. H. and Wiesel, T. N. (1968). Receptive fields and functional architecture of monkey striate cortex. *Journal of Physiology*, **195**, 215–243.

Hull, C. L. (1943). *Principles of behavior: an introduction to behavior theory*. New York: Appleton-Century-Crofts.

Hume, D. (1896). A treatise of human nature. In: L. A. Selby-Bigge (ed.), *Hume's treatise*. Oxford, UK: Clarendon Press. (Original work published 1739.)

Humphreys, G. W. (1999). Neural representation of objects in space. In: G. W. Humphreys, J. Duncan, and A. M. Treisman (eds), *Attention, space, and action*, pp. 165–182. Oxford, UK: Oxford University Press.

Humphreys, G. W. and Müller, H. J. (1993). Search via recursive rejection (SERR): a connectionist model of visual search. *Cognitive Psychology*, **25**, 43–110.

Hung, J., Driver, J., and Walsh, V. (2005). Visual selection and posterior parietal cortex: effects of repetitive transcranial magnetic stimulation on partial report analyzed by Bundesen's theory of visual attention. *Journal of Neuroscience*, **25**, 9602–9612.

Husain, M. and Kennard, C. (1996). Visual neglect associated with frontal-lobe infarction. *Journal of Neurology*, **243**, 652–657.

Husain, M. and Rorden, C. (2003). Non-spatially lateralized mechanisms in hemispatial neglect. *Nature Reviews Neuroscience*, **4**, 26–36.

Husain, M., Shapiro, K., Martin, J., and Kennard, C. (1997). Abnormal temporal dynamics of visual attention in spatial neglect patients. *Nature*, **385**, 154–156.

Intriligator, J. and Cavanagh, P. (2001). The spatial resolution of visual attention. *Cognitive Psychology*, **43**, 171–216.

Isaak, M. I., Shapiro, K. L., and Martin, J. (1999). The attentional blink reflects retrieval competition among multiple rapid serial visual presentation items: tests of an interference model. *Journal of Experimental Psychology: Human Perception and Performance*, **25**, 1774–1792.

Ittelson, W. H. (1951). Size as a cue to distance: static localization. *American Journal of Psychology*, **64**, 54–67.

Johnston, W. A. and Dark, V. J. (1986). Selective attention. *Annual Review of Psychology*, **37**, 43–75.

Johnston, W. A. and Heinz, S. P. (1978). Flexibility and capacity demands of attention. *Journal of Experimental Psychology: General*, **107**, 420–435.

Jolicoeur, P. (1990). Orientation congruency effects on the identification of disoriented shapes. *Journal of Experimental Psychology: Human Perception and Performance*, **16**, 351–364.

Jonides, J. (1981). Voluntary versus automatic control over the mind's eye's movement. In: J. Long and A. Baddeley (eds), *Attention and performance IX*, pp. 187–203. Hillsdale, NJ: Lawrence Erlbaum Associates.

Jonides, J. and Yantis, S. (1988). Uniqueness of abrupt visual onset in capturing attention. *Perception & Psychophysics*, **43**, 346–354.

Julesz, B. (1981). A theory of preattentive texture discrimination based on first-order statistics of textons. *Biological Cybernetics*, **41**, 131–138.

Kahneman, D. (1973). *Attention and effort*. Englewood Cliffs, NJ: Prentice-Hall.

Kahneman, D. and Henik, A. (1981). Perceptual organization and attention. In: M. Kubovy and J. R. Pomerantz (eds), *Perceptual organization*, pp. 181–211. Hillsdale, NJ: Lawrence Erlbaum Associates.

Karnath, H.-O. (1988). Deficits of attention in acute and recovered hemi-neglect. *Neuropsychologia*, **20**, 27–43.

Karnath, H.-O., Ferber, S., and Himmelbach, M. (2001). Spatial awareness is a function of the temporal not the posterior parietal lobe. *Nature*, **411**, 950–953.

Karnath, H.-O., Himmelbach, M., and Rorden, C. (2002a). The subcortical anatomy of human spatial neglect: putamen, caudate nucleus and pulvinar. *Brain*, **125**, 350–360.

Karnath, H.-O., Milner, D., and Vallar, G. (eds) (2002b). *The cognitive and neural bases of spatial neglect*. Oxford, UK: Oxford University Press.

Karnath, H.-O., Berger, M. F., Küker, W., and Rorden, C. (2004). The anatomy of spatial neglect based on voxelwise statistical analysis: a study of 140 patients. *Cerebral Cortex*, **14**, 1164–1172.

Kastner, S., De Weerd, P., Desimone, R., and Ungerleider, L. G. (1998). Mechanisms of directed attention in the human extrastriate cortex as revealed by functional MRI. *Science*, **282**, 108–111.

Kastner, S., Pinsk, M. A., De Weerd, P., Desimone, R., and Ungerleider, L. G. (1999). Increased activity in human visual cortex during directed attention in the absence of visual stimulation. *Neuron*, **22**, 751–761.

Kastner, S., De Weerd, P., Pinsk, M. A., Elizondo, M. I., Desimone, R., and Ungerleider, L. G. (2001). Modulation of sensory suppression: implications for receptive field sizes in the human visual cortex. *Journal of Neurophysiology*, **86**, 1398–1411.

Kastner, S., O'Connor, D. H., Fukui, M. M., Fehd, H. M., Herwig, U., and Pinsk, M. A. (2004). Functional imaging of the human lateral geniculate nucleus and pulvinar. *Journal of Neurophysiology*, **91**, 438–448.

Kim, Y. H., Gittelman, D. R., Nobre, A. C., Parrish, T. B., LaBar, K. S., and Mesulam, M.-M. (1999). The large-scale neural network for spatial attention displays multifunctional overlap but differential asymmetry. *NeuroImage*, **9**, 269–277.

Kinsbourne, M. (1993). Orientation bias model of unilateral neglect: evidence from attentional gradients within hemispace. In: I. H. Robertson and J. C. Marshall (eds), *Unilateral neglect: clinical and experimental studies*, pp. 63–86. Hove, UK: Lawrence Erlbaum Associates.

Kinsbourne, M. and Warrington, E. K. (1962). A disorder of simultaneous form perception. *Brain*, **85**, 461–486.

Kramer, A. F. and Jacobson, A. (1991). Perceptual organization and focused attention: the role of objects and proximity in visual processing. *Perception & Psychophysics*, **50**, 267–284.

Krueger, L. E. and Shapiro, R. G. (1980). Repeating the target neither speeds nor slows its detection: evidence for independent channels in letter processing. *Perception & Psychophysics*, **28**, 68–76.

Kyllingsbæk, S. (2006). Modeling visual attention. *Behavior Research Methods*, **38**, 123–133.

Kyllingsbæk, S. and Bundesen, C. (2007). Parallel processing in a multi-feature whole-report paradigm. *Journal of Experimental Psychology: Human Perception and Performance*, **33**, 64–82.

Kyllingsbæk, S., Schneider, W. X., and Bundesen, C. (2001). Automatic attraction of attention to former targets in visual displays of letters. *Perception & Psychophysics*, **63**, 85–98.

Kyllingsbæk, S., Valla, C., Vanrie, J., and Bundesen, C. (2007). Effects of spatial separation between stimuli in whole report from brief visual displays. *Perception & Psychophysics*, **69**, 1040–1050.

LaBerge, D. and Brown, V. (1989). Theory of attentional operations in shape identification. *Psychological Review*, **96**, 101–124.

LaBerge, D. and Buchsbaum, M. S. (1990). Positron emission tomographic measurements of pulvinar activity during an attention task. *Journal of Neuroscience*, **10**, 613–619.

Larsen, A. and Bundesen, C. (1978). Size scaling in visual pattern recognition. *Journal of Experimental Psychology: Human Perception and Performance*, **4**, 1–20.

Larsen, A. and Bundesen, C. (1998). Effects of spatial separation in visual pattern matching: evidence on the role of mental translation. *Journal of Experimental Psychology: Human Perception and Performance*, **24**, 719–731.

Lashley, K. S. (1950). In search of the engram. *Symposia of the Society for Experimental Biology*, **4**, 454–482.

Lavie, N. (1995). Perceptual load as a necessary condition for selective attention. *Journal of Experimental Psychology: Human Perception and Performance*, **21**, 451–468.

Lee, D. and Chun, M. M. (2001). What are the units of visual short-term memory, objects or spatial locations? *Perception & Psychophysics*, **63**, 253–257.

Leibniz, G. W. (1996). *New essays concerning human understanding*. Cambridge, UK: Cambridge University Press. (Original work published 1765.)

Lezak, M. D. (1995). *Neuropsychological assessment*, (3rd edn). Oxford, UK: Oxford University Press.

Li, L., Miller, E. K., and Desimone, R. (1993). The representation of stimulus familiarity in anterior inferior temporal cortex. *Journal of Neurophysiology*, **69**, 1918–1929.

Logan, G. D. (1988). Toward an instance theory of automatization. *Psychological Review*, **95**, 492–527.

Logan, G. D. (1996). The CODE theory of visual attention: an integration of space-based and object-based attention. *Psychological Review*, **103**, 603–649.

Logan, G. D. (2002*a*). An instance theory of attention and memory. *Psychological Review*, **109**, 376–400.

Logan, G. D. (2002*b*). Parallel and serial processes. In: H. Pashler and J. Wixted (eds), *Stevens' handbook of experimental psychology: vol. 4. Methodology in experimental psychology*, (3rd edn), pp. 271–300. New York: John Wiley & Sons.

Logan, G. D. (2004). Cumulative progress in formal theories of attention. *Annual Review of Psychology*, **55**, 207–234.

Logan, G. D. (2005). The time it takes to switch attention. *Psychonomic Bulletin & Review*, **12**, 647–653.

Logan, G. D. and Bundesen, C. (1996). Spatial effects in the partial report paradigm: a challenge for theories of visual spatial attention. In: D. L. Medin (ed.), *The psychology of learning and motivation: vol. 35*, pp. 243–282. San Diego, CA: Academic Press.

Logan, G. D. and Bundesen, C. (2003). Clever homunculus: is there an endogenous act of control in the explicit task cuing procedure? *Journal of Experimental Psychology: Human Perception and Performance*, **29**, 575–599.

Logan, G. D. and Bundesen, C. (2004). Very clever homunculus: compound stimulus strategies for the explicit task-cuing procedure. *Psychonomic Bulletin & Review*, **11**, 832–840.

Logan, G. D. and Gordon, R. D. (2001). Executive control of visual attention in dual-task situations. *Psychological Review*, **108**, 393–434.

Logan, G. D., Schneider, D. W., and Bundesen, C. (2007). Still clever after all these years: searching for the homunculus in explicitly cued task switching. *Journal of Experimental Psychology: Human Perception and Performance*, **33**, 978–994.

Logothetis, N. K. (2003). The underpinnings of the BOLD functional magnetic resonance imaging signal. *Journal of Neuroscience*, **23**, 3963–3971.

Logothetis, N. K., Pauls, J., Augath, M., Trinath, T., and Oeltermann, A. (2001). Neurophysiological investigation of the basis of the fMRI signal. *Nature*, **412**, 150–157.

Luce, R. D. (1959). *Individual choice behavior*. New York: John Wiley & Sons.

Luce, R. D. (1963). Detection and recognition. In: R. D. Luce, R. R. Bush, and E. Galanter (eds), *Handbook of mathematical psychology*, vol. 1, pp. 103–189. New York: John Wiley & Sons.

Luce, R. D. (1986). *Response times: their role in inferring elementary mental organization*. New York: Oxford University Press.

Luck, S. J. and Girelli, M. (1998). Electrophysiological approaches to the study of selective attention in the human brain. In: R. Parasuraman (ed.), *The attentive brain*, pp. 71–94. Cambridge, MA: MIT Press.

Luck, S. J. and Vogel, E. K. (1997). The capacity of visual working memory for features and conjunctions. *Nature*, **390**, 279–281.

Luck, S. J., Chelazzi, L., Hillyard, S. A., and Desimone, R. (1997). Neural mechanisms of spatial selective attention in areas V1, V2 and V4 of macaque visual cortex. *Journal of Neurophysiology*, **77**, 24–42.

Lupker, S. J. (1979). On the nature of perceptual information during letter perception. *Perception & Psychophysics*, **25**, 303–312.

Luria, A. R. (1959). Disorders of 'simultaneous perception' in a case of bilateral occipito-parietal brain injury. *Brain*, **82**, 437–449.

Luria, A. R. (1973). *The working brain*. Oxford, UK: Basis Books.

Mackworth, J. F. (1963). The relation between the visual image and post-perceptual immediate memory. *Journal of Verbal Learning and Verbal Behavior*, **2**, 75–85.

MacLeod, C. M. (1991). Half a century of research on the Stroop effect: an integrative review. *Psychological Bulletin*, **109**, 163–203.

Manes, F., Paradiso, S., Springer, J. A., Lamberty, G., and Robinson, R. G. (1999). Neglect after right insular cortex infarction. *Stroke*, **30**, 946–948.

Mangun, G. R., Hillyard, S. A., and Luck, S. J. (1993). Electrocortical substrates of visual selective attention. In: D. Meyer and S. Kornblum (eds), *Attention and performance XIV*, pp. 219–243. Cambridge, MA: MIT Press.

Marocco, R. T. and Davidson, M. C. (1998). Neurochemistry of attention. In: R. Parasuraman (ed.), *The attentive brain*, pp. 35–50. Cambridge, MA: MIT Press.

Marois, R., Chun, M. M., and Gore, J. C. (2000). Neural correlates of the attentional blink. *Neuron*, **28**, 299–308.

Marr, D. (1982). *Vision*. San Francisco: Freeman.

Martínez, A. and Hillyard, S. A. (2005). Electrophysiological and neuroimaging approaches to the study of visual attention. In: L. Itti, G. Rees, and J. K. Tsotsos (eds), *Neurobiology of attention*, pp. 507–513. London: Elsevier Academic Press.

Martínez, A., Anllo-Vento, L., Sereno, M. I., Frank, L. R., Buxton, R. B., Dubowitz, D. J., *et al.* (1999). Involvement of striate and extrastriate visual cortical areas in spatial attention. *Nature Neuroscience*, **2**, 364–369.

Martinez-Trujillo, J. C. and Treue, S. (2002). Attentional modulation strength in cortical area MT depends on stimulus contrast. *Neuron*, **35**, 365–370.

Martinez-Trujillo, J. C. and Treue, S. (2004). Feature-based attention increases the selectivity of population responses in primate visual cortex. *Current Biology*, **14**, 744–751.

Martinez-Trujillo, J. C. and Treue, S. (2005). The feature similarity gain model of attention: unifying multiplicative effect of spatial and feature-based attention. In: L. Itti, G. Rees, and J. K. Tsotsos (eds), *Neurobiology of attention*, pp. 300–304. London: Elsevier Academic Press.

Marzi, C. A., Girelli, M., Natale, E., and Miniussi, C. (2001). What exactly is extinguished in unilateral extinction? Neurophysiological evidence. *Neuropsychologia*, **39**, 1354–1366.

Maunsell, J. H. R. and McAdams, C. J. (2001). Effects of attention on the responsiveness and selectivity of individual neurons in visual cerebral cortex. In: J. Braun, C. Koch, and J. L. Davis (eds), *Visual attention and cortical circuits*, pp. 103–120. Cambridge, MA: MIT Press.

May, C. P., Kane, M. J., and Hasher, L. (1995). Determinants of negative priming. *Psychological Bulletin*, **118**, 35–54.

McAdams, C. J. and Maunsell, J. H. R. (1999*a*). Effects of attention on orientation-tuning functions of single neurons in macaque cortical area V4. *Journal of Neuroscience*, **19**, 431–441.

McAdams, C. J. and Maunsell, J. H. R. (1999*b*). Effects of attention on the reliability of individual neurons in monkey visual cortex. *Neuron*, **23**, 765–773.

McAdams, C. J. and Maunsell, J. H. R. (2000). Attention to both space and feature modulates neuronal responses in macaque area V4. *Journal of Neurophysiology*, **83**, 1751–1755.

McCarley, J. S., Wang, R. F., Kramer, A. F., Irwin, D. E., and Peterson, M. S. (2003). How much memory does oculomotor search have? *Psychological Science*, **14**, 422–426.

McClelland, J. L. and Rumelhart, D. E. (eds) (1986). *Parallel distributed processing*, vol. 2. Cambridge, MA: MIT Press.

McIntyre, C., Fox, R., and Neale, J. (1970). Effects of noise similarity and redundancy on the information processed from brief visual displays. *Perception & Psychophysics*, **7**, 328–332.

McLaughlin, E. N., Shore, D. I., and Klein, R. M. (2001). The attentional blink is immune to masking-induced data limits. *Quarterly Journal of Experimental Psychology*, **54A**, 169–196.

McMains, S. A. and Somers, D. C. (2004). Multiple spotlights of attentional selection in human visual cortex. *Neuron*, **42**, 677–686.

McMains, S. A. and Somers, D. C. (2005). Processing efficiency of divided spatial attention mechanisms in human visual cortex. *Journal of Neuroscience*, **25**, 9444–9448.

Merikle, P. M., Coltheart, M., and Lowe, D. G. (1971). On the selective effects of a patterned masking stimulus. *Canadian Journal of Psychology*, **25**, 264–279.

Mesulam, M.-M. (1981). A cortical network for directed attention and unilateral neglect. *Annals of Neurology*, **10**, 309–325.

Mesulam, M.-M. (1990). Large-scale neurocognitive networks and distributed processing for attention, language, and memory. *Annals of Neurology*, **28**, 597–613.

Mesulam, M.-M. (2000). Attentional networks, confusional states, and neglect syndromes. In: M.-M. Mesulam (ed.), *Principles of behavioural and cognitive neurology*, (2nd edn), pp. 174–256. Oxford, UK: Oxford University Press.

Mevorach, C., Humphreys, G. W., and Shalev, L. (2006). Opposite biases in salience-based selection for the left and right posterior parietal cortex. *Nature Neuroscience*, **9**, 740–742.

Miller, E. K., Li, L., and Desimone, R. (1993). Activity of neurons in anterior inferior temporal cortex during a short-term memory task. *Journal of Neuroscience*, **13**, 1460–1478.

Miller, E. K., Erickson, C. A., and Desimone, R. (1996). Neural mechanisms of visual working memory in prefrontal cortex of the macaque. *Journal of Neuroscience*, **16**, 5154–5167.

Miller, J. (1982). Divided attention: evidence for coactivation with redundant signals. *Cognitive Psychology*, **14**, 247–279.

Milliken, B. and Tipper, S. P. (1998). Attention and inhibition. In: H. Pashler (ed.), *Attention,* pp. 13–75. Hove, UK: Psychology Press.

Milner, A. D. and Goodale, M. A. (1995). *The visual brain in action.* Oxford, UK: Oxford University Press.

Miyashita, Y. and Chang, H. S. (1988). Neuronal correlate of pictorial short-term memory in the primate temporal cortex. *Nature,* **331,** 68–70.

Monsell, S. and Mizon, G. A. (2006). Can the task-cuing paradigm measure an endogenous task-set reconfiguration process? *Journal of Experimental Psychology: Human Perception and Performance,* **32,** 493–516.

Moore, C. M., Egeth, H., Berglon, L. R., and Luck, S. J. (1996). Are attentional dwell times inconsistent with serial visual search? *Psychonomic Bulletin & Review,* **3,** 360–365.

Moore, T. and Armstrong, K. M. (2003). Selective gating of visual signals by microstimulation of frontal cortex. *Nature,* **421,** 370–373.

Moran, J. and Desimone, R. (1985). Selective attention gates visual processing in the extrastriate cortex. *Science,* **229,** 782–784.

Moray, N. (1959). Attention in dichotic listening: affective cues and the influence of instructions. *Quarterly Journal of Experimental Psychology,* **11,** 56–60.

Mort, D. J., Malhotra, P., Mannan, S. K., Rorden, C., Pambakian, A., Kennard, C., and Husain, M. (2003). The anatomy of visual neglect. *Brain,* **126,** 1986–1997.

Moruzzi, G. and Magoun, H. W. (1949). Brainstem reticular formation and activation of the EEG. *Electroencephalographic Clinical Neurophysiology,* **1,** 455–473.

Motter, B. C. (1993). Focal attention produces spatially selective processing in visual cortical areas V1, V2 and V4 in the presence of competing stimuli. *Journal of Neurophysiology,* **70,** 909–919.

Motter, B. C. (1994*a*). Neural correlates of attentive selection for color or luminance in extrastriate area V4. *Journal of Neuroscience,* **14,** 2178–2189.

Motter, B. C. (1994*b*). Neural correlates of feature selective memory and pop-out in extrastriate area V4. *Journal of Neuroscience,* **14,** 2190–2199.

Mozer, M. C. (1991). *The perception of multiple objects: a connectionist approach.* Cambridge, MA: MIT Press.

Muggleton, N. G., Postma, P., Moutsopoulou, K., Nimmo-Smith, I., Marcel, A., and Walsh, V. (2006). TMS over right posterior parietal cortex induces neglect in a scene-based frame of reference. *Neuropsychologia,* **44,** 1222–1229.

Nakayama, K. and Silverman, G. H. (1986). Serial and parallel processing of visual feature conjunctions. *Nature,* **320,** 264–265.

Neill, W. T. (1977). Inhibitory and facilitatory processes in selective attention. *Journal of Experimental Psychology: Human Perception and Performance,* **3,** 444–450.

Neisser, U. (1963). Decision-time without reaction-time: experiments in visual scanning. *American Journal of Psychology,* **76,** 376–385.

Neisser, U. (1967). *Cognitive psychology.* New York: Appleton-Century-Crofts.

Nickerson, R. S. (1966). Response times with a memory-dependent decision task. *Journal of Experimental Psychology,* **72,** 761–769.

Nobre, A. C., Sebestyen, G. N., Gitelman, D. R., Mesulam, M.-M., Frackowiak, R. S., and Frith, C. D. (1997). Functional localization of the system for visuospatial attention using positron emission tomography. *Brain,* **120,** 515–533.

Norman, D. A. (1968). Toward a theory of memory and attention. *Psychological Review*, **75**, 522–536.

Nosofsky, R. M. (1984). Choice, similarity, and the context theory of classification. *Journal of Experimental Psychology: Learning, Memory, and Cognition*, **10**, 104–114.

Nosofsky, R. M. (1986). Attention, similarity, and the identification–categorization relationship. *Journal of Experimental Psychology: General*, **115**, 39–57.

Nosofsky, R. M. and Palmeri, T. J. (1997). An exemplar-based random walk model of speeded classification. *Psychological Review*, **104**, 266–300.

O'Connor, D. H., Fukui, M. M., Pinsk, M. A., and Kastner, S. (2002). Attention modulates responses in the human lateral geniculate nucleus. *Nature Neuroscience*, **5**, 1203–1209.

Oliveri, M., Rossini, P. M., Traversa, R., Cicinelli, P., Filippi, M. M., Pasqualetti, P., *et al.* (1999). Left frontal transcranial magnetic stimulation reduces contralesional extinction in patients with unilateral right brain damage. *Brain*, **122**, 1731–1739.

Olshausen, B. A., Anderson, C. H., and van Essen, D. C. (1993). A neurobiological model of visual attention and invariant pattern recognition based on dynamic routing of information. *Journal of Neuroscience*, **13**, 4700–4719.

Owen, A. M., Epstein, R., and Johnsrude, I. S. (2003). fMRI: applications in cognitive neuroscience. In: P. Jezzard, P. M. Matthews, and S. M. Smith (eds), *Functional MRI: an introduction to methods*, pp. 311–328. Oxford, UK: Oxford University Press.

Page, M. P. A. (2000). Connectionist modelling in psychology: a localist manifesto. *Behavioral and Brain Sciences*, **23**, 443–467.

Palmer, J. (1995). Attention in visual search: distinguishing four causes of a set-size effect. *Current Directions in Psychological Science*, **4**, 118–123.

Palmer, J., Verghese, P., and Pavel, M. (2000). The psychophysics of visual search. *Vision Research*, **40**, 1227–1268.

Palmer, S. E. (1977). Hierarchical structure in perceptual representation. *Cognitive Psychology*, **9**, 441–474.

Paquet, L. and Lortie, C. (1990). Evidence for early selection: precuing target location reduces interference from same-category distractors. *Perception and Psychophysics*, **48**, 382–388.

Parker, A. J. and Newsome, W. T. (1998). Sense and the single neuron: probing the physiology of perception. *Annual Review of Neuroscience*, **21**, 227–277.

Parzen, E. (1962). *Stochastic processes*. San Francisco: Holden-Day.

Pascual-Leone, A., Walsh, V., and Rothwell, J. (2000). Transcranial magnetic stimulation in cognitive neuroscience–virtual lesion, chronometry, and functional connectivity. *Current Opinion in Neurobiology*, **10**, 232–237.

Pashler, H. (1987a). Detecting conjunctions of color and form: reassessing the serial search hypothesis. *Perception & Psychophysics*, **41**, 191–201.

Pashler, H. (1987b). Target–distractor discriminability in visual search. *Perception & Psychophysics*, **41**, 285–292.

Pashler, H. and Badgio, P. C. (1987). Attentional issues in the identification of alphanumeric characters. In: M. Coltheart (ed.), *Attention and performance XII: the psychology of reading*, pp. 63–81. Hillsdale, NJ: Lawrence Erlbaum Associates.

Paus, T. (1999). Imaging the brain before, during, and after transcranial magnetic stimulation. *Neuropsychologia*, **37**, 219–224.

Peers, P. V., Ludwig, C. J. H., Rorden, C., Cusack, R., Bonfiglioli, C., Bundesen, C., *et al.* (2005). Attentional functions of parietal and frontal cortex. *Cerebral Cortex*, **15**, 1469–1484.

Pelli, D. G., Palomares, M., and Majaj, N. J. (2004). Crowding is unlike ordinary masking: distinguishing feature integration from detection. *Journal of Vision*, **4**, 1136–1169.

Petersen, S. E., Robinson, D. L., and Keys, W. (1985). Pulvinar nuclei of the behaving rhesus monkey: visual responses and their modulations. *Journal of Neurophysiology*, **54**, 867–886.

Petersen, S. E., Robinson, D. L., and Morris, D. (1987). Contributions of the pulvinar to visual spatial attention. *Neuropsychologia*, **25**, 97–105.

Peterson, M. S., Kramer, A. F., Wang, R. F., Irwin, D. E., and McCarley, J. S. (2001). Visual search has memory. *Psychological Science*, **12**, 287–292.

Phaf, R. H., van der Heijden, A. H. C., and Hudson, P. T. W. (1990). SLAM: a connectionist model for attention in visual selection tasks. *Cognitive Psychology*, **22**, 273–341.

Podgorny, P. and Shepard, R. N. (1978). Functional representations common to visual perception and imagination. *Journal of Experimental Psychology: Human Perception and Performance*, **4**, 21–35.

Podgorny, P. and Shepard, R. N. (1983). Distribution of visual attention over space. *Journal of Experimental Psychology: Human Perception and Performance*, **9**, 380–393.

Pomerantz, J. R. (1981). Perceptual organization in information processing. In: M. Kubovy and J. R. Pomerantz (eds), *Perceptual organization*, pp. 141–180. Hillsdale, NJ: Lawrence Erlbaum Associates.

Posner, M. I. (1978). *Chronometric explorations of mind*. Hillsdale, NJ: Lawrence Erlbaum Associates.

Posner, M. I. (1980). Orienting of attention. *Quarterly Journal of Experimental Psychology*, **32**, 3–25.

Posner, M. I. and Boies, S. J. (1971). Components of attention. *Psychological Review*, **78**, 391–408.

Posner, M. I. and Cohen, Y. (1984). Components of visual orienting. In: H. Bouma and D. G. Bouwhuis (eds), *Attention and performance X: control of language processes*, pp. 531–556. Hillsdale, NJ: Lawrence Erlbaum Associates.

Posner, M. I. and Driver, J. (1992). The neurobiology of selective attention. *Current Opinion in Neurobiology*, **2**, 165–169.

Posner, M. I. and Keele, S. W. (1967). Decay of visual information from a single letter. *Science*, **158**, 137–139.

Posner, M. I. and Petersen, S. E. (1990). The attention system of the human brain. *Annual Review of Neuroscience*, **13**, 25–42.

Posner, M. I., Boies, S. J., Eichelman, W. H., and Taylor, R. L. (1969). Retention of visual and name codes of single letters. *Journal of Experimental Psychology Monograph*, **79** (1, Pt 2).

Posner, M. I., Nissen, M. J., and Ogden, W. C. (1978). Attended and unattended processing modes: the role of set for spatial location. In: H. L. Pick and I. J. Saltzman (eds), *Modes of perceiving and processing information*, pp. 137–157. Hillsdale, NJ: Lawrence Erlbaum Associates.

Posner, M. I., Snyder, C. R. R., and Davidson, B. J. (1980). Attention and the detection of signals. *Journal of Experimental Psychology: General*, **109**, 160–174.

Posner, M. I., Walker, J. A., Friedrich, F. J., and Rafal, R. D. (1984). Effects of parietal injury on covert orienting of attention. *Journal of Neuroscience*, **4**, 1863–1874.

Posner, M. I., Walker, J.A., Friedrich, F. A., and Rafal, R.D. (1987). How do the parietal lobes direct covert attention? *Neuropsychologia*, **25**, 135–145.

Pratt, J. and Abrams, R. A. (1999). Inhibition of return in discrimination tasks. *Journal of Experimental Psychology: Human Perception and Performance*, **25**, 229–242.

Prinzmetal, W. (1981). Principles of feature integration in visual perception. *Perception & Psychophysics*, **30**, 330–340.

Prinzmetal, W. and Banks, W. P. (1977). Good continuation affects visual detection. *Perception & Psychophysics*, **21**, 389–395.

Rafal, R. D. (1994). Neglect. *Current Opinion in Neurobiology*, **4**, 231–236.

Rainer, G., Rao, S. C., and Miller, E. K. (1999). Prospective coding for objects in primate prefrontal cortex. *Journal of Neuroscience*, **19**, 5493–5505.

Ratcliff, R. and McKoon, G. (1997). A counter model for implicit priming in perceptual word identification. *Psychological Review*, **104**, 319–343.

Raymond, J. E., Shapiro, K. L., and Arnell, K. M. (1992). Temporary suppression of visual processing in an RSVP task: an attentional blink? *Journal of Experimental Psychology: Human Perception and Performance*, **18**, 849–860.

Rayner, K. (1998). Eye movements in reading and information processing: 20 years of research. *Psychological Bulletin*, **124**, 372–422.

Rees, G., Wojciulik, E., Clarke, K., Husain, M., Frith, C., and Driver J. (2000). Unconscious activation of visual cortex in the damaged right hemisphere of a patient with extinction. *Brain*, **123**, 1624–1633.

Reeves, A. and Sperling, G. (1986). Attention gating in short-term visual memory. *Psychological Review*, **93**, 180–206.

Remington, R. and Pierce, L. (1984). Moving attention: evidence for time-invariant shifts of visual selective attention. *Perception & Psychophysics*, **35**, 393–399.

Remington, R. W., Johnston, J. C., and Yantis, S. (1992). Involuntary attention capture by abrupt onsets. *Perception & Psychophysics*, **51**, 279–290.

Reynolds, J. H. (2005). Visual cortical circuits and spatial attention. In: L. Itti, G. Rees, and J. K. Tsotsos (eds), *Neurobiology of attention*, pp. 42–49. London: Elsevier Academic Press.

Reynolds, J. H. and Chelazzi, L. (2004). Attentional modulation of visual processing. *Annual Review of Neuroscience*, **27**, 611–647.

Reynolds, J. H. and Desimone, R. (2003). Interacting roles of attention and visual salience in V4. *Neuron*, **37**, 853–863.

Reynolds, J. H., Chelazzi, L., and Desimone, R. (1999). Competitive mechanisms subserve attention in macaque areas V2 and V4. *Journal of Neuroscience*, **19**, 1736–1753.

Reynolds, J. H., Pasternak, T., and Desimone, R. (2000). Attention increases sensitivity of V4 neurons. *Neuron*, **26**, 703–714.

Robertson, I. H. (1993). The relation between lateralised and non-lateralised deficits. In: I. H. Robertson and J. C. Marshall (eds), *Unilateral neglect: clinical and experimental studies*, pp. 257–278. Hove, UK: Lawrence Erlbaum Associates.

Robertson, I. H. and Manly, T. (1999). Sustained attention deficits in time and space. In: G. W. Humphreys, J. Duncan, and A. Treisman (eds), *Attention, space, and action*, pp. 297–310. Oxford, UK: Oxford University Press.

Robertson, L. C., Lamb, M. R., and Knight, R. T. (1988). Effects of lesions of temporal–parietal junction on perceptual and attentional processing in humans. *Journal of Neuroscience*, **8**, 3757–3769.

Robertson, L. C., Treisman, A., Friedmann-Hill, S., and Grabowecky, M. (1997). The interaction of spatial and object pathways: evidence from Balint's syndrome. *Journal of Cognitive Neuroscience*, **9**, 295–318.

Robinson, D. L. and Cowie, R. J. (1997). The primate pulvinar: structural, functional, and behavioral components of visual salience. In: M. Steriade, E. G. Jones, and D. A. McCormick (eds), *Thalamus*, vol. 2, pp. 53–92. Amsterdam: Elsevier.

Robinson, D. L. and Petersen, S. E. (1992). The pulvinar and visual salience. *Trends in Neurosciences*, **15**, 127–132.

Rosenthal, C. R., Walsh, V., Mannan, S. K., Anderson, E. J., Hawken, M. B., and Kennard, C. (2006). Temporal dynamics of parietal cortex involvement in visual search. *Neuropsychologia*, **44**, 731–743.

Rossetti, Y., Pisella, L., and Vighetto, A. (2003). Optic ataxia revisited: visually guided action versus immediate visuomotor control. *Experimental Brain Research*, **153**, 171–179.

Rubin, E. (1965). Die Nichtexistenz der Aufmerksamkeit [The nonexistence of attention]. *Psykologiske tekster*, vol. 1, pp. 195–198. Copenhagen, Denmark: Akademisk Forlag. (Original work published 1925.)

Ruff, C. C., Blankenburg, F., Bjoertomt, O., Bestmann, S., Freeman, E., Haynes, J. D., *et al.* (2006). Concurrent TMS-fMRI and psychophysics reveal frontal influences on human retinotopic visual cortex. *Current Biology*, **16**, 1479–1488.

Rumelhart, D. E. (1970). A multicomponent theory of the perception of briefly exposed visual displays. *Journal of Mathematical Psychology*, **7**, 191–218.

Rumelhart, D. E. and McClelland, J. L. (eds) (1986). *Parallel distributed processing*, vol. 1. Cambridge, MA: MIT Press.

Saenz, M., Buracas, G. T., and Boynton, G. M. (2002). Global effects of feature-based attention in human visual cortex. *Nature Neuroscience*, **5**, 631–632.

Salinas, E. and Sejnowski, T.J. (2000). Impact of correlated synaptic input on output firing rate and variability in simple neuronal models. *Journal of Neuroscience*, **20**, 6193–6209.

Schall, J. D. and Thompson, K. G. (1999). Neural selection and control of visually guided eye movements. *Annual Review of Neuroscience*, **22**, 241–259.

Schneider, W. (1985). Toward a model of attention and the development of automatic processing. In: M. I. Posner and O. S. M. Marin (eds), *Attention and performance XI*, pp. 475–492. Hillsdale, NJ: Lawrence Erlbaum Associates.

Schneider, W. and Fisk, A. D. (1982). Degree of consistent training: improvements in search performance and automatic process development. *Perception & Psychophysics*, **31**, 160–168.

Schneider, W. and Shiffrin, R. M. (1977). Controlled and automatic human information processing: I. Detection, search, and attention. *Psychological Review*, **84**, 1–66.

Schneider, W., Dumais, S. T., and Shiffrin, R. M. (1984). Automatic and control processing and attention. In: R. Parasuraman and D. R. Davies (eds), *Varieties of attention*, pp. 1–27. New York: Academic Press.

Schneider, W. X. (1995). VAM: a neuro-cognitive model for visual attention, control of segmentation, object recognition, and space-based motor action. *Visual Cognition*, **2**, 331–375.

Schneider, W. X. and Deubel, H. (2002). Selection-for-perception and selection-for-spatial-motor-action are coupled by visual attention: a review of recent findings and new evidence from stimulus-driven saccade control. In: W. Prinz and B. Hommel (eds), *Attention and performance XIX: common mechanisms in perception and action*, pp. 609–627. Oxford: Oxford University Press.

Sclar, G. and Freeman, R. D. (1982). Orientation selectivity in the cat's striate cortex is invariant with stimulus contrast. *Experimental Brain Research*, **46**, 457–461.

Shapiro, K. L., Raymond, J. E., and Arnell, K. M. (1994). Attention to visual pattern information produces the attentional blink in rapid serial visual presentation. *Journal of Experimental Psychology: Human Perception and Performance*, **20**, 357–371.

Shapiro, K. L., Driver, J., Ward, R., and Sorensen, R. E. (1997). Priming from the attentional blink: a failure to extract visual tokens but not visual types. *Psychological Science*, **8**, 95–100.

Shaw, M. L. (1978). A capacity allocation model for reaction time. *Journal of Experimental Psychology: Human Perception and Performance*, **4**, 586–598.

Shaw, M. (1980). Identifying attentional and decision-making components in information processing. In: R. S. Nickerson (ed.), *Attention and performance VIII*, pp. 277–296. Hillsdale, NJ: Lawrence Erlbaum Associates.

Shaw, M. (1984). Division of attention among spatial locations: a fundamental difference between detection of letters and detection of luminance increments. In: H. Bouma and D. G. Bouwhuis (eds), *Attention and performance X: control of language processes*, pp. 109–121. Hillsdale, NJ: Lawrence Erlbaum Associates.

Shaw, M. L. and Shaw, P. (1977). Optimal allocation of cognitive resources to spatial locations. *Journal of Experimental Psychology: Human Perception and Performance*, **3**, 201–211.

Shelton, P. A., Bowers, D., and Heilman, K. M. (1990). Peripersonal and vertical neglect. *Brain*, **113**, 191–205.

Shepard, R. N. (1957). Stimulus and response generalization: a stochastic model relating generalization to distance in psychological space. *Psychometrika*, **22**, 325–345.

Shepard, R. N. and Cooper, L. A. (1982). *Mental images and their transformations*. Cambridge, MA: MIT Press.

Sherman, S. M. and Guillery, R. W. (2001). *Exploring the thalamus*. San Diego: Academic Press.

Shibuya, H. (1993). Efficiency of visual selection in duplex and conjunction conditions in partial report. *Perception and Psychophysics*, **54**, 716–732.

Shibuya, H. and Bundesen, C. (1988). Visual selection from multielement displays: measuring and modeling effects of exposure duration. *Journal of Experimental Psychology: Human Perception and Performance*, **14**, 591–600.

Shiffrin, R. M. and Czerwinski, M. P. (1988). A model of automatic attention attraction when mapping is partially consistent. *Journal of Experimental Psychology: Learning, Memory, and Cognition*, **14**, 562–569.

Shiffrin, R. M. and Dumais, S. T. (1981). The development of automatism. In: J. R. Anderson (ed.), *Cognitive skills and their acquisition*, pp. 111–140. Hillsdale, NJ: Lawrence Erlbaum Associates.

Shiffrin, R. M. and Schneider, W. (1977). Controlled and automatic human information processing: II. Perceptual learning, automatic attending, and a general theory. *Psychological Review*, **84**, 127–190.

Shiffrin, R. M., Dumais, S. T., and Schneider, W. (1981). Characteristics of automatism. In: J. Long and A. Baddeley (eds), *Attention and performance IX*, pp. 223–238. Hillsdale, NJ: Lawrence Erlbaum Associates.

Shih, S.-I. (in press). The attention cascade model and attentional blink. *Cognitive Psychology*.

Shih, S.-I. and Sperling, G. (2002). Measuring and modeling the trajectory of visual spatial attention. *Psychological Review*, **109**, 260–305.

Shulman, G. L., Ollinger, J. M., Akbudak, E., Conturo, T. E., Snyder, A. Z., Petersen, S. E., and Corbetta, M. (1999). Areas involved in encoding and applying directional expectations to moving objects. *Journal of Neuroscience*, **19**, 9480–9496.

Smania, N., Martini, M. C., Gambina, G., Tomelleri, G., Palamara, A., Natale, E., *et al.* (1998). The spatial distribution of visual attention in hemineglect and extinction patients. *Brain*, **121**, 1759–1770.

Smith, J. E. K. (1980). Models of identification. In: R. S. Nickerson (ed.), *Attention and performance VIII*, pp. 129–158. Hillsdale, NJ: Lawrence Erlbaum Associates.

~ Sperling, G. (1960). The information available in brief visual presentations. *Psychological Monographs*, **74** (11, Whole No. 498).

~ Sperling, G. (1963). A model for visual memory tasks. *Human Factors*, **5**, 19–31.

Sperling, G. (1967). Successive approximations to a model for short-term memory. *Acta Psychologica*, **27**, 285–292.

Sperling, G. (1984). A unified theory of attention and signal detection. In: R. Parasuraman and D. R. Davies (eds), *Varieties of attention*, pp. 103–181. New York: Academic Press.

Sperling, G. and Reeves, A. (1980). Measuring the reaction time of a shift of visual attention. In: R. S. Nickerson (ed.), *Attention and performance VIII*, pp. 347–360. Hillsdale, NJ: Lawrence Erlbaum Associates.

Sperling, G. and Speelman, R. G. (1970). Acoustic similarity and auditory short-term memory: experiments and a model. In: D. A. Norman (ed.), *Models of human memory*, pp. 151–202. New York: Academic Press.

Sperling, G. and Weichselgartner, E. (1995). Episodic theory of the dynamics of spatial attention. *Psychological Review*, **102**, 503–532.

Sperling, G., Budiansky, J., Spivak, J. G., and Johnson, M. C. (1971). Extremely rapid visual search: the maximum rate of scanning letters for the presence of a numeral. *Science*, **174**, 307–311.

Spitzer, H., Desimone, R., and Moran, J. (1988). Increased attention enhances both behavioral and neuronal performance. *Science*, **240**, 338–340.

Sprague, J. M., Chambers, W. W., and Stellar, E. (1961). Attentive, affective and adaptive behaviour in the cat. *Science*, **133**, 165–173.

Spratling, M. W. and Johnson, M. H. (2004). A feedback model of visual attention. *Journal of Cognitive Neuroscience*, **16**, 219–237.

Sternberg, S. (1966). High-speed scanning in human memory. *Science*, **153**, 652–654.

Sternberg, S. (1967). Scanning a persisting visual image versus a memorized list. Paper presented at the Annual Meeting of the Eastern Psychological Association.

Sternberg, S. (1969a). Memory-scanning: mental processes revealed by reaction-time experiments. *American Scientist*, **57**, 421–457.

Sternberg, S. (1969b). The discovery of processing stages: extensions of Donders' method. *Acta Psychologica*, **30**, 276–315.

Sternberg, S. (1998). Discovering mental processing stages: the method of additive factors. In: D. Scarborough and S. Sternberg (eds), *An invitation to cognitive science: Vol. 4. Methods, models, and conceptual issues*, pp. 365–454. Cambridge, MA: MIT Press.

Stone, S. P., Patel, P., Greenwood, R. J., and Halligan, P. W. (1992). Measuring visual neglect in acute stroke and predicting its recovery: the visual neglect recovery index. *Journal of Neurology, Neurosurgery and Psychiatry*, 55, 431–436.

Strasburger, H. (2005). Unfocussed spatial attention underlies the crowding effect in indirect form vision. *Journal of Vision*, 5, 1024–1037.

Stroop, J. R. (1935). Studies of interference in serial verbal reactions. *Journal of Experimental Psychology*, 18, 643–662.

Sturm, W., de Simone, A., Krause, B. J., Specht, K., Hesselmann, V., Radermacher, I. *et al.* (1999). Functional anatomy of intrinsic alertness: evidence for a fronto-parietal–thalamic–brainstem network in the right hemisphere. *Neuropsychologia*, 37, 797–805.

Swets, J. A., Tanner, W. P. Jr, and Birdsall, T. G. (1961). Decision processes in perception. *Psychological Review*, 68, 301–340.

Tanaka, K. (1996). Inferotemporal cortex and object vision. *Annual Review of Neuroscience*, 19, 109–139.

Tanaka, K. (2003). Columns for complex visual object features in the inferotemporal cortex: clustering of cells with similar but slightly different stimulus selectivities. *Cerebral Cortex*, 13, 90–99.

Tanner, W. P. Jr. and Swets, J. A. (1954). A decision making theory of visual detection. *Psychological Review*, 61, 401–409.

Tarr, M. J. and Bülthoff, H. H. (1995). Is human object recognition better described by geon-structural-descriptions or by multiple-views? *Journal of Experimental Psychology: Human Perception and Performance*, 21, 1494–1505.

Theeuwes, J. (1992). Perceptual selectivity for color and form. *Perception & Psychophysics*, 51, 599–606.

Theeuwes, J. (1994). Stimulus-driven capture and attentional set: selective search for color and visual abrupt onsets. *Journal of Experimental Psychology: Human Perception and Performance*, 20, 799–806.

Theeuwes, J. (1995). Temporal and spatial characteristics of preattentive and attentive processing. *Visual Cognition*, 2, 221–233.

Theeuwes, J. (1996). Perceptual selectivity for color and form: on the nature of the interference effect. In: A. F. Kramer, M. G. H. Coles, and G. D. Logan (eds), *Converging operations in the study of visual selective attention*, pp. 297–314. Washington, DC: American Psychological Association.

Thornton, T. L. and Gilden, D. L. (2007). Parallel and serial processes in visual search. *Psychological Review*, 114, 71–103.

Thurstone, L. L. (1927). A law of comparative judgment. *Psychological Review*, 34, 273–286.

Tipper, S. P. (1985). The negative priming effect: inhibitory priming by ignored objects. *Quarterly Journal of Experimental Psychology*, 37A, 571–590.

Tipper, S. P. (2001). Does negative priming reflect inhibitory mechanisms? A review and integration of conflicting views. *Quarterly Journal of Experimental Psychology*, 37A, 321–343.

Tipper, S. P. and Cranston, M. (1985). Selective attention and priming: inhibitory and facilitatory effects of ignored primes. *Quarterly Journal of Experimental Psychology*, 37A, 591–611.

Todd, J. J. and Marois, R. (2004). Capacity limit of visual short-term memory in human posterior parietal cortex. *Nature*, **428**, 751–754.

Townsend, J. T. (1969). Mock parallel and serial models and experimental detection of these. In: *Purdue Centennial Symposium on Information Processing*, pp. 617–628. Purdue University.

Townsend, J. T. (1971*a*). Theoretical analysis of an alphabetic confusion matrix. *Perception & Psychophysics*, **9**, 40–50.

Townsend, J. T. (1971*b*). Alphabetic confusion: a test of models for individuals. *Perception & Psychophysics*, **9**, 449–454.

Townsend, J. T. and Ashby, F. G. (1982). Experimental test of contemporary mathematical models of visual letter recognition. *Journal of Experimental Psychology: Human Perception and Performance*, **8**, 834–864.

Townsend, J. T. and Ashby, F. G. (1983). *The stochastic modeling of elementary psychological processes*. Cambridge, UK: Cambridge University Press.

Townsend, J. T. and Landon, D. E. (1982). An experimental and theoretical investigation of the constant-ratio rule and other models of visual letter confusion. *Journal of Mathematical Psychology*, **25**, 119–162.

Treisman, A. M. (1964*a*). Verbal cues, language, and meaning in selective attention. *American Journal of Psychology*, **77**, 206–219.

Treisman, A. M. (1964*b*). The effect of irrelevant material on the efficiency of selective listening. *American Journal of Psychology*, **77**, 533–546.

Treisman, A. M. (1969). Strategies and models of selective attention. *Psychological Review*, **76**, 282–299.

Treisman, A. M. (1988). Features and objects: the fourteenth Bartlett memorial lecture. *Quarterly Journal of Experimental Psychology*, **40A**, 201–237.

Treisman, A. M. (1999). Feature binding, attention and object perception. In: G. W. Humphreys, J. Duncan, and A. M. Treisman (eds), *Attention, space, and action*, pp. 91–111. Oxford, UK: Oxford University Press.

Treisman, A. M. and Gelade, G. (1980). A feature-integration theory of attention. *Cognitive Psychology*, **12**, 97–136.

Treisman, A. M. and Gormican, S. (1988). Feature analysis in early vision: evidence from search asymmetries. *Psychological Review*, **95**, 15–48.

Treisman, A. M. and Paterson, R. (1984). Emergent features, attention, and object perception. *Journal of Experimental Psychology: Human Perception and Performance*, **10**, 12–31.

Treisman, A. M. and Sato, S. (1990). Conjunction search revisited. *Journal of Experimental Psychology: Human Perception and Performance*, **16**, 459–478.

Treisman, A. and Schmidt, H. (1982). Illusory conjunctions in the perception of objects. *Cognitive Psychology*, **14**, 107–141.

Treisman, A. M., Sykes, M., and Gelade, G. (1977). Selective attention and stimulus integration. In: S. Dornic (ed.), *Attention and performance VI*, pp. 333–361. Hillsdale, NJ: Lawrence Erlbaum Associates.

Treisman, A. M., Kahneman, D., and Burkell, J. (1983). Perceptual objects and the cost of filtering. *Perception & Psychophysics*, **33**, 527–532.

Treue, S. and Martinez-Trujillo, J. C. M. (1999). Feature-based attention influences motion processing gain in macaque visual cortex. *Nature*, **399**, 575–579.

Tripathy, S. P. and Cavanagh, P. (2002). The extent of crowding in peripheral vision does not scale with target size. *Vision Research*, **42**, 2357–2369.

Tsal, Y. (1983). Movements of attention across the visual field. *Journal of Experimental Psychology: Human Perception and Performance*, **9**, 523–530.

Tsal, Y., Merian, N., and Lavie, N. (1994). The role of attention in illusory conjunctions. *Perception & Psychophysics*, **55**, 350–358.

Ullman, S. (1996). *High-level vision: object recognition and visual cognition*. Cambridge, MA: MIT Press.

Ungerleider, L. G. and Mishkin, M. (1982). Two cortical visual systems. In: D. J. Ingle, M. A. Goodale and R. J. W. Mansfield (eds), *Analysis of visual behaviour*, pp. 549–586. Cambridge, MA: MIT Press.

Usher, M. and Niebur, E. (1996). Modelling the temporal dynamics of IT neurons in visual search: a mechanism for top-down selective attention. *Journal of Cognitive Neuroscience*, **8**, 311–327.

Uttal, W. R. (2001). *The new phrenology*. Cambridge, MA: MIT Press.

Vallar, G. and Perani, D. (1986). The anatomy of unilateral neglect after right-hemisphere stroke lesions. A clinical/CT-scan correlation study in man. *Neuropsychologia*, **24**, 609–622.

Vallar, G., Sandroni, P., Rusconi, M. L., and Barbieri, S. (1991). Hemianopia, hemianesthesia, and spatial neglect: a study with evoked potentials. *Neurology*, **41**, 1918–1922.

Vallar, G., Rusconi, M. L., Bignamini, L., Germiniani, G., and Perani, D. (1994). Anatomical correlates of visual and tactile extinction in humans: a clinical CT scan study. *Journal of Neurology, Neurosurgery, and Psychiatry*, **57**, 464–470.

Vandenberghe, R., Duncan, J., Dupont, P., Ward, R., Poline, J. B., Bormans, G. *et al.* (1997). Attention to one or two features in left or right visual field: a positron emission tomography study. *Journal of Neuroscience*, **17**, 3739–3750.

van der Heijden, A. H. C. (1981). *Short-term visual information forgetting*. London: Routledge and Kegan Paul.

van der Heijden, A. H. C. (1992). *Selective attention in vision*. London: Routledge.

van der Heijden, A. H. C. (2004). *Attention in vision: perception, communication and action*. Hove, UK: Psychology Press.

van der Heijden, A. H. C., La Heij, W., and Boer, J. P. A. (1983). Parallel processing of redundant targets in simple visual search tasks. *Psychological Research*, **45**, 235–254.

van der Heijden, A. H. C., Schreuder, R., Maris, L., and Neerincx, M. (1984). Some evidence for correlated separate activation in a simple letter-detection task. *Perception & Psychophysics*, **36**, 577–585.

van der Heijden, A. H. C., Schreuder, R., and Wolters, G. (1985). Enhancing single-item recognition accuracy by cueing spatial locations in vision. *Quarterly Journal of Experimental Psychology*, **37A**, 427–434.

van Oeffelen, M. P. and Vos, P. G. (1982). Configurational effects on the enumeration of dots: counting by groups. *Memory & Cognition*, **10**, 396–404.

van Oeffelen, M. P. and Vos, P. G. (1983). An algorithm for pattern description on the level of relative proximity. *Pattern Recognition*, **16**, 341–348.

van Zomeren, A. H. and Brouwer, W. H. (1987). Head injury and concepts of attention. In: H. S. Levin, J. Grafman, and H. M. Eisenberg (eds), *Neurobehavioral recovery from head injury*. Oxford, UK: Oxford University Press.

van Zomeren, A. H. and Brouwer, W. H. (1994). *Clinical neuropsychology of attention*. Oxford, UK: Oxford University Press.

Vogel, E. K., Luck, S. J., and Shapiro, K. L. (1998). Electrophysiological evidence for a post-perceptual locus of suppression during the attentional blink. *Journal of Experimental Psychology: Human Perception and Performance*, **24**, 1656–1674.

Vogel, E. K., Woodman, G. F., and Luck, S. J. (2001). Storage of features, conjunctions, and objects in visual working memory. *Journal of Experimental Psychology: Human Perception and Performance*, **27**, 92–114.

von Mühlenen, A., Müller, H. J., and Müller, D. (2003). Sit-and-wait strategies in dynamic visual search. *Psychological Science*, **14**, 309–314.

von Wright, J. M. (1968). Selection in immediate visual memory. *Quarterly Journal of Experimental Psychology*, **20**, 62–68.

von Wright, J. M. (1970). On selection in visual immediate memory. *Acta Psychologica*, **33**, 280–292.

Vuilleumier, P. and Driver, J. (2007). Modulation of visual processing by attention and emotion: windows on causal interactions between human brain regions. *Philosophical Transactions of the Royal Society of London, Series B, Biological Sciences*, **362**, 837–855.

Wagemans, J., Wichmann, F. A., and Op de Beeck, H. (2005). Visual perception I: Basic principles. In: K. Lamberts and R. L. Goldstone (eds), *The handbook of cognition*, pp. 3–47. London, UK: Sage.

Walsh, V. and Rushworth, M. (1999). A primer of magnetic stimulation as a tool for neuropsychology. *Neuropsychologia*, **37**, 125–135.

Walsh, V., Ellison, A., Battelli, L., and Cowey, A. (1998). Task-specific impairments and enhancements induced by magnetic stimulation of human visual area V5. *Proceedings of the Royal Society, Series B*, **265**, 537–543.

Ward, R., Duncan, J., and Shapiro, K. (1996). The slow time-course of visual attention. *Cognitive Psychology*, **30**, 79–109.

Washburn, M. F. and Gillette, A. (1933). Motor factors in voluntary control of cube perspective fluctuations and retinal rivalry fluctuations. *American Journal of Psychology*, **45**, 315–319.

Watson, R. T. and Heilman, K. M. (1979). Thalamic neglect. *Neurology*, **29**, 690–694.

Watson, R. T., Heilman, K. M., Cauthen, J. C., and King, F. A. (1973). Neglect after cingulectomy. *Neurology*, **23**, 1003–1007.

Weichselgartner, E. and Sperling, G. (1987). Dynamics of automatic and controlled visual attention. *Science*, **238**, 778–780.

Weiskrantz, L. (1997). *Consciousness lost and found: a neuropsychological exploration*. Oxford, UK: Oxford University Press.

Wernicke, C. (1874). *Der aphasische Symptomenkomplex: Eine psychologische Studie auf anatomischer Basis*. Breslau: Cohn und Weigert.

Wertheimer, M. (1923). Untersuchungen zur Lehre von der Gestalt II. *Psychologische Forschung*, **4**, 301–350.

Wilken, P. and Ma, W. J. (2004). A detection theory account of change detection. *Journal of Vision*, **4**, 1120–1135.

Williford, T. and Maunsell, J. H. R. (2006). Effects of spatial attention on contrast response functions in macaque area V4. *Journal of Neurophysiology*, **96**, 40–54.

Wittgenstein, L. (1953). *Philosophical investigations*. Oxford, UK: Blackwell.

Wojciulik, E. and Kanwisher, N. (1999). The generality of parietal involvement in visual attention. *Neuron*, **23**, 747–764.

Wojciulik, E., Husain, M., Clarke, K., and Driver, J. (2001). Spatial working memory deficit in unilateral neglect. *Neuropsychologia*, **39**, 390–396.

Wolfe, J. M. (1994). Guided Search 2.0: a revised model of visual search. *Psychonomic Bulletin and Review*, **1**, 202–238.

Wolfe, J. M. (1998). What can 1 million trials tell us about visual search? *Psychological Science*, **9**, 33–39.

Wolfe, J. M., Cave, K. R., and Franzel, S. L. (1989). Guided search: an alternative to the feature integration model for visual search. *Journal of Experimental Psychology: Human Perception and Performance*, **15**, 419–433.

Womelsdorf, T., Fries, P., Mitra, P. P., and Desimone, R. (2006). Gamma-band synchronization in visual cortex predicts speed of change detection. *Nature*, **439**, 733–736.

Woodman, G. F. and Luck, S. J. (1999). Electrophysiological measurement of rapid shifts of attention during visual search. *Nature*, **400**, 867–869.

Xu, Y. and Chun, M. M. (2006). Dissociable neural mechanisms supporting visual short-term memory for objects. *Nature*, **440**, 91–95.

Yantis, S. (1993). Stimulus-driven attentional capture and attentional control settings. *Journal of Experimental Psychology: Human Perception and Performance*, **19**, 676–681.

Yantis, S. and Hillstrom, A. P. (1994). Stimulus-driven attentional capture: evidence from equiluminant visual objects. *Journal of Experimental Psychology: Human Perception and Performance*, **20**, 95–107.

Yantis, S. and Jonides, J. (1984). Abrupt visual onsets and selective attention: evidence from visual search. *Journal of Experimental Psychology: Human Perception and Performance*, **10**, 601–621.

Yantis, S. and Jonides, J. (1990). Abrupt visual onsets and selective attention: voluntary versus automatic allocation. *Journal of Experimental Psychology: Human Perception and Performance*, **16**, 121–134.

Zeki, S. (1993). *A vision of the brain*. Oxford, UK: Blackwell.

Index